W9-DHK-246

INDEX OF PRINTED
MIDDLE ENGLISH PROSE

R.E. Lewis
N.F. Blake
A.S.G. Edwards

GARLAND PUBLISHING INC. • NEW YORK & LONDON
1985

Library of Congress Cataloging-in-Publication Data

Lewis, Robert E.
Index of printed Middle English prose.

(Garland reference library of the humanities ;
vol. 537)
Includes indexes.
1. English prose literature—Middle English, 1100–
1500—Bibliography. 2. English prose literature—
Middle English, 1100–1500—Indexes. 3. English language
—Middle English, 1100–1500—Texts—Bibliography.
4. English language—Middle English, 1100–1500—
Texts—Indexes. I. Blake, N. F. (Norman Francis)
II. Edwards, A. S. G. (Anthony Stockwell Garfield),
1942– . III. Title. IV. Series: Garland
reference library of the humanities ; v. 537.
Z2014.P795L49 1985 [PR255] 016.828'108 84-45383
ISBN 0-8240-8839-5 (alk. paper)

Printed on acid-free, 250-year-life paper
Manufactured in the United States of America

INDEX OF PRINTED
MIDDLE ENGLISH PROSE

GARLAND REFERENCE LIBRARY
OF THE HUMANITIES
(VOL. 537)

CONTENTS

PREFACE

We have tried to be complete in our listing of texts and editions through 1982, including for 1983 and 1984 only those that we knew about or that came to hand in the course of our work, but inevitably there will be some errors and omissions. We would be grateful to receive notices of such errors and omissions for a possible supplement; they may be sent to Lewis at the Middle English Dictionary, University of Michigan, Ann Arbor. We learned of several new entries after the indices were programmed and printed out. Rather than renumber every entry to accommodate these additions, with the resultant possibility of introducing new errors, we have introduced the decimal system used in the supplement to The Index of Middle English Verse and similar works; any further entries can be added in the same way.

For answering queries, checking information, or sharing their knowledge or expertise with us, we are grateful to Cynthia R. Bland, K.D. Borris, Peter Brown, Sarah Cureton, Sigmund Eisner, Jeremy Griffiths, Ralph Hanna III, Kate Harris, Anne Hudson, George R. Keiser, Stephen F. Lappert, Geoffrey Lester, Julie Lewis, Lister M. Matheson, Vincent P. McCarren, Katharine F. Pantzer, David Parkinson, Derek Pearsall, John Reidy, Anne Rooney, Linda E. Voigts, and Edward Wilson.

We owe special thanks to A.I. Doyle for reading a draft of the index and giving us the benefit of his expert knowledge of Middle English prose; to Delores J. Kuzma for designing the format of the text and entering it into the computer; and for Marilyn S. Miller for programming the numbering system and the indices. Edwards gratefully acknowledges a research grant from the Social Sciences and Humanities Research Council of Canada in connection with his work on the index; Lewis gratefully acknowledges a fellowship from the American Council of Learned Societies, on which his work on the index was begun, and grants from the Faculty Assistance Fund of the College of Literature, Science, and the Arts at the University of Michigan to prepare the index for the press.

ABBREVIATIONS

Addl.	Additional
Aldine (1845), rev.ed. (1866)	Pickering's Aldine Poets, 2 and 3 (1845), rev.ed. by R. Morris (1866)
Allen, English (1931)	H.E. Allen, English Writings of Richard Rolle, Hermit of Hampole (1931)
Allen, Writings (1927)	H.E. Allen, Writings Ascribed to Richard Rolle Hermit of Hampole and Materials for His Biography (1927)
Ames (1749)	J. Ames, Typographical Antiquities (1749)
Ampe (1964)	A. Ampe, Dr.L. Reypens Album (1964)
Anderson (1793)	R. Anderson, The Works of the British Poets, 1 (1793)
Archiv	Archiv für das Studium der neueren Sprachen und Literaturen
Aungier (1840)	G.J. Aungier, The History and Antiquities of Syon Monastery (1840)
Aurner (1926)	N.S. Aurner, Caxton, Mirrour of Fifteenth-Century Letters (1926)
Ayling (1869)	S. Ayling, The Fifteen O's and Other Prayers (1869)
Baillie-Grohman (1904)	W.A. and F. Baillie-Grohman, The Master of Game (1904)
Baugh (1956)	N.S. Baugh, A Worcestershire Miscellany, Compiled by John Northwood, c. 1400, Edited from British Museum MS. Add. 37,787 (1956)
Bazire and Colledge (1957)	J. Bazire and E. Colledge, The Chastising of God's Children and the Treatise of Perfection of the Sons of God (1957)
J. Bell (1782)	J. Bell, The Poets of Great Britain Complete from Chaucer to Churchill, 2-5 (1782)
R. Bell (1854-56), rev.ed. (1878)	R. Bell, Bell's Annotated Editions of the English Poets, 1-4 (1854-56), rev.ed. (1878)
Bentley (1833)	S. Bentley, Excerpta Historica, or Illustrations of English History

Bibl.
BL
Blackwood (1880?)

Blades, Biography (1877),
2nd ed. (1882)

Blades, Boke (1881, 1905)

Blades, Life (1861-63)

Blake, Caxton (1969)

Blake, COP (1973)

Blake, CT (1980)

Blake, MERP (1972)

Blake, Selections (1973)

Bliss (1857), 2nd ed. (1869)

BN
Bodl
Boyd (1978)

Bradshaw (1889)

Braekman (1980)

Brewer (1978)

Buchanan-Brown (1966)

Bühler (1973)

Burrell (1908), rev.ed. (1912)

(1833)
Bibliothèque
London British Library
Blackwood, The Poetical Works of Chaucer (1880?)
W. Blades, The Biography and Typography of William Caxton, England's First Printer (1877), 2nd ed. (1882)
W. Blades, The Boke of Saint Albans (1881, 1905)
W. Blades, The Life and Typography of William Caxton, England's First Printer, 2 vols. (1861-63)
N.F. Blake, Caxton and His World (1969)
N.F. Blake, Caxton's Own Prose (1973)
N.F. Blake, The Canterbury Tales (1980)
N.F. Blake, Middle English Religious Prose (1972)
N.F. Blake, Selections from William Caxton (1973)
P. Bliss, Reliquiae Hearnianae: The Remains of Thomas Hearne (1857), 2nd ed. (1869)
Bibliothèque Nationale
Oxford Bodleian Library
B. Boyd, Chaucer According to William Caxton (1978)
Collected Papers of Henry Bradshaw (1889)
W.L. Braekman, The Treatise on Angling in The Boke of St. Albans (1496), Scripta, 1 (1980)
D.S. Brewer, Chaucer: The Critical Heritage, Volume I 1385-1837 (1978)
J. Buchanan-Brown, The Remains of Thomas Hearne Reliquiae Hearnianae (1966)
C.F. Bühler, Early Books and Manuscripts Forty Years of Research (1973)
A. Burrell, Chaucer's Canterbury Tales (1908), rev. ed. (1912)

x

c.	century
ca.	circa
Cawley (1958)	A.C. Cawley, The Canterbury Tales (1958)
CCC	Corpus Christi College
CCCC	Cambridge Corpus Christi College
Cf.	Compare
Chalmers (1810)	A. Chalmers, The Works of the English Poets from Chaucer to Cowper, 1 (1810)
Chap(s.	Chapter(s
Chaucer and Middle English Studies (1974)	B. Rowland, Chaucer and Middle English Studies in Honour of Rossell Hope Robbins (1974)
Clermont (1869)	T. Fortescue, Lord Clermont, The Works of Sir J. Fortescue, 2 vols. (1869)
col.	column
Colledge and Walsh (1978)	E. Colledge and J. Walsh, A Book of Showings to the Anchoress Julian of Norwich, 2 vols. (1978)
cols.	columns
Complete Works (1930)	Geoffrey Chaucer, Complete Works in Poetry and Prose (1930)
Cooke and Wordsworth (1902)	W. Cooke and C. Wordsworth, Ordinale Sarum sive Directorium Sacerdotum, 2 (1902)
Coxe (1840)	H.O. Coxe, Forms of Bidding Prayer (1840)
Cripps-Day (1918)	F.H. Cripps-Day, The History of the Tournament in England and France (1918)
CUL	Cambridge University Library
d'Ardenne (1977)	S.R.T.O. d'Ardenne, The Katherine Group Edited from MS. Bodley 34 (1977)
Deanesly (1920)	M. Deanesly, The Lollard Bible (1920)
Dibdin, BS, IV (1815)	T.F. Dibdin, Bibliotheca Spenceriana, IV (1815)
Dibdin, TA, I (1810), II (1812)	T.F. Dibdin, Typographical Antiquities I-II (1810-12)
Doble (1886)	C.E. Doble, Remarks and Collections of Thomas Hearne, 2 (1886)

Dobson (1970), 2nd ed. (1983) R.B. Dobson, The Peasants' Revolt of 1381 (1970), 2nd ed. (1983)

Dodgson, English (1936) C. Dodgson, English Woodcuts of the Fifteenth Century (1936)

Dodgson, Woodcuts (1929) C. Dodgson, Woodcuts of the Fifteenth Century in the Ashmolean Museum, Oxford (1929)

Duff (1917) E.G. Duff, Fifteenth Century English Books (1917)

Duff, WC (1905) E. G. Duff, William Caxton (1905)

ed. edition; edited by

eds. editors

EETS es, os, ss Early English Text Society extra series, original series, supplementary series

EHR English Historical Review

Ellis (1896) F.S. Ellis, The Kelmscott Chaucer (1896)

ELN English Language Notes

Emerson (1905, etc.) O.F. Emerson, Middle English Reader (1905, 1915, 1932)

EPS English Philological Studies

ES Englische Studien

ex. end

f. folio

Festschrift (1906) Festschrift zum XII. allgemeinen deutschen Neuphilologentage in München, ed. E. Stollreither (1906)

ff. folios

Fifth Report (1876) Fifth Report of the Royal Commission on Historical Manuscripts (1876), Appendix

Fisher (1977) J.H. Fisher, The Complete Poetry and Prose of Geoffrey Chaucer (1977)

Flügel (1895) E. Flügel, Neuenglisches Lesebuch, 1 (1895)

Forshall and Madden (1850) J. Forshall and F. Madden, The Holy Bible Containing the Old and New Testaments, 4 vols. (1850)

Foxe (1563, etc.) J. Foxe, Actes and Monuments (1563-1684)

Franciplegius (1965)

J.B. Bessinger and R.P. Creed, Franciplegius: Medieval and Linguistic Studies in Honor of Francis Peabody Magoun, Jr. (1965)

Gairdner (1872-75; rptd.1908), rev. ed. (1904)

J. Gairdner, The Paston Letters, 1 (1872-75; rptd. 1908), rev. ed., 3 (1904)

Garbaty (1984)

T.J. Garbaty, Medieval English Literature (1984)

Genet (1977)

J.-P. Genet, Four English Political Tracts of the Later Middle Ages, Camden Fourth Series, 18 (1977)

Geoffrey Chaucer (1929-30)

Geoffrey Chaucer: The Canterbury Tales, 2 vols. (1929-30)

Gilman (1880)

A. Gilman, Poetical Works of Geoffrey Chaucer, 3 vols. (1880)

Globe (1898)

A.W. Pollard et alii, The Works of Geoffrey Chaucer (1898)

Grisdale (1939)

D.M. Grisdale, Three Middle English Sermons from the Worcester Chapter Manuscript F. 10 (1939)

Hall (1920)

J. Hall, Selections from Early Middle English, 2 vols. (1920)

Halliwell, Miscellanies (1855)

J.O. Halliwell, Early English Miscellanies in Prose and Verse (1855)

Halliwell, Rara (1839)

J.O. Halliwell, Rara Mathematica (1839)

Hanna (1984)

R. Hanna III, A Handlist of Manuscripts Containing Middle English Prose in the Henry E. Huntington Library, The Index of Middle English Prose, Handlist I (1984)

Harley and Bickley (1928)

J. Harley and F. Bickley, Report on the Manuscripts of the Late Reginald Rawdon Hastings Esq. of The Manor House, Ashby de la Zouche, 1, Historical Manuscripts Commission Report 78 (1928)

Haslewood (1810-11)

J. Haslewood, The Book Contain-

	ing the Treatises of Hawking; Hunting; Coat-Armour; Fishing; and Blasing of Arms (1810-11)
Hawking (1972)	Hawking, Hunting, Fouling, and Fishing, with the True Measures of Blowing (1972)
Hearne (1729)	T. Hearne, Historia Vitae et Regni Ricardi II (1729)
Henslow (1899)	G. Henslow, Medical Works of the Fourteenth Century (1899)
Herbert, I (1785)	W. Herbert, Typographical Antiquities, I (1785)
HLQ	Huntington Library Quarterly
Hodgson (1982)	P. Hodgson, The Cloud of Unknowing and Related Treatises (1982)
Hogg (1980)	J. Hogg, The Rewyll of Seynt Sauioure and Other Middle English Brigittine Legislative Texts, 3 and 4 (1980)
Hudson (1978)	A. Hudson, Selections from English Wycliffite Writings (1978)
Hulme (1918)	W.H. Hulme, Richard Rolle of Hampole's Mending of Life (1918)
IMEV	C. Brown and R.H. Robbins, The Index of Middle English Verse (1943) with Supplement by Robbins and J.L. Cutler (1965)
in.	beginning
JBAA	Journal of the British Archaeological Association
JEGP	Journal of English and Germanic Philology
Jolliffe	P.S. Jolliffe, A Check-List of Middle English Prose Writings of Spiritual Guidance (1974)
Kaiser (1958)	R. Kaiser, Medieval English, 3rd ed. (1958)
Kemble (1848)	J.M. Kemble, The Dialogue of Salomon and Saturnus (1848)
Ker	N.R. Ker, Catalogue of Manuscripts Containing Anglo-Saxon (1957)

Kingsford, EHL (1913

Kluge (1904, etc.)

Koch (1915)

Krochalis and Peters (1975)

Lambeth Palace
Lamond (1890)

Legg (1899)

Lewis (1720), rev.ed. (1820)

Lewis (1737)

Lindberg (1978)

Louis (1980)

Lounsbury (1900)

MacCracken, College (1913)

MacCracken, CT (1928)

MÆ
Mätzner, I, 2 (1869)

Manly-Rickert (1940)

Maskell (1846-47), 2nd ed.
(1882)

C.L. Kingsford, English Histori-
cal Literature in the Fifteenth
Century (1913)
F. Kluge, Mittelenglisches Lese-
buch (1904, 1912)
J. Koch, Canterbury Tales nach
dem Ellesmere MS (1915)
J. Krochalis and E. Peters, The
World of Piers Plowman (1975)

London Lambeth Palace
E. Lamond, Walter of Henley's
Husbandry (1890)
J.W. Legg, The Processional of
the Nuns of Chester, Henry
Bradshaw Society 18 (1899)
J. Lewis, The History of the Life
and Sufferings of the Reverend
and Learned John Wicliffe,
D.D. (1720, 1723), rev. ed.
(1820)
J. Lewis, The Life of Mayster
Wyllyam Caxton, of the Weald
of Kent (1737)
C. Lindberg, The Middle English
Bible Prefatory Epistles of St.
Jerome (1978)
C. Louis, The Commonplace Book
of Robert Reynes of Acle An
Edition of Tanner MS 407 (1980)
Chaucer's Complete Works, with
introduction by T.R. Louns-
bury, 2 vols. (1900)

H.N. MacCracken, The College
Chaucer (1913)
H.N. MacCracken, Canterbury
Tales by Geoffrey Chaucer
(1928)
Medium Ævum
E. Mätzner, Altenglische Sprach-
proben nebst einem Wör-
terbuche, I, 2 (1869)
J.M. Manly and E. Rickert, The
Text of the Canterbury Tales, 3
and 4 (1940)
W. Maskell, Monumenta Ritualia
Ecclesiae Anglicanae, 3 vols.

Maskell (1846-47), 2nd ed. (1882) — W. Maskell, _Monumenta Ritualia Ecclesiae Anglicanae_, 3 vols. (1846-47), 2nd ed. (1882)

Mass. — Massachusetts

ME — Middle English

med. — middle

MET — Middle English Texts

Meyrick (1824) — S.R. Meyrick, _A Critical Inquiry into Antient Armour_ (1824)

MLN — _Modern Language Notes_

Moore (1942) — G.E. Moore, _The Middle English Verse Life of Edward the Confessor_ (1942)

Morell (1737) — T. Morell, _The Canterbury Tales of Chaucer_ (1737)

Morley (1889) — H. Morley, _Early Prose Romances_ (1889)

Mott (1933) — A.S. Mott, _The Noble & Joyous Boke Entytled Le Morte Darthur_, 2 vols. (1933)

MP — _Modern Philology_

MS — _Mediaeval Studies_

MS(S — manuscript(s

N&Q — _Notes and Queries_

n.d. — no date

Needham (1976) — P. Needham, _Sir Thomas Malory: Le Morte Darthur_ (1976)

Nichols (1860) — J.G. Nichols, _The Boke of Noblesse Addressed to King Edward the Fourth on His Invasion of France in 1475_, Roxburghe Club (1860)

NLS — National Library of Scotland

NLW — National Library of Wales

NM — _Neuphilologische Mitteilungen_

n.s. — new series

OE — Old English

Oldys (1737) — W. Oldys, _The British Librarian_ (1737)

Origins of Angling (1963) — J. McDonald, _The Origins of Angling_ (1963)

p. — page

Paues (1904) — A.C. Paues, _A Fourteenth Century English Biblical Version_, rev. ed. (1904)

PBSA	Papers of the Bibliographical Society of America
Pegge (1780)	S. Pegge, The Forme of Cury (1780)
Plummer (1885)	C. Plummer, The Governance of England ... by Sir John Fortescue, Kt. (1885)
PMLA	PMLA: Publications of the Modern Language Association of America
Poetical (n.d. [1880])	The Poetical Works of Geoffrey Chaucer (n.d. = 1880)
Pollard (1886-87), 2nd ed. (1931)	A.W. Pollard, Chaucer's Canterbury Tales (1886-87), 2nd ed. (1931)
pp.	pages
PQ	Philological Quarterly
Pratt (1974)	R.A. Pratt, Geoffrey Chaucer The Tales of Canterbury Complete (1974)
Price (1877)	F.C. Price, Fac-similes of Examples from the Press of William Caxton at Westminster (1877)
PRO	Public Record Office
r	recto (of a folio)
Rel. Ant., I (1841), II (1843)	T. Wright and J.O. Halliwell, Reliquiae Antiquae, 2 vols. (1841-43)
RES	Review of English Studies
rev.	revised
Revell	P. Revell, Fifteenth Century English Prayers and Meditations A Descriptive List of Manuscripts in the British Library (1975)
Robinson (1933), 2nd ed.(1957)	F.N. Robinson, The Complete Works of Geoffrey Chaucer (1933), 2nd ed. (1957)
Rolls	Rolls Series
Roxburghe	Roxburghe Club
rptd.	reprinted
Ruggiers (1979)	P.G. Ruggiers, Geoffrey Chaucer The Canterbury Tales (1979)
s.	century
Schreiber, Handbuch (1926-30)	W.L. Schreiber, Handbuch der Holz- und Metallschnitte des xv Jahrhunderts, 8 vols. (1926-30)

Schreiber, Manuel, I (1891), VI (1893)	W.L. Schreiber, Manuel de l'amateur de la gravure sur bois et sur métal au xve siècle, 6 vols. (1891-93)
SEW (1869-71)	T. Arnold, ed., Select English Works of Wyclif, 3 vols. (1869-71)
Shakespeare Head (1929)	The Works of Geoffrey Chaucer, 6 vols. (1929)
Sisam (1921)	K. Sisam, Fourteenth Century Verse & Prose (1921)
Skeat, Chaucerian (1897)	W.W. Skeat, Chaucerian and Other Pieces (1897)
Skeat, Complete (1894), 2nd ed. (1900)	W.W. Skeat, The Complete Works of Geoffrey Chaucer, 6 vols. (1894), 2nd ed. (1900)
SN	Studia Neophilologica
Soc.	Society
Sommer (1889)	H.O. Sommer, Le Morte Darthur by Syr Thomas Malory, 1 (1889)
Southey (1817)	R. Southey, The Byrth, Lyf, and Actes of Kyng Arthur, 2 vols. (1817)
SP	Studies in Philology
Speght (1598), 2nd ed. (1602), 3rd ed. (1687)	T. Speght, The Workes of Our Antient and Lerned English Poet Geffrey Chaucer (1598), 2nd ed. (1602), 3rd ed. (1687)
Spisak and Matthews (1983)	J.W. Spisak and W. Matthews, Caxton's Malory (1983)
Spurgeon (1914)	C.F.E. Spurgeon, Five Hundred Years of Chaucer Criticism and Allusion (1357-1900), Part 1, Chaucer Soc., 2nd series 48 (1914)
STC	A.W. Pollard and G.R. Redgrave, A Short-Title Catalogue of Books Printed in England, Scotland, & Ireland and of English Books Printed Abroad 1475-1640 (1926); 2nd ed. of Part II by W.A. Jackson, F.S. Ferguson, and K.F. Pantzer (1976)
Stow (1561)	J. Stow, The Workes of Geffrey Chaucer (1561)
STS	Scottish Text Society

Takamiya (1980)   T. Takamiya, _Two Minor Works of Walter Hilton Eight Chapters on Perfection and Of Angels' Song_ (1980)

TCC   Cambridge Trinity College

TCD   Dublin Trinity College

Thoms (1828)   W.J. Thoms, _A Collection of Early Prose Romances_ (1828)

Thoms, 2nd ed. (1858), enlarged ed. (1906, 1907)   W.J. Thoms, _Early English Prose Romances_ (1858), enlarged ed. (1906, 1907)

Thomson (1984)   D. Thomson, _An Edition of the Middle English Grammatical Texts_ (1984)

Thynne (1532), 2nd ed. (1542), 3rd ed. ([1545?])   W. Thynne, _The Workes of Geffrey Chaucer_ (1532), 2nd ed. (1542), 3rd ed. ([1545?])

Thynne (1905)   W. Thynne, _The Works of Geoffrey Chaucer and Others_ (1905)

Tilander (1956)   G. Tilander, _La Vénerie de Twiti_, Cynegetica II (1956)

Todd (1851)   J.H. Todd, _Three Treatises by John Wycklyffe, D.D._ (1851)

Trans.   Transactions

Twysden (1652)   R. Twysden, _Henry Knighton's Chronica_, in _Historiae Anglicanae Scriptores_, 10 (1652)

Tyrwhitt (1775), 2nd ed.(1798)   T. Tyrwhitt, _The Canterbury Tales of Chaucer_, 4 vols. (1775), 2nd ed., 2 vols. (1798)

Urry (1721)   J. Urry, _The Works of Geoffrey Chaucer_ (1721)

v   verso (of a folio)

Vaughan, John (1853)   R. Vaughan, _John de Wycliffe, D.D._ (1853)

Vaughan, Life (1828), 2nd ed. (1831)   R. Vaughan, _The Life and Opinions of J. de Wycliffe_, 2 vols. (1828), 2nd ed. (1831)

Vinaver, Malory (1954), 2nd ed. (1971)   E. Vinaver, _The Works of Sir Thomas Malory_ (1954); 2nd ed., _Malory Works_ (1971)

Vinaver, Works (1947), 2nd ed. (1967)   E. Vinaver, _The Works of Sir Thomas Malory_ 3 vols. (1947), 2nd ed. (1967)

Voigts and McVaugh (1984)   L.E. Voigts and M.R. McVaugh,

A Latin Technical Phlebotomy and Its Middle English Translation, Transactions of the American Philosophical Society, 74, 2 (1984)

Wallner (1954) B. Wallner, An Exposition of Qui Habitat and Bonum Est in English (1954)

Warner (1791) R. Warner, Antiquitates Culinariae (1791)

Whiting B.J. Whiting, Proverbs, Sentences, and Proverbial Phrases from English Writings Mainly Before 1500 (1968)

Wing D. Wing, Short-Title Catalogue of Books Printed in England, Scotland, Ireland, Wales, and British America and of English Books Printed in Other Countries 1641-1700, 3 vols. (1945-51), 2nd ed. of 1 and 2 (1972-82)

Winn (1929) H.E. Winn, Wyclif Select English Writings (1929)

Winterich (1958) J.T. Winterich, The Works of Geoffrey Chaucer (facsimile of Ellis) (1958)

Wordsworth (1901) C. Wordsworth, Ceremonies and Processions of the Cathedral Church of Salisbury (1901)

Wright (1847-51) T. Wright, The Canterbury Tales of Geoffrey Chaucer, Percy Soc., 3 vols. (1847-51)

Wülcker (1874, 1879) R. Wülcker, Altenglische Lesebuch, 2 vols. (1874, 1879)

YW, I (1895), II (1896) C. Horstman, Yorkshire Writers Richard Rolle of Hampole An English Father of the Church and His Followers, I (1895) and II (1896)

Zupitza (1874 and later editions) J. Zupitza, Altenglisches Übungs buch (1874); Zupitza et alii, Alt- und mittelenglisches Übungsbuch (1882, etc.)

INTRODUCTION

An index of Middle English prose may well create the impression that there is a clearly defined entity "Middle English prose" which has certain characteristics marking it off from other writings of the period. Unfortunately this is far from being the case. On the one side the boundary between prose and poetry is ill-defined for much of the Middle English period, and on the other side the division between literary and non-literary prose is even more difficult to make for a period like Middle English than it is for Modern English, for the concept of what is literary prose is a fluid one. Thus sermons are accepted as literature up to the eighteenth century or even beyond, but few people today would want to categorize them in that way.

As will be explained more fully later in this introduction, the practical distinction between prose and poetry for this volume has been made for us since there is in existence The Index of Middle English Verse (IMEV).(1) The index of prose has taken within its orbit everything which is not included in the index of verse, including a few pieces which modern editors now print as prose. The division into two indices is an unhappy one in that it encourages the view that there is a recognizable difference between the two media both technically and aesthetically. As Jonathan Culler has suggested, if we today take a piece of prose and divide it up into lines of free verse to make it seem like a poem, we immediately bring different concepts and associations to the way in which we read the same words.(2) This is because we regard prose as the appropriate medium for everyday communication whereas poetry is for the more heightened forms of discourse. This in turn implies that prose is composed in an almost thoughtless way, while the words of poetry have to be chosen with great care to achieve the desired effect. This is not a situation which applies to the medieval period. Prose was a sophisticated medium which was intimately linked to the intellectual tradition of theological and historical scholarship in Latin. Much prose was very close to Latin versions through translation or through using the same rhetorical forms of composition in imitation of Latin. Verse could be as didactic as prose, but because of the medium it was often more ephemeral in that fashions in poetry changed more quickly. Perhaps because of its oral background poetry was often considered then more suitable for elementary forms of instruction; the poetic rhythms made it easier to memorize than prose. Certainly one can find many different kinds of expository works which today would appear in prose. Sometimes the same work is found in both poetic and prose forms. With the Forme of Lyvyng (35) the original prose version is intended for a more sophisticated and learned audience than the poetry, which has simplified the matter by cutting out what was not part of traditional teaching such as the expression of mystical states.(3) The poetic version has been reduced to a treatise suitable for the average man. In the fifteenth century a trend to convert poetic texts into prose set in. This trend commenced in the Duchy of Burgundy and became established in England as well. There is no indication that the prose versions were meant for a less elevated audience, for many of them were made in Burgundy for the Dukes and their courtiers. Many of the works Caxton printed started life as poems, but his prose editions were meant to appeal to the snobbery of his clientele and were clearly not designed as inferior in any way to poetry.

In the early Middle English period the relation between poetry and prose was blurred because of the nature of alliterative style. Alliterative poetry does not have a set number of syllables per line; it demands only that there are a certain number of alliterative words in a line, though that number was not constant. On occasions when the verse writing becomes less taut, the alliterative stresses may fall below what one might regard as the minimum alliteration for a line of poetry. On the other hand, alliteration was a device encouraged by the rhetorical handbooks to enrich writing and so prose writers often employed it for that purpose. Thus what is today considered heightened prose may well be more alliterative than what is now taken to be verse. This applies to sections of Rolle's "Ego Dormio" (160). It is indeed difficult to determine whether a given piece should be labelled prose or poetry because of the uncertainty of the criteria to be applied. Even in late Old English this is exemplified with some of the lives of Ælfric, and in the later Middle English period the problem is still present in the series of tracts associated with "Jack Upland" (782). In fact, in this period one can detect works that are highly alliterative which are poetic at one end of the spectrum and at the other end works which have no alliteration and which are clearly prose. In between come many works which could be (and sometimes have been) categorized as either prose or poetry. A categorization into one or the other forces the material into molds which have little relevance for the medieval period, and users of this index should always use IMEV as well to look for comparable material.

A decision as to what constitutes the more literary types of prose, to which this volume is generally confined, is also difficult. Such a consideration did not arise in the compilation of the verse index because anything which was in verse was included. Even so, verse was used in medieval times for a whole range of topics which today would almost certainly be in prose. Thus the basic facts of many disciplines -- the traditional knowledge of plants, for example -- and the abstract rules and concepts found in intellectual discussions could as readily be found in verse as prose.(4) While this is perhaps more characteristic of Latin than English, it nevertheless remains true for English. The difference between verse and prose in this respect can be gauged by considering the English pieces found in the Fasciculus Morum, which have recently been edited by Siegfried Wenzel.(5) An index of verse would seek to include all the verse passages which are quoted in the Latin text even though they may be no more than two lines long and even though they were composed by the composer of the

Latin text to illustrate his theme at that point. No literary judgment or evaluation of length is involved. An index of prose could not hope to include the occasional English sentences which are included in this text and others like it although they fulfill precisely the same purpose as the English verses. They may have been written by the composer of the text or they may be traditional sayings; in some cases it is even possible to assume that they are single lines of a poetic couplet. The point we wish to emphasize is that an index of prose will be less complete, and this might create the impression that verse is inherently superior because all verse is collected. The same general approach would apply to a macaronic text. The question of length and what is embedded in a text in a different language represents one side of the problem of composing a prose index. The other is how to define texts as literary for a period where such a distinction cannot be said to exist. It is possible to suggest that anything which could have appeared in verse should by that token be considered literary, and this would mean that recipes, chronicles, and technical tracts on such subjects as warfare and the keeping of horses are included. In fact, the policy of inclusion or exclusion is determined by other criteria which are explained elsewhere in this introduction, but the question of what is a literary text as such is one that the user of this index has to keep in mind.

A further difficulty that has emerged in the compilation of a prose index is to decide what precisely constitutes a complete and integral work. This problem arises because medieval authors borrow copiously from other works. When they do so in verse, they usually have to adapt what they borrow to the rhythm and meter of their own poems. The simple borrowing of whole passages in verse is thus rarely encountered, though Chaucer's Gentilesse was incorporated by Scogan in one of his poems. With prose this is less true, for it is quite easy to copy whole sections or even complete works into a different text. This applies particularly to short texts like prayers, curses, recipes, and so on. The compilers of this index have naturally followed modern printed editions in deciding what constitutes a complete work, but it should be remembered that a text may include other complete works within it. The Gret Sentence (122), for example, may be found in other works as a subsidiary section.

Not unnaturally there is more material from the latter part of the Middle English period included in the index. Not only is this more accessible to modern readers and hence more likely to be edited, but the introduction of printing and the beginning of the process of standardization of the language meant that far more was written in the vernacular at that time.

It is also more difficult to chart the progress of prose than that of poetry because it appears in a variety of styles. This is because so much prose is based on translation and so reflects the language and style of the original. Furthermore, although prose was subject to the same impetus to elaborate style as poetry, it was also subjected to calls for simplicity in style so that it could be readily understood by a wider range of people. The result is that there is a myriad of both styles and subject matter in the prose of the medieval period.

There is no obvious link between style and subject matter in the Middle English period and so it is not easy to characterize the variations in style found then. At the beginning of the period the predominant, or indeed only, style is the alliterative one, though alliteration is not obtrusive in such works as the Ancrene Wisse (559). Because so much of what was written in English in this period was of a religious or spiritual nature, there developed an English tradition of spiritual writing which was linked with certain religious foundations, principally Cistercian at first and later Carthusian and Brigittine. In the first case the influence of St. Bernard was important, and in the second the newness of many of the houses of the order. In the late thirteenth and fourteenth centuries the spread of religious houses in the North and North Midlands gave a great spiritual impetus to religious life there, and this was reflected in many of the writings produced. Although Rolle is the most prolific writer of the time, there were many other important writers as well as the continued transmission of spiritual texts from the previous century. This religious writing built on the work of previous writers so that there was a real sense of continuity. In the fifteenth century the foundation of such houses as Syon and Sheen led to the London area becoming the main center for spiritual writing. Although the writers of this time used earlier English works, they were more influenced by the writings of Continental mystics and by the new style associated with London and the court. Hence religious writing tended to lose its own special style and fell in more with the stylistic fashions of the capital. Secular writing had been sporadic before the fourteenth century. Where it occurs it is straight translation from Latin and French so that it tends to reflect the style of its original. In the fifteenth century the influence of Burgundy in cultural matters led to the adoption of the highly ornate style associated with the ducal court. This style relies on a pompous vocabulary, the use of doublets and triplets, and the employment of convoluted syntax. The elegance and force of the alliterative tradition were lost. By the end of our period this was the dominant style, but other styles such as the simpler Wycliffite style are also found.

Although it is possible to divide Middle English prose up into a variety of genres, the overlap between them is considerable because so much of what was written was intended both to instruct and to entertain.(6) Thus the majority of secular works could be regarded as either romances or histories. But a reader of a Charlemagne romance might feel he was reading history, just as a reader of Trevisa's translation of Higden's Polychronicon (605) might feel it was more like romance in parts. A special type of historical writing is the legendary material and saints' lives, which may be historical in intention but were largely imaginative in execution. The majority of prose works in the period are intended for instruction, which may be either primary or secondary. Primary instruction is that in which the author has a particular audience in mind and his intention is unusually clear: the explanation of Christian teaching or the laying down of rules for the conduct of life. Secondary instruction is more generalized in that the audience is not specific; the text is arranged to handle general problems which may affect a wide variety of people. Works of this type had to be made interesting and readable, since the author had to keep the attention of his audience. The reader of a primary work of instruction presumably needed the instruction and so the material can be presented in a more direct way. Some works are affective in that they appeal more to the emotions of the listener; this appeal may be to frighten him or to attract him to reconsider his way of life. Often these works rely on pathos and may make use of the human life of Christ or other saints. A more specialized type of affective work is that which tries to make the reader see some emotional affinity between himself and Christ as in the form of a spiritual marriage. Other material can be polemical as is so much of the complaint literature of the time. All these types will be found in the index, though religious material is not unnaturally more common than other varieties.

This index records only what medieval texts have been printed; and this is a rather uneven record, for how a text gets into print is haphazard. Print confers some popularity which may be quite spurious. The best way for a text to become popular was for it to be printed by one of the fifteenth-century printers. A text like the Ancrene Wisse (559), which was well known among religious from the early thirteenth to the middle of the fifteenth centuries, did not find a printer and so became much less familiar until it was revived through an early nineteenth-century edition. On the other hand, a text like the Historye of Reynard the Fox (388), which was translated and printed by Caxton at the end of the fifteenth century, was frequently reprinted and adapted throughout the following centuries because it was available in printed form. It is a sobering fact to realize that without this edition, the story of Reynard, which was little known in England beforehand, would probably have been familiar in England only from specialized episodes such as the one found in Chaucer's Nun's Priest's Tale. The romances popularized by Caxton at the end of the fifteenth century were largely new to England, but because later printers found it easier to reprint from a book than a manuscript they had a better chance of being republished. Caxton's version of the history of Troy (825) becomes the predominant version for the following centuries. The texts which were printed in the fifteenth century were romances, which were often new, courtly poetry such as the poems of Chaucer, which encouraged the printing of his prose works as well, and the books of elementary or primary instruction. These latter had a wide appeal and were generally not too complicated. Thus Mirk's Festivall (734) was constantly reprinted, but the Clowde of Unknowyng (320), which was for a more specialized audience, was not printed at all. These latter texts are printed in fifteenth-century forms and it is only gradually being worked out how much they owe to earlier versions. With the sixteenth century new interests arose. Religion became more polemical and many of the older texts fell into disuse. Romances and histories continue to be reprinted, but they too gradually give way to more fashionable texts. The result is that there is little medieval prose printed in the seventeenth and eighteenth centuries, though there are some notable exceptions. Versions of the Historye of Reynard the Fox (388) and the works of Geoffrey Chaucer continue to appear, and the works of Wyclif begin to appear. The nineteenth century witnessed a revival of interest in the medieval period, and the formation of such societies as the Early English Text Society led to the publication of many medieval texts. But poetry tended to take precedence over prose so that even today large amounts of prose have remained uncatalogued, let alone read. The reason for an Index of Middle English Prose, and for the present index as a first stage in this work, is to remedy this situation.

Our aim in the present index is twofold. First, we try to provide a bibliographical overview of editorial work completed on Middle English prose texts. Second, we seek to provide a bibliographical tool of assistance to scholars and students working with Middle English prose materials, particularly with such materials in manuscript forms; it will provide them for the first time with a comprehensive means of identifying texts and relating them to other manuscript copies or printed versions.(7) To these ends we have given two full indices, one of authors, titles, and genres and the other of manuscripts. We hope thereby to provide an index that will be of maximum utility to editors and bibliographers of Middle English prose.

Our intention has been to include all Middle English prose that has been printed which was written from the second half of the twelfth century to circa 1500. For the earlier date we have generally taken N.R. Ker's Catalogue of Manuscripts Containing Anglo-Saxon (Oxford: Clarendon Press, 1957) as our criterion for exclusion.(8) Material described in Ker is generally not included in the present work. This has not led to absolute consistency. We have included some items which could be considered Old English, such as the texts in Harley 6258b (289, 663, 849),(9) as well as continuations of texts begun in the Old English period like the Peterborough Chronicle (752). Our later date, circa 1500, has inevitably posed some difficulties which also resist consistent resolution. We have generally relied on the conclusions of editors as to the dating of the texts, unless substantial evidence exists to cast doubt on their conclusions. In cases where there is uncertainty we have included the work. We have included a few texts which belong to the early sixteenth century, primarily those whose authors are known to have begun writing in the fifteenth century and for which we have been unable to establish a precise compositional date. Richard Atkynson and Margaret Countess of Richmond's translation of Thomas à Kempis (838) is an example. We have also included post-medieval transcripts of Middle English prose texts which in some cases provide the sole authority for a text.

Certain categories of prose material are not included. We have generally omitted material of a documentary nature. This omitted material includes parish records, accounts, receipts, charter deeds, petitions, assize rolls, bailiff rolls, close rolls, bench books, bursar's books, ledger books, calendars and inventories, cartularies, custumals, muniments, guild books, subsidy rolls, and yearbooks. Such materials are more appropriately dealt with by calendaring rather than by a first-line index. Their inclusion would also have greatly extended the completion time of our work and increased its bulk for very limited gains, since our work is primarily concerned with texts rather than documents.(10)

Other classes of material excluded include glossaries, glosses, lists, and letters. It would be difficult, once again, to arrive at any satisfactory method of indexing these classes of material. The non-inclusion of letters is a matter for some regret; but fortunately the major collections have been published. To include individual letters would have served little purpose. On the one hand, letters in general tend to be unique documents and hence there are unlikely to be difficulties of identification or of multiple texts; on the other hand, they nearly always begin formulaically and thus are difficult to distinguish adequately in a work such as ours. We have, however, included literary works that designate themselves as "letters" (e.g., 444, 562), as well as a few items that are borderline (412, 425).

We have not included brief passages of Middle English prose in texts primarily in foreign languages. Deciding where to make exclusions is inevitably a matter of judgment. We have, for example, excluded isolated phrases of Middle English in certain sermon texts and prose rubrics to verse texts, but we have included some extended prose passages which appear in prologues or epilogues to verse texts (e.g., 828) and prose passages in Roger Dymmok's Liber Contra XII Errores et Hereses Lollardorum (807) and Henry Knighton's Chronicle (e.g., 802), both of which are primarily in Latin. In effect, we have included passages which seem sufficiently substantial and sufficiently self-contained to possess some claim to an independent validity as Middle English prose texts.

There has been considerable debate over one class of material -- alliterative prose -- and whether it is, in fact, prose at all, as we mentioned earlier. At times, some of it has been printed as verse. We have, in general, included as prose texts such items as are not classified as verse by IMEV.

We have excluded (with one large exception) all modernizations of Middle English prose texts, though some texts, only the orthography of which has been normalized, have found their way in. The exception is texts found in A.W. Pollard and G.R. Redgrave's Short-Title Catalogue of Books Printed in England, Scotland, & Ireland and of

English _Books_ _Printed_ _Abroad_ 1475-1640, I (1926) and II, 2nd ed.
(1976). Early printers inevitably did some modernizing of medieval
texts, but we have included their editions because they illustrate the
early printing history, reception, and popularity of medieval texts and
because in a number of cases they are the only printed editions.
Finally, we have excluded all texts that are selections made by
modern editors. It is not always easy to decide with confidence what
is an editorial selection. For example, we have of course included
cycles or groups of sermons, but we have not included individual
sermons unless they circulated separately in medieval manuscripts.
We have included single recipes if they circulated separately, but have
generally excluded single recipes or groups of them when they have been
extracted from a context of related material. Such kinds of material
do raise problems about unity which resist a confident resolution, and
we have not found it possible or practicable to be absolutely consistent
here. When a collection of sermons or recipes has been edited from a
single manuscript, we have indexed it by the first entry only and have
not given separate references for individual sermons or recipes. And
when there is any degree of uncertainty as to whether the published text
is complete, we have generally included it unless we could establish
grounds for exclusion. This principle of excluding editorial selections
has occasionally meant that we have had to leave out a work of
importance such as Geoffrey Shepherd's edition of the _Ancrene_ _Wisse_,
Parts VI and VII (1959), or some of the editions of selections in the
Middle English Texts series. But since one of the main aims of our
index is to assist scholars working with manuscript material, there
would be little purpose in including a version of a text that has no
distinct manuscript status.

The index is arranged alphabetically by first lines, both numbered main entries and unnumbered cross-referenced entries, and the
format is for each main entry to contain at least two and often three
sections following the first line.(11) In _IMEV_ there was no problem
with the first line: if the poem was in rhyming couplets, the first two
lines were given; if the poem was in alliterative verse, the first line was
given. For this index we did not have that convenience, and the first
question we had to answer was how many words to print. As a
general rule, we have given twenty to thirty, which for most texts is
enough to give a sense of the beginning and to produce a line that can
stand on its own syntactically, though occasionally we have given
fewer (e.g., 116, 636). In transcribing the first line we have omitted
all punctuation but have retained capital letters (except in the first
word); we have used a capital letter at the beginning of the line, except
when it begins imperfectly, whether or not it has one in the printed
edition. We have reproduced the words of the line exactly as they
appear in the printed edition, but we have not reproduced italicized
suspensions, superscript marks and letters, and the like.

The first line is the incipit of the actual Middle English text,
omitting titles, introductory rubrics, and tables of contents. That

sounds easy in theory but is difficult in practice, and where there was any question about which of two competing incipits was the actual incipit, as often happens with recipes, we have given one as the main entry and the other as an unnumbered entry with a cross reference to the main one. If an introductory rubric seems to appear in the index, it is because it is the incipit of a substantive prologue or preface, or the actual beginning of the text proper. If an English work has a substantive prologue or preface, that provides the main (and only) incipit. If a translator has a prologue or preface, that provides the main incipit, with the incipit to the text proper appearing as an unnumbered entry. If one author has provided a prologue (or epilogue) for the work of another author (Caxton is the best example), the prologue (or epilogue) is indexed separately, with a cross reference to the other work. Acephalous texts are included as main entries in the alphabetical scheme, as with the supplement to IMEV, though separately edited fragments from main entries beginning imperfectly do not have their incipits listed as unnumbered entries.

If a Middle English prose text begins with Latin or French, we have given the first few words of the Latin or French but have omitted the rest (if there is any more), as indicated by a three-dot ellipsis, and have then given the English incipit as an unnumbered entry. If, however, an unnumbered incipit begins with Latin or French, we have usually not given a further unnumbered incipit beginning with the English.

The incipit has usually been taken from the first edition listed in the edition category. Exceptions are of two kinds: the first, and more frequent, is when it seemed more appropriate to use an incipit from an edition of a manuscript rather than from an early printed edition or when the first edition began imperfectly; the second is when we did not have access to the first printed edition. For all exceptions we have indicated from which edition we took the incipit with the formula "(from plus edition number)"; if no formula appears, it can be assumed that the incipit has been taken from the first edition listed.

The English incipits have been listed alphabetically according to the modern English spelling of the words involved. We have admitted archaic words into this scheme (e.g., lief, nim) as well as the -eth verb ending, both singular and plural, but obsolete words have been listed under their nearest modern English equivalent (e.g., ӡehur under Hear, onʒinneþ under beginneth, and ileue under believe). Numbers have been alphabetized with the spelling they would have in modern English if written out as words. The interjection oh is alphabetized under O, though the interjection ah is alphabetized under Ah to avoid confusion with the article a. Latin and French incipits are alphabetized as they appear in the printed editions. Errors or partial words in incipits of texts that begin imperfectly have been left as they appear in the printed edition (e.g., 635, 791).

One of the most difficult questions we had to answer was whether to list the incipits of all edited manuscripts of a given text.

Each case had to be decided individually, but in principle we decided that if an incipit differed substantively from the main incipit in the first five to ten words, we would list it as a separate but unnumbered entry with a cross reference to the main entry. In practice, however, we have seldom given unnumbered incipits, even if they differed substantively, when the main entry either preceded or followed or was very close, (12) unless they were incipits to separate versions of the main entry (e.g., 143, 308). We have been much more liberal with incipits that appear far from their main entry (e.g., 171, 313), and indeed an important feature of our index, which should be particularly useful to scholars and students working with Middle English prose materials in manuscript form, is the number of unnumbered cross-referenced entries (nearly 400, or circa thirty per cent of the total).

The first section following the incipit contains the following information, in order: author, title, genre, and date of composition. The author's name appears without comment when it is clear who he or she is (e.g., 183, 450), a question mark appears after the author's name when it is probable though not absolutely certain who he is (e.g., 205, 554), and square brackets around the author's name indicate that a work has been attributed to him but that it is unlikely that he wrote it (e.g., 362, 635). If none of these three permutations appears, the work is anonymous.

The second item in the section is the title. An underlined title means that it comes from an edited manuscript or, if such a title does not appear, from an early printed edition if one exists. If a title is excessively long, we occasionally omit unnecessary words in it (e.g., 65, 678). Occasionally we give two underlined titles, especially if they are quite different but both have manuscript authority or if one is Latin (e.g., 157, 452). In all underlined titles the spelling of i/j and u/v is normalized according to modern English usage. Any title within quotation marks is a modern creation, usually made by the editor and accepted in the scholarship. When a manuscript title is unfamiliar or differs considerably from the modern title, we also add the modern title in parentheses after the manuscript title (e.g., 71, 506).

The third item is genre. For this we normally give a generic term or phrase and then add to it whatever further brief information we think might be useful to the user of the index. Most typically this is information on the language or work from which a translation has been made (e.g., 387, 528). If the nature of the work is evident from its title, we often omit a generic description (e.g., 344, 421).

The last item is date of composition, and here we have simply followed informed opinion, which is usually that of the editor, on the matter. If a precise date is possible, we give it. Otherwise we use the following abbreviations: s.xiv in., the beginning of the fourteenth century; s. xiv (1), the first half of the same century; s. xiv med., the middle of the century; s. xiv (2), the second half of the century; s. xiv ex., the end of the century; s. xiv, an undetermined date in the century; s. xiv/xv, the turn of the century; s. xiv-xv, an undetermined period from the end of the century to the beginning of the next.

The second section following the incipit contains a numbered listing, arranged chronologically, of all editions of the complete work. The dates are given for all editions, both because they enable the user of the index to locate the editions, especially in series and journals, and because they illustrate at a glance the printing history of a work. In parentheses following each edition is the base manuscript used by the editor (if we know what it is), with folio or page numbers if we know them (they are omitted intentionally if the work occupies the whole of the manuscript); for the second (or third, etc.) occurrence of a base manuscript we refer to the first for the necessary information with the formula "(as in plus edition number)."

We have tried to examine all the editions we list, but occasionally we have been unable to lay our hands on certain editions (this is especially true of frequently reprinted works listed in STC). We have included as separate items second (and third, etc.) editions, but we have omitted reprints; we have done the same for STC editions even though strictly speaking many may be reprints. We have also included facsimile and diplomatic editions of STC editions. Unless dissertations have actually been printed (as is the case with some German ones from the late nineteenth and early twentieth centuries), they have been omitted.

Some refinements are inevitable, particularly refinements to conserve space. A work that has been edited in a journal or a series does not have the editor's name but only the name of the journal or series, usually abbreviated. If only the editor's name appears, it indicates that the title of the edition is similar to the title of the Middle English work in question; only when the title of the edition differs considerably from the title of the work do we give it. Any edition that appears in two or more main entries is abbreviated, either by author or by title or by both, for which see the list of abbreviations. For anthologies like Emerson or Kluge or Zupitza (and including also Foxe's Actes and Monuments) we give only one appearance, with the dates of later editions in parentheses following the date of the first edition. (13)

The third section following the incipit, when it appears, usually contains other manuscripts of the work in question arranged alphabetically by city, library, and shelfmark, (14) but it can also contain cross references to other entries in the index, bibliographical data (including Jolliffe numbers), references to Old English prose and Middle English verse versions of the same work, and other relevant information.

NOTES

(1)   By C. Brown and R.H. Robbins (New York: Columbia Uni-
        versity Press for the Index Society, 1943), with supplement by
        Robbins and J.L. Cutler (Lexington: University of Kentucky
        Press, 1965).
(2)   Structuralist Poetics (London: Routledge & Kegan Paul, 1975),
        chapter 8.
(3)   N.F. Blake, "The Form of Living in Prose and Poetry,"
        Archiv, 211 (1974), 300-308. Boldfaced numbers in paren-
        theses henceforth refer to entries in the index proper.
(4)   Cf. L. Thorndike, "Unde Versus," Traditio, 11 (1955), 163-
        93.
(5)   Verses in Sermons: Fasciculus Morum and Its Middle English
        Poems (Cambridge, Mass.: Medieval Academy of America,
        1978).
(6)   Cf. N.F. Blake, "Varieties of Middle English Religious
        Prose," in Chaucer and Middle English Studies in Honour of
        Rossell Hope Robbins, ed. B. Rowland (London: George Allen
        & Unwin, 1974), pp. 348-56.
(7)   We stress "comprehensive" to distinguish the scope of our work
        from P.S. Jolliffe's more limited but invaluable Check-List of
        Middle English Prose Writings of Spiritual Guidance (Toronto:
        Pontifical Institute of Mediaeval Studies, 1974).
(8)   With "Supplement" in Anglo-Saxon England, 5 (1976), 121-
        131.
(9)   Usually this is a matter of interpretation, depending on whether
        one emphasizes the date of the manuscript or the language of the
        text. For discussion of the problems posed by Harley 6258b see
        Ker, p. xix, and L.E. Voigts, "One Anglo-Saxon View of the
        Classical Gods," Studies in Iconography, 3 (1977), 13 note 14.
(10)   Once again, absolute consistency on this point has not seemed
        desirable; we have, for example, included early printed editions
        of the Statutes (686) and some papal bulls (518, 586).
(11)   Much of the following has been adapted from Lewis's "Editorial
        Technique in the Index of Middle English Prose," in Middle
        English Prose: Essays on Bibliographical Problems, ed.
        A.S.G. Edwards and D. Pearsall (New York: Garland Pub-
        lishing, Inc., 1981), pp. 43-64, with refinements to accommo-
        date decisions we have made on the index since 1980.
(12)   For example, the incipit to version D of 733 adds the word trew
        before lenght, but this variant did not seem significant enough
        to warrant listing the additional incipit. On the other hand,
        the substantive variant sixe in the incipit to edition 5 of 287
        seemed important enough to list, and in order to save space we
        inserted it in brackets in the main incipit.
(13)   When an author has written more than one version of a work or
        when it has proved impossible to establish the independence of

two or more versions of a work, it has seemed appropriate to arrange the relevant edition secions by versions (e.g., **308, 618**), but the principles and refinements just enumerated for the normal edition sections hold for them as well.

(14)   References to manuscripts, both in the third section and in parentheses following editions in the second secion, are somewhat abbreviated, with "Library" usually omitted and "College" always omitted for Oxford and Cambridge college libraries; full references will be found in the Manuscript Index.

Index of Printed
Middle English Prose

A Contrey ther was in which it happed that a wyse knyght whiche longe
had mayntened the ordre of chyualrye And that by the force and
noblesse   Incipit to text proper of **794**.

1 A curatt hadde in his parisshe a paryshene rebell vnbuxom and maili-
   cious that did till him many Iniurijes and harmys

   Fifteen short legends of the Virgin, s. xv.

   1. Anglia, 3 (1880), 320-25 (Lambeth Palace 432, ff. 85-89v).

   A good be-gynnyng makyth a god ende   See **116**.

2 A gode begynnyng makyth a gode endyng Felix principium finem facit
   esse beatum Hyt ys as ryȝth as a ramyeys horne Hoc est ita rectum sicut
   cornu

   Proverbs, with Latin equivalents, s. xiv (2).

   1. Franciplegius (1965), pp. 277-79 (BL Addl. 37075, ff. 70-
   71).

3 A good horsse must have xv propertyes and condicions that is to witte
   iij of a man iij of a woman iij of a fox iij of an hare iij of an asse

   XV Condycyons That a Goode Hors Schuld Have, s. xv.

   1. Rel. Ant., I (1841), 232-33 (BL Lansdowne 762, f. 16); 2.
   EETS es 100 (1907), p. xxv note (as in 1); 3. ed. A.G. Rigg, A
   Glastonbury Miscellany of the Fifteenth Century (1968), p. 74
   (TCC O.9.38, f. 49); 4. MÆ, 41 (1972), 238 (Bodl Wood
   empt. 18, f. 60), condensed version.

   Also in Aberystwyth NLW Porkington 10 and New York Columbia University Plimpton Add. 2. Also appears in the Boke of
   Hunting (IMEV 4064) from the Boke of St. Albans and as Chap.
   2 of **718**. Other ME prose versions in **9**, BL Cotton Galba E.
   IX, and Oxford Balliol 354.

4 A Grete clarke that men calle Rycharde of saynt Vyctor In a boke that
   he maketh þer of studye of wysdome wytnesseth and saythe that ij
   myghtes are in a mannes soule

[Richard Rolle], Benyamyn, a free and abridged translation of Richard of St. Victor's De Preparatione Animi ad Contemplationem, s. xiv ex.

1. H. Pepwell, 1521 (STC 20972, Part 1); 2. YW, I (1895), 162-72 (BL Harley 1022, ff. 74-99); 3. EETS os 231 (1955), pp. 12-46 (BL Harley 674, ff. 111-21); 4. Hodgson (1982), pp. 129-45 (as in 3).

Also in CCCC 385, CUL Ff.6.33, CUL Ii.6.39, CUL Kk.6.26, Cambridge (Mass.) Harvard University Richardson 22, Glasgow University Hunterian 258, BL Arundel 286, BL Harley 2373, London Westminster School 3, San Marino Huntington HM 127. Cf. 5.

5   A Grete clerk þat men cals Ricard of Saynt Victor settes in a buke þat he makes of contemplacioun thre wyrkyngs of cristen mans saule þat er þere

[Richard Rolle], Off Thre Wyrkyngs in Man's Saule, epistle on thought, thinking, and contemplation based on Richard of St. Victor's De Preparatione Animi ad Contemplationem, I.3, s. xiv ex.

1. YW, I (1895), 82 (CUL Dd.5.64, f. 142v, fragmentary text).

Also in Cambridge Magdalene Pepys 2125, TCC O.8.26, BL Sloane 1009 (abridged). Jolliffe M.5/O.15. Cf. 4.

6   A Grete differens es be-twene prechynge and techynge Prechynge es in a place where es clepynge to-gedyr or folwynge of pepyl in holy dayes in chyrches

Speculum Christiani, compilation of religious knowledge, with introductory prayer, s. xiv (2).

1. EETS os 182 (1933), pp. 2-140 (even pages only) (BL Harley 6580, ff. 2-62).

Harley 6580 is entirely in English; the other MSS (at least sixty six), as well as the early printed editions, are mainly Latin, with English prose in the Fifth Tabula (for an edition see EETS os 182, pp. 3-241, odd pages only).

7   A Grete reule to all lerned men was sette be Seint Paule in þe first
     capitle Ad Romanos where he saide þat he was dettour on to wise men
     and onwise Wise men clepid he gretly lerned and onwise simple ydiotis

     John Capgrave, Lif of Seynt Augustyn, ca. 1450.

     1. EETS os 140 (1910), pp. 1-60 (BL Addl. 36704, ff. 5-45).

8   A holy woman in France rawiste in spret sagh a Cownteyse to wome
     scho was full homle be drane to hell with deuls

     [Richard Rolle], exemplum from De Dono Timoris, s. xiv.

     1. YW, I (1895), 157 (BL Harley 1022, f. lv).

9   A horse hath xviij proprietees iij of an ox iij of an asse iij of a fox iij of
     an hare and vi of a woman

     "Eighteen Properties of a Horse", s. xv (2).

     1. Harley and Bickley (1928), p. 421 (San Marino Huntington
     HU 1051, f. 62v); 2. Hanna (1984), p. 52 (as in 1).

     Other ME prose versions in 3, BL Cotton Galba E. IX, and
     Oxford Balliol 354.

10   A lernid man in the lawe of this lande come late to the same Sir John
     Fortescu sayinge in this wise Sir while ye were in Scotelande with
     Henry

     John Fortescue, Declaracion upon Certayn Wrytinges Sent Oute
     of Scotteland, s. xv (2).

     1. Clermont (1869), I, 523-41 (BL Royal 17 D.xv).

     Also in Holkham Hall Earl of Leicester MS, BL Harley 537, BL
     Harley 1757, BL Addl. 48020, BL Addl. 48079, Lambeth Palace
     262, Bodl Cherry 20 (1), Bodl Digby 198, San Marino Hunting-
     ton EL 34 C 18.

A maydene thare was fro here berth gracyouslye blessede of oure lorde
Godde insomoche that hytt semede to alle folke that this chosene childe
schulde have gyevene uppe the spyrite   Incipit to text proper of 658.

5

A man that dremeth that byrdys ffyghten   See **100**.

11   A man þat wylneþ for to profyȝte in þe wey of perfeccyon and
souereynly to plese god he muste bysylye studye to haue þe maters of
þise IX poyntys in hys herte

IX Poyntys, short treatise on the nine points best pleasing to
God, s. xiv.

1. YW, II (1896), 375-77 (BL Harley 1706, ff. 151-54v).

Also in TCC B.15.39. Jolliffe I.26. For verse versions see
IMEV 212 and 1188; other prose versions in BL Harley 1704,
Bodl Eng. poet. a. 1, Bodl Rawlinson C. 285.

12   . . . a meruulus wytt þat bothe he was a nobyl werryur of knightly
prowes alle the dayis of this present lyfe eke a nobyl phylysophyr

Johannes de Caritate, Boke of þe Privyte of Privyteis, book of
instruction translated from the full Latin Secreta Secretorum, s.
xv (2).

1. EETS os 276 (1977), pp. 114-202 (formerly San Juan Capistrano, California, Honeyman MS, ff. 4-109v, beginning imperfectly).

13   A nedefull thynge to knaw god all-myghty er þe tene Comandementis
þat god has gifen vs Of þe whilke tene þe thre þat er first aw vs haly to
hald onence oure god

John Gaytryge, "Of the Ten Commandments", extract from his
sermon circulating as a separate item, s. xiv (2).

1. YW, I (1895), 108-9 (Bodl Rawlinson C. 285, ff. 61v-62v).

See **71**.

14   A nobile knowinge of nature ys þe whiche enserchiþ qualities within a
man by fformes withoute and þat doþe þe tretis of þe science of
phisonomye

Þe Booke of Phisonomye, treatise on physiognomy, s. xiv (?).

1. Krochalis and Peters (1975), pp. 219-28 (CUL Ll.4.14,

6

ending imperfectly).

A scolere at pares had done many full synnys þe whylke he hade schame to schryfe hym of   Incipit to text proper of **58**.

15   A simple maid of the Realm [of Englonde now] in exile within the Realm of [Scottis knowyng the] Title by the which Edwarde (from 2)

John Fortescue, "On the Title of the House of York", legal tract, s. xv (2).

    1. Clermont (1869), I, 497-502 (BL Cotton Julius F. VI), beginning and ending imperfectly; 2. Plummer (1885), pp. 355-56 (BL Cotton Vespasian F. IX, f. 122), ending imperfectly.

A soule þat is reised vp wiþ heunli and gostli desires and affecciouns to þe worship of God and to þe helþe of mannes soule   Incipit to text proper of **561**.

16   A special frend in God axiþ bi charite þes fyve questiouns of a mek prest in God First what is love Aftirward where is love þe þridd tyme he axiþ hou God schuld medefully be loved

"Five Questions of Love", Wycliffite tract, s. xiv (2).

    1. <u>SEW</u>, III (1871), 183-85 (Oxford New 95, ff. 127v-35); 2. Winn (1929), pp. 110-12 (as in 1).

17   A woman solatarie and recluse coueytinge to knowe the nommbre of the woundes of Oure Lorde Ihesu Crist oftyn preyd to God of speciall grace þat He wolde wouchesaffe to schewe her hem

"A Woman Recluse and the Wounds of Jesus", legend commonly found in <u>Horae</u>, s. xv (2).

    1. Louis (1980), pp. 264-68 (Bodl Tanner 407, ff. 42-43).

    Another version in BL Harley 2869. Latin versions in CUL Ii.6.43, BL Arundel 506, and BL Addl. 37787.

A ȝonge mane a chanone at parys vn-chastely and delycyousely lyfande and full of many syynys laye seke to þe dede   Incipit to text proper

18 A Yong man that called was Mellebeus the whiche was mighty and
    riche begat a doughter vpon his wyf that Callyd was Prudence

Geoffrey Chaucer, Chaucers Tale of Melibee, from the "Canterbury Tales", s. xiv ex.

1. W. Caxton, [1477?] (STC 5082); 2. W. Caxton, [1483?]
(STC 5083); 3. R. Pynson, [1492?] (STC 5084); 4. W. de
Worde, 1498 (STC 5085); 5. R. Pynson, 1526 (STC 5086); 6.
Thynne (1532; STC 5068); 7. Thynne, 2nd ed. (1542; STC
5069); 8. Thynne, 3rd ed. ([1545?]; STC 5071); 9. Stow (1561;
STC 5075); 10. Speght (1598; STC 5077); 11. Speght, 2nd ed.
(1602; STC 5080); 12. Speght, 3rd ed. (1687); 13. Urry (1721);
14. Morell (1737); 15. Tyrwhitt (1775); 16. J. Bell (1782); 17.
Anderson (1793); 18. Tyrwhitt, 2nd ed. (1798); 19. Chalmers
(1810); 20. Aldine (1845); 21. Wright (1847-51) (BL Harley
7334); 22. R. Bell (1854-56), 4 (as in 21); 23. Aldine, rev. ed.
(1866); 24. Mätzner, I, 2 (1869); 25. Chaucer Soc., 1st series
25 (1872) (Aberystwyth NLW Peniarth 392, CUL Gg.4.27, BL
Lansdowne 851, Oxford CCC 198, Petworth House Lord Leconfield 7, San Marino Huntington EL 26 C 9); 26. Chaucer Soc.,
1st series 32 (1874) (San Marino Huntington El 26 C 9); 27.
Chaucer Soc., 1st series 33 (1874) (CUL Gg.4.27); 28. Chaucer
Soc., 1st series 39 (1875) (Aberystwyth NLW Peniarth 392); 29.
Chaucer Soc., 1st series 41 (1875) (Oxford CCC 198); 30.
Chaucer Soc., 1st series 42 (1875) (Petworth House Lord Leconfield 7); 31. Chaucer Soc., 1st series 43 (1875) (BL Lansdowne
851); 32. R. Bell, rev. ed. (1878); 33. Gilman (1880); 34.
Poetical ([1880]); 35. Blackwood (1880?); 36. Pollard (1886-
87); 37. Skeat, Complete (1894), 4, 199-240; 38. Ellis (1896);
39. Globe (1898); 40. Lounsbury (1900); 41. Skeat, Complete,
2nd ed. (1900); 42. Chaucer Soc., 1st series 96 (1902) (CUL
Dd.4.24); 43. Thynne (1905) (facsimile of 6); 44. Works of
Chaucer (1906); 45. Burrell (1908); 46. Burrell, rev. ed.
(1912); 47. Koch (1915) (as in 26); 48. MacCracken, CT
(1928); 49. Shakespeare Head (1929); 50. Geoffrey Chaucer
(1929-30); 51. Complete Works (1930); 52. Pollard, 2nd ed.
(1931); 53. Robinson (1933), pp. 201-26 (as in 26); 54. Manly-
Rickert (1940), 4, 152-215 (as in 28, etc.); 55. Robinson, 2nd
ed. (1957), pp. 167-88 (as in 26); 56. Cawley (1958); 57.
Winterich (1958) (facsimile of 38); 58. Scolar Press (1969)
(facsimile of 6); 59. (1972) (facsimile of 2); 60. Pratt (1974),
pp. 167-207 (as in 26 supplemented by 28); 61. Fisher (1977),
pp. 253-80 (as in 26); 62. Ruggiers (1979), pp. 858-933 (as in
28); 63. Blake, CT (1980), pp. 491-529 (as in 28).

Also in Alnwick Castle Duke of Northumberland MS, Austin University of Texas 143, Cambridge Fitzwilliam Museum Mc-Clean 181, Cambridge Magdalene Pepys 2006, TCC R.3.3, TCC R.3.15, CUL Ii.3.26, CUL Mm.2.5, Chicago University 564, Chatsworth Duke of Devonshire MS (Christie's 6 June 1974 to L.D. Feldman), Geneva Bodmer Foundation Cod. 48, Glasgow University Hunterian 197, Holkham Hall Earl of Leicester 667, Lichfield Cathedral 29, Lincoln Cathedral 110, BL Arundel 140, BL Egerton 2726, BL Egerton 2863, BL Egerton 2864, BL Harley 1758, BL Harley 7333, BL Royal 17 D.xv, BL Royal 18 C.ii, BL Sloane 1009, BL Sloane 1685, BL Sloane 1686, BL Addl. 5140, BL Addl. 25178 (imperfect), BL Addl. 35286, London Royal College of Physicians 388, Manchester Chetham 152, Manchester Rylands English 113, New York Morgan M 249, Bodl Barlow 20, Bodl Bodley 414, Bodl Hatton Donat. 1, Bodl Laud Miscellaneous 600, Bodl Rawlinson poet. 141, Bodl Rawlinson poet. 149, Bodl Rawlinson poet. 223, Bodl Selden Arch. B. 14, Oxford Christ Church 152, Oxford New 314, Oxford Trinity 49, Paris BN anglais 39, Philadelphia Rosenbach Foundation 1084/1 (Phillipps 8137, imperfect), Princeton University 100, San Marino Huntington HM 144, Stonyhurst College B.xxiii. Melibee circulated separately in BL Arundel 140, BL Sloane 1009, and Stonyhurst College B.xxiii. Many reprints of the various editions in the 18th, 19th, and early 20th centuries.

19 Abbas Make the signe for age and also for a woman Aftirward Meue thy fore fynger of thy right hand vndir the litle fynger of thy lefte hande

Thomas Betson, The Boke of Sygnes, a table of signs used during the hours of silence by the sisters and brothers of Syon Abbey, s. xv.

1. Bentley (1833), pp. 415-19 (London St. Paul's Cathedral 5, ff. 69-72); 2. Aungier (1840), pp. 405-9 (as in 1); 3. Hogg (1980), 3, 134-44 (as in 1).

20 Abbas non debet esse nimis rigidus . . . Som tyme þer was ane abbott þat asked councell of Saynt Anselme & sayd vnto hym what sall we do with childer þat er nurysshid & broght vpp in our clostre

"An Alphabet of Tales", collection of exempla translated from the Latin Alphabetum Narrationum of Etienne de Besançon, s. xv.

1. EETS os 126 (1904) and 127 (1905) (BL Addl. 25719).

21 Aboute Candelmasse last a chapelein of my lorde of Clarence called
maistr John Barnby & with him John Clare preste cam to my lord
Confession of Sir Robert Welles (1470), ca. 1470.

1. Bentley (1833), pp. 282-84 (BL Harley 283, f. 283).

Aboute the dawnynge of the day whan the first cleerte of the sun and
nature is content of the rest of the nyght   Incipit to text proper of
778.

22 About þo [glorious] mayden of qwam oure lord Ihesu Crist toke flesch
& blode we may vmthynke vs of hir lyfe

[Richard Rolle], Þe Reule of þe Liif of Oure Lady, translation of
Chap. 3 of St. Bonaventure's Meditationes Vite Christi, s. xiv.

1. YW, I (1895), 158-61 (BL Harley 1022, ff. 64-65); 2. YW, I
(1895), 158-59 (Bodl Bodley 938, f. 262).

Also in Cambridge Magdalene Pepys 2125, BL Harley 2339, BL
Royal 8 C.i, London Westminster School 3, Bodl Ashmole 41.

Aboute the sprynge of the day whanne the sune shewyth his furst light
and nature content through kyndly rest of the nyght   Incipit to text
proper of 779.

23 Accipe red fenell rede rose rew march beteyn eufrace fylage endyne
ocularis and celidone flowyris off wodbynd rotys off pyony or þe leuys
off þe wȝyte wyn-tre off ech quantyte

John of Burgundy, Practica Phisicalis, medical recipes, s. xv
(?).

1. ed. H. Schöffler, Beiträge zur mittelenglischen Medizinlitera-
tur (1919), pp. 192-260 (Bodl Rawlinson D. 251, ff. 72v-113).

24 Accipiant repromissionem Vocati . . . I rede in Genesi the firste book
of holi write 12 16 & 17 capitulis þat God thorw þe heȝe loue þat he
had in-to þe progenie and te posterite of Abraham

Hugh Legat, Hugonis Legat in Passione Domine, sermon, ca.
1389-1404.

1. Grisdale (1939), pp. 1-21 (Worcester Cathedral F. 10, ff. 8-13v).

Ach off hede   See **447**.

Ad confortandum lumen oculorum   See **640**.

25 Adam was made of oure lord god in the same place that Jhesu was
borne in that is to seye in the cite of Bethleem

Tretys of Adam and Eve (from B), devotional treatise, s. xiv.

A. Standard version (containing Corpus Adae and Vita Adae et
Evae): 1. Archiv, 74 (1885), 345-53 (Bodl Bodley 596, ff. 1-
12).

B. Expanded version (s. xiv/xv) circulating separately: 1. Archiv, 74 (1885), 353-65 (BL Harley 4775, ff. 258v-64, as part of
the Gilte Legende collection); 2. EETS os 155 (1921), pp. 76-99
(BL Addl. 39574, ff. 59v-88).

Another MS of A: TCC R.3.21. Other MSS of B: BL Harley
1704, BL Harley 2388, Bodl Ashmole 244, Bodl Ashmole 802,
Bodl Douce 15; B also appears in some MSS of the Gilte
Legende: BL Egerton 876, BL Addl. 35298, Lambeth Palace 72,
Bodl Douce 372.

26 Adest nomen tuum et munera tua accepta erunt . . . Good men and
wymmen that Lord þat made all thynge of now3th and man aftur ys
owne similitude and liknesse

Sermon collection, ca. 1378-1417.

1. EETS os 209 (1940) (BL Royal 18 B.xxiii, ff. 51-72, 74-148,
149v-57).

27 After dyuerse werkes made translated and achieued hauyng noo werke
in hande I sittyng in my studye where as laye many dyuerse paunflettis
and bookys

William Caxton, Eneydos, translation of the Livre des Eneydes,
a French version of an Italian paraphrase of parts of Virgil's
Æneid, ca. 1490.

11

1. W. Caxton, 1490? (STC 24796); 2. EETS es 57 (1890) (as in 1).

Princeton University 128 (ca. 1600) made from Caxton's edition.

28   After I had drawe þe martirdom of the holy virgyn and martir seynt Kateryne from latyn into englesshe as hit is wryton in legendis þat are compleet

þe Lyf and Martirdom of Seynt Kateryne (of Alexandria), saint's life from the Gilte Legende circulating separately, 1438.

1. Roxburghe 112 (1884), pp. 1-67 (Cambridge (Mass.) Harvard University Richardson 44, ff. 22-125).

Also in Cambridge Gonville and Caius 390/610 and BL Addl. 33510. Three other versions: (a) in Aberystwyth NLW Porkington 10, Edinburgh NLS Advocates 19.3.1, BL Cotton Titus A. XXVI, BL Harley 5259, Manchester Chetham 8009, and Oxford CCC 237; (b) in CCCC 142, Cambridge Fitzwilliam Museum McClean 129, TCC O.9.1, and Stonyhurst College B.xliii in addition to complete MSS of the Gilte Legende; (c) in BL Harley 4012. Cf. 138 and 727.

29   Efter ure lauerdes pine ant his passiun ant his deaþ o rode ant his ariste of deaþ ant efter his upastihunge as he steah to heouene weren monie martyrs wepme ba ant wummen (from 2)

þe Liflade ant te Passiun of Seinte Margarete, saint's life, ca. 1200.

1. ed. O. Cockayne (1862), reprinted as EETS os 13 (1866), pp. 1-23 (BL Royal 17 A.xxvii, ff. 37-56); 2. EETS os 193 (1934), even pages (Bodl Bodley 34, ff. 18-36v); 3. EETS os 193 (1934), odd pages (as in 1); 4. d'Ardenne (1977), pp. 53-94 (as in 2).

After solempne and wyse wryters of Arte and of scyence that had swetenes and lykyng al her lyf tyme to studye and to trauaille aboute connyng and knowleche   Incipit to text proper of 605.

30   After that I had accomplysshed and fynysshed dyuers hystoryes as wel of contemplacyon as of other hystoryal and worldly actes of grete conquerours and prynces

William Caxton, prologue to Malory's Morte d'Arthur, 1485.

1. W. Caxton, 1485 (STC 801); 2. W. de Worde, 1498 (STC 802); 3. W. de Worde, 1529 (STC 803), beginning imperfectly; 4. W. Copland, [1557] (STC 804); 5. T. East, 1578 (STC 805); 6. Ames (1749), pp. 43-45 (as in 1); 7. Herbert, I (1785), 57-60 (as in 1); 8. Southey (1817), I, i-vi (as in 1); 9. Blades, Life, I (1861), 177-81 (as in 1); 10. Sommer, I (1889), 1-5 (as in 1); 11. Aurner (1926), pp. 271-75 (as in 1); 12. EETS os 176 (1928), pp. 92-95 (as in 1); 13. Mott (1933), I (as in 1); 14. Vinaver, Works (1947), I, cxi-cxiv (as in 1); 15. Vinaver, Malory (1954), pp. xv-xviii (as in 1); 16. Vinaver, Works, 2nd ed. (1967), I, cxliii-cxlvi (as in 1); 17. ed. A.G. Rigg, The English Language (1968), pp. 217-19 (as in 1); 18. Vinaver, Malory, 2nd ed. (1971), pp. xiii-xv (as in 1); 19. Blake, COP (1973), pp. 106-10 (as in 1); 20. Blake, Selections (1973), pp. 5-8 (as in 1); 21. Needham (1976) (facsimile of 1); 22. Spisak and Matthews (1983) (as in 1).

31 Afftir þat I haue first ȝolden þankyngis to almyȝti god þe ȝeuere boþe of euerlastyng lijf of soulis & helþe of bodies þat heeliþ alle oure grete soris

An Inventarie or a Collectarie in þe Cirurgical Partie of Medi-cyn, partial translation of Guy de Chauliac's Inventarium seu Collectorium in Parte Cyrurgicali Medicine, s. xv.

1. ed. B. Wallner (1970), pp. 3-34 (Cambridge Gonville and Caius 336/725, ff. 1-16).

There are three other Middle English translations of the Inventa-rium, two complete and one interpolated. One complete trans-lation is 32; the other is partially edited by B. Wallner (1964, 1969, 1976, 1979, 1982) from New York Academy of Medicine 12.

32 After þat I schall firste ȝeue þonkynges to God ȝeuynge euerlastynge lif of soules and helþe of bodyes and helynge grete sikenesses by þe grace whiche He offrede to all fleisshe

Cyrurgie of Maistre Guydo de Cauliaco, translation of Guy de Chauliac's Inventarium seu Collectorium in Parte Cyrurgicali Medicine, s. xv in.

1. EETS os 265 (1971) (Paris BN anglais 25, ff. 2-191v).

13

There are three other Middle English translations of the Inventarium, one complete, one interpolated, and one partial. The complete translation is partially edited by B. Wallner (1964, 1969, 1976, 1979, 1982) from New York Academy of Medicine 12. For the partial translation see 31.

33 Aftir the crucifiyng of oure lord Ihesu crist and that the holy cristen feith was magnified and augmented in alle the Reaumes that at this day be cristened

"Three Kings' Sons", romance translated from French, s. xv.

1. EETS es 67 (1895) (BL Harley 326, ff. 8-123v).

34 Aftyr the fyrst mone of thepyphany comyte x days and the nexte sonday after ys loken alleluia then weddyng

Notes on the calendar, s. xv ex.

1. Hanna (1984), p. 36 (San Marino Huntington HM 1086, f. 176v).

35 After the nowble wryters of artes to whom hit was a pleasure in this life presente to fixe theire studies and laboures abowte the knowlege of thynges and virtues moralle

"Polychronicon", translation of Ranulph Higden's Polychronicon, continued to 1401, s. xv in.

1. Rolls 41, 8 vols. (1865-1882), odd pages, lower halves (BL Harley 2261).

See 605.

36 Aftre the synne off Adam expulsed and put out of the place of Paradice for the synne While he cried in to the mercyes of the Lord he was clad with periȝomate

"Legend of the Cross Before Christ", translation of the Latin Legenda (s. xiii), s. xv.

1. MÆ, 34 (1965), 212-22 (Worcester Cathedral F. 172, ff. 13-16).

After the Tyme that man was exyled oute of the hyghe Cyte of heuene by the rightwys dome of almyghty god souerayne kynge   Incipit to text proper of 553.

37   Agens hem that seyn that hooli wrigt schulde not or may not be drawun in to Engliche we maken thes resouns (from 6)

John Purvey (?), "The Compendyous Treatise", Wycliffite tract on Bible translation, s. xv in.

1. H. Luft, 1530 (STC 3021); 2. H. Luft, 1530 (STC 1462.5, Part 2; 6813, Part 2); 3. R. Banckes, [ca. 1538?] (STC 3022); 4. Foxe (1563), pp. 452-55 (as in 1 plus BL Harley 425, ff. 1-2v); 5. ed. F. Fry (1863; rptd. 1871) (facsimile of 2); 6. Deanesly (1920), pp. 439-45 (TCC B.14.50, ff. 26-30v); 7. MÆ, 7 (1938), 170-79 (as in 6).

Also in CCCC 100, CCCC 298, TCC B.1.26, BL Cotton Vitellius D. VII, Lambeth Palace 594, New York Morgan M 648. Cf. 601.

38   Agnus castus is an herbe þat men clepyn totsane or parkleuys and þis herbe haȝt lewys sumqwat reddysch lyke to þe lewys of orage and þis herbe haȝt senewys in his lewys (from 10)

Herbal ("Agnus Castus"), s. xv (1).

1. R. Banckes, 1525 (STC 4720); 2. R. Banckes, 1526 (STC 4721); 3. R. Redman, [1530?] (STC 4722); 4. R. Redman, [1541?] (STC 4723); 5. T. Petyt, 1541 (STC 4724); 6. W. Middleton, 1546 (STC 4725); 7. W. Copland, [1552?] (STC 4726); 8. W. Copland, [1533?] (STC 4727); 9. J. Kynge, [1560?] (STC 4728); 10. ed. G. Brodin (1950) (Stockholm Kungliga Biblioteket X.90, pp. 156-216, with insertions from various other MSS).

Also in Aberystwyth NLW Peniarth 207, Aberystwyth NLW Peniarth 369B, TCC R.14.32, BL Arundel 272, BL Harley 3840, BL Royal 18 A.vi (two copies), BL Sloane 7 (fragment), BL Sloane 120, BL Sloane 135, BL Sloane 297, BL Sloane 962, BL Sloane 1315, BL Sloane 2460, BL Sloane 2948, BL Sloane 3160 (fragments), BL Sloane 3489, BL Addl. 4698, BL Addl. 4797, Oxford Balliol 329, Bodl Ashmole 1432, Bodl Ashmole 1447, Bodl Bodley 483, Bodl Bodley 536, Bodl Bodley 1031, Bodl Digby 95, Bodl Laud Miscellaneous 553, Bodl Wood D. 8, Bodl Addl. A. 106 (three copies, one a fragment), York Minster

39   A dere brethir and systirs I see þat many walde be in religyone bot þat may noghte owthir for pouerte or for drede of thaire kyne or for band of maryage (from 4)

þe Abbey of þe Holy Gost, devotional treatise translated from French, 1350-70.

1. W. de Worde, [1496]; 2. W. de Worde, 1497 (STC 13609); 3. W. de Worde, [1521] (STC 13610); 4. EETS os 26 (1867), pp. 48-58 (Lincoln Cathedral 91, ff. 271-76); 5. YW, I (1895), 321-37 (as in 4); 6. EETS os 26, rev. ed. (1914), pp. 51-62 (as in 4); 7. Blake, MERP (1972), pp. 88-102 (Bodl Laud Miscellaneous 210, ff. 180-86v).

Also in Aberystwyth NLW Peniarth 334A, Cambridge Jesus 46, TCC O.1.29, CUL Dd.11.89, CUL Ii.4.9, CUL Ll.5.18, Hopton Hall Chandos-Pole-Gell MS, BL Cotton Vespasian D. XIII, BL Egerton 3245, BL Harley 1704, BL Harley 2406, BL Harley 5272, BL Stowe 39, BL Addl. 22283, BL Addl. 36983, Lambeth Palace 432, Longleat Marquis of Bath 4, Bodl Douce 141, Bodl Douce 323, Bodl Eng. poet. a. 1, Oxford CCC 155, Stonyhurst College B.xxiii, Tokyo Takamiya 65, Winchester College 33. Jolliffe H.16. Cf. 590, which is usually joined in MS with the Abbey.

40   A Good curteys aungell ordeyned to my gouernale I knowe well my feblenes & my vnconnynnge also well I wote þat strength haue I none

Prayer to guardian angel, s. xiv (2) (?).

1. W. de Worde, 1506 (STC 21259); 2. W. de Worde, [1519?] (STC 21260); 3. Maskell, II (1846), 270 (BL Harley 2445, f. 94); 4. YW, II (1896), 105 (as in 1); 5. Maskell, 2nd ed., III (1882), 291-92 (as in 3).

Also in CUL Addl. 6686, Nijmegen Universiteit 194, San Marino Huntington HM 147. Cf. 487.

41   A my broþir if þou coueitist to wite þouȝ J with not how moost parfijt and fullest riȝtwisnes is for to loue god wiþ al þe herte and wiþ al þe wille

A Tretiis þat Seynt Austin Made to an Eerl Clepid Julian, trans-

lation of the De Salutaribus Documentis/Exhortationes Beati
Augustini ad Julianum Comitem of Pseudo-Augustine, s. xiv
ex.

1. ed. S.L. Fristedt, The Wycliffe Bible, II (1969), 1-60 (BL
Harley 2330, ff. 1-66).

Also in CUL Ii.6.55, Cambridge (Mass.) Harvard University
Richardson 3, and Oxford All Souls 24.

42   Alas for sorwe grete prestis sittinge in derkenessis and in schadewe of
deep noȝt hauynge him þat openly crieþ al þis I wille ȝeue ȝif þou
auaunce me

On the Last Age of the Chirche, Wycliffite tract, s. xiv (2).

1. ed. J.H. Todd (1840) (TCD 244, ff. 208-10v).

Alas fortune alas I that som tyme in delycyous houres was wont to
enioy blysful stoundes am nowe dryue by vnhappy heuynesse to
bewayle my sondrye yuels in tene   Incipit to text proper of 451.

43   Allas I wepyng am constrained to begynne vers of soroufull matere
That whylom in flourisshing studye made delitable ditees For lo rend-
yng muses of poetes enditen to me thinges to be writen

Geoffrey Chaucer, Boecius de Consolacione Philosophie/Boke of
Consolacion of Philosophie, consolatory literature, ca. 1380.

1. W. Caxton, 1478? (STC 3199), with epilogue by Caxton; 2.
Thynne (1532; STC 5068); 3. Thynne, 2nd ed. (1542; STC
5069); 4. Thynne, 3rd ed. ([1545?]; STC 5071); 5. Stow (1561;
STC 5075); 6. Speght (1598; STC 5077); 7. Speght, 2nd ed.
(1602; STC 5080); 8. Speght, 3rd ed. (1687); 9. Urry (1721);
10. Chalmers (1810); 11. EETS es 5 (1868) (BL Addl. 10340, ff.
3-40); 12. Chaucer Soc., 1st series 75 (1886) (CUL Ii.3.21, ff.
1-180); 13. Skeat, Complete (1894), 2, 1-151 (as in 12); 14.
Ellis (1896); 15. Globe (1898), pp. 352-437 (CUL Ii.1.38, ff.
1-69); 16. Lounsbury (1900); 17. Skeat, Complete, 2nd ed.
(1900); 18. Thynne (1905) (facsimile of 2); 19. MacCracken,
College (1913); 20. Shakespeare Head (1929) (as in 15); 21.
Complete Works (1930); 22. Robinson (1933), pp. 374-448 (as
in 15); 23. Robinson, 2nd ed. (1957), pp. 320-84 (as in 15); 24.
Winterich (1958) (facsimile of 14); 25. Scolar Press (1969)
(facsimile of 2); 26. Fisher (1977), pp. 816-903 (as in 12); 27.

17

Boyd (1978), pp. 40-75 (as in 1); 28. Studies in the Age of Chaucer, 1 (1979), 145-46 (Columbia University of Missouri Fragmenta Manuscripta 150).

Also in Aberystwyth NLW Peniarth 393D (fragment), Cambridge Pembroke 215, BL Harley 2421, BL Addl. 16165, Bodl Bodley 797, Salisbury Cathedral 13. Bodl Auct. F.3.5 is a commentary using Chaucerian text as lemma only. For a verse translation by John Walton see IMEV 1597.

44   Alas that euer I synned in my lyfe to me is come this day þe dredfull tydynges that euer I herde

> Treatyse of the Dyenge Creature, didactic and consolatory tract, s. xv ex. (?).

> 1. W. de Worde, 1507 (STC 6034); 2. W. de Worde, 1514 (STC 6035); 3. W. de Worde, [n.d.] (STC 6035a).

Allebehitt this booke maye be clepede the booke of reuelacions ande of vysiouns ande thowe hitt be profytabelle ande lernynge that ye schalle fynde thareyn   Incipit to second prologue of 658.

45   Alixander þe grete conquerour in alle his conquest and werres was reuled by Aristotel þe worthiest philosopher þat euer was

> Certeyne Rewles of Phisnomy, followed by A Calculacion to Knowe by of Tuo Men Feghtynge, translation of the physiognomy and onomancy sections of the Latin Secreta Secretorum, s. xiv ex.

> 1. EETS os 276 (1977), pp. 10-17 (BL Sloane 213, ff. 118v-21).

46   Al for wondrid of owre self auȝte vs for to be ȝif we be þouȝte vs innerly of þe grete vnmesurable loue þat god to vs hath shewed

> Walter Hilton (?), Prickynge of Love, devotional treatise translated and abridged from the Stimulus Amoris attributed to St. Bonaventure, s. xiv ex.

> 1. ed. H. Kane, 2 vols. (1983) (BL Harley 2254, ff. 1-72v).

> Also in TCC B.14.19, CUL Hh.1.11 (selections), CUL Hh.1.12 (selections), Downside Abbey 26542, Durham Univer-

sity Cosin V.III.8, Leeds University Brotherton 501 (selections), BL Harley 2415, BL Addl. 22283, Bodl Ashmole 1286 (selections), Bodl Bodley 480, Bodl Eng. poet. a. 1, New Haven Yale University 223, Paris BN anglais 41 (selections), Philadelphia University of Pennsylvania English 8, Taunton Somerset Record Office Heneage 3084 (selections).

47 Al Ingratitude vtterly settyng apart we owe to calle to our myndes the manyfolde gyftes of grace with the benefaittis that our lorde of his moost plentiueuse bonte hath ymen [sic] vs wretches in this present transitoire lif

Anthony Woodville, Cordyal, translation from Jean Mielot's Quatre Derrenieres Choses (with epilogue by William Caxton), 1478.

1. W. Caxton, 1479 (STC 5758); 2. [W. de Worde, n.d.] (STC 5759); 3. ed. J.A. Mulders ([1962]) (as in 1).

Two MSS copied from 1: CUL Nn.3.10, s. xv/xvi, and BL Sloane 779, 1484.

Alle manere men schulde holde Goddis comaundementis for wiþoute keping and rulyng bi hem mai no man be saued   Incipit to edition B.3 of 49.

48 Alle maner of men schulden holde Godes biddynges For withouten holdynge of hem mai no mon beo saued

Ten Comaundementes, orthodox commentary on the ten commandments, s. xiv (2).

1. EETS os 217 (1942), pp. 317-33 (BL Addl. 22283, ff. 92-93, inserted in 668.

Also in Cambridge Emmanuel 246, BL Harley 218, BL Harley 2346, BL Royal 17 A.xxvi, London Westminster School 3, Bodl Laud Miscellaneous 524, Oxford University 97, Paris Bibl. Ste.-Geneviève 3390, Princeton University Deposit 1459, San Marino Huntington HM 744.   Cf. 49 and 650.

49 Alle manere of men schulde holde þe comaundementis of God for wiþouten holdynge of hem may no man be savyd And so þe gospel telliþ how oon askide Crist what he schulde do for to come to hevene

19

John Wyclif (?), Þe Ten Comaundementis, commentary on the ten commandments, s. xiv (2).

A. Original version: 1. SEW, III (1871), 82-92 (Bodl Bodley 789, ff. 108 ff.)

B. Compressed versions: 1. EETS os 118 (1901), pp. 33-57 (odd pages only) and 58-59 (Lambeth Palace 408, ff. 6v-12); 2. PMLA, 69 (1954), 688-92 (New York Morgan M 861, ff. 1-3v); 3. Bulletin of the John Rylands Library, 42 (1959-60), 371-76 (Manchester Rylands English 85, ff. 2v-9); 4. Bühler (1973), pp. 498-502 (as in 2).

Other MSS of A: BL Arundel 268, BL Harley 2346, London Society of Antiquaries 681, Bodl Rawlinson A. 381, Bodl Rawlinson A. 423. Other MSS of B: Glasgow University Gen. 223, New York Columbia University Plimpton Add. 3, Bodl Douce 246. Expanded versions appear in TCD 245, BL Harley 2398, and York Minster XVI.L.12. Cf. 48 and 650.

50   Alle manere of thyng þat es by-gun þat may turne to the profyte of mannes saule to god allonely and to oure lady saynte Marie be þe wirchipe gyffene and to none othir erthely mane ne womane

      A Revelaycyone Schewed to ane Holy Womane Now One Late Tyme, dream visit from a certain Margaret from Purgatory in 1422, s. xv med.

      1. YW, I (1895), 383-92 (Lincoln Cathedral 91, ff. 250v-57v).

      Also in Longleat Marquis of Bath 29, Bodl Eng. th. c. 58.

51   Al men þat wyll her of þe sege of Jerusalem her ȝe may her of gret meraculs þat almytty God wroȝt to schow his goodnys and of gret vengans þat he toke for syn

      Sege of Jerusaleme, romance based on an abridged version of Titus and Vespasian (IMEV 1881), s. xv (2).

      1. ed. A. Kurvinen (1969) (Aberystwyth NLW Porkington 10, ff. 157v-84).

      Another prose version in Cleveland Public Library W q091.92-C468, John G. White Collection (formerly Aldenham). Verse versions in IMEV 1583 and 1881. Cf. 241.

Alle men þat wol liuen in þis world cristenliche schall suffre persecucions as þe Apostel seiþ or from withouten be malice of men or from
withinne bi temptacion of þe fend   See 554.

52   All Prynces and other Lordes that take pleasure for to rede all bookes I
     wyl recounte vnto you the lyfe of the two chyualrous Lordes Valentyne
     and Orson (from 5)

     Henry Watson, The Hystory of the Two Valyaunte Brethren
     Valentyne and Orson, romance translated from French, s. xvi
     in.

     1. [W. de Worde, ca. 1510] (STC 24571.3), fragment; 2. W.
     Copland, [ca. 1555] (STC 24571.7); 3. W. Copland, [ca. 1565]
     (STC 24572); 4. EETS os 204 (1937), pp. 18-32 (even pages) (as
     in 1); 5. EETS os 204 (1937), rest of book (as in 2 supplemented
     by 3).

     Alle scriptures and wrytyngis ben they good or evyll ben wreton for our
     prouffyt and doctrine The good to thende to take ensample by them to
     do well   Incipit to text proper of 783.

53   Alle þat bileeuen on Jhesu Crist lusteneþ and ȝe mowen heere how
     muche is þe miht of vre heuene kyng Furst he schop heuene

     Lyff of Adam and Eve, devotional treatise, s. xiv.

     1. ed. C. Horstmann, Sammlung altenglischer Legenden (1878),
     pp. 220-27 (Bodl Eng. poet. a. 1, f. 393); 2. Blake, MERP
     (1972), pp. 103-18 (as in 1).

     Probably originally in verse but in prose by the time of the MS.
     For another version in prose see 25; many verse versions.

54   Alle þes holy namys of alle myȝtty god seynt Leo þe pope of Rome
     wrote to kyng Charulse & sayde who-so breit þis letter with hym he þar
     not drede hym of hys emny to be ouercome

     "The Names of God", letter from Pope Leo to Charlemagne, s.
     xiv.

     1. Baugh (1956), p. 154 (BL Addl. 37787, ff. 175v-76).

21

Alle tho that wyn lerne of huntyge I schal teth hom as I have lerned
byfor this tyme   Incipit to edition 3 of **763**.

Alle vertuouse doctryne and techynge had and lerned of suche as haue
endeuoured   Incipit to Prologue of **385**.

55   Almiȝti god yaf ten hestes ine þe laȝe of iewes þet Moyses onderuing
ine þe helle of Synay ine tuo tables of ston þet were i-write mid godes
vingre (from 2)

   Dan Michel of Northgate, Ayenbite of Inwyt, translation of
   Friar Lorens's Somme le roi, 1340.

   1. ed. J. Stevenson (1855) (BL Arundel 57, ff. 13-94); 2. EETS
   os 23 (1866) (as in 1); 3. EETS os 23, rev. ed. (1965) (as in 1),
   supplemented by EETS os 278 (1979).

   For other translations see **668** and **824**.

56   Almighty God kepe oure souerain lord Kyng of England and of Fraunce
and of all his trewe and humble subgettes that they live in prosperite
and ferme pece

   John Shirley, Governance of Prynces Seyd the Secrete of Secretes, book of instruction translated from a French version of the
   Secreta Secretorum, ca. 1450.

   1. EETS os 276 (1977), pp. 229-313 (lower portion of odd pages)
   (BL Addl. 5467, ff. 211-24v, ending imperfectly).

57   Almyȝty God saue þi puple fro erryng in ymagis þat longe haþ durit in
rude wittis of many forgetyng þe meruelouse and precious werkis þat
han ben done by þee

   A Tretyse of Ymagis, Wycliffite tract, s. xiv ex.

   1. Hudson (1978), pp. 83-88 (BL Addl. 24202, ff. 26-28v).

   Also in TCC B.14.50 and Bodl Eng. th. f. 39.

Almyȝty god þe trinyte fadir sonne and holy gooste boþe in þe olde
lawe and þe newe haþ fowndid his chirche up on þre statis   See **247**.

58   All-swa he reherces a-nothyre tale of verraye contrecyone þat þe same
      clerke Cesarius says He tellys þat A scolere at pares had done many full
      synnys þe whylke he hade schame to schryfe hym of

      Richard Rolle (?), Tale of Verraye Contrecyone, exemplum from
      Cesarius of Heisterbach's Dialogus Miraculorum, s. xiv.

      1. EETS os 20 (1866), p. 7 (Lincoln Cathedral 91, f. 194); 2.
      YW, I (1895), 193 (as in 1); 3. EETS os 20, rev. ed. (1921), p.
      7 (as in 1).

      Also in Bodl Ashmole 751. Cf. **564** and **126**.

59   Alswa Heraclides þe clerke telles þat a maydene forsuke hir Cete and
      satte in a sepulcre and tuke hir mete at a lyttill hole ten ȝere scho saghe
      neuer mane ne womane ne þay hir face

      Richard Rolle (?), De Vita Cuiusdam Puelle Incluse Propter
      Amorem Christi, exemplum, s. xiv.

      1. YW, I (1895), 194 (Lincoln Cathedral 91, f. 194v); 2. EETS
      os 20, rev. ed. (1921), p. 9 (as in 1); 3. Garbaty (1984), pp.
      796-97 (as in 1).

60   Also veraly as God is and was and chal be and als verali as þat he sayd
      was sothe

      Charme of Seynte William, charm for worms, canker, wounds,
      and gouts, s. xv.

      1. Chaucer and Middle English Studies (1974), p. 68 (BL Sloane
      962, f. 72).

      A similar charm in a collection in Stockholm Kungliga Biblioteket
      X.90 (see **173**).

61   Alwey I am myndeful of the also among the perels and doubtes of our
      batels most diere comandour and after my moder and susters most
      acceptable

      Epistola Alexandri Magni Regis Macedonis ad Magistrum Suum
      Aristotilem ("Letter of Alexander to Aristotle"), translation
      from the Latin Epistola, s. xv (1).

      1. Costerus, n.s. 13 (1978), pp. 50-110 (even only) (Worcester

Cathedral F. 172, ff. 138-46v); 2. MS, 41 (1979), 117-45 (odd only) (as in 1).

For an OE translation see Ker 216.

Amonge all creatures that euer god of his endeles myght made was there none þat he so loued as he dyd mankynde   Incipit to text proper of 362.

62   Amonge all the euyll condicions and signes that may be in a man the first and þe grettest is whan he feereth not ne dredeth to displese and make wroth god by synne

William Caxton, Game and Playe of the Chesse, moral allegorization of chess pieces translated from French versions of Jacobus de Cessolis's Latin original, 1474.

1. W. Caxton, 1474 (STC 4920), with dedication to Duke of Clarence; 2. W. Caxton, 1483? (STC 4921), with new prologue; 3. ed. V. Figgins (1855) (facsimile of 2); 4. ed. W.E.A. Axon (1883) (as in 1); 5. ed. N.F. Blake (1976) (facsimile of 2).

BL Sloane 779 (1484) made from edition 1.

Ymonges [sic] many ylles of them that be professed to crystes relygyon one there is ferre out of of [sic] the waye of helthe that we were institute in   Incipit to preface to edition 1 of 561.

Amonge other vertuous commendynges of the holy virgyne cecylle it is wreton that she bare al weythe gospel of cryste hydde in her brest Incipit to text proper of 553.

Anciently the kynges and princes of hye felicite were attendaunt and awayted whan their seed shold bringe forth generacion   Incipit to Chap. 1 of 226.

ancte   See 586.

63   And by asmoch as the mone is brighter than other sterres and thurgh the good radiacion of the sonne more shynynger in so moche the clernesse of your engyne and science passeth all others

24

Secrete of Secretes, book of instruction translated from the full Latin Secreta Secretorum, s. xv (1).

1. EETS os 276 (1977), pp. 18-113 (Bodl Ashmole 396, ff. 1-47).

Also in Bodl Lyell 36.

And here I make an ende of this mater for this tyme Prayeng and requyryng all theym that in this sayd werke shal haue ony playsyre Incipit to 81 as it appears in editions 2-4.

64 And if þou be nogth styrd agaynes þe persone be angre or felle cheer outward ne be na pryue haat in þi hert for to despyse hym or deme hym

Walter Hilton, Be Whate Takynes Þou Sal Knaw If Þou Luf Þin Ennemy, Chap. 70 of the Ladder of Perfeccion circulating as a separate item, s. xiv.

1. YW, I (1895), 104-5 (Bodl Rawlinson C. 285, ff. 57v-58v).

See 255.

65 And our lorde wyll that there shal be shewed iiij tokens after doctours sayng For oure lorde is so mercyful that hy wyl not punisshe vs but hy wyl shewe somme tokes afore

Jan de Doesborch, Lytill Treatyse Called the XV Tokens, treatise on the four, then fifteen signs before doomsday, followed by observations on the number of footsteps of Jesus at the time of his passion, translated from Dutch, ca. 1500.

1. J. de Doesborch, [1505?] (STC 793.3, 24222); 2. R. Wyer [1535?] (STC 14505), first four signs only.

66 And þat þou may do þe better and þe mare redely if þou be bisy for to sette þi hert mast opon a thyng and þat thyng es nogth ellis bot a gastly desire to god

Walter Hilton, What Thyng Helpes Mast a Mans Knawyng, Chap. 91 of the Ladder of Perfeccion circulating as a separate item. s. xiv.

1. YW, I (1895), 105-6 (Bodl Rawlinson C. 285, ff. 58v-59).

See 255.

Annas and Cayphas Symeon Datan Gamalyell Iudas Leuy Nepcalym Alyzaundyr zaryus and many other Iewes   Incipit to text proper of 395.

67   Anno 1376 there was a parlyment at London whiche began about the octave of St. George and contynewed 9 weekes

Chronicle of the reign of Edward III, s. xv.

1. Archaeologia, 22 (1829), 212-84 (BL Harley 6217 and BL Harley 247).

Ante omnia fratres charissimi diligatur deus deinde proximus . . . whiche sentence we haue thus translated indyfferently vnto bothe the sexes or kyndes   Incipit to version B of 268.

68   Antony for sothe of nobulle & religyous fader & moder I-getyn of partyes of Egipt wyt so grete besynes kept in cloes þat nothyng he knew bot hys fader & moder & hyre menʒe

Þe Fyndyng of the Glorios Confessour Antone, saint's life, s. xv.

1. Anglia, 4 (1881), 116-38 (BL Royal 17 C.xvii, ff. 124v-33).

Also in TCC R.3.21.

69   . . . æni mann mai don Alle hie bieð forsakene on godes awene muðe ðe ðus seið Vade prius reconciliari fratri tuo Ga arst and seihtle wið ðine broðer

"Vices and Virtues", dialogue between the Soul and Reason, ca. 1200.

1. EETS os 89 (1888), odd pages (BL Stowe 240, beginning imperfectly).

70   As a gret clerk tellys and schewys in his bokys Of alle þe creaturis þat god made in heuyn and in erthe in water and in eyre or in ouʒt ellys

26

<u>Mandatum</u> <u>Domini</u> <u>Johannis</u> de <u>Thoresby</u>, Wycliffite adaptation
and expansion of John Gaytryge's <u>Sermon</u>, s. xiv ex.

1. EETS os 118 (1901), primarily odd pages (Lambeth Palace
408, ff. 1-17).

Also in York Minster XVI.L.12. This text is listed in <u>IMEV</u>,
as 406B, but it is more accurate to call it semi-alliterative prose. -
For the original English sermon see **71**.

71   Als a grett Doctour schewes in his buke of all þe creatours þat Gode
made in Heuene and in erthe in water and in ayere or in oghte ellse

John Gaytryge, <u>Sermon</u> ("Lay Folks' Catechism"), translation
from the Latin catechism of Archbishop Thoresby of York, 1357.

1. EETS os 26 (1867), pp. 1-14 (Lincoln Cathedral 91, ff. 213v-
18v); 2. EETS os 118 (1901), primarily even pages (York Minster Archbishop Thoresby's Register, ff. 295 ff.); 3. EETS os
26, rev. ed. (1914), pp. 1-15 (as in 1); 4. Blake, <u>MERP</u> (1972),
pp. 73-87 (as in 1).

Parts of the sermon appear in CUL Dd.12.39, BL Addl. 24202,
Bodl Rawlinson C. 285. For Thoresby's Latin see EETS os 118
(1901), lower halves of even pages. The ME translation is listed
by <u>IMEV</u>, as 406A, but it is more accurate to call it semi-
alliterative prose. For a Wycliffite adaptation of Gaytryge's
<u>Sermon</u> see **70**.

72   As almyȝtty god in trinyte ordeyneþ men to come to þe blisse of heuene
bi þre groundis bi knowynge of þe trinyte bi sad feiþ bi treue kepynge of
goddis hestis

<u>Hou</u> <u>Sathanas</u> <u>and</u> <u>His</u> <u>Prestis</u>, Wycliffite tract, s. xiv (2).

1. EETS os 74 (1880, 1902), pp. 264-74 (CCCC 296, pp. 213-
21).

Also in TCD 244.

As Auntyent wryters haue wryten ther be xxv bokes of the old
testament whych be bokes of fayth and fully bokes of holy wryte
Incipit to edition 1 of **205**.

73 As for alle thynges that folowe referre them to my copey in whyche is
wretyn a remanente lyke to this forseyd werke

[John Warkworth], chronicle of the years 1461-1473, s. xv ex.

1. Camden Soc. 10 (1839), pp. 1-27 (Cambridge Peterhouse
190, ff. 214v-25).

Also in Glasgow University Hunterian 83.

As for to speke of noblesse spyrytuall it is the moost grete noblesse that
is and that man may haue   Incipit to brief introduction to **454**.

74 As Haly wyttnessyth the gret astrologere off days namyd cretyk the
qwyche the calkyllyd and drop owte be gret conclusyonnys off astronomye qwyche schuld be moste fortunate to the vse of man as the days of
yche mone

John Metham, lunary, s. xv.

1. EETS os 132 (1916), pp. 148-56 (Princeton University Garrett
141, ff. 79-83v).

75 As I laye in a seint laurence nyght slepynge in my bedde me bifelle a full
merueylous dreme whiche I shal rehercen

Dreme of the Pilgrymage of the Sowle/Grace Dieu, didactic text
translated from a French prose version of the Pélerinage de l'ame
by Guillaume de Deguilleville, partially in verse, 1413.

1. W. Caxton, 1483 (STC 6473); 2. ed. K.I. Cust (1859) (as in
1).

In Cambridge Gonville and Caius 124/61, CUL Kk.1.7, Hatfield House Marquis of Salisbury MS, BL Egerton 615, BL Addl.
34193, Melbourne Victoria Public Library MS, New York Public
Library Spencer 19, Bodl Bodley 770, Oxford CCC 237, Oxford
University 181.

76 As I was occupied on a day in bodyly traueyle and thouȝt on gostly
werkys that were nedefulle to Goddis seruauntys foure gostly werkes
comme soon to my mynde

A Ladder of Foure Ronges, devotional treatise translated from the Scala Paradisi attributed to Guigo II, ninth Prior of the Grande Chartreuse, s. xv.

1. EETS os 231 (1955), pp. 100-17 (CUL Ff.6.33, ff. 115-38).

Also in BL Harley 1706, Bodl Douce 322.

As Iheronimus sheweth In this begynnynge so wyll I wryte of the iiij Tokens   Introductory rubric to edition 2 only of 65.

As it is redde in thystoryes of the troians After the dystructyon of the noble cyte of Troye there was a kyng moche noble named francus the whyche was felowe of Eneas   Incipit to text proper of 582.

Alse longe as i liue i þis werld i schal þenkin of þe michele suink þat Iesu Crist þolede in spellinge   See 552.

77   As houre lord ihesu crist ordeynede to make his gospel sadly knowen and meyntened aȝenst heretikis and men out of bileue bi wittynge of his foure euangelistis so þe deuel sathanas castiþ bi anticrist

Hou Anticrist and His Clerkis Traveilen to Distroie Holy Writt, Wycliffite tract, s. xiv (2).

1. EETS os 74 (1880, 1902), pp. 255-62 (CCCC 296, pp. 209-13).

Also in TCD 244.

As Romulus harde say of his broder Remus and of the towne of Raynes than he was uery heuy for the wales of Raynes was so hygh   Incipit to text proper of 739.

78   As seint Jerom þe holy doctour seiþ in a bibil þat he made hit is harde to turne a language into a noþer worde for worde

Þe Lyfe of Seint Elizabeth of Spalbeck, saint's life, s. xv.

1. Anglia, 8 (1885), 107-18 (Bodl Douce 114, ff. 1-12).

[A]s that a gret clerk shewes in his bokes Et est secundo sentenciarum

29

distinctione prima Of all the creatures that god made in heuen   Incipit to edition 2 of 71.

79   As the noble and worthi clerke Guydo writeth in his boke and declareth and so doeth þe famous clerk Dares also how that sometyme in Thesaile there was a king called Eson

    Sege of Troye, romance, s. xv (1).

    1. PMLA, 22 (1907), 174-200 (Bodl Rawlinson D. 82, ff. 11-24); 2. Archiv, 130 (1913), 272-85 (as in 1).

80   As the Philosopher in the fyrit [sic] booke of hys methafysyque sayth þat euery man naturaly desireth to know and to con new thynges (from 4)

    William Caxton, Historie of the Foure Sonnes of Aimon, romance translated from a French prose version of Les Quatre Filz Aymon, ca. 1489.

    1. W. Caxton, 1489 (STC 1007), imperfect at beginning; 2. W. de Worde, [1504] (STC 1008), fragment; 3. [W. Copland? n.d.] (STC 1009), fragment; 4. W. Copland, 1554 (STC 1010); 5. EETS es 44, 45 (1884-5) (as in 1 supplemented by 4).

81   As touchyng the sentence dyffnytyf gyuen by the Senate aftir thise two noble knyghtes had purposed and shewed theyr Oracions I fynde none

    William Caxton, epilogue to John Tiptoft's translation, Oracionis, ca. 1481.

    1. W. Caxton, 1481 (STC 5293, Part 3); 2. Oldys (1737), pp. 260-61 (as in 1); 3. Ames (1749), p. 27 (as in 1); 4. Herbert, I (1785), 34 (as in 1); 5. Blades, Life, I (1861), 163-64 (as in 1); 6. Aurner (1926), pp. 248-49 (as in 1); 7. EETS os 176 (1928), pp. 46-47 (as in 1); 8. Blake, COP (1973), pp. 124-25 (as in 1); 9. (1977) (facsimile of 1).

    See 830.

82   As touchyng tythynges please it to you to wite that at the Princes comyng to Wyndesore the Duc of Buk toke hym in his armes and presented hym to the Kyng

John Stodeley, newsletter concerning the events of 1453-54,
1454.

1. Gairdner (1872-75; rptd. 1908), I, 263-68 (BL Egerton 914);
2. Gairdner, rev. ed. (1904), II, 295-99 (as in 1).

As wyse folkes sayen there ben thre signes of very loue & frenshyp One
is a persone wyll be gladde to speke well of whom they loue beste
Incipit to "Three Signs of True Love and Friendship" = Part 4 of the
Tretyse of Love (751), a devotional tract probably appended to the
original Tretyse.

83   Asculta o fili Son Herkyn þe commandementis of þe mastir & lay to þe
      eere of thy herte

      Reule of Sain Benet, translation of Benedictine Rule for religious
      (monks in Prologue and Chaps. 1-2, nuns thereafter), s. xv in.

      1. EETS os 120 (1902), pp. 1-47 (BL Lansdowne 378, ff. 1v-
      42v).

      For other versions see 98 and 281.

84   Ate begynnyng do bynd hys fete to-gyder and hyde his eyen and þan
      sege in his ere O þow Egle mannes frend now i sle þe to hele of man

      Vertues of þe Egle/Virtute Aquile, collection of medical recipes,
      translated from a Latin translation of the Greek Kyranides, s.
      xv.

      1. Tulane Studies in English, 22 (1977), 21-28 (BL Addl. 34111,
      ff. 195-96v).

85   At Calays ye shal haue as many plackys for half a noble englysshe or
      for a dukate xxiiij plackes That is beste moneye vnto Brugis

      Informacion for Pylgrymes unto the Holy Londe, account of
      route to the Holy Land, preceded by lists of cities and mileages,
      s. xv ex. (?).

      1. [W. de Worde, 1500?] (STC 14081); 2. W. de Worde, 1515
      (STC 14082); 3. W. de Worde, 1524 (STC 14083); 4. Rox-
      burghe (1824) (as in 1); 5. ES, 8 (1885), 277-84 (BL Cotton
      Appendix VIII, ff. 108-12); 6. ed. E.G. Duff (1893) (facsimile

of 1).

86   At Calyse ye schal haue for a dim nowbyl Englysche or for a doket
     xxiiij plackys that ys best money vn to Brugys At Brugeys ye schal haue
     as many of plackys for a dim nowbyl or a doket as ye had at Calyse

     William Wey, Chaunges of Money from Englond to Rome and
     Venyse, proem to his Itineraries (IMEV 883), after 1458.

     1. Roxburghe 76 (1857), pp. 1-7 (Bodl Bodley 565, ff. 8 ff.).

     Also in Bodl Douce 389.

87   At morne whan þou risist oute of þe bed haue Myȝel in þi mynde and
     þou schal haue al þat day glad to þe

     Charm involving angels, s. xv.

     1. Chaucer and Middle English Studies (1974), p. 58 (BL Sloane
     2584, f. 37).

     At the bygynnyng god and haly kirk corses al thais that the friunches of
     halykirk brekes or disturbes   Incipit to edition F.2 of 122.

88   At the deuoute and dylygent request of the ryght reuerende fader in god
     and lorde Rycharde bysshop of Dureham and lord pryueseall of Eng-
     londe

          Contemplacyon of Synners, with prose prologue to a series of
          meditations for each day in a mixture of English verse and Latin
          prose, s. xv ex.

          1. W. de Worde, 1499 (STC 5643).

89   At þe first begynnyng þe mese salbe of oure lady þe offece of þe mese
     salbe Salve sancta parens þe epistil and þe godspel and all þe tother
     salbe als þe tyme of þe ȝer askes

          Manere forto Make a Nun, ritual for the ordination of nuns, s.
          xv in.

          1. Maskell, 2nd ed., III (1882), 360-63 (BL Cotton Vespasian
          A. XXV, ff. 120-24v); 2. EETS os 120 (1902), pp. 145-50 (as

in 1).

Cf. 178, 366, and 862.

At the Hart rather then at any other beast wher for he is the most
mervelous for he bearethe grease cretethe and Roungethe and so doe
nonne other   Incipit to edition 2 of 485.

90   At the honour and the reuerence of God Almichty his glore and louyng
      of his prouidence the quhilk is souerane lord and syre de toutes choses

            Gilbert of the Haye, The Buke of the Ordre of Knychthede,
            translation of Le Livre de l'ordre de chevalerie, a French version
            of Ramon Lull's Libre del orde de cauayleria, 1456.

            1. ed. B. Botfield (1847) (Abbotsford Scott Collection 1-3, ff.
            85-103); 2. STS, 1st series 62 (1908), pp. 1-70 (as in 1).

            Cf. 794.

91   At the reuerence and worschip of the blessed trinite and of the glorious
      Virgyn saynt Marye and the conseruacion of the comyn wele of alle
      cristen people

            Bengt Knutsson (Canutus), Bishop of Vesterås, Passing Gode
            Lityll Boke Necessarye and Behouefull Azenst the Pestilence,
            translation from Latin, s. xv (2).

            1. [W. de Machlinia, ca. 1486] (STC 4589); 2. [W. de Machli-
            nia, ca. 1488] (STC 4590); 3. [W. de Machlinia, ca. 1490]
            (STC 4591); 4. W. de Worde, [ca. 1510] (STC 4592); 5. [J. de
            Doesborch, ca. 1520] (STC 4593); 6. T. Gybson, 1536.

92   At þe reuerence of oure lorde Ihesu criste to þe askynge of þi desyre
      Syster Margarete couetynge a-sethe to make for encrece also of gostely
      comforth to þe and mo þat curiuste of latyn vnderstandes noght

            Richard Misyn, Fyer of Lufe, translation of Richard Rolle's
            Incendium Amoris, 1435.

            1. EETS os 106 (1896), pp. 1-104 (Oxford CCC 236, ff. 1-44).

            Also in BL Addl. 37790.

33

93   At this present tyme shall be wryten of the ferefull sygnes that shall
      happen before the comynge of oure lorde Ihesu cryst to the Iugement at
      the dredefull daye of dome

      Byrthe and Comynge of Antechryst, account of the life and death
      of Antichrist, followed by the fifteen signs before doomsday, s.
      xv ex. (?).

      1. W. de Worde, [1520?] (STC 670).

      Atte wrastlinge mi lemman i ches and atte ston-kasting i him for-les
      Text for the sermon in 432.

94   Attendite a fermento phariseorum quod est ypocrisis . . . Crist
      comandiþ to his disciplis and to alle cristene men to vndirstonde and
      flee þe sowrdow of pharisees þe wiche is ypocrisie

      "Of the Leaven of Pharisees", Wycliffite tract, ca. 1383.

      1. EETS os 74 (1880, 1902), pp. 2-27 (CCCC 296, pp. 1-22).

      Also in TCD 244.

95   Avdi filia et uide et inclina aurem tuam . . . Dauið þe psalm wruhte
      spekið i þe sawter towart godes spuse þet is euch meiden þet haueð
      meiið þeawes (from 2)

      Epistel of Meidenhad ("Hali Meidenhad"), homiletic treatise,
      ca. 1200.

      1. EETS os 18 (1866), odd pages (BL Cotton Titus D. XVIII,
      ff. 112v-27); 2. EETS os 18, 2nd ed. (1922), even pages (Bodl
      Bodley 34, ff. 52-71v); 3. EETS os 18, 2nd ed. (1922), odd
      pages (as in 1); 4. ed. A.F. Colburn (1940), odd pages (as in 2);
      5. ed. A.F. Colburn (1940), even pages (as in 1); 6. Blake,
      MERP (1972), pp. 35-60 (as in 2); 7. d'Ardenne (1977), pp.
      127-65 (as in 2); 8. EETS os 284 (1982) (as in 2).

96   Audi filia et vide Here doughter and see fructuous example of vertuous
      liuinge to edyfycacion of thy sowle and to comforte and encrese of thy
      gostly labour in all werkis of pyte

      Lyf of Saint Katherin of Senis, saint's life translated from the
      Latin of Raimundus de Vineis, s. xv med.

1. [W. de Worde, 1492?] (STC 24766, Part 1); 2. W. de Worde, [1500?] (STC 24766.3); 3. Archiv, 76 (1886), 33-112, 265-314, 353-91 (as in 1).

Cf. 121.

97 Augustinus Arguam te nescis þe holy doctour seynt austyn spekyng in þe persone of crist vnto synful men seiþ in þis wise I schal reproue þe

"Arguam Te Nescis", Wycliffite tract, s. xiv (2).

1. EETS os 74 (1880, 1902), p. 281 (CCCC 296, pp. 238-39).

98 Ausculta o filia precepta magistri . . . Ʒehur ðu min bearn beboda þines lareowes and onhyld þinre hurte eare and þines arfæstan fæder mynaʒunga lustlice underfoh

Reʒolan Sanctes Benedictes, translation of Benedictine Rule made for the nuns of Winteney, with Latin and English interspersed, 1220-1225.

1. ed. M.M.A. Schröer, Die Winteney-Version der Regula S. Benedicti (1883) (BL Cotton Claudius D. III, ff. 50-138).

For other versions see 83 and 281; another prose version (for women) is in Washington Library of Congress 4, ff. 1-36, s. xv. For a verse version see IMEV 218. A second translation for the nuns of Winteney was made by Bishop Richard Fox in 1516 (see R. Pynson, 1516?, STC 1859). For OE translations see (1) Ker 41B, 109, 117, 154B, 186 item 25, 200, 353; (2) Ker 395; (3) Ker 186 item 1.

99 Ave holie & grete fader in hevine Do wee aske grete meercyes from thi hand and unto [us] geve all thynges whyche in thi bountyfull gudeness thi hand may seem fytt

Prayer, s. xiv (?).

1. N&Q, 12th series, 10 (1922), 128 (Norton-on-Tees Grove House Fairfax-Blakeborough MS).

100 Aues A man that dremeth that byrdys ffyghten with hym it be-tokneth wrath Aues A man that dremeth that he letyth byrdys gon it be-tokneth wynnyng

35

The Interpretacions of Daniel the Prophete, dream book, translation of the Somniale Danielis, s. xv.

1. Archiv, 127 (1911), 52-84 (even pages only) (BL Sloane 1609, ff. 29v-32), supplemented by Anglia, 80 (1962), 271-72 (BL Royal 12 E.xvi, f. 2v).

Also in TCC O.9.37. For another translation see 337.

Aye þe uondingges of þe dyeule zay þis þet uolȝeþ Zuete iesu þin holy blod þet pou sseddest ane þe rod uor me and and uor mankende Incipit to preface to 55.

101   Baltesar be the grace of Mahounde son of þe kynge of Sarsyn of Clefery dyssendynge of þe kynge profet Ihesu of Nazarethe

Satirical proclamation by Lucifer to the Duke of Burgundy, s. xv med.

1. MLN, 71 (1956), 243-44 (Aberystwyth NLW Porkington 10, ff. 193v-94v).

Cf. 315.

102   Be hyt had yn mynde that the cite of Garnartho the whiche sometyme was Crysten and after were renegates and so contynued the space of vijc yere

Account of the capitulation of Granada (1492), s. xv ex.

1. Camden Soc., n.s. 28 (1880), pp. 86-87 (Lambeth Palace 306, f. 141).

103   Be yt knowen & hadde in mynde that the xxj day of May the xxxiij zere [sic] of the Regne of Kyng Herry the sext

Bellum apud Seynt Albons, account of the first battle of St. Albans (1455), s. xv (2).

1. Archaeologia, 20 (1824), 519-23 (London PRO Chancery Misc. 37, File III.4-11); 2. Gairdner (1872-75; rptd. 1908), I, 327-31 (as in 1); 3. Gairdner, rev. ed. (1904), III, 25-29 (as in 1).

Cf. 701.

104   Be it knowen to alle true cristen peple to whom this present writyng
      shal come se or here Thomas whete Prioure of the place of Croced
      Freres besyde the Tour of London

      Indulgence for charitable giving to said convent, s. xv ex.

      1. [R. Pynson, 1491] (STC 14077c.51).

105   Be it knowen tall wele disposed people having will to understande the
      trewthe that thoughe it so were the Righte of the Crownes of Englande
      and of Fraunce (from 2)

      John Fortescue, The Replicacion Made Agenste the Title and
      Clayme by the Duc of Yorke, ca. 1461.

      1. Clermont (1869), I, 517-18 (Phillipps 13783), beginning
      imperfectly; 2. Plummer (1885), pp. 353-54 (BL Addl. 48031).

      Also in BL Harley 543 and BL Harley 545.

106   By cause that hardynes is so moche necessarye to entrepryse hye
      thynges whiche without that shold neuer be enprysed That same is
      couenable to me at this present werke to put it forth without other
      thyng

      William Caxton, Book of Fayttes of Armes and of Chyvalrye,
      translation from the French of Christine de Pisan of the Latin De
      Re Militari by Vegetius, 1489.

      1. W. Caxton, 1489 (STC 7269); 2. EETS os 189 (1932) (as in
      1); 3. EETS os 189, corrected ed. (1937) (as in 1); 4. (1968)
      (facsimile of 1).

107   Bycause that I desyre ye hye and notable fayttes of ryght noble and
      ryght valyaunt men of honour and prowesse for to brynge them in to
      memorye

      Henry Watson, The Hystorye of Olyver of Castylle and of the
      Fayre Helayne, romance translated from French, s. xvi in.

      1. W. de Worde, 1518 (STC 18808); 2. ed. R.E. Graves,
      Roxburghe 136 (1898) (as in 1).

108   Bifore þe resceyuynge of cristis body syxe þingis þer ben to concidere
The firste is þat a man knowe by vertu of discressioun what he schal
resceyue

A Preciouse Mater How a Man Schal Make Hym Cleer and
Perfite Clene Bifore þe Resseyuynge of þe Sacramente of þe
Auter, ca. 1400.

1. EETS os 71 (1879), pp. 122-27 (Bodl Ashmole 1286, ff. 223-
26).

109   Byhold specially in þe fyue mooste notable woundes two in his blessed
hoondys & two in his blessed feet and þe mooste opene wounde in his
riȝt syde

A Meditacion of þe Fyve Woundes of Jhesu Crist, s. xiv.

1. YW, II (1896), 440-41 (Oxford University 97, ff. 131v-33).

Also in BL Addl. 22283.

Biholde ye the foulis of hevene for bi hem men lerne how thei schulden
love god   See 563.

Beyng in worthenes aarmes for to beere by the Royall blode in
ordynance all nobull and gentyll men from the hyest degre to the lawyst
Incipit to text proper of 302.

110   Belevest thowe fully alle the pryncipalle articles of the Feithe and also
alle holy scripturs in alle thynges after the exposicione of the holy &
trewe doctours of holy Chirche

VII Specialle Interrogacions, seven questions to be asked by a
curate of a dying man, s. xv.

1. EETS os 31 (1868), pp. 63-65 (BL Lansdowne 762, ff. 21v-
22v); 2. EETS os 31, rev. ed. (1902), pp. 69-71 (as in 1).

Jolliffe L.2/N.2 For other versions see 111 and 460.

111   Beleuyst þow in god fader almythi makere of heuene and of erthe

Questions to be asked of a dying man, taken from the Office for the Visitation of the Sick, followed by a form of confession, s. xv.

1. EETS es 90 (1903), pp. 6-9 (BL Addl. 30506, ff. 50v-52).

For other versions see 110 and 460.

112   Benedictus dominus deus israel . . . Blissid bee lord god of israel for he haþ visited and made þe biynge of his folk The hooli man zacarias

Walter Hilton (?), Benedictus, commentary on the Benedictus, s. xiv (2).

1. ed. B. Wallner, A Commentary on the 'Benedictus' (1957) (Lambeth Palace 472, ff. 252v-59v).

Also in London Dawson of Pall Mall and Newcastle-upon-Tyne Public Library TH. 1678.

113   Berwik lieth south and north of Golden stonys the Ilonde and Berwik haven lien west north west and Est South est

Pilot book containing navigational instructions, s. xv (2).

1. Hakluyt Soc., 79 (1889), pp. 11-22 (BL Lansdowne 285, ff. 138-42); 2. ed. D.W. Waters, The Rutters of the Sea (1967), pp. 181-95, 449-67 (as in 1).

Also in New York Morgan M 75 and Bodl Rawlinson D. 328.

Blessyd be god our souerayn creatour and dyrectour Infallyble whyche woll that all mankynde sholde be sauyd and come to the perfyghte knowlege of trouthe   Incipit to text proper of 222.

Blissid bee lord god of israel for he haþ visited and made þe biynge of his folk The hooli man zaxarias fader of seynt Jhon   See 112.

114   Blesced be þe man þat зede nouзt in þe counseil of wicked ne stode nouзt in þe waie of sinзeres ne sat nauзt in fals iugement

Psalterium, psalms followed by the twelve canticles, s. xiv (1).

1. EETS os 97 (1891) (BL Addl. 17376, ff. 1-149v).

39

Also in Cambridge Magdalene Pepys 2498, TCD 69, and Princeton University Scheide 43.

115 Boys seying in the begynnyng of his Arsemetrike Alle thynges that bene fro the first begynnyng of thynges have procedede and come forthe And by resoun of nombre ben formede

Art of Nombryng, arithmetic translated from the De Arte Numerandi attributed to John of Holywood (Sacrobosco), s. xv.

1. EETS es 118 (1922), pp. 33-51 (Bodl Ashmole 396, ff. 48-56).

115.5 Bonum est confiteri domino . . . Hit is good to schriuen to vre lord and singen to þi name þou allerhiȝest No man mai liuen in þis lyf þat he ne schal sinne sum-tyme

Walter Hilton (?), Bonum Est Confiteri Domino, commentary on Psalm 91, s. xiv (2).

1. Wallner (1954), pp. 51-92 (Bodl Eng. poet. a. 1, ff. 340v-42).

Also in CUL Dd.1.1, CUL Hh.1.11, BL Harley 2397, Lambeth Palace 472. Cf. 544.

116 Bonum principum facit bonum finem A good be-gynnyng makyth a god ende

Proverbia, proverbs and sayings (83 in all), alternating Latin and English, s. xv.

1. MP, 38 (1940), 117-26 (Bodl Rawlinson D. 238, ff. 140-44v).

Brethirne and susteryne bodely and goostely two maner of states ther bene in holy chirche be the which cristen soules plesyne god and gettyn hem the blisse of hevene   Incipit to 6 and 9 of 147.

117 Bridalis wern maad in þe Chana of Galilee and Ihesus modir was þere and Ihesus wt his disciples was clepid to þe bridale

Sermon on John ii illustrating the fourfold method of interpreta-

40

tion, s. xv.

1. PMLA, 65 (1950), 594-600 (BL Harley 2276, ff. 32v-35v).

118 . . . Bretayn þat cristendom was destroied and all þe bretons dreven
out and the lond left vnto saxons

Commentary on Geoffrey of Monmouth's Prophetia Merlini, s.
xv.

1. ed. C.D. Eckhardt (1982) (University Park Pennsylvania
State University PS. V-3, ff. 1-5, beginning and ending imperfectly).

119 Brother Ambrose to me thi litel ʒiftis perfitli berynge hath brouʒt with
and riʒt swete lettres the whiche han shewid sothfastnes of now proued
feith (from A.2)

Goddis Storie, Wycliffite translation of the Bible, preceded by
the prefatory Epistle of St. Jerome, 1380-96.

A. Earlier version, 1380-84: 1. ed. L. Wilson, The New
Testament in English (1848), New Testament only (Manchester
Rylands English 81); 2. Forshall and Madden (1850), Old and
New Testaments (BL Royal 1 B.vi, Bodl Douce 369, Bodl Douce
370, and Oxford CCC 4 supplemented by other MSS); 3. ed. C.
Lindberg, MS. Bodley 959, 5 vols. (1959-69), and The Earlier
Version of the Wycliffite Bible (1973), Old Testament only (Bodl
Bodley 959 supplemented by Oxford Christ Church 145); 4.
Lindberg (1978), even pages, Epistle of St. Jerome only (Oxford
Christ Church 145).

B. Revision traditionally attributed to John Purvey, 1384-
1395/6: 1. ed. J. Lewis (1731, 1810) (Bodl Gough Eccl. Top. 5
and London British and Foreign Bible Society 1, 2); 2. ed. S.
Bagster, The English Hexapla (1841) (Manchester Rylands English 77); 3. Forshall and Madden (1850), Old and New Testaments (BL Royal 1 C.viii); 4. ed. W.W. Skeat, The New
Testament in English (1879), New Testament only (as in 3); 5.
Lindberg (1978), odd pages, Epistle of St. Jerome only (Oxford
New 66).

Earlier version (all or parts) also in Cambridge Jesus 30, Cambridge Magdalene 6, Cambridge Sidney Sussex 99, CUL
Dd.1.27, CUL Ee.1.10, CUL Addl. 6681-6682, TCD 66, TCD
75, Durham University Cosin V.V.1, Edinburgh NLS 6127,

41

Edinburgh NLS Advocates 18.6.7, Glasgow University Gen. 223, Lichfield Cathedral 10, BL Arundel 254, BL Cotton Claudius E. II, BL Egerton 617-618, BL Royal 17 A.xxvi, BL Addl. 11858, BL Addl. 15580, Lambeth Palace 25, Longleat Marquis of Bath 3, Manchester Rylands English 84, Manchester Rylands English 89, Manchester Rylands English 92, New Haven Yale University 125, New York Columbia University Plimpton 308, New York Public Library 67, Bodl Bodley 183, Bodl Bodley 277, Bodl Bodley 771, Bodl Bodley 978, Bodl Fairfax 2, Bodl Hatton 111, Bodl Rawlinson C. 258-C. 259, Oxford New 66-67, Oxford Queen's 369, Philadelphia University of Pennsylvania English 6, San Marino Huntington HM 134, Wolfenbüttel Herzog-August-Bibliothek Aug. A.2. Revision (all or parts) also in Aberystwyth NLW 7855A, Alnwick Castle Duke of Northumberland 788, Berkeley University of California Helmingham 45, Bristol Baptist College Z.d.37, Cambridge Christ's 10, CCCC 147, CCCC 440, Cambridge Emmanuel 21, Cambridge Emmanuel 34, Cambridge Emmanuel 108, Cambridge Gonville and Caius 179/212, Cambridge Gonville and Caius 343/539, Cambridge Jesus 30, Cambridge Jesus 47, Cambridge Magdalene 6, Cambridge Magdalene Pepys 15-16, Cambridge Magdalene Pepys 1603, Cambridge Magdalene Pepys 2073, Cambridge St. John's 116-117, Cambridge St. John's 121, Cambridge St. John's 194, Cambridge St. John's 242, Cambridge St. John's 267 no. 72, Cambridge Sidney Sussex 99, TCC B.2.8, TCC B.10.7, TCC B.10.20, TCC O.7.26, CUL Dd.1.27, CUL Gg.6.8, CUL Gg.6.23, CUL Kk.1.8, CUL Ll.1.13, CUL Mm.2.15, CUL Addl. 6680, CUL Addl. 6683-6684, Cambridge (Mass.) Harvard University Richardson 3, Canterbury Cathedral 103, Covington (Virginia) Harry A. Walton Jr. A-2, Dresden Sächsische Landesbibliothek Od 83, TCD 67, TCD 73-76, Dunedin (New Zealand) Public Library 8, Eton College 24, Glasgow University Hunterian 176, Glasgow University Hunterian 189, Glasgow University Hunterian 191, Glasgow Unversity Hunterian 337, Gloucester Diocesan Record Office 8, Hereford Cathedral O.VII.1, Lincoln Cathedral 245, London British and Foreign Bible Society 3, BL Arundel 104, BL Burney 30, BL Cotton Claudius E. II, BL Egerton 1165, BL Egerton 1171, BL Harley 272, BL Harley 327, BL Harley 940, BL Harley 984, BL Harley 1212, BL Harley 1666, BL Harley 1896, BL Harley 2249, BL Harley 2309, BL Harley 3903, BL Harley 4027, BL Harley 4890, BL Harley 5017, BL Harley 5767-5768, BL Harley 6333, BL Lansdowne 407, BL Lansdowne 454-455, BL Royal 1 A.iv, BL Royal 1 A.x, BL Royal 1 A.xii, BL Royal 1 B.ix, BL Royal 1 C.ix, BL Addl. 5890-5902, BL Addl. 10046-10047, BL Addl. 10596, BL Addl. 11858, BL Addl. 15517, BL Addl. 28256, BL Addl. 31044, Lambeth Palace 25, Lambeth Palace 369, Lambeth Palace 532, Lambeth Palace 547, Lambeth Palace 1033, Lambeth

Palace 1150-1151, Lambeth Palace 1366, London Sion College Arc. L 40.2/E.1-E.2, London Westminster Abbey 8, London Dr. Williams' Library Anc. 7, Longleat Marquis of Bath 5, Manchester Chetham 6723, Manchester Rylands English 3, Manchester Rylands English 75-76, Manchester Rylands English 78-80, Manchester Rylands English 82-84, Manchester Rylands English 88-89, Manchester Rylands English 91, Manchester Rylands English 902, New York Columbia University Plimpton 269, New York Columbia University Plimpton 308, New York Morgan M 362, New York Morgan M 400, New York Public Library 64-66, Norwich Public Library TC 27/5, Bodl Ashmole 1517, Bodl Bodley 183, Bodl Bodley 277, Bodl Bodley 296, Bodl Bodley 531, Bodl Bodley 554, Bodl Bodley 665, Bodl Bodley 978-979, Bodl Douce 36, Bodl Douce 240, Bodl Douce 265, Bodl Dugdale 46, Bodl e Mus. 110, Bodl Eng. misc. c. 27, Bodl Fairfax 2, Bodl Fairfax 11, Bodl Fairfax 21, Bodl Junius 29, Bodl Laud Miscellaneous 24-25, Bodl Laud Miscellaneous 33, Bodl Laud Miscellaneous 36, Bodl Laud Miscellaneous 182, Bodl Laud Miscellaneous 207, Bodl Laud Miscellaneous 361, Bodl Lyell 26-27, Bodl Rawlinson C. 237-C. 238, Bodl Rawlinson C. 257, Bodl Rawlinson C. 259, Bodl Rawlinson C. 752, Bodl Rawlinson C. 883, Bodl Selden Supra 49, Bodl Selden Supra 51, Oxford Brasenose 10, Oxford Christ Church 146-147, Oxford CCC 20, Oxford Lincoln Lat. 119, Oxford New 66, Oxford New 320, Oxford Oriel 80, Oxford Queen's 23, Oxford St. John's 7, Oxford St. John's 79, Oxford University 96, Oxford Worcester E.5.10 (binding fragment), Princeton University Scheide 12-13, San Marino Huntington HM 134, San Marino Huntington HM 501, Taunton Somerset Record Office Heneage 3182, Tokyo Takamiya 28, Tokyo Takamiya Boies Penrose MS, Tokyo Takamiya fragments (2), Winchester St. Mary's College 2, Windsor St. George's Chapel MS, Worcester Cathedral F. 172, Worcester Cathedral Q. 84, York Minster XVI.N.7, York Minster XVI.O.1. Other MSS whose current locations are unknown: Dr. Cardwell MS (Harmsworth sale, Sotheby's 15 October 1945, lot 2036, to Maggs), H.O. Coxe MS, Sir George Dashwood MS, George Goyder MSS (2, one of which is from Harmsworth sale, lot 2034), Sir Leicester Harmsworth MS (Sotheby's 16 October 1945, lot 2035, to Quaritch), Marquis of Hastings MS, Thomas Kerslake MS, Sotheby's June 1950 lot 218, Sotheby's 3 December 1951 lot 18, J.H. Todd MS, Conrad von Uffenbach MS. On the MSS in general see <u>SN</u>, 42 (1970), 333-47.

120 Brother or sustere that desyrest to come to the endeles blysse that mankynde was ordeyned to in hys fyrst creacion whyche oure fadere Adame lost thorow brekyng off the commaundement off oure lorde

gode

A Tretyse of Gostly Batayle, devotional tract, s. xv.

1. YW, II (1896), 421-36 (BL Harley 1706, ff. 36v-47v).

Also in CCCC 142, BL Royal 17 C.xviii, Manchester Rylands English 94, Bodl Douce 322, Bodl Rawlinson C. 894, Oxford CCC 220. Jolliffe H.3.

121 Broþer Stephen of Senys pryour þof vnworþy of þe hous of the Charteus ordyr nere Papy greteþ wel in hym þat is verray hele of alle

A Letter Touchynge þe Lyfe of Seint Kateryn of Senys, s. xv.

1. Anglia, 8 (1885), 184-96 (Bodl Douce 114, ff. 76-89v).

Cf. 96.

But here þe menours seyn þat þei ben not holden þer-to for a man haþ not lordschipe ne iurisdiccion vpon his pere   Incipit to commentary on 522.

122 By auttorite of god almiȝti ffader & Son & holy gost And of al þe Seyntes of heuen ffirst we accursen al them that broken the pece of holy chirch

The Gret Sentence/Magna Sentencia Excommunicationis, recited by parish priests three or four times a year, various versions from s. xiv to s. xv ex.

A. Version inserted in John Mirk's Instructions for Parish Priests, ca. 1400: 1. EETS os 31 (1868), pp. 21-24 (Bodl Douce 103, ff. 134v-36v); 2. EETS os 31, rev. ed. (1902), pp. 60-67, conflation of versions A and B (BL Cotton Claudius A. II, ff. 125v-28); 3. ed. G. Kristensson, John Mirk's Instructions for Parish Priests (1974), pp. 104-7 (Bodl Douce 60, ff. 161-63).

B. Version in a manual for parish priests, s. xv in.: 1. ed. A. Pothman, Zur Textkritik von John Myrk's Pars Oculi (1914), pp. 49-56 (BL Burney 356, ff. 50v-53).

C. Version issued by Archbishop Henry Chichele, 1434: 1. ed. W. Lyndwood, Provinciale seu Constitutiones Anglicæ (1679), appendix, pp. 73-74 (Eton College 98, ff. 331v-32); 2. Words-

44

worth (1901), pp. 44-46 (Salisbury Cathedral 148, ff. 19v-20v); 3. ed. E.F. Jacob, The Register of Henry Chichele, III (1945), 257-58 (Lambeth Palace Reg. H. Chichele, II, f. 100v).

D. Version of the later Sarum Manuals, s. xiv/xv: 1. Maskell, II (1846), 286-301 (STC 16148.2); 2. Surtees Soc. 63 (1875), pp. 86*-94* (STC 16140.7); 3.Maskell, 2nd ed., III (1882), 309-26 (as in 1); 4. Wordsworth (1901), pp. 245-54 (STC 16145).

E. Version, with exposition, incorporated into Fons Jacob ("Jacob's Well"), Chaps. 3-9, ca. 1445: 1. EETS os 115 (1900), pp. 13-63 (Salisbury Cathedral 103, ff. 9v-22v).

F. Version in the York Manuals, s. xiv-xv: 1. Surtees Soc. 63 (1875), pp. xvi-xvii, 119-22 (STC 16160 supplemented by York Minster XVI.M.4, pp. 166-72 and flyleaf); 2. Fifth Report (1876), pp. 305-6 (Cambridge (Mass.) Harvard University Widener 1, ff. 101v-4v).

G. Version appearing as part 2 of Quattuor Sermones, s. xv (see 689).

H. Version prefixed to the Englyssh Register of Godstow Nunnery (see The wyseman towht hys chyld), s. xv: 1. EETS os 129 (1905), pp. 1-3 (Bodl Rawlinson B. 408, f. 2r-v, beginning imperfectly).

I. Scottish version, ca. 1491-92: 1. ed. A.P. Forbes, Liber Ecclesie Beati Terrenani de Arbuthnott: Missale Secundum Usum Ecclesiae Sancti Andreae in Scotia (1864), pp. lxx-lxxi (unspecified MS); 2. ed. J. Robertson, Concilia Scotiae: Ecclesiae Scoticanae Statuta, Bannatyne Club 113 (1866), II, 6-8 (as in 1); 3. ed. D. Patrick, Statutes of the Scottish Church 1225-1559, Scottish Historical Soc. 54 (1907), pp. 5-7 (as in 1).

B also in BL Harley 4172, Bodl Bodley 110, Bodl Bodley 736, Oxford Trinity 7; C also in Cambridge Sidney Sussex 55, BL Royal 11 A.i (fragment), Sotheby's 4 April 1939 lot 295, Sotheby's 4-5 July 1955 lot 87; D also in CCCC 142, BL Harley 335, BL Harley 2399 (fragment), BL Addl. 33784, London Society of Antiquaries 687, Bodl Ashmole 750, Bodl e Mus. 212, Oxford Trinity 86, and in printed Sarum Manuals up to 1543 (STC 16138 to 16150); F also in CUL Ee.4.19, Durham University Cosin V.IV.2, London Society of Antiquaries 285 (fragment), and STC 16161 ([1530?]); G appears separately in Bodl Rawlinson A. 381, ff. 1v-2v. Other versions appear in: (1) Lambeth

Palace 172; (2) London Dulwich College 22 (fragment); (3) BL Arundel 130 (fragment), BL Burney 356 (again), Oxford Trinity E. 86 (again); (4) Edinburgh NLS Advocates 18.3.6, Lincoln Cathedral 229; (5) Durham University Cosin V.IV.2 (again, fragment); (6) Cambridge Emmanuel 248; (7) Bodl Bodley 123; (8) BL Harley 2383; (9) BL Harley 2283 (again); (10) Lincoln Cathedral 66; (11) BL Harley 665 (fragment). For a Wycliffite tract on the Gret Sentence see 175. On the versions in general see Leeds Studies in English, n.s. 12 (1981), 229-44.

Be his awne propre blode he entred in Blode kyndely maketh a tree þat is drie fruteful Hit maketh mennes bodies þat bene seke heleful   See 538.

Be holy cherche it is ordeynid þat curatys of mannys soule owyn to schewyn iiij tymes in þe ȝere or do schewe to here peryschenys þe artycles of þe sentens of þe grete curs   Incipit to version E of 122.

By the autorite of oure holi fader the pope N and alle his cardenallis Archebisshopes bishopes and alle holy chirche   Incipit to edition C.3 of 122.

123   Be the dyscression and ordenaunce of all the roialme of England the lordys spiritual and temporall of alle maner of weyghtis and mesures

"Weights and Measures", specifications for various weights, s. xv (2).

1. Louis (1980), pp. 315-18 (Bodl Tanner 407, f. 60r-v).

Cf. 124.

124   By the discrecion and ordynaunce of oure Lorde the king weight and mesure were made It is to be knowen that an Englisse penny which is called a rounde sterlyng and without clyppyng

Weight and Mesure, account of weights and measures, s. xv.

1. Rel. Ant., I (1841), 232 (BL Lansdowne 762, f. 2v).

Cf. 123.

125   C for B D for C F for D G for F H for G K for H L for K

"Directions for Writing in Cipher", s. xv.

1. Rel. Ant., II (1843), 15 (BL Sloane 351, f. 15v).

Canticum beate marie de dolore suo in passione filii sui Plenitudo legis
est dilectio The apostel seinte poule seyth The fulfyllyng of the lawe ys
loue   Incipit to text proper of 751.

126   Cesarius tels þat a prest þat had cure of sawle sagh a woman clade in
sere clethyngs & hade a long tayle þat scho drogh after here

[Richard Rolle], exemplum from Cesarius of Heisterbach's Dialogus Miraculorum, s. xiv.

1. YW, I (1895), 157 (BL Harley 1022, f. 1v).

127   Christ biddiþ us be ware wiþ þese false prophetis þat comen in cloþinge
of sheep and ben wolves of raveyne And þes ben speciali men of þes
sewe ordris

Exposicioun of þe Text of Matheu ("Vae Octuplex"), Wycliffite
sermon, s. xiv (2).

1. SEW, II (1871), 379-89 (Bodl Bodley 788, ff. 90v-96); 2.
Hudson (1978), pp. 75-83 (BL Royal 18 B.ix, ff. 191v-94v).

Also in Cambridge Christ's 7, Cambridge Pembroke 237, Cam-
bridge St. John's 193, TCC B.4.20, TCD 245, Leicester Old
Town Hall 3, Leicester Wyggeston Hospital 10.D.34/6, BL
Addl. 40672, Lambeth Palace 1149, Bodl Don.c.13, Bodl Laud
Miscellaneous 314, and Princeton Robert H. Taylor MS.

Crist comandiþ to his disciplis and to alle cristene men to vndirstonde
and flee þe sowrdow of pharisees   See 94.

128   Crist oure goode hed of al holichirche and vre god he tauhte vs to preye
þe Pater Noster

Exposicion of þe Pater Noster, s. xiv.

1. EETS os 217 (1942), pp. 334-36 (BL Addl. 22283, f. 101).

Also in Oxford University 97.

Crist telliþ in þis parable how richessis ben perilouse for liʒtli wole a riche man use hem unto moche lust A parable is a word of stori þat bi þat hydeþ a spirituall witt   See **304**.

Crist þat deyde vp on þe crosse for sauacion of mankynde Graunt vs grace so to a skapyn þe sley ensaylingis of þe fende That we be not for synne lost in owr last ende   Invocation to **789**.

129 Crist þou arte now soþfastely conteyned heere in þis mooste excellent sacrament I knowlich þee my lord god wiþ my mouþe

   Prayer to the Eucharist appended to Contemplacyons of the Drede and Love of God, s. xv (?).

   1. The Library Chronicle (University of Pennsylvania), 42 (1977), 17-18 (Philadelphia University of Pennsylvania English 2, ff. 132-34v).

   See **362**.

130 Cristene men preien mekely and deuoutly to almyʒty god þat he graunte his grace for his hendeles mercy to oure religious boþe possessioneris and mendynauntis

   How Religious Men Sholde Kepe Certayne Articles, Wycliffite tract, s. xiv (2).

   1. EETS os 74 (1880, 1902), pp. 220-25 (CCCC 296, pp. 185-90).

   Also in TCD 244.

131 Cristen mennes bileeue tauʒt of Iesu Crist God and man and hise apostles and seynt Austyn seynt Ierome and seynt Ambrose and of þe court of Rome and alle treue men is þis

   Wycliffite tract on the Eucharist, s. xiv ex.

   1. Hudson (1978), pp. 110-12 (TCD 245, ff. 145-46v).

Crysten peple thier wordis þat I af take to speke of at this tyem er þe wordis of Seynt Powl   See **435**.

Cristyn þe worschepful virgyne of Criste was goten and borne of honest fadir and modir in þe toune of seinte Trudous in Hasban   Incipit to text proper of **808**.

132   Cristis chirche is his spouse that haþ thre partis Þe first part is in bliss wiþ Crist hed of þe chirche and conteyneþ aungelis and blessid men þat nowe ben in heuene

        Of þe Chirche and Hir Membris, Wycliffite treatise, s. xiv (2).

        1. Todd (1851), pp. iii-lxxx (TCD 245, ff. 63v-75v); 2. SEW, III (1871), 339-65 (Bodl Bodley 788, ff. 328-36).

        Also in Leicester Wyggeston Hospital 10.D.34/6, BL Royal 18 B.ix, and BL Addl. 40672.

133   Clerkis possessioneris fordon presthod knyȝthod and comineris for þei taken þe ordre of presthod and bynden hem to kepe þis ordre and holi lif and techynge of goddis peple

        Of Clerkis Possessioneris, Wycliffite tract, s. xiv (2).

        1. EETS os 74 (1880, 1902), pp. 116-40 (CCCC 296, pp. 107-23).

        Also in TCD 244.

Come to me seythe our mercyfull lorde all that laboreth and be charged and I shal gyue vnto you refeccyon   Incipit to prologue to Margaret Countess of Richmond's translation of Book 4 of De Imitatione Christi (**838**)

134   Confitebor tibi Domine quia iratus es michi . . . I schall schryve to þee Lord for þou art wraþþ to me turnyd is þi breeþ and þou cumfortidst me

        "Super Cantica Sacra", Wycliffite version of the twelve canticles with commentary, ca. 1400.

        1. SEW, III (1871), 5-81 (Bodl Bodley 288).

Also complete in Aberdeen University D2.7.35, TCC B.5.25,
Lincoln Cathedral 35, BL Harley 1806, Bodl Bodley 877, Bodl
Bodley 953, Bodl Laud Miscellaneous 448, Oxford Magdalen 52,
Oxford New 320 (without commentary), Oxford University 56;
excerpts in Bodl Bodley 554, Bodl Bodley 938, Bodl Douce 258,
Bodl Fairfax 2, Bodl Laud Miscellaneous 174, Oxford New 95.

Confitebor tibi domine quoniam iratus es michi . . . . I sall shrife til the
lord for thou ert wrethid til me turnyd is thi breth and thou me
comfortid   Incipit to canticles in 271.

135   Confiteor Deo coeli . . . . I knowleche to God of heuene and vnto the
blessid Marye and vnto alle his halewis and unto thee fadre for that I
wreche synner

A form of confession, s. xv.

1. Maskell, II (1846), 282 (Bodl Douce 246); 2. Maskell, 2nd
ed., III (1882), 304 (as in 1).

Cf. Jolliffe C.24-30.

136   Confiteor Deo . . . Specyally I haske God mercy that I haue not kepytt
his commandments and the councellis of the gospell

A Compendius Forme of Dayly Confessions, s. xv.

1. Maskell, II (1846), 279-81 (BL Cotton Nero A. III, ff.
135v-37); 2. Maskell, 2nd ed., III (1882), 301-3 (as in 1).

Jolliffe C.42.

136.7 Considerith thopynyons sentences and diffinicions of wyse Philosophers and other sage persoones auncient and autentike that is to sey in
the bible the Wise Parables of Salamon

III Consideracions Right Necesserye to the Good Governaunce of
a Prince, political tract translated from French, s. xv med.

1. Genet (1977), pp. 180-209 (Oxford University 85, pp. 136-
79).

Also in TCC O.5.6 and Cambridge (Mass.) Harvard University
English 530.

137 Consideryng that wordes ben perisshyng vayne and forgeteful And
writynges duelle and abide permanent as I rede Vox audita perit littera
scripta manet

William Caxton, Myrrour of the Worlde, encyclopaedic work
translated from French prose version (BL Royal 19 A.ix), 1481.

1. W. Caxton, 1481? (STC 24762); 2. W. Caxton, 1490? (STC
24763); 3. EETS es 110 (1913) (as in 1); 4. Kentfield/Allen
(1964) (as in 1); 5. 1979 (facsimile of 1).

138 Constantin & Maxence weren on a time as in Keiseres stude behest in
Rome Ah Constentin ferde þurh þe burh-menne reaδ into Fronc londe
& wunede sum hwile þear

Þe Martyrdom of Sancte Katerine (of Alexandria), saint's life, s.
xiii in.

1. ed. J. Morton, Abbotsford Club (1841) (BL Cotton Titus D.
XVIII, ff. 133v-47v); 2. ed. C. Hardwick, An Historical
Inquiry Touching St. Catharine of Alexandria, Cambridge Antiquarian Society (1849), pp. 21-40 (as in 1); 3. EETS os 80
(1884) (BL Royal 17 A.xxvii, ff. 11-37); 4. Roxburghe 112
(1884), Appendix (as in 3); 5. d'Ardenne (1977), pp. 17-53
(Bodl Bodley 34, ff. 1-18); 6. EETS ss 7 (1981) (as in 1, 3, and
5).

Cf. 28.

139 Continuel meditacione of þe passione of Cryste sall rewle a man in
spekynge in thynkynge in wyrkynge and rayse hym into gastly felynge

Bone Aventure, quotations from St. Bonaventure, Rolle, and
others, s. xiv.

1. YW, I (1895), 129-31 (Bodl Rawlinson C. 285, f. 39v); 2.
YW, I (1895), 129-31 (CUL Dd.5.55, f. 93).

Cum   See [Q]uum

Cumanimaduerterem quam plurimos homines errare in via morum . . .
Whan I remembre and consydere in my corage that moche peple erre
greuously in the way of maners and of good doctrynes   Incipit to
text proper of 793.

140   Cvm natus esset ihesus in betleem iude in diebus herodis regis . . . We
       redeth i þo holi godespelle of te dai ase ure louerd god almichti i-bore
       was of ure lauedi seinte Marie

       Sermons (5) in Kentish dialect translated from the French of
       Maurice de Sully, beginning with Epiphany, s. xiii (1).

       1. EETS os 49 (1872), pp. 26-36 (Bodl Laud Miscellaneous 471,
       ff. 128v-33v); 2. Kluge (1904, 1912), pp. 19-25 (as in 1); 3.
       Hall (1920), I, 214-22 (as in 1).

       Da nobis auxilium de tribulacione . . . Þo holy prophete spekeþ in þe
       persoune of mankynde þat is sette in tribulacions & aduersitees of þis
       world   Incipit to version B of 143.

141   Da nobis auxilium domine de tribulacione Þou soule tribulid and
       temptid to þe is þis word shewid þat þou lere wherof tribulacion serues
       and þat þou not onely susteyne hom suffraandely but also gladely

       [Richard Rolle], "Twelve Profits of Tribulacion", translation of
       De XII Utilitatibus Tribulationis ascribed to Peter of Blois, s.
       xiv.

       1. YW, II (1896), 45-60 (BL Royal 17 B.xvii, ff. 49v-67).

       Also in Bodl Laud Miscellaneous 210; Jolliffe J.3.c. For an-
       other translation of the Latin see 142; for a verse translation see
       IMEV 257. For a translation from French see 143.

142   Da nobis domine auxilium de tribulacione Lord god graunte us helpe of
       tribulacion To þe soule þat art distroublid and temptid to þe is purposed
       þat þou schalt lerne wherof tribulacions seruen (from 4)

       Þe XII Prophetis and Avauntegis of Tribulacion, translation of
       De XII Utilitatibus Tribulationis ascribed to Peter of Blois, s.
       xiv.

       1. W. Caxton, [1491] (STC 3305, Part 2); 2. W. de Worde,
       [1499] (STC 20412); 3. W. de Worde, 1530 (STC 20413); 4.
       YW, II (1896), 391-406 (Bodl Rawlinson C. 894, ff. 2v-18).

       Also in BL Harley 1706, BL Royal 17 C.xviii, Manchester
       Rylands English 94, Bodl Douce 322, Oxford CCC 220; Jolliffe
       J.3.b. For another translation of the Latin see 141; for a verse
       translation see IMEV 257. For a translation from French see

143 Da nobis domine auxilium de tribulacione To the soule that art
delyuered to temptacions and to tribulacions of this lyf is ordeyned the
wisdom of this world

> The Boke of Tribulacyon, devotional treatise translated from the
> French Livre de tribulacion (s. xiii), s. xiv ex.
>
> A. Longer version: 1. MET 15 (1983), pp. 38-131 (Bodl Bodley
> 423, ff. 205-26).
>
> B. Abbreviated version: 1. MET 15 (1983), pp. 134-43 (BL
> Arundel 286, ff. 100-15).
>
> Another MS of A: BL Harley 1197; Jolliffe J.3.e. Version B is
> Jolliffe J.3.a. Another translation of the French is in Cam-
> bridge St. John's 188 and New York Columbia University Plimp-
> ton 256; Jolliffe J.3.d. For three translations from Latin see
> **141, 142,** and IMEV 257.

144 Dauid seiþ Lord sett þou a lawe maker vpon hem Hit semyþ to me seiþ
Austyn þat þis signifieþ antecrist of whom þe apostle seiþ

> Of Antecrist and His Meynee, Wycliffite tract, s. xv in.
>
> 1. Todd (1851), pp. cxv-cliv (TCD 245, ff. 117-27).

David the prophete saith that the Iuggements and the punysshinges of
god ben as abysmes without bottom and without ryuage   Incipit to
text proper (from edition 2) of **363.**

Dauið þe psalm wruhte spekeð i þe sawter   See **95.**

145 De quadam muliere luxuriosa þat wold not shryue hur of hur synnes
and at þe last shuld die

> Exemplum based on a story in the Speculum Laicorum, s. xv.
>
> 1. NM, 72 (1971), 98-99 (BL Royal 18 B.xxiii, f. 50v).

Dere beloued relygious frendes ye must aboue all thynges loue almyghty

god & than þe neyghbour   Incipit to text proper of both versions of
268.

146   Dere brother in Cryste I haue vnderstandynge by thyne owne speche
and also by tellynge of another man þat thou yernest and desyrest
gretely for to haue more knowledge and vnderstandynge then thou hast
of aungelles songe

Walter Hilton (?), The Anehede of Godd with Mannis Saule/Of
the Songe of Aungells, treatise on the purity of souls, s. xiv (2).

1. H. Pepwell, 1521 (STC 20972, Part 5); 2. EETS os 20
(1866), pp. 14-19 (Lincoln Cathedral 91, ff. 219v-21v); 3.
Mätzner, 2 (1869), 133-37 (as in 2); 4. YW, I (1895), 175-82
(CUL Dd.5.55, ff. 94v-99v); 5. YW, I (1895), 175-82 (as in
2); 6. EETS os 20, rev. ed. (1921), pp. 15-20 (as in 2); 7.
Studies in English Literature, 54, no. 3 (1977), 9-15 (BL Addl.
27592, ff. 57v-61v); 8. Takamiya (1980), pp. 9-15 (as in 7).

Also in CUL Ff.5.40, Bodl Bodley 576, Tokyo Takamiya 3;
probably also in Bodl Rawlinson C. 285 originally.

147   Dere brother in cryst two maner of states there are in holy chyrche by
þe whiche crysten soules plesen god & geten hem the blysse of heuen
(from 2)

Walter Hilton, Medled Lyfe/Vita Mixta, devotional treatise in
epistle form, s. xiv (2).

1. [W. de Worde], 1494 (STC 14042, Part 2); 2. J. Notary,
1507 (STC 14043, Part 2); 3. R. Pynson, 1516 (STC 4602, Part
3); 4. W. de Worde, 1525 (STC 14044, Part 2); 5. R. Wyer,
ca. 1530 (STC 14041); 6. W. de Worde, 1533 (STC 14045, Part
2); 7. EETS os 20 (1866), pp. 19-42 (Lincoln Cathedral 91, ff.
223-28v supplemented by BL Royal 17 C.xviii); 8. YW, I
(1892), 264-92 (Bodl Eng. poet. a. 1, ff. 353-55); 9. YW, I
(1892), 270-92 (Lincoln Cathedral 91, as in 6); 10. EETS os 20,
rev. ed. (1921), pp. 21-43 (as in 6).

Also in Cambridge Fitzwilliam Museum Bradfer-Lawrence De-
posit 10, CUL Ff.5.40, Hopton Hall MS, BL Harley 2254, BL
Harley 2397, BL Addl. 22283, Lambeth Palace 472, Longleat
Marquis of Bath 29, Manchester Chetham 6690, New York
Columbia University Plimpton 271, Bodl Ashmole 751 (por-
tions), Bodl Rawlinson A. 355, Bodl Rawlinson A. 356, Bodl
Rawlinson C. 894, Tokyo Takamiya 66.

148 Dere brothyr in ihesu crist I pray ʒou hertyly for þe loue of god and of oure lady seynt Marye godys modyr and virgyne

Revelacio, vision addressed to a monk, s. xv (1).

1. Speculum, 59 (1984), 104-5 (TCD 281, f. 161).

149 Dere brothyr þow walde gladly wyte qwilke is venial synne and qwilke dedly synne for þe thynke qwen a man can knawe þe tane fra þe toþir he may be more war for to flee þam

[Walter Hilton], "Of Deadly and Venial Sin", epistle discussing the two classes of sin, s. xiv.

1. YW, I (1895), 182-83 (CUL Dd.5.55, ff. 100-101v).

Also in CUL Ff.5.40. Jolliffe F.3.

Dere ffrende wit þou wele þat þe ende and þe soueraynte of perfeccione standes in a verray anehede of Godd and of manes saule by perfyte charyte   Incipit to editions 2, 3, 5, and 6 of 146.

Der frendes ye sall make a speciall prayer unto gode allmyghty   Incipit to edition 11 of 857.

150 Dere sistir þou wost wel þe more a man haþ vndirstondyng of riʒtwisnesse and þe openlier þat he knowiþ God þe more likyng he haþ and þe more he it loueþ ʒif he be good

[Richard Rolle], Pater Noster of Richard Ermyte, exposition of the Pater Noster, s. xv in.

1. ed. F.G.A.M. Aarts (1967), pp. 3-56 (London Westminster School 3, ff. 1-67v).

Also in Cambridge Sidney Sussex 74, TCC O.1.29, CUL Ii.6.40, Durham Cathedral A.IV.22 (beginning imperfectly), Bodl Laud Miscellaneous 104.

151 Demeþ nouʒt by þe face but riʒtful doom ʒe deme John 8o co Holy fader in þe begynnyng of my sermoun ich make a protestacioun þat is is nouʒt myn entent

John Trevisa, translation of Richard FitzRalph's sermon <u>Defensio Curatorum</u>, s. xiv (2).

1. EETS os 167 (1925), pp. 39-93 (BL Harley 1900, ff. 6-21).

Also in Cambridge St. John's 204, BL Stowe 65, BL Addl. 24194, Manchester Chetham 11379, San Marino Huntington HM 28561.

152   Demaunde who bare þe best burden that euer was borne Response That bare þe asse whan our lady fled with our lorde in to egypte

Demaundes Joyous, dialogue translated from French, s. xv ex. (?).

1. W. de Worde, 1511 (STC 6573); 2. Rel. Ant., II (1843), 72-75 (as in 1); 3. Kemble (1848), pp. 287-92 (as in 1).

Deprecemur Deum Patrem omnipotentem   Incipit to editions 2, 4, 9, and 12 of 857.

153   Diamonde comes from Inde and some from Arabie that wich cometh from Inde is clipped males ye other female

Lapidary, translation of an Anglo-Norman version, s. xv (?).

1. EETS os 190 (1933), pp. 119-30 (BL Sloane 2628, ff. 14v-29v).

154   Dias saise let a fox see an almonde and he schall die The oyle of almundis sleys longe wormes in þe wombe and purgis menstruall blode

John Trevisa, <u>De Arboribus et Herbis</u>, extracts from Book XVII of his translation of <u>De Proprietatibus Rerum</u> circulating separately, s. xv in.

1. Anglia, 91 (1973), 21-34 (BL Sloane 983, ff. 95-103).

See 785.

155   Diliges dominum deum tuum ex toto corde tuo . . . Thou schalt loue thi lord thi god of al thyn herte of al thy lyf of al thi mynde and of al thi strengthes or myghtes and thyn neighebor as thi-self

Exposition of "Diliges dominum deum tuum", s. xiv.

1. YW, II (1896), 454-55 (Oxford University 97, ff. 97-98).

Also in BL Harley 2385, London Westminster School 3, Bodl Douce 246, Bodl Laud Miscellaneous 210. Jolliffe G.26.

156   Diues et Pauper obuiauerunt sibi vtriusque operator est dominus . . . These ben the wordes of Salomon this moche to say in englyssh The riche and the pore mette to themself the lorde is worcher of euireither

> "Dives et Pauper", exposition of the ten commandments, preceded by a dialogue on holy poverty, ca. 1405-10.
>
> 1. R. Pynson, 1493 (STC 19212) (Bodl Eng. th. d. 36); 2. W. de Worde, 1496 (STC 19213) (as in 1); 3. T. Berthelet, 1536 (STC 19214) (as in 1); 4. EETS os 275 (1976) and os 280 (1980) (Glasgow University Hunterian 270 supplemented by Lichfield Cathedral 35 and Bodl Eng. th. d. 36).
>
> Also in BL Harley 149, BL Royal 17 C.xx, BL Royal 17 C.xxi, BL Addl. 10053 (fragment), New Haven Yale University 228, Oscott College MS (pastedown), Bodl Ashmole 750 (5) (excerpts), Bodl Douce 295, Bodl Eng. th. e. 1 (fragment).

Doo to a nother as thou wold be done vnto This commaundement haue we of our lorde Ihesu criste in his gospell of Mathew the viij chapytre Incipit to "A shorte exhortacyon ofte to be shewed to the peple," which is added to Mirk's Festivall (734) in editions 3-13 at least.

157   Domine labia Lord thou schalt opyne myn lippis And my mouth schal schewe thi prisyng God take heede to myn help Lord hiȝe thee to helpe me

> The Prymer/Matyns of Our Ladi, translation of the Sarum Breviary, s. xiv ex.
>
> 1. Maskell, II (1846), xxxvii, 3-242 (BL Addl. 36683, with excerpts from BL Harley 2343, William Maskell MS, Bodl Bodley 85, Bodl Douce 246, and Bodl Douce 275); 2. Maskell, 2nd ed., III (1882), xxxix-xl, 3-247 (as in 1); 3. ed. H. Littlehales (1891), Part I (Cambridge St. John's 192); 4. EETS os 105 (1895) (CUL Dd.11.82).
>
> Also in Cambridge Emmanuel 246, Glasgow University Hunter-

ian 157, BL Addl. 17010, BL Addl. 17011, BL Addl. 27592, Bodl Ashmole 1288, Bodl Rawlinson C. 699, Oxford Queen's 324.

Domine labia mea aperies Lord opene þou my lippis And my mouþ schal telle þi preisyng   Incipit to edition 4 of 157.

Dominus noster Iesus Christus humiliauit semetipsum pro nobis . . . Iesu Iesu Iesu haue marcy on me ₌   Incipit to edition 16 of 355.

158   . . . doun in to þe dyke and thare he felle & was all to-frusched and þan Alexander said vn-to hym one this wyse

Vita Alexandry Magni Conquestoris/Lyf of Gret Alexander, romance, slightly abridged from the Latin Historia de Preliis, s. xv (1).

1. EETS os 143 (1913) (Lincoln Cathedral 91, ff. 1-49).

159   Ecce uenit rex occurramus obuiam saluatori nostro To dai is cumen ðe holie tid þat me clepeð aduent þanked be ure louerd ihesu crist þit haueð isend

Sermon collection, s. xii ex.

1. EETS os 53 (1873), pp. 3-219 (odd pages only) (TCC B.14.52, pp. 1-157).

160   Ego dormio et cor meum uigilat Þou þat lyste lufe herken & here of luf In þe sang of luf it es writen I slepe & my hert wakes

Richard Rolle, "Ego Dormio", epistle written to a woman, 1343-48.

1. YW, I (1895), 50-61 (CUL Dd.5.64, ff. 22v-29); 2. YW, I (1895), 50-61 (Bodl Rawlinson A. 389, ff. 77-95, and Bodl Eng. poet. a. 1, ff. 369-70); 3. YW, I (1895), 415-16 (BL Arundel 507, ff. 40-40v, ending imperfectly), abridged version; 4. Allen, English (1931), pp. 61-72 (as in 1); 5. MS, 43 (1981), 230-48 (as in 1).

Also in Cambridge Fitzwilliam Museum Bradfer-Lawrence Deposit 10, Cambridge Magdalene Pepys 2125, TCD 155, BL

Addl. 22283, BL Addl. 37790, London Westminster School 3, Longleat Marquis of Bath 29, Paris Bibl. Ste.-Geneviève 3390, Tokyo Takamiya 66. A Latin version appears in Cambridge Gonville and Caius 140/80.

161 Ego sum creatura Dei creatoris mei What noumbre and person is the verbe sum The syngler noumbre

John Jones, grammatical treatise related to Ego sum creatura Dei, ca. 1440.

1. Thomson (1984), pp. 193-207 (BL Addl. 19046, ff. 49-63, ending imperfectly).

162 Ego sum creatura Dei This verbe sum is þe syngler nombyr and the fyrst person for so is his nominatyfe case ego

John Cobbow (?), Formula Gramaticis, grammatical treatise revised from the Informacio (see 349), s. xv in.

A. Early version: 1. Thomson (1984), pp. 148-63 (BL Harley 1002, ff. 1-2).

B. Version by Walter Pollard (1444-83): 1. Thomson (1984), pp. 164-76 (Bodl Rawlinson D. 328, ff. 76-79v).

C. Version by John Clavering (s. xv [2]): 1. Thomson (1984), pp. 140-47 (BL Addl. 37075, ff. 30v-37, 41).

D. Version by William Hampshire (1475-79): 1. Thomson (1984), pp. 131-39 (CCCC 233, ff. 164-69v).

Ego sum vitis vera . . . As comune þing is betere and bifore oþer þingis so þis gospel þat is red in comun story shulden men knowe sum what Incipit to Commune Sanctorum series of 304.

163 Engle lond is eyhte hundred Myle long from penwyþ steorte þat is fyftene Mylen by-yonde Mihhales steowe on cornwale fort þat cume to katenes

Þe Syren and þe Hundredes of Engelonde, s. xiii.

1. EETS os 49 (1872), pp. 145-46 (Oxford Jesus 29, f. 267r-v); 2. Kluge (1904, 1912), pp. 26-27 (as in 1).

erylle   See 539.

164   Esdras the profate sayth that when the day of the kalendys of Januare
       ys vppon the sunday

       Prognostic, s. xv.

       1. Archiv, 128 (1912), 295 (Bodl Digby 88, ff. 25-26).

165   Every creature resonable vnto whome god hath gyuen mynde and
       vnderstandynge and wyll Hym ought to knowe serue and loue with all
       his myght

           Ordynarye of Crysten Men, compendium of religious knowledge
           in five parts translated from French, ca. 1467 (?).

           1. W. de Worde, 1502 (STC 5198); 2. W. de Worde, 1506 (STC
           5199).

       Euery proud persone wold compare hym self to god in so moche as they
       gloryfye them self in the goddes that they haue   Incipit to text
       proper of 820.

166   Euery wise man þat cleymeþ his eritage eiþir askeþ gret pardoun kepiþ
       bisili & haþ ofte mynde vpon þe chartre of his calenge (from 2)

           A Good Tretys of a Notable Chartour of Pardoun of Oure Lorde
           Ihesu Crist, tract from Pore Caitif circulating separately, s. xiv
           ex.

           1. R. Lant, [1542?] (STC 19187); 2. ed. M.C. Spalding, The
           Middle English Charters of Christ (1914), pp. 100-2 (CUL
           Ff.6.34, ff. 72-74v).

           The tract appears separately in CUL Ii.6.40, Cambridge (Mass.)
           Harvard University English 701, BL Harley 1706, BL Harley
           4012, London Westminster School 3, Manchester Rylands Eng-
           lish 85, Bodl Douce 322 (imperfect), Bodl Eng. th. c. 50
           (fragment).   See Jolliffe B.

       Exiguum et cum tedio est tempus vite nostre . . . Sythen that by
       naturall course the date of mannes lyf is short and as experyence
       sheweth the processe of the same is full of peryls   Incipit to text

proper of **88.**

167   Faciamus hominem ad ymaginem nostram . . . that is to seye God seith Make we man to oure liknesse to haue lordship aboue the creatures of the erthe and by whom the setis of paradise that ben voide maye be fulfilled

       Translation of Chapters 5-23 of the Bible en françois (s. xiii) by Roger d'Argenteuil, didactic work, ca. 1470.

       1. MET 6 (1977) (Cleveland Public Library W q091.92-C468, ff. 77-99v).

168   Facti sunt filii mei perditi quia invaluit inimicus that is to seie in Englisch thus My sones ben maad lost for the enemye hath had the maistrie

       Reginald Pecock, "The Book of Faith", ca. 1456.

       1. ed. J.L. Morison (1909) (TCC B.14.45, ending imperfectly).

169   Fayre Sir I aske yow whether ye hadde leuyr reioye wt out desyrynge or to desyre wt oute reioyinge

       The Demaundes of Love, translation from French, 1487.

       1. ed. W. Braekman (1982) (BL Addl. 60577, ff. 95-106).

170   False confessouris ben cause of alle þe synne þat regneþ among clerkis among lordis among communes for þei taken þe charge to hele alle men of synne and don not here power þer to

       Þre Þingis Distroien Þis World, Wycliffite tract, s. xiv (2).

       1. EETS os 74 (1880, 1902), pp. 181-86 (CCCC 296, pp. 160-64).

       Also in TCD 244 and Bodl Bodley 938.

171   Fadre oure þat art in heve i-halgeed bee þi nome i-cume þi kinereiche (from 3)

       Pater Noster ("Lord's Prayer"), various dates from s. xii (1) to

1. Rel. Ant., I (1841), 42 (BL Arundel 57, f. 94); 2. Rel. Ant., I (1841), 204 (BL Cotton Vitellius A. XII, f. 181v); 3. Rel. Ant., I (1841), 282 (Cambridge Gonville and Caius 52/29); 4. Maskell, II (1846), 238 (as in 3); 5. Maskell, II (1846), 238-39 (BL Royal 5 C.v, blank leaf at end); 6. Maskell, II (1846), 239 (Cambridge St. John's 142); 7. Maskell, II (1846), 239 (Bodl Douce 246, f. 15); 8. Mätzner, I, 2 (1869), 3-4 (as in 3); 9. ES, 1 (1877), 215 (Salisbury Cathedral 82, f. 271v); 10. Maskell, 2nd ed., III (1882), 248 (as in 3); 11. Maskell, 2nd ed., III (1882), 249 (as in 5); 12. Maskell, 2nd ed., III (1882), 249 (as in 6); 13. Maskell, 2nd ed., III (1882), 249 (as in 7); 14. N&Q, 12th series 10 (1922), 128 (Norton-on-Tees Grove House Fairfax-Blakeborough MS); 15. MLN, 49 (1934), 236 (Pavia Biblioteca Universitaria 69, f. 41v).

Also included in 157 and various other ME works.

Fader þat hart in heuene blesed be þi name Incipit to edition 15 of 171.

172   Felician regnyd emperour in the Cyte of Rome In the empeire of whom þer was a knyȝt þat hadde weddid a yong damesell to wif

Gesta Romanorum, collection of exempla translated from Latin, s. xv (1).

1. W. de Worde, [1502?] (STC 21286.2); 2. W. de Worde, [ca. 1510] (STC 21286.3); 3. [W. de Worde, ca. 1515] (STC 21286.5); 4. [W. de Worde, ca. 1525] (STC 21286.7); 5. J. Kynge, 1557 (STC 21287); 6. ed. F. Madden (1838) (CUL Kk.1.6, ff. 216-45v; BL Harley 7333, ff. 150-203; BL Addl. 9066; supplemented by 2); 7. EETS es 33 (1879) (as in 6); 8. ed. K.I. Sandred (1971) (Gloucester Cathedral 22, pp. 723-87, beginning and ending imperfectly).

The Gloucester Cathedral MS is partly a different translation from that in the other MSS. Many modernized and chapbook versions from 1595 into the eighteenth century.

173   Fylle a potte of old reed wyn and doo þere inne powdir of canell gyllofre gingefre peletre

Medical recipes, s. xv.

1. ed. G. Müller, Aus mittelenglischen Medizintexten (1929) (Stockholm Kungliga Biblioteket X.90).

174 First how be it that our souveraigne lorde as a prince enclined to shew his mercy and pite to his subgettes raither then rigure and straitenesse of his laweʒ

A Remembrance of Suche Acteʒ and Dedes, chronicle of the rebellion in Lincolnshire (1470), ca. 1470.

1. Camden Soc. 39 (1847), pp. 5-18 (London College of Arms Vincent 435, item 9).

175 First alle heretikis aʒenst þe feiþ of holy writt ben cursed solempnely foure tymes in þe ʒer and also meyntenouris and consentoris to heresie or heretikis in here errour

Þe Grete Sentence of Curs Expouned, Wycliffite tract, s. xiv ex.

1. SEW, III (1871), 271-337 (CCCC 296, pp. 239-88).

Cf. 122.

176 First and formest yf alle thei that ouʒte to sewe to this court be here present or no and ho lakketh present here defautes

Statutes and the Lawes of the Kynges Forestes, appended to the Maystere of Game in one MS, s. xv (?).

1. Baillie-Grohman (1904), pp. 241-42 (Bodl Douce 335, ff. 72-73v).

See 775.

177 First as Galfride saith this lande was named Albion after the name of Albyne the oldest doughter of Dioclesian and had xxxij sustres

John Trevisa, Descripcion of Britayne, an extract from his English version of Higden's Polychronicon (with brief prologue and epilogue by Caxton), 1398.

1. W. Caxton, 1480 (STC 13440a, 9991 Part 2); 2. W. de Worde, 1498 (STC 13440b, 9996 Part 2); 3. W. de Worde, 1502 (STC 9997, Part 2); 4. J. Notary, 1504 (STC 9998, Part 2); 5.

R. Pynson, 1510 (STC 9999, Part 2); 6. J. Notary, 1515 (STC 10000, Part 2); 7. W. de Worde, 1515 (STC 9985, Part 2); 8. W. de Worde, 1520 (STC 10001, Part 2); 9. W. de Worde, 1528 (STC 10002, Part 2).

178 First at the houre conuenient the bisshop wyth his ministres indued and arrayed after their accustumable maner shall come to the hygh aulter

Fourme and Order of the Cerimonies Perteignyng to the Solempne Profession, Benediction, and Consecracion of Holy Virgyns, ritual for the ordination of nuns, s. xv ex.

1. Maskell, II (1846), 308-31 (CUL Mm.3.13, ff. 16-18v); 2. Maskell, 2nd ed., III (1882), 333-59 (as in 1).

Cf. **89, 366,** and **862.**

179 First begynneth the lyf of Esope with alle his fortune how he was subtyll wyse and borne in Grece not ferre fro Troye the graunt in a Towue named Amoneo

William Caxton, Subtyl Historyes and Fables of Esope, translated from French and slightly modified, 1483.

1. W. Caxton, 1484 (STC 175); 2. R. Pynson, [1497?] (STC 176), Fables only but probably both originally; 3. R. Pynson, [1500?] (STC 177); 4. ed. J. Jacobs (1889), II (as in 1), Fables only; 5. Grabham Press ed. (1930) (as in 1); 6. Gregynog Press ed. (1931) (as in 1), Fables only; 7. ed. R.T. Lenaghan (1967) (as in 1); 8. (1972) (facsimile of 1); 9. ed. D. Gray (1975) (facsimile of 1); 10. ed. E. Hodnett (1976) (facsimile of 1).

180 First byhoues þe ask þe name of man or of woman for whan þow will say Ga than in to þe kirke and say thar þi charme

Charm for stanching blood, s. xv.

1. Chaucer and Middle English Studies (1974), p. 62 (BL Royal 17 A.viii, f. 48v).

Fyrste byþenke þe howe þou myȝte holde þi selfe wrechyde foule and vnworþi to eny benefyce of god Also studye howe þou myȝte dysplese þi selfe and desyre to plese god aloone   Incipit to text proper of 11.

181   First by the meane of the Kynge of Fraunce the sayd Erle of Warwick
       purchased a pardon of the Quene Margarete and of her sonne

       The Maner and Gwidynge of the Erle of Warwick at Aungiers
       (1470), newsletter, ca. 1470.

       1. ed. H. Ellis, Original Letters Illustrative of English History,
       2nd series 1 (1827), 132-35 (BL Harley 543, ff. 168-69).

182   First crist comaundiþ men of power to fede hungry pore men þe fend
       and his techen to make costly festis and waste many goodis on lordis
       and riche men

       Hou Sathanas and His Children Turnen Werkis of Mercy Upso-
       doun, Wycliffite tract, s. xiv (2).

       1. EETS os 74 (1880, 1902), pp. 210-18 (CCCC 296, pp. 179-
       85); 2. Blake, MERP (1972), pp. 139-50 (as in 1).

       Also in TCD 244.

183   Ffyrst Englond hath three Ryverse with in hym selffe comyng owte of
       the See in to the myddes of the londe

       John Fortescue, The Comodytes of Englond, s. xv med.

       1. Clermont (1869), I, 549-54 (Bodl Laud Miscellaneous 593).

184   Firste euery day in the ere hosumeuer cometh to the saide monastary
       deuotly geuyng sumwhat to the reparacions of the saide monastery

       The Pardon of the Monastery of Shene, indulgences, s. xv (2).

       1. ed. T. Hearne, Johannis de Fordun Scotichronicon Genuinum
       (1722), V, 1399-1402 (BL Harley 4012, ff. 110-13); 2. Aungier
       (1840), pp. 422-26 (as in 1).

185   Ferst for þe sithgt of descaunt it is to wete as it is a-for-seide þat ther
       be 9 a-cordis of descant

       A Litil Tretise Acording to þe Ferst Tretise of þe Sight of
       Descant, treatise on counterpoint, s. xv.

       1. Speculum, 10 (1935), 258-65 (BL Lansdowne 763, ff. 112v-

15v).

186 Firste forasmoche as many of the lordes and other menne in lower
estate whiche in this tyme of the kinges grete trouble haue done hym
good service

John Fortescue, Certeyne Advertisementes, articles of advice
from the Duke of Clarence to the Earl of Warwick, 1470.

1. Plummer (1885), pp. 348-53 (BL Addl. 48031).

Also in BL Harley 543.

187 First Friars seyen that there Religion founden of sinful men is more
perfit then that Religion or order the which Christ himselfe made that is
both God and man

John Purvey (?), "Fifty Heresies and Errors of Friars", Wycliffite tract, s. xiv ex.

1. ed. T. James (J. Barnes, 1608; STC 25589, Part 2) (Bodl
Bodley 647, ff. 86-107); 2. SEW, III (1871), 367-401 (as in 1).

Also in CCCC 296 and TCD 244.

188 First I witnes bifor God Almiȝty and ale trewe cristunmen and wommen and ȝowe þat I haue not ben nor is nor neuer schal of myn entent
ne purpos

"An Apology for Lollard Doctrines", Wycliffite tract, s. xv in.

1. Camden Soc. 20 (1842) (TCD 245, ff. 164-218).

189 Ffirst in servise of all thyngys in pantery and botery and also for the
ewery ffirst table-clothis towelles longe and shorte covertours and
napkyns

"For to Serve a Lord", treatise on serving at table and carving, s.
xv/xvi.

1. EETS os 32 (1868, 1904), pp. 367-77 (W.W. Skeat's copy of
Arthur Davenport Bromley MS).

190 First in the worship of the holy Trinite bring to mynde to calle in the begynnyng of every good work for grace And sithe this little epistle is wrote and entitled to courage and comfort noble men in armes

William Worcester, Boke of Noblesse, revision of an epistle of 1451 addressed to Edward IV on his invasion of France, 1475.

1. Nichols (1860), pp. 1-85 (BL Royal 18 B.xxii, ff. 1-43).

191 First it is to knaw to a prince or a chiftain of weir that smythis wrychtis massonys ar profitable to battell warkis

De Bello Campestra, partial translation of Vegetius's De Re Militari, s. xv.

1. Studies in Scottish Literature, 8 (1970-71), 177-83 (BL Harley 6149, ff. 128-32v).

First it was shewed by the comens in the sayd parliament assembled that where in the parlianent of the right noble prynce henry the vj late kyng of englond   Incipit to text proper of 4 Henry VII of 686.

192 First kepe wel in þin herte alle þi wittis and þat is esy to do Aftyrward beþenke þe what peyne cryst sufferd in herte

Meditation on the five wits attached to end of Contemplacyons of the Drede and Love of God, s. xv (?).

1. The Library Chronicle (University of Pennsylvania), 42 (1977), 13-15 (Philadelphia University of Pennsylvania English 8, ff. 145v-46v).

See 362.

193 First seruauntis schullen trewely and gladly serue to here lordis or maistris and not be fals ne idel ne grucchynge ne heuey in here seruyce doynge

Of Servauntis and Lordis How Eche Schal Kepe His Degree, Wycliffite tract, ca. 1382.

1. EETS os 74 (1880, 1902), pp. 227-43 (CCCC 296, pp. 190-203).

Also in TCD 244.

194   First she is an ey and discloseth and hath haukes And thou maist sey An hauke eyred in the woode and hath branchers And beth y take with nettez

> The Maner of Keping of Sparhauke and Goshauke, treatise on hawking perhaps translated from French or Latin, s. xv.
>
> 1. SN, 22 (1949-50), 139-45 (BL Sloane 3488, ff. 1-3, ending imperfectly).
>
> For another translation see 741. Both translations were probably used by the author of 391.

First take a pocioun of lynne cloþ and 3 ellyn   See 291.

195   Fyrst take and geve hym yelow antes otherwyse called pysmerys as nere as ye may and the white ante or pysmers egges be best bothe wynter and somer

> Dyete for a Nyghtyngale, s. xv.
>
> 1. Rel. Ant., I (1841), 203-4 (Lambeth Palace 306, f. 177).

First that where dyuerse of the kynges subgettes hauyng cause of accyon by Fermedowne in the descendre or elles in the remayndre   Incipit to text proper of 1 Henry VII (as in edition 1) of 686.

First the kyng our sayd souereyn lord remembreth how bi vnlawfull mayntenaunces gyuynges of liueres signes and tokens and reteyndres Incipit to text proper of 3 Henry VII of 686.

196   First the kynge oure sovereyne lorde writith oute lettris un to certeyne squyers of this rewme and desirynge them for to make them redy for to receyve the hye and worshipfull ordir of knyghthode (from 2)

> How Knyghtis of the Bath Shulde Be Made, s. xiv ex.
>
> 1. Archaeological Journal, 5 (1848), 258-66 (New York Morgan M 775, ff. 195v-98v); 2. Archaeologia, 57 (1900), 67-69 (as in 1).

Also in BL Cotton Tiberius B. VIII, BL Lansdowne 254, BL
Lansdowne 285, BL Addl. 6113, BL Addl. 10106, London
College of Arms L.5, Bodl Ashmole 863.

197 Firste the prince that is newe to be crownid the day before his
     coronacion shall be apparaylid and clothid with most nobill and fayrest
     clothinge

     Maner and Forme of the Coronacion of Kyngis and Quenes in
     Engelonde, s. xv med.

     1. Archaeologia, 57 (1900), 47-55 (New York Morgan M 775,
     ff. 16-23).

     Also in BL Cotton Tiberius E. VIII, BL Lansdowne 254, BL
     Lansdowne 260, BL Lansdowne 285, BL Addl. 6113, BL Addl.
     10106, London College of Arms L.4, Bodl Ashmole 863.

198 Ffirst the seide lorde departid oute of Caleis to Guynes by watir thee
     tuisday aftir Cristmas day for to take the eire and disporte of the
     Countrey

     Account of the feat of arms performed by Richard Beauchamp,
     Earl of Warwick, against three French knights (1415), ca. 1415.

     1. PMLA, 22 (1907), 601-3 (BL Lansdowne 285, ff. 16-17v);
     2. Cripps-Day (1918), pp. xxxvi-xxxviii (as in 1).

     Also in London College of Arms L.5.

199 First the Usher must see that the Hall be trymmed in every poynt and
     that the Cloth of estate be hanged in the Hall and that foure Quyshions
     of estate be set in order upon the Benche

     The Great Feast at the Intronization of George Nevell, Arch-
     bishop of York and Chauncelour of Englande, instructions for
     the feast preceded by lists of guests and courses, 1465.

     1. ed. T. Hearne, Joannis Lelandi Antiquarii De Rebus Britanni-
     cus Collectanea (1770), 6, 7-14 (unspecified MS); 2. Warner
     (1791), pp. 92-105 (as in 1).

     [F]yrste yei be accursyd that presume to take away or pryse any
     Chirche the right yat longyth yereto   Incipit to edition C.1 of 122.

200   First þei seyn þat prechynge of þe gospel makiþ discencion and enemyte
        and siþ cristene men schulde make pees and charite as þe gospel seiþ þei
        schulden cesse of prechynge

        Speculum de Antichristo, Wycliffite tract, s. xiv (2).

        1. EETS os 74 (1880, 1902), pp. 109-13 (CCCC 296, pp. 103-
        6).

        Also in TCD 244.

201   Friste þis boke tellith how many hevenes þer beth and afterwarde he
        pronuncyth and declared of þe cours and þe governaunce of þe planetys

        The Wyse Boke of Philosophie and Astronomye, astronomical
        treatise, s. xiv (?).

        1. Krochalis and Peters (1975), pp. 5-17 (CUL Ll.4.14, ff.
        143-46).

        Also in Cambridge Gonville and Caius 457/395, Cambridge
        Magdalene Pepys 878, TCC R.14.51, BL Egerton 827, BL
        Egerton 2433, BL Royal 17 A.iii, BL Royal 17 A.xxxii, BL
        Sloane 965, BL Sloane 1317, BL Sloane 1609, BL Sloane 2453,
        BL Sloane 3553, BL Addl. 12195, London University College
        Angl. 6, London Wellcome Historical Medical Library 411, New
        Haven Yale University 163, New York Columbia University
        Plimpton 260, Bodl Ashmole 189, Bodl Ashmole 1405, Bodl
        Ashmole 1443, Bodl Ashmole 1477, Bodl Rawlinson D. 242
        (imperfect), Bodl Rawlinson D. 1220, Bodl Selden Supra 73,
        Bodl Addl. B. 17, San Marino Huntington HM 64, Tokyo
        Takamiya 39.

202   First þou schalt þinke how þis world is passing & nat duryng Also þinke
        on þi bygyninge & on þi midle age & how þou hast lyved þi lyfe

        [Richard Rolle], A Devout Meditacioun of Ric. Hampole, inter-
        polated version of parts of the Speculum Ecclesie of Edmund of
        Abingdon, s. xiv.

        1. PMLA, 40 (1925), 241-51 (CUL Ii.6.40, ff. 207v-20v); 2.
        ed. H.W. Robbins, Le Merure de Seinte Eglise (1925), pp. 82-
        92 (as in 1).

        Also in Longleat Marquis of Bath 32. Related to extracts from
        the Speculum Ecclesie in Cambridge Magdalene Pepys 2125, BL

Arundel 286, and San Marino Huntington HM 502. For other translations see **800**.

Furst to Caleys and through Flaundres Almyne the hye and the lowe
Incipit to edition 5 of **85**.

203   First whanne þou risist or fulli wakist þenk on þe goodnesse of God ffor
his owne goodnesse and non oþer nede he made al þing of nouȝt

    <u>A</u> Schort <u>Reule</u> of <u>Lif</u>, Wycliffite tract, s. xiv (2).

    1. <u>SEW</u>, III (1871), 204-8 (Bodl Laud Miscellaneous 174).

    Also in CCCC 296, BL Harley 2398, London Westminster School
    3, Bodl Bodley 9, Bodl Bodley 938, Bodl Eng. th. f. 39.

204   First whanne trewe men techen bi goddis lawe wit and reson þat eche
prest owiþ to do his myȝt his wit and his wille to preche cristis gospel
þe fend blyndiþ ypocritis to excuse hem

    <u>Of</u> <u>Feyned</u> <u>Contemplatif</u> <u>Lif</u>, Wycliffite tract, s. xiv (2).

    1. EETS os 74 (1880, 1902), pp. 188-96 (CCCC 296, pp. 165-
    70, 298-300); 2. Sisam (1921), pp. 119-28 (as in 1).

    Also in TCD 244.

205   Fyue and twenty bookis of the olde testament ben bookis of feith and
fulli bookis of holy writ the first is Genesis the ij is Exodi (from 3)

    John Purvey (?), <u>A</u> <u>Prolog</u> <u>for</u> <u>Alle</u> the <u>Bokis</u> of the <u>Bible</u> of the
    <u>Oolde</u> <u>Testament</u>, 1395 or 1396.

    1. J. Gough, 1540 (STC 3033, 25587.5); 2. R. Crawley, 1550
    (STC 25588) (CUL Mm.2.15); 3. Forshall and Madden, (1850),
    I, 1-60 (as in 2 and BL Harley 1666).

    Also in CCCC 147, CUL Kk.1.8, TCD 75, BL Harley 6333, BL
    Royal 1 C.viii, Manchester Rylands English 77, Bodl Bodley
    277, Oxford Lincoln 15, Oxford University G.3.

206   For ache of heued þat comeþ of fleumatyk betokeneþ þe nose ystoppyd
and þe eyen watery and heuy of slepe

<u>Experimentes</u> of <u>Cophon</u> þe <u>Leche</u> of <u>Salerne</u>, medical recipes, s. xv.

1. ed. P. Fordyn (1983), pp. 19-69 (BL Addl. 34111, ff. 218-30v).

207 For brekynge of þe fyrste heeste God turned alle þe waters of Egipt into blood boþe freische water and salt alle was blood

<u>Þe Ten</u> <u>Veniauncis</u> <u>Þat</u> <u>God</u> <u>Toke</u> <u>uppon</u> <u>Men</u> of <u>Egipt</u>, plagues visited on Egyptians based on Exodus 7, s. xv.

1. <u>PMLA</u>, 69 (1954), 692 (New York Morgan M 861, ff. 3v-4);
2. Bühler (1973), pp. 502-3 (as in 1).

208 For fals men multiplien mony bokes of þe Chirche nowe reendynge byleve and nowe clowtyng heresies þerfore men schulden be ware of þese two perilles þat fals men pynchyn in þe Pater noster

<u>Septem</u> <u>Hereses</u> <u>Contra</u> <u>Septem</u> <u>Peticiones</u>/<u>Speculum</u> <u>Vite</u> <u>Christiane</u>, Wycliffite tract, s. xiv (2).

1. <u>SEW</u>, III (1871), 441-46 (Bodl Douce 274, ff. 10v ff.).

Also in TCD 245, BL Harley 2385, and York Minster XVI.L.12.

For full many for defaute of gud gouernance in dietynge falles in þis sekenes thare-fore þat tyme vse none excesse nor surfete in mete & drynke   Incipit to edition 5 of 659.

For it is seide in holdynge of oure haly day þat we schulde ocupie þe tyme in prechynge and preiynge   See 595.

209 Fore hit is so þat all mankynde in this world nys but in exile and wildernesse out of his kyndely contre or as is a pilgrym or a weyfaring man in a strang londe

<u>A</u> <u>Myrour</u> <u>to</u> <u>Lewde</u> <u>Men</u> <u>and</u> <u>Wymmen</u>, a prose version of the <u>Speculum</u> <u>Vite</u> (<u>IMEV</u> 245) and related to Friar Lorens's <u>Somme</u> <u>le</u> <u>roi</u>, ca. 1400.

1. MET 14 (1981) (BL Harley 45, ff. 1-167v).

Also in Bodl e Mus. 35, Bodl Rawlinson A. 356, Philadelphia University of Pennsylvania English 3; Jolliffe A.3.

210   For many beres heuy þat freris ben clepid pseudo or ypocritis antecristis or fendis or ony siche name it were to tell what goddis lawe seyþ here

Tractatus de Pseudo-Freris, Wycliffite tract, s. xiv (2).

1. EETS os 74 (1880, 1902), pp. 296-324 (TCD 245, ff. 81-95v).

211   For of aftyr a nown substantyve verbe substantyve ys syne of the genityue case

John Clavering, grammatical treatise, s. xv (2).

1. Thomson (1984), p. 208 (BL Addl. 37075, f. 72).

212   For that in the accomptynge of the yeres of the worlde from the Creacion of Adam vnto the incarnacion of Crist been many and sundry oppynyons (from 6)

Robert Fabian, Cronecarum, chronicle of England and France to 1495, s. xvi in.

1. R. Pynson, 1516 (STC 10659); 2. W. Rastell, 1533 (STC 10660); 3. W. Bonham, 1542 (STC 10661); 4. J. Reynes, 1542 (STC 10662); 5. J. Kingston, 1559 (STC 10663, 10664); 6. ed. H. Ellis, The New Chronicles of England and France (1811), pp. 1-677 (as in 1 & BL Cotton Nero C. XI).

Also in Holkham Hall Earl of Leicester 671. Related to 365.

For that in tyme past hystoriagraphes dayly wrote and dyurnally do the hygh feates of nobles   Incipit to translator's prologue to 361.

213   For þat we been in the wey of this failyng lyf ande oure dayes passen as a schadewe þerfore it nedeth ful ofte to recorde in oure mynde that oure freelte and oure deedly seeknesse maketh vs so ofte to forȝete

Myrour of Synneres, translation of the Speculum Peccatoris ascribed variously to St. Augustine, St. Bernard, and Rolle, s. xiv.

73

1. <u>YW</u>, II (1896), 436-40 (Oxford University 97, ff. 127-31v).

Also in Cambridge Magdalene Pepys 2125, CUL Ff.5.45, CUL Ff.6.55, Coughton Court Throckmorton MS, Glasgow University Hunterian 496, Glasgow University Hunterian 520, BL Harley 1706, BL Harley 2339, BL Harley 4012, BL Addl. 22283, BL Addl. 60577, London Society of Antiquaries 300, Longleat Marquis of Bath 32, Manchester Rylands English 85, Manchester Rylands English 412, Bodl Bodley 3, Bodl Douce 13, Bodl Laud Miscellaneous 23, Bodl Laud Miscellaneous 174, Bodl Lyell 29, Bodl Tanner 336. Jolliffe F.8.

For the fallynge evill   See **643**.

For þe heuyd   See **446**.

214   For ye loue of kyng phelypp of Fraunce ye whych god kepe is thys buke of precious stones Ibegynne and he yt purchased yis buke serched many Abbay and wyth many clerkes spak

     <u>Buke</u> <u>of</u> <u>Precious</u> <u>Stones</u>, translation of the French Lapidary of King Philip, s. xv.

     1. EETS os 190 (1933), pp. 38-57 (Bodl Addl. A. 106, ff. 44-47, 126-36).

     For another translation see **215**.

215   For the loue of Philippe Kyng of Fraunce þat God hath in his kepyng was made this boke þat is clepid the boke of stones

     <u>Boke</u> <u>of</u> <u>Stones</u>, translation of the French Lapidary of King Philip, s. xv.

     1. EETS os 190 (1933), pp. 17-37 (Bodl Douce 291, ff. 121-35v); 2. ed. G.R. Keiser (1984), even pages (as in 1); 3. ed. G.R. Keiser (1984), odd pages (Chicago Newberry 32.9, Part II, pp. 1-29).

     For another translation see **214**.

For þe molde þat is fallyn doun   See **645**.

For the more declaracion of the truth it is to be had in mind that Edward was occupying the croune of Englande by a pretended title   Incipit to edition 1 of 105.

216   For þe office of curatis is ordeyned of god and fewe don it wele and many ful euyle þerfore telle we summe defautis to amende hem wiþ goddis helpe

Hou þe Office of Curatis Is Ordeyned of God, Wycliffite tract, s. xiv ex.

1. EETS os 74 (1880, 1902), pp. 143-63 (CCCC 296, pp. 123-36).

Also in TCD 244.

217   For þe ordre of presthod is ordeyned of god boþe in þe olde lawe and þe newe And many prestis kepen it ful euele telle we summe errours of prestis to amende hem

Ordre of Presthod, Wycliffite tract, s. xiv (2).

1. EETS os 74 (1880, 1902), pp. 166-79 (CCCC 296, pp. 136-44).

Also in TCD 244.

For þe propirtees of þinges folewyth þe substaunce þe ordre and þe distinccioun of propirtees schal be ordeyned to ordir and distinccioun of þe substaunce þerof   Incipit to prologue in edition 4 of 785.

218   For þis unkouþe discencioun þat is bitwixe þes popes semeþ to signyfie þe perillous tyme þat Poul seiþ schulde come in þes laste dayes

"De Pontificum Romanorum Schismate", Wycliffite tract, s. xiv (2).

1. SEW, III (1871), 242-66 (TCD 244, ff. 193v-208).

For to begyn than this werke it is clerely knowen to all good and true catholyke crysten men to the ende that there sholde be perpetuall memory of the holy wordes and vertuous operacyons of our redemptoure Ihesu cryst   Incipit to text proper of 712.

For to haue and to come vnto the knowleche of the x comandementes of
the lawe   Incipit to text proper of **824**.

For to here opene and declare the matere of whiche here after shall be
made mencyon It behoueth to presuppose that Troye the grete capitall
cyte   Incipit to text proper of **27**.

For to make a drinke that men cal dwale to make a man to slepe   See
558.

For to make blak ynke   See **632**.

Vor te make Cynople   See **626**.

For to make pelotus of antioche For wounds   See **629**.

219   Uor to sseawy þe lokynge of man wyþ-inne þellyche ane uorbysne oure
lhord ihesu crist zayþ Þis uorzoþe ywyteþ þet yef þe uader of þe house
wyste huyche time þe þyef were comynde

Dan Michel of Northgate, translation of Pseudo-Anselm, De
Custodia Interioris Hominis, ca. 1340.

1. EETS os 23 (1866), pp. 263-69 (BL Arundel 57, ff. 94v-
96v); 2. EETS os 23, rev. ed. (1965), pp. 263-69 (as in 1).

220   For to wite cleerly what is doon pryncipaly in this book folewing and in
the oþere bookis to hym perteynyng and for what eende and purpos þei
were maad it is to wite þat foure þingis ben necessarie to ech mannys
good lyvyng

Reginald Pecock, Reule of Crysten Religioun, ca. 1444.

1. EETS os 171 (1927) (New York Morgan M 519, ff. 1-192v).

Forto witte how this boke was makyd ye shal vndyrstonde that aftyr
Alexander had conquerit al the landis of Pers and Mede he Passyd wyth
his retenue towards the londe of Inde to gete hit   Incipit to text
proper of **358**.

76

221 For why it is to wite to us moost dere breþeren how in þe begynnyng
God made of nouȝt heuene & erþe & by hym alle þingis beþ made

John Trevisa (?), Of þe Begynnyng of þe World and þe Rewmes
Bitwixe, translation of a work attributed to Methodius, s. xiv
(2).

1. EETS os 167 (1925), pp. 94-112 (upper halves only) (BL
Harley 1900, ff. 21v-23v).

Also in San Marino Huntington HM 28561. Cf. 404.

For werke and vanytee in þe hede   See 647.

222 For as moche as dayly amonge the Infenyte multytude of mortall people
is seen but fewe of theym that lyue vertuously And the contrarye many
in grete nombre lyuen voluptuously

William Caxton, Vitas Patrum/Lyff of the Olde Auncyent Holy
Faders Hermytes, lives of saints translated from French (with
epilogue by Wynkyn de Worde), ca. 1491.

1. W. de Worde, 1495 (STC 14507).

223 Forasmoch as I John haue late in this worldes ende perceyued in saule
many Gentilnes in armes blasyng

Tretis on Armes, heraldic treatise, s. xv.

1. ed. E.J. Jones, Medieval Heraldry (1943), pp. 213-20 (BL
Addl. 34648).

Also in BL Harley 6097, Bodl Laud Miscellaneous 733.

224 For as moche as in the englische boke the whiche y haue compiled of
legenda and of oþer famous legendes at the instaunce of my specialle
frendis and for edificacioun and comfort of alle

Osbern Bokenham, Mappula Anglie, partial translation of Higden's Polychronicon, s. xv.

1. ES, 10 (1887), 6-34 (BL Harley 4011, ff. 144-63).

For as moche as it is notriously known that the kyng to his grete costis and charges hath sent his Ambassiatours to Charlis his aduersary of Fraunce to haue had acconuenyent peas with hym   Incipit to 7 Henry VII (as in edition 3) of **686.**

225   For as moche as it is often seen þat mannys reason wherby he shulde decern the good from the euyl and the right from the wronge is many tymes by seduction of the deuyl worldly coueitise and sensual appetites repressed and vanquysshed

Statutes and Ordenaunces of Warre, 1492.

1. [R. Pynson, 1493] (STC 9332).

226   For as moche as late by the comaundement of the right hye and noble princesse my right redoubted lady My lady Margarete by the grace of god Duchesse of Bourgoyne Brabant et cetera

William Caxton, Boke of th'Istories of Jason, romance translated from the French of Raoul Lefevre (printed by Caxton 1475?), ca. 1477.

1. W. Caxton, 1477? (STC 15383); 2. G. Leeu, 1492 (STC 15384); 3. EETS es 111 (1913) (as in 1).

Two MSS copied from 1: CUL Dd.3.45, s. xv ex., and Glasgow University Hunterian 410, s. xv/xvi.

227   For als mykil as mannes saule es made euer to life for-þi es man halden to serue god & lufe god euer with-outen ende

Note on the bond that binds man to serve God, s. xiv ex.

1. YW, I (1895), 156 (BL Arundel 507, f. 36v, bottom margin).

228   For as moche as oftentymes grete doubtes and doubtefull thynges deceyueth the reders therfore all doubtes sette a parte ye shall se dyuers thynges

Lyfe of Joseph of Armathy, saint's life based on Capgrave's Nova Legenda Anglie, s. xv ex. (?).

1. W. de Worde, [1511?] (STC 14806); 2. EETS os 44 (1871), pp. 27-32 (as in 1).

For verse lives see <u>IMEV</u> 130, 1778, 3117.4.

229 For as muche as seint Austin seiþ to Peter in þe Booc of be-leeue Þat is
a Miracle what heih þing oþur vncostumable þing so comeþ ouur
Monnus faculte to þe strengþing of vr feiþ

Spiritu <u>Gwydonis</u>, tale of the revelation of the spirit of Guy to
his wife, translated from Latin, s. xiv (1).

1. <u>YW</u>, II (1896), 292-333 (Bodl Eng. poet. a. 1, ff. 363 ff.);
2. ed. G. Schleich, <u>Palaestra</u>, 1 (1898), p. xvii (Cambridge
Gonville and Caius 175/96, f. 156, fragment); 3. <u>Beiträge zur</u>
<u>englische Philologie</u>, 32 (1938) (Oxford Queen's 383, ff. 135-
64v).

For two verse versions see <u>IMEV</u> 2725 and 3028; a possible third
is <u>IMEV</u> 554.3.

230 For asmoche as thappostle sayth yat we may not pleyse god wythout
good fayth

"Remedies Against Temptations", translation of William Flete's
<u>De</u> <u>Remediis</u> <u>contra</u> <u>Temptaciones</u>, s. xiv med.

1. [W. de Worde, ca. 1492] (STC 5065, Part 2).

In Bristol Public Library 6, CUL Hh.1.11, Glasgow University
Hunterian 520, Leeds University Brotherton 501, BL Harley
6615, BL Addl. 37049, Longleat Marquis of Bath 29. Jolliffe
K.8.b. Two other English translations: (1) 528 and (2) in
Beeleigh Abbey Foyle MS, BL Harley 6615, BL Harley 2409, BL
Royal 18 A.x, and Bodl Bodley 131 (Jolliffe K.8.a).

231 For as moche as þe book ycallid þe reule of cristen religioun with þe
oþire bokis to him perteynyng is made to renne vpon vij maters moost
necessary to eche cristen lyuer to be knowun and þese maters ben
þerynne so tariyngli tretid

Reginald Pecock, <u>Donet</u> <u>of</u> <u>Cristen</u> <u>Religioun</u>, 1443-49.

1. EETS os 156 (1921), pp. 1-214 (Bodl Bodley 916, ff. 1-
106v).

232 For als moche as the lond beȝonde the see þat is to seye the holy lond

79

þat men callen the lond of promyssioun or of beheste passynge alle oþere londes it is the most worthi lond (from 6)

"Mandeville's Travels", travel literature, conflation of a lost manuscript of 233 and a French manuscript, ca. 1400.

1. (1725) (BL Cotton Titus C. XVI); 2. (1727) (as in 1); 3. ed. J.O. Halliwell (1839) (as in 1); 4. ed. J.O. Halliwell, 2nd ed. (1866) (as in 1); 5. ed. J.O. Halliwell, 3rd ed. (1883) (as in 1); 6. EETS os 153 (1919) (as in 1); 7. (1928) (as in 1); 8. ed. M.C. Seymour (1967) (as in 1); 9. ed. M.C. Seymour (1968) (as in 1).

For other translations see 233, 239, and 599. Verse translations in IMEV 248.5 and 3117.6.

233   For as moche as the Lande ouer the see that is to say the holy lande that men call the lande of hetynge amonge all other landes it is mooste worthy lande

"Mandeville's Travels", travel literature, translation from French (known as the "defective version"), s. xiv ex.

1. R. Pynson, [1496] (STC 17246); 2. W. de Worde, 1499 (STC 17247); 3. [W. de Worde, 1503] (STC 17249); 4. [W. de Worde, 1510?] (STC 17249.5); 5. T. East, 1568 (STC 17250); 6. T. East, [1582?] (STC 17251); 7. T. Snodham, 1612 (STC 17251.5); 8. T. Snodham, 1618 (STC 17252); 9. T. Snodham, 1625 (STC 17253); 10. W. Stansby, 1632 (STC 17253.5); 11. R. Bishop, [1639?] (STC 17254); 12. R. B[ishop], 1650 (Wing M 412); 13. R. B[ishop], 1657 (Wing M 413); 14. (1670) (Wing M 414); 15. (1677) (Wing M 415); 16. (1684) (Wing M 416); 17. (1696) (Wing M 417); 18. R. Chiswell, 1704; 19. R. Chiswell, 1705; 20. [1710]; 21. A. Wilde, 1722; 22. ed. J. Ashton (1887) (as in 5); 23. ed. J. Bramont (as in 5); 24. (1932) (as in 5); 25. English Studies, 38 (1957), 263-64 (Ripon Cathedral MS, fragment); 26. Anglia, 84 (1966), 30-48 (BL Addl. 37049, ff. 3-9, an epitome); 27 English Studies in Africa, 4 (1961), 150-58 (Bodl Ashmole 751, ff. 48-50, 142v-43, extracts); 28. ed. M.C. Seymour (1980) (facsimile of 1).

Also in Cambridge Fitzwilliam Museum Bradfer-Lawrence Deposit 7, Cambridge Magdalene Pepys 1955, TCC R.4.20, CUL Dd.1.17, CUL Ff.5.35, CUL Gg.1.34.3, Corning Museum of Glass 6, TCD 604, Edinburgh NLS Advocates 19.1.11, BL Arundel 140, BL Harley 2386, BL Harley 3954, BL Royal 17 B.xliii, BL Royal 17 C.xxxviii, BL Sloane 2319, BL Addl.

33758, Manchester Chetham 6711, Oxford Balliol 239, Bodl
Digby 88 (extract), Bodl Douce 33, Bodl Douce 109, Bodl e
Mus. 124, Bodl Lat. misc. e. 85 (fragment), Bodl Rawlinson B.
216, Bodl Rawlinson D. 100, Bodl Rawlinson D. 101, Bodl
Rawlinson D. 652, Bodl Tanner 405, Bodl Addl. C. 285,
Oxford Queen's 383, Penrose MS (fragment), Rugby School
Bloxam 1008, San Marino Huntington HM 144. For other
translations see 232, 239, and 599. Verse translations in IMEV
248.5 and 3117.6.

234   For as much as þe passage of deth owt of the wrecchidnesse of the exile
of this world for vnkunnyng of dyinge not oonly to lewd men but also
to religiouse men & deuoute personys

        Boke of Crafte of Dyinge, translation from the Latin De Arte
        Moriendi, s. xiv (2).

        1. YW, II (1896), 406-20 (Bodl Rawlinson C. 894, ff. 18v-33).

        Also in Beeleigh Abbey Foyle MS, TCC R.3.21, CUL Ff.5.45,
        BL Harley 1706, BL Harley 4011, BL Royal 17 C.xviii, BL
        Addl. 10596, Manchester Rylands English 94, Bodl Bodley 423,
        Bodl Douce 322, Oxford CCC 220.

        Jolliffe L.4.a. For another translation see 603.   Cf. 818 and
        826.

235   For as moche as ther ben manye women that hauen many diuers
maladies and sekenesses nygh to þe deth and thei als ben shamefull to
schewen

        Liber Trotularis, treatise on gynecology and obstetrics, s. xv (1).

        1. ed. B. Rowland, A Medieval Woman's Guide to Health
        (1981), even pages only (BL Sloane 2463, ff. 194-232).

        Also in BL Sloane 249, London Royal College of Physicians
        129a.i.5.

236   For asmoche as we offend in many thinges it is nedeful that in many
wyses we be correcte therfor wherfor whan the ordinary chaptyr is
holde the president schal come so rathe ther to

        "Additions to the Rule of St. Saviour", a translation from Latin
        for use of the sisters and brothers of the Brigittine Order at Syon

Abbey, ca. 1431.

1. Aungier (1840), pp. 249-404 (BL Arundel 146, ff. 1-104, supplemented by London St. Paul's Cathedral 5, ff. 6-55v); 2. Hogg (1980), 3, 1-133 (London St. Paul's Cathedral 5, ff. 6-55v); 3. Hogg (1980), 4, 1-206 (BL Arundel 146, ff. 1-104).

237 For Asmoche that the meritory and notable operacyons of famose goode and deuoute faders yn God sholde be remembred for Instruccion of aftyr cummers to theyr consolacioun and encres of deuocion

"The Book of the Foundation of St. Bartholomew's, London", history of the hospital translated from Latin (ca. 1180), ca. 1400.

1. EETS os 163 (1923) (BL Cotton Vespasian B. IX, ff. 41-77v).

238 . . . fo[ur]me of cury was compiled of the chef Maister Cokes of kyng Richard the Secunde kyng of ynglond aftir the Conquest the which was acounted þe best and ryallest vyand

Fourme of Cury, recipes for cooking, s. xiv ex.

1. Pegge (1780), pp. 1-89 (BL Addl. 5016 roll).

Also in Durham University Cosin V.III.11, BL Cotton Julius D. VIII, BL Harley 1605, Manchester Rylands English 7, New York C.F. Bühler 36.

Forsoþe after þat I haue first done louynges or thankynges vn-to god giffyng boþe perpetuale life of soules & helþe of bodies & leching Incipit to complete translation of Guy de Chauliac's Inventarium partially edited by B. Wallner (1964); see notes to 31 and 32.

239 For thy that many men desireth and coveytith to hire of the holy londe and of the londes byჳonde the see that is to seye be esten in dyuers parties of the worlde

Liber Qui Vocatur Maundevile/Tractatus de Mirabilibus Mundi, travel literature, abridgment of a lost English translation, s. xv in.

1. Hakluyt Soc., series 2, 102 (1953), pp. 419-81 (Bodl Raw-

linson D. 99, ff. 1-31v); 2. EETS os 253 (1963), odd pages (Bodl e Mus. 116, ff. 6-49v).

For other translations see **232, 233** and **599**. Verse translations in IMEV 248.5 and 3117.6.

240   For-þi þat þer ben diuerse kindes of spirites þerfore it is needful to us discrete knowing of hem siþ it so is þat we ben lernid of þe apostle Seinte Iohun not to bileue to alle spirites (from 2)

     A Tretis of Discrescyon of Spirites, devotional treatise, s. xiv ex.

     1. H. Pepwell, 1521 (STC 20972, Part 7); 2. EETS os 231 (1955), pp. 80-93 (BL Harley 674, ff. 1-5v); 3. Hodgson (1982), pp. 147-53 (as in 2).

     Also in Bristol Public Library 6, CUL Ff.6.31, CUL Kk.6.26, BL Harley 993, BL Harley 2373, Bodl Bodley 576.

241   Forty yere after that our lorde Ihesu crist was put on the crosse in Iherusalem Vaspasyan that was then Emperoure of Rome of Almayne and of all Lombardye

     Dystruccyon of Iherusalem by Vaspazian and Tytus, historical romance translated from a French prose version, s. xv ex.

     1. W. de Worde, 1510? (STC 14518); 2. R. Pynson, 1513? (STC 14517); 3. W. de Worde, 1528 (STC 14519).

     Cf. **51**; for verse versions see IMEV 1583 and 1881.

242   Foure thinges nedes man til knowe if he sal he right disposid in bodi & saule Þe first what thinge files him Þat oþer what makes him clene

     "Four Things", treatise extracted from Chapter 6 of Rolle's Forme of Lyvyng, s. xiv.

     1. YW, I (1895), 412-15 (BL Arundel 507, ff. 36-38v).

     See **351**.

Fracture of bone as is said aboue in þe wondes of bones after G in 6 cerapeutice is said after grek tonge euery maner solucioun of continuite made in a bone   Incipit to Book V of complete translation of Guy de Chauliac's <u>Inventarium</u> partially edited by B. Wallner (1969); see notes to **31** and **32**.

243   Frend in Crist as Seynt Poule seiþ we ne hauen here no cyte þat is dwelling but we sechen on þat is to come hereafter

    <u>Þe Lyfe of Soule</u>, didactic treatise, s. xiv (2).

    1. ed. H.M. Moon (1978) (Bodl Laud Miscellaneous 210, ff. 114-32v).

    Also in BL Arundel 286 and San Marino Huntington HM 502.

    Frendys ye cawse of our commyng at yis tyme es for ye worthy sacrament off Matrimone   Incipit to edition 3 of **313**.

    Fryndis this is to seye to your lewde undurstandyng that hoote wordes erased crusstes makeyn sofft harde wortes   See **456**.

    Fro Nazareth to tho Mount Thabor is iii myle Ther Oure Lord transfigured Hym byfore Petur Ion and James   Incipit to second extract in edition 27 of **233**.

244   Ffrom the party of the pore plentyff in love wyth many yers of probacion professyd to be trewe To al the holy ffraternite

    [John Lydgate], <u>The Epystel in Prose</u>, epistle added at the end of the "Venus Mass" (<u>IMEV</u> 4186), s. xv.

    1. EETS os 71 (1879), pp. 394-95 (Bodl Fairfax 16, ff. 316v-17v); 2. <u>JEGP</u>, 7 (1907-8), 102-4 (as in 1); 3. ed. E.P. Hammond, <u>English Verse Between Chaucer and Surrey</u> (1927), pp. 212-13 (as in 1).

    Cf. **787** and **835**.

245   Fvll prouffitable ben to vs traueylyng pylgrymes and freyll synners the fruytfull werkes and treatyses of holy faders the whyche call vs fro the waye of derknesse and synne

    Student of Cambridge, <u>Medytacions of Saynt Bernarde</u>, translation of Pseudo-Bernard's <u>Meditationes</u>, a treatise on knowing oneself, 1495.

1. W. de Worde, 1496 (STC 1916); 2. W. de Worde, [1499?] (STC 1917); 3. W. de Worde, 1525 (STC 1918).

246   Fvll wrothe and angry was the Deuell whan that oure lorde hadde ben in helle and had take oute Adam and Eve and other at his plesier

"Merlin", romance translated from the French prose <u>Merlin</u>, ca. 1450.

1. EETS os 10 (1865), 21 (1866), 36 (1869) (CUL Ff.3.11).

247   Fundamentum aliud nemo potest ponere preter id quod positum est . . . Almyȝty god þe trinyte fadir sonne and holy gooste boþe in þe olde lawe and þe newe haþ fowndid his chirche up on þre statis

"The Clergy May Not Hold Property", Wycliffite tract, s. xiv (2).

1. EETS os 74 (1880, 1902), pp. 362-404 (Lambeth Palace 551, ff. 2-59v).

Parts of this version were printed ca. 1530 (STC 1462.3) and in 1530 (STC 1462.5; 6813). Another, longer version in CUL Dd.14.30, CUL Ff.6.2, BL Egerton 2820, and San Marino Huntington HM 503.

248   Galien sais þat hit is spedefull to known that the hed his departid in iiii parties Blode hase maistur in the forhed and colera in the ryght syde

John Trevisa, <u>Abstractus Bartholomei de Proprietatibus Rerum</u>, summary of Book VII of his translation of the <u>De Proprietatibus Rerum</u> circulating separately, s. xiv ex.

1. <u>Anglia</u>, 87 (1969), 4-25 (BL Sloane 983, ff. 81-94v).

Cf. **785.**

249   Geometri es saide of þis greke worde geos þat es erthe on englisch and of þis greke worde metros þat es mesure on englisch

<u>A Tretis of Geometrie</u>, s. xv (?).

1. Halliwell, Rara (1839), pp. 56-71 (BL Sloane 213, ff. 120 ff.).

250 Goostly frende in God as touching þin askyng of me how þou schalt reule þin hert in tyme of þi preier I answere vnto þee febely as I kan (from 2)

A Pistle of Preier, devotional treatise in epistle form, s. xiv ex.

1. H. Pepwell, 1521 (STC 20972, Part 4); 2. EETS os 231 (1955), pp. 48-59 (BL Harley 674, ff. 12v-17); 3. Hodgson (1982), pp. 101-7 (as in 2).

Also in CUL Ff.6.31, CUL Kk.6.26, Liverpool University F. 4. 10, BL Harley 2373, Bodl Bodley 576.

251 Goostly freende in God as touching þin inward ocupacion as me þink þee disposid I speke at þis tyme in specyall to þi self and not to alle þoo þat þis writyng scholen here in general

Book of Prive Counseling, devotional treatise in epistle form, s. xiv ex.

1. EETS os 218 (1944), pp. 135-72 (BL Harley 674, ff. 91v-110v); 2. Hodgson (1982), pp. 75-99 (as in 1).

Also in Ampleforth Abbey 42, CUL Ff.6.41, CUL Ii.6.31, CUL Kk.6.26, Downside Abbey 10, Downside Abbey 14, TCD 122, BL Harley 2373, Bodl Bodley 576, Bodl Douce 262, St. Hugh's Charterhouse (Sussex) Parkminster D. 176, Stanbrook Abbey 3.

252 Goostly freend in God þat same grace & ioie þat I wil to myself I will to þee at Goddes wile Þou askist me counsel of silence and of spekyng (from 2)

A Pistle of Discrecioun of Stirings, devotional treatise in epistle form, s. xiv ex.

1. H. Pepwell, 1521 (STC 20972, Part 6); 2. EETS os 231 (1955), pp. 62-77 (BL Harley 674, ff. 5v-12v); 3. Blake, MERP (1972), pp. 119-31 (CUL Ff.6.31, ff. 53-68); 4. Hodgson (1982), pp. 109-18 (as in 2).

Also in CUL Kk.6.26, BL Harley 2373.

Goostly freende in God þou schalt wel vnderstonde þat I fynde in my boistous beholdyng foure degrees & fourmes of Cristen mens leuyng Incipit to text proper of **320.**

253 Gastly gladnes in Ihesu & ioy in hert with swetnes in sawle of þe sauor of heuen in hope es helth in til heie

Richard Rolle, Cantica Divini Amoris, a prose lyric consisting of alliterative sentences, ca. 1343.

1. YW, I (1895), 81 (CUL Dd.5.64, f. 141v); 2. Allen, Writings (1927), p. 273 (Longleat Marquis of Bath 29, f. 49); 3. Allen, English (1931), pp. 51-52 (as in 1).

254 Gostly syster in Ihesu Cryste I trowe hyt be not ȝytt fro ȝoure mynde that whenne we spake laste togyderys I behette ȝow a medytacyon of the passyon of oure lorde

A Carthusian of Sheen, Myrowre to Devot Peple/Speculum Devotorum, the life of Jesus arranged as devotional material, s. xv (2).

1. Analecta Cartusiana, 12-13 (1973-74) (CUL Gg.1.6, ff. 1-117, supplemented by Beeleigh Abbey Foyle MS).

255 Ghosti suster in Ihesu cryst I praye the that in the callyng whiche our lorde hath callid the to his seruyse thou holde the payd

Walter Hilton, Ladder of Perfeccion/Scala Perfectionis, mystical text, s. xiv (2).

1. [W. de Worde], 1494 (STC 14042, Part 1); 2. J. Notary, 1507 (STC 14043, Part 1); 3. W. de Worde, 1525 (STC 14044, Part 1); 4. W. de Worde, 1533 (STC 14045, Part 1); 5. G.D., 1653 (Wing H 3881).

In Brussels Bibl. Royale 2544-2545, CCCC 268, Cambridge Magdalene F. 4. 17, Cambridge St. John's 202, TCC B.15.18, TCC O.7.47, CUL Dd.5.55, CUL Ee.4.30, CUL Ff.5.40, CUL Addl. 6686, Chatsworth Duke of Devonshire MS, TCD 122, TCD 352, Edinburgh NLS 6126, Edinburgh NLS fragments, Lincoln Cathedral 91, Liverpool University F. 4. 10, BL Harley 330, BL Harley 1022, BL Harley 1035, BL Harley 2387, BL Harley 2397, BL Harley 6573, BL Harley 6579, BL Lansdowne 362, BL Addl. 11748, BL Addl. 22283, London Inner Temple

Petyt 524, Lambeth Palace 472, London Westminster Cathedral Treasury 4, London Westminster School 3, Longleat Marquis of Bath 298, New York Columbia University Plimpton 257, New York Morgan Aldenham MS (copy of edition 1), Oxford All Souls 25, Bodl Bodley 100, Bodl Bodley 592, Bodl Eng. poet. a. 1, Bodl Laud Miscellaneous 602, Bodl Rawlinson C. 285, Bodl Rawlinson C. 894, Oxford University 28, Philadelphia University of Pennsylvania English 8, San Marino Huntington HM 112, San Marino Huntington HM 266, Stonyhurst College A.vi.24, Tokyo Takamiya MS, Worcester Cathedral F. 172.

256   Yeve thy almes unto poore folke whilest thowe livest for that pleaseth me more than thowe gavest a grete hill of golde after thy deth

The IX Answers Which God Gave to a Certeyn Creture, treatise on the nine virtues, s. xv.

1. Rel. Ant., I (1841), 245-46 (BL Lansdowne 762, f. 9r-v).

Also in CUL Ff.6.33. Jolliffe I.12.g,j. For other versions see **410** and **847**.

257   Gloriouse maister y praie þee to answere me to my questiouns þat y desyre to aske to þe worschipe of god & profijt of mennes soules

Lucidarie, translation of Book I and part of Book II of the Latin Elucidarium by Honorius of Autun, s. xv.

1. ed. F. Schmitt, Die mittelenglische Version des Elucidariums des Honorius Augustodunensis (1909) (Cambridge St. John's 174, ff. 1-16, ending imperfectly).

Also in CUL Ii.6.26 (incomplete). For an OE translation of portions of the Latin in BL Cotton Vespasian D. XIV see Ker 209. Andrew Chertsey made a translation from the French version early in the 16th c. (see STC 13686).

258   God almyghty al wytty al lovely in whome is al goodnes the wel of mercy & grace the gloryous trynyte one god & persones thre (from 2)

Richard Methley, To Hew Heremyte a Pystyl of Solytary Lyfe, mystical treatise, s. xv/xvi.

1. ed. F.W. Nugent, The Thought & Culture of the English Renaissance (1956), pp. 388-93 (London PRO SP I/239, ff.

262-65v); 2. Analecta Cartusiana, 31 (1977), pp. 112-19 (as in 1).

259 [G]od allmyghty hathe graunted that what man or woman or child redith this preyer that folouth euery sonday or yeueth any almes to a poor man

Commendations for a Latin prayer to St. Erasmus, s. xv ex.

1. Hanna (1984), p. 36 (San Marino Huntington HM 1159, ff. 9v-10).

260 God almyghty kepe oure kyng and conferme his Rewme in the lawe of god and make him regne in gladnes in lovyng and in worshipe of god I that am servitoure of the kyng haue put in execucioun his comaundement and travaylid forto gete the book of good thewes to him

The Book of the Governaunce of Kyngis and of Pryncis Callid the Secrete of Secretes, book of instruction translated from French version of the Secreta Secretorum, s. xv.

1. EETS es 74 (1898), pp. 1-39 (BL Royal 18 A.vii, ff. 1-42v).

261 God almyȝty kepe oure kynge to ioye of his ligeys and make fast his kyngdome to defende þe lawe of god and make hym dwellynge to enhye þe worschipe & louynge of gode men

Þe Treetys of þe Secreet of Secreetȝ off Aristotyll, book of instruction translated from the Latin Secreta Secretorum, s. xv in.

1. EETS es 74 (1898), pp. 41-118 (Lambeth Palace 501, ff. 1-42).

God almyghty kepe oure kynge to the glorye of trew Cristen men in bileve and conferme his kyngdom in kepyng of Goddes lawe   Incipit to text proper of 63.

262 God allmighty preserue oure kynge and the prosperite of his true subgites and stablissh his reame to the perfeccion of the feith of Criste

Booke of the Governaunce of Kinges and Princes Called the Secret of Secreetes, book of instruction translated from a

89

French version of the Secreta Secretorum, s. xv med.

1. EETS os 276 (1977), pp. 252-384 (even pages only) (Oxford University 85, ff. 36-68v).

263 God made mankynde aftur his owne ymage and lyknesse and put hym in paradys þat was a lond of blysse and ʒef hym þat lond to haue y-woned þer-ynne euer more and neuer to han be ded

New Testament Epistles, with Acts and part of Matthew, with prologue, rearranged and translated for a female religious, s. xiv (2).

1. ed. A.C. Paues, A Fourteenth Century English Biblical Version (1902) (Cambridge Selwyn 108. L. 19); 2. Paues (1904), pp. 1-208 (as in 1).

Also complete in CCCC 434 and partial in CUL Dd.12.39, Holkham Hall Earl of Leicester 672, and Bodl Douce 250. Cf. 413.

264 God seiþ bi ieremye þat he wakide eerly to his puple and criede his lawe bi his prophetis þat weren martrid in goddis cause and for profit of his chirche

De Papa, Wycliffite tract, s. xiv ex.

1. EETS os 74 (1880, 1902), pp. 460-82 (Manchester Rylands English 86, ff. 25-34v).

God seith Make we man to oure liknesse to haue lordship aboue the creatures of the erthe and by whom the setis of paradise that ben voide maye be fulfilled   See 167.

265 Godd spede you saue ʒou or rest mery Saluete Salue Saluus sis chrito Iubeo te saluere Thow art welcom

John Anwykyll, Vulgaria, English sentences with Latin translations (excerpted and adapted from Terence) for use in school, 1480-83.

1. [T. Rood, 1483] (STC 696, Part 2).

May also have been in STC 695, but it is now a fragment.

266 God þat is good in him silf faire in hise aungelis merveilouse in his
seintis and merciful vpon synners haue merci on vs now and euer and
ȝeue vs grace to holde þe weye of truþe (from 2)

Lanterne of Liȝt, Wycliffite treatise, s. xv in.

1. R. Redman, [1535?] (STC 15225); 2. EETS os 151 (1917) (BL
Harley 2324, ff. 1-128v).

Also in BL Harley 6613 (defective).

God unto whom alle hertes ben open and unto whom all wille spekiþ
and unto whom no priue þing is hid I beseche þee   Introductory
prayer to 320.

Goodfaders and goodmoders and all that be here about say in the
worshyppe of god and our ladye   Incipit to editions 2 and 9 of 468.

Good brother in criste two maner of states there are   See 147.

Good deuoute chrystyens let vs fyrst consydre that all we ben mortall
as well the ryche as the poore the yonge as the olde   Incipit to text
proper of 833.

267 Good deuout religious doughter you haue often and instantly required
me to write vnto you & vnto your systers some good lesson of religion

Richard Whitford, The Pype or Tonne of the Lyfe of Perfection,
devotional treatise, s. xv ex./xvi in. (?).

1. R. Redman, 1532 (STC 25421); 2. ed. J. Hogg, 3 vols.
(1979) (as in 1).

268 Good deuout relygyous doughters ye haue here sende vnto me your rule
of saynt Augustyn and done requyre me other to amende and reforme þe
englysshe or els to translate þe rule of newe

Richard Whitford, The Rule of Saynt Augustyn, translation done
for the nuns of Syon Abbey, s. xv ex./xvi in. (?).

A. First edition: 1. W. de Worde, 1525? (STC 922.3, Part 1;
25417, Part 1); 2. W. de Worde, 1527 (STC 922.4, Part 1;

25419, Part 1).

B. Second edition, with expositions by Hugh of St. Victor and Whitford: 1. W. de Worde, 1525 (STC 13925): 2. W. de Worde, 1525? (STC 922.3, Part 2; 25417, Part 2); 3. W. de Worde, 1527 (STC 922.4, Part 2; 25419, Part 2).

Godemen and wymmen as for the most party of ӡow þat here beth habbuþ y herd of banes that habbeþ ben yasked   Incipit to edition 9 of **313**.

269   Good men and women y charge yow by the Auctoryte of holy churche that no man nother woman that this day proposyth here to be comenyd

An exhortation before communion, s. xv.

1. Maskell, III (1847), 348-49 (BL Harley 2383, ff. 60v-61); 2. Maskell, 2nd. ed., III (1882), 408-9 (as in 1).

Jolliffe C.11.

Gode men and women I do you to understande we tha[t] have care of your soulles be commaundet of our ordinaries   Incipit to MS version of edition G of **122**.

Godmen et wymmen it is ordeyned by the counseil of al holy chirche First of oure holy fader the Pope of Rome   Incipit to version D of **122**.

Good men and wymmen that Lord þat made all thynge of nowӡth and man aftur ys owne similitude and liknesse   See **26**.

Good men and wymmen þys day as ӡe knowen well ys cleped Sonenday yn þe Aduent þat ys þe Sonenday of Cristys comyng   Incipit to edition 24 of **734**.

Good men and wymmen this day is callid the firste sonday in aduente werfore hooly churche makith mencion of the comyng of criste goddis sone   Altenate incipit to text proper as it appears in all editions of **734**, beginning with 2, before 1500 and in nearly all subsequent ones.

Gode men hit is an heste dei to dei þe is on xii monþe þis godspel sed hu
þe helend nehlechede to-ward ierusalem   See 556.

Gowd men þees poyntes and artycles þat j shal to ʒow shewe of
corsynge or mansynge beþ y-ordeyned and y-stabeled and y-confermyd
of popes   Incipit to version B and similar to incipit to edition A.2 of
122.

270   Good morowe Bonum tibi huius diei sit primordium Good nyght Bona
    nox tranquilla nox optata requies Good spede

        John Stanbridge, Vulgaria, English sentences with Latin transla-
        tions for use in school, preceded by Latin-English vocabulary, s.
        xvi in.

        1. W. de Worde, [1509?] (STC 23195.5); 2. W. de Worde,
        1515 (STC 23196); 3. W. de Worde, [1517?] (STC 23196.2); 4.
        [J. Scolar, 1518?] (STC 23196.4); 5. W. de Worde, [1519?]
        (STC 23196.6); 6. W. de Worde, 1519 (STC 23196.8); 7. W.
        de Worde, [1520?] (STC 23196a); 8. [R. Pynson, ca. 1520]
        (STC 23196a.2); 9. R. Pynson, 1523 (STC 23196a.4); 10. W.
        de Worde, [1524?] (STC 23196a.5); 11. W. de Worde, [1525?]
        (STC 23196a.6); 12. W. de Worde, [1526?] (STC 23196a.7);
        13. W. de Worde, [1527?] (STC 23197); 14. W. de Worde,
        [1529?] (STC 23198); 15. J. Skot [1529?] (STC 23199); 16. P.
        Treveris, [1530?] (STC 23198.3); 17. [W. de Worde, 1534?]
        (STC 23198.7); 18. EETS os 187 (1932), pp. 1-30 (as in 6).

        Cf. 593.

271   Grete haboundance of gastly comfort and ioy in god comes in the hertes
    of thaim at says or synges deuotly the psalmes in louynge of ihesu crist

        Richard Rolle, Psalterium David Regis, psalms and first seven
        canticles with commentary, 1337-49.

        1. ed. H.R. Bramley (1884) (Oxford University 64, ff. 6-137v,
        supplemented by Bodl Laud Miscellaneous 286).

        Also in Aberdeen University 243, Barnbougle Castle Lord Rose-
        bery MS, CCCC 387, Cambridge Sidney Sussex 89, Eton College
        10, BL Arundel 158, BL Harley 1806, Newcastle-upon-Tyne
        Public Library TH. 1678, Bodl Bodley 467, Bodl Bodley 953,
        Bodl Hatton 12, Bodl Laud Miscellaneous 448, Bodl Tanner 1,
        Oxford Magdalen 52, Oxford University 56, San Marino Hunt-

ington HM 148, Vatican Biblioteca Apostolica Vaticana Regin. 320, Worcester Cathedral F. 158. A Lollard version in eight MSS, other interpolated versions in five MSS, and six unclassified MSS, for all of which see A Manual of the Writings in Middle English 1050-1500, ed. J.B. Severs, 2 (1970), 538. For a verse prologue in one MS see IMEV 3576.

Grete awayte ought eueribodi to haue vp on theymself þat they retorne not ayen vnto those synnes that they haue ben reconsiled of   Incipit to "An Exhortation by Faith," devotional tract (Part 7) incorporated into 751.

272   Grete thankynges lawde and honoure we merytoryously ben bounde to yelde and offre vnto wryters of hystoryes whiche gretely haue prouffyted oure mortal lyf

William Caxton, prologue to Trevisa's translation of the Polychronicon, ca. 1482.

1. W. Caxton, 1482 (STC 13438); 2. W. de Worde, 1495 (STC 13439); 3. P. Treveris, 1527 (STC 13440); 4. Blades, Life, I (1861), 191-94 (as in 1); 5. Aurner (1926), pp. 288-92 (as in 1); 6. EETS os 176 (1928), pp. 64-67 (as in 1); 7. Blake, COP (1973), pp. 128-32 (as in 1); 8. Blake, Selections (1973), pp. 1-5 (as in 1).

See 605.

273   Grete thankes lawde and honour ought to be gyuen vnto the clerkes poetes and historiographs that haue wreton many noble bokes of wysedom

William Caxton, prologue to his second edition of Chaucer's "Canterbury Tales", ca. 1483.

1. W. Caxton, 1483? (STC 5083); 2. R. Pynson, [1492?] (STC 5084), slightly modified; 3. W. de Worde, 1498 (STC 5085); 4. R. Pynson, 1526 (STC 5086), slightly modified; 5. Ames (1749), pp. 55-6 (as in 1); 6. Herbert, I (1785), 73-4 (as in 1); 7. Blades, Life, I (1861), 173-74 (as in 1); 8. Flügel, I (1895), 6-7 (as in 1); 9. Spurgeon (1914), pp. 61-63 (as in 1); 10. Aurner (1926), pp. 266-67 (as in 1); 11. EETS os 176 (1928), pp. 90-91 (as in 1); 12. R. Kaiser, Alt- und mittelenglische Anthologie (1954, 1955), pp. 462-63 (as in 1); 13. Kaiser (1958), pp. 566-67 (as in 1); 14. Blake, Caxton (1969), p. 160

(as in 1); 13. Kaiser (1958), pp. 566-67 (as in 1); 14. Blake, Caxton (1969), p. 160 (as in 1); 15. (1972), f. a iir-v (facsimile of 1); 16. Blake, COP (1973), pp. 61-63 (as in 1); 17. Brewer (1978), pp. 76-77 (as in 1).

274 Greuous es þe vice of bostynge & pride and full perilous it es ffor it castes doun saules fra þe heygthnes of perfeccyone

[Walter Hilton], Epistill of Saynt Johann þe Ermyte, treatise against boasting and pride, s. xiv.

1. YW, I (1895), 122-24 (Bodl Rawlinson C. 285, ff. 68v-71v).

Also in CUL Ff.5.40, BL Addl. 33971, Bodl Rawlinson D. 913 (fragment), San Marino Huntington HM 148, Savile MS (now lost). Jolliffe F.10 and O.16.

275 Guthelinus kyng guthelyne or keneln hole kyng of grete Brytayn that comprehendyth Englond Walys and Scotlond he was a vertuus man and a grete bylder

John Rous, The Rows Rol, history of the Earls of Warwick, 1484.

1. ed. W. Courthope (1845-59) (BL Addl. 48976); 2. ed. C. Ross (1980) (as in 1).

A copy probably from s. xvi (2) is in BL Lansdowne 882, edited in Hearne (1729), pp. 217-39; a Latin version is in London College of Arms MS.

276 Heil be þou marie ful of grace þe lord is wiþ þe blissed be þou among wymmen and blissed be þe fruyt of þi wombe

Ave Maria, Wycliffite exposition of the Ave Maria, s. xiv (2).

1. EETS os 74 (1880, 1902), pp. 204-8 (CCCC 296, pp. 175-78).

Also in Cambridge Sidney Sussex 74, London Westminster School 3, Norwich Castle Museum 158.926 4g.3. Cf. 455.

277 Hail be yow holie crowche blesfolle Hail be yow holie crowche

dereworye Aze wesleche aze owre lord iesu crist his holie bodi fowchete sauf as he wolde

Prayer to ease childbirth, s. xiii.

1. N&Q, 225 (1980), 292 (Bodl Ashmole 1280, f. 192v).

Hayl godes moder Marie Mayde uol of þonke   Incipit to editions 4 and 7 of 279.

Heile holyest body of oure lord Ihesu Crist that arte nowe sothefastly conteyned here in thys mooste excellent sacrament   Incipit to prayer added to 553.

278   Heyl Ihesu Crist Word of þe Fadir Sone of þe Virgyn Lomb of God Heelþe of this world sacrid Oost Welle of pytee Word and Flesch boren of þe Virgyn Modir

A Devoute Prayer, to be said at the Elevation of the Host, translated from Latin, s. xiv/xv.

1. EETS os 155 (1921), p. 100 (BL Addl. 39574, f. 88r-v).

279   Hayl Marie fol of milce God is mit the þu blessede among wymmen

Ave Maria/"Hail Mary", s. xiv (1).

1. Rel. Ant., I (1841), 42 (BL Arundel 57, f. 94); 2. Rel. Ant., I (1841), 282 (Cambridge Gonville and Caius 52/29); 3. EETS os 23 (1866), p. 263 (as in 1); 4. EETS os 23 (1866), p. 271 (BL Arundel 57, f. 96v); 5. Mätzner, I, 2 (1869), 4 (as in 2); 6. EETS os 23, rev. ed. (1965), p. 263 (as in 1); 7. EETS os 23 (1965), p. 271 (as in 4).

Also included in 157 and in various other ME works.

Heil qweene modir of merci   See 585.

280   Haue on god in worship Take not his name in veyne Halow þin halyday Worship þi fadir and modir Sle no man Doo no lechery

A collection of eight catechisms and exhortations, beginning with

Þe X Commowndmentis of God, s. xv (?).

1. Archiv, 90 (1893), 297-98 (CUL Hh.3.13, f. 119).

He most take a hanfvll of rewe a hanfvll of marygoldis halfe a hanfvll
of fetherfev   Incipit to text proper of 743.

281 He or she þat is to be made hede or souereyn in a monestary in whom
all the hole congregacion in one acorde after god consentyth

Rule of Saynte Benet, an abbreviated translation of the Benedictine Rule for men and women (with prologue by Caxton), s. xv
ex.

1. W. Caxton, 1491? (STC 3305, Part 3); 2. EETS os 120
(1902), pp. 119-40 (as in 1).

See 297; cf. 98.

282 He schal have noo schirte up on him but a dowbelet of ffustean lynyd
with satene cutte full of hoolis (from 5)

How a Man Schall Be Armyd at His Ese, instructions for arming
a man to fight on foot, s. xv med.

1. Archaeologia, 17 (1814), 295-96 (BL Lansdowne 285, f. 9r-
v); 2. Meyrick (1824), II, 191-93 (as in 1); 3. Archaeological
Journal, 4 (1847), 234-5 (New York Morgan M 775, ff. 122v-
23v); 4. Historic Society of Lancashire and Cheshire, 2 (1850),
209-10 (as in 1); 5. Archaeologia, 57 (1900), 43-44 (as in 3); 6.
Cripps-Day (1918), p. xxxiii (as in 1).

Also in BL Addl. 46354.

He þat a lytul me ȝeuyth to me wyllyth longe lyffe Qui modicum mihi
dat mihi vitam longius optat   Prose incipit to edition 1 of 840.

283 He þat devotely sayse þis Orysone dayly sall hafe remyssyone of alle his
synnys and that daye he ne sall noghte dy none euylle dede

Preface to a Latin prayer, s. xv (?).

1. YW, I (1895), 376 (Lincoln Cathedral 91, f. 177).

. . . He þat doth as can Blame hym no man   Verse incipit (IMEV 1147.2) to edition 1 of **840**.

284   He that foloweth me sayth Cryste our Sauyoure walkyth not in darkenes but he shall haue the lyghte of lyfe

Richard Whitford, The Folowynge of Cryste, translation of Thomas à Kempis, De Imitatione Christi, s. xvi in.

1. R. Wyer, [1531?] (STC 23961); 2. T. Godfray, [1531?] (STC 23963); 3. [R. Redman, 1531?] (STC 23964); 4. [R. Redman, 1531?] (STC 23964.3); 5. [R. Redman, 1535?] (STC 23964.7); 6. W. Myddylton, [1545?] (STC 23965); 7. J. Cawood, 1556 (STC 23966); 8. J. Cawood, 1566 (STC 23967.5); 9. [W. Carter, ca. 1575] (STC 23967); 10. [G. L'Oyselet], 1585 (STC 23968).

285   He þat wolde begyn to kepe þe fo[. . .] of helthfull lyfe and come to perfec[. . .] sholde kepe thyse lytel doctrynes þat fo[. . .]eth to his power

Mirroure of Conscyence, didactic tract, s. xv ex. (?).

1. [U. Mylner, 1517?] (STC 17979.5), fragment.

Here doughter and see fructuous example of vertuous liuinge to edyfycacion of thy sowle   See **96**.

3ehur ðu min bearn beboda þines lareowes   See **98**.

Hereth of these iij worshipfull and glorious kynges in all the world frome the arysyng of the sonne to the downe going   Incipit to edition 5 of **290**.

286   Here begynne medicinys þat good lechys haue made and drawyn out of here auctourys as out Galion Acclepias and ypocras qheche wore þe beste lechys of þe world in here dayis

Bonas Medicinas, medical recipes (19) followed by a charm, s. xiv.

1. Henslow (1899), pp. 139-45 (BL Sloane 521, ff. 232-72

98

passim).

287 Here begynneth a lytill shorte treatyse that tellyth how there were vij
[sixe in edition 5] maystere assembled togydre euerycheone asked other
what thynge they myghte best speke of that myght plese god

> [Adam the Carthusian], A Litil Schort Tretice, devotional trea-
> tise, s. xiv.
>
> 1. W. Caxton, [1491] (STC 3305, Part 2); 2. W. de Worde,
> [1499] (STC 20412); 3. W. de Worde, 1530 (STC 20413); 4.
> EETS os 42 (1870), pp. 35-36 (CUL Kk.1.5.4, ff. 34v-35); 5.
> YW, II (1896), 390 (BL Royal 17 A.xxv, ff. 62-63v).
>
> Also in CUL Ii.4.9, BL Cotton Cleopatra D. VII, BL Harley
> 1706, BL Harley 4012, BL Royal 17 C.xviii, BL Addl. 60577,
> Lambeth Palace 523, Manchester Rylands English 94, Bodl
> Douce 322, Bodl Rawlinson C. 894, Oxford CCC 220, Oxford
> St. John's 147, Oxford University 142, San Marino Huntington
> HM 140; Jolliffe J.2.c. Often precedes 142. Another trans-
> lation (from French) is incorporated into 751, beginning "There
> were sixe mayster togyder."

Here begynneth a noble boke of festes ryalle and Cokery a boke for a
pryncis housholde or any other estates and the makyage therof accordynge as ye shall fynde more playnly within this boke   Introduction
to 630.

Here begynyth A shorte extracte and tellyth how þar ware sex masterys
asemblede ande eche one askede oþer quhat thing þai sholde spek of
gode   Incipit to edition 4 of 287.

288 Here begynnyth a schort tretys and a comfortabyl for synful wrecchys
wher-in þei may haue gret solas and comfort to hem and vndyrstondyn
þe hy & vnspecabyl mercy of ower souereyn Sauyowr Cryst Ihesu

> Margery Kempe, "Book of Margery Kempe", autobiography, s.
> xv (1).
>
> 1. EETS os 212 (1940) (BL Addl. 61823, ff. 1-123).
>
> For extracts circulating separately see 592.

Here begynneþe gode medycyns for al maner yuellis that euery man hath gode lechys drawen owt off þe bokys that men clepe Archippus Preface to **447**.

Here be-gynnyth medicynis þat good lechis haue made and drawyn out of his bokys Galien Asclipius and Ipocras   See **446**.

289   Her onginþ seo boc peri didaxeon þæt ys seo swytelunȝ hu fela ȝera wæs behuded se læcecræft And be his ȝewitnesse þa ȝelæredusþan læce ȝewislice smeadon

Peri Didaxeon, medical recipes, ca. 1150.

1. ed. M. Löweneck (1896) (BL Harley 6258b, ff. 83v-98v).

Heere bigynneþ þe kalender eiþer þe table of þe chapitels of þis tretys heere aftir suyng þe whiche tretys is clepid þe chastisyng of goddis children   See **343**.

Here begynneth the grete substaunce of the chapytre of þe rule of saynt Ierome the whiche he wrote at þe age nyghe of an C yere as he shewith in his prologue to the blyssed virgyn Eustoch   Incipit to preface to **815**.

290   Here begynnyth the lyfe of the thre kynges of Coleyn fro that tyme they sought our lorde god almyghty and came to Bedleem and worshypped hym

Lyfe of the Thre Kynges of Coleyn/Historia et Vita III Regum Indie, abridged translation of the Latin legend Historia Trium Regum by John of Hildesheim, ca. 1400.

1. W. de Worde, [1496] (STC 5572); 2. W. de Worde, [ca. 1499] (STC 5573); 3. W. de Worde, 1511 (STC 5574); 4. W. de Worde, 1526 (STC 5575); 5. ed. T. Wright, The Chester Plays, 1 (1843), 266-304 (BL Harley 1704, ff. 49v ff.); 6. EETS os 85 (1886), even pages (CUL Ee.4.32, ff. 1-23v); 7. EETS os 85 (1886), odd pages (BL Royal 18 A.x, ff. 87-119).

Also in Astor A. 2, Cambridge Magdalene Pepys 2006, TCC R.5.43 (1), CUL Kk.1.3, CUL Addl. 43, Cambridge (Mass.) Harvard University English 530, Durham Cathedral Hunter 15.2, BL Cotton Titus A. XXV, BL Cotton Vespasian E. XVI, BL

Stowe 951, BL Addl. 36983, Lambeth Palace 72, Bodl Ashmole 59, Bodl Douce 301, Bodl Eng. th. c. 58, Bodl Laud Miscellaneous 658, Bodl Laud Miscellaneous 749, San Marino Huntington HM 114, Stonyhurst College B.xxiii, Whalley MS. For a ME verse version see IMEV 854.3.

291 Here by-gynyth þe maner of steynyng of lynne cloþ Furst take a pocioun of lynne cloþ and 3 ellyn or as moche as þou wolt and euer more to viii ellyn of cloþ take a pound of alyme

Miscellaneous recipes (23), s. xiv.

1. Henslow (1899), pp. 1-8 (MS formerly in Henslow's possession, ff. 26-31).

292 Here begynneth the prohemye vpon the reducynge both out of latyn as of frensshe in to our englyssh tongue of the polytyque book named Tullius de senectute

William Caxton, prologue to the anonymous translation, Tullius de Senectute, ca. 1481.

1. W. Caxton, 1481 (STC 5293, Part 1); 2. Oldys (1737), pp. 255-58 (as in 1); 3. Ames (1749), pp. 23-25 (as in 1); 4. Herbert, I (1785), 30-32 (as in 1); 5. Blades, Life, I (1861), 159-61 (as in 1); 6. Aurner (1926), pp. 244-47 (as in 1); 7. EETS os 176 (1928), pp. 41-44 (as in 1); 8. Blake, COP (1973), pp. 120-23 (as in 1); 9. (1977) (facsimile of 1).

See 466.

Here begynneth the prologue or prohemye of the book callid Caton whiche booke hath ben translated in to Englysshe by Mayster Benet Burgh   Incipit to brief introduction to 793.

293 Her begyneth the retenewe of the dowty kynge K Edward the thirde and how he went to the sege of Callis with his oste

Account of the siege of Calais (1346), s. xv.

1. Camden Soc., n.s. 28 (1880), pp. 81-85 (Lambeth Palace 306, f. 139).

101

Here begynneth the ten commaundements of God þe whiche euery man mote kepe if he wulle come to blysse   Incipit to brief introduction to edition B.2 of 49.

Here begynneth the volume intituled and named the recuyell of the historyes of Troye   Brief introduction by Caxton to 825.

Here bigynneth the wyse boke of philosophie and astronomye conteyned and made of the wyseste philosophre and astronomer   Incipit to brief introduction to 201.

294   Here declaris the autour of this buke that a clerk callit Fair Pateris wys in all langagis fand in Grece kepit within a temple callit the Temple of the Soune

   Gilbert of the Haye, The Buke of the Governaunce of Princis, translation of French version of Liber de Regimine Principum, 1456.

   1. STS, 1st series 62 (1908), pp. 71-165 (Abbotsford Scott Collection 1-3, ff. 103-29).

295   Here endeth the book named the dictes or sayengis of the philosophhres enprynted by me william Caxton at westmestre

   William Caxton, epilogue with additional sayings concerning women to Anthony Woodville's Dictes or Sayengis of the Philosophhres, 1477.

   1. W. Caxton, 1477 (STC 6826); 2. W. Caxton, 1480? (STC 6828); 3. W. Caxton, 1489? (STC 6829); 4. W. de Worde, 1528 (STC 6830); 5. Ames (1749), pp. 9-12 (as in 1); 6. Herbert, I (1785), 15-17 (as in 1); 7. Blades, Life, I (1861), 141-48 (as in 1, 2, 3); 8. ed. W. Blades (1877) (facsimile of 1); 9. Price (1877), plates III-VIII (facsimile of 1); 10. Aurner (1926), pp. 234-36 (as in 1); 11. EETS os 176 (1928), pp. 18-31 (as in 1, 2, 3); 12. Blake, COP (1973), pp. 73-76 (as in 1).

296   Here endeth het [sic] discripcion of Britayne the whiche conteyneth englond wales and scotland and also bicause Irlonde is vnder the reule of englond

   William Caxton, epilogue to the Descripcion of Britayne, ca.

1480.

1. W. Caxton, 1480 (STC 13440a, 9991 Part 2); 2. W. de
Worde, 1498 (STC 13440b, 9996 Part 2); 3. W. de Worde, 1502
(STC 9997, Part 2); 4. J. Notary, 1504 (STC 9998, Part 2); 5.
R. Pynson, 1510 (STC 9999, Part 2); 6. J. Notary, 1515 (STC
10000, Part 2); 7. W. de Worde, 1515 (STC 9985, Part 2); 8.
W. de Worde, 1520 (STC 10001, Part 2); 9. W. de Worde, 1528
(STC 10002, Part 2); 10. Blades, Life, I (1861), 164 (as in 1);
11. ed. E.J.L. Scott, The Schoolmaster Printer of St. Albans
(1878), Part 1, 763 (as in 1); 12. Aurner (1926), p. 250 (as in
1); 13. EETS os 176 (1928), p. 40 (as in 1); 14. Blake, COP
(1973), pp. 72-73 (as in 1).

See 177.

297   Here felowyth a compendious abstracte translate in to englysshe out of
       the holy rule of saynte Benet for men and wymmen of the habyte therof

       William Caxton, prologue to Rule of Saynte Benet, ca. 1491.

       1. W. Caxton, 1491? (STC 3305, Part 3); 2. EETS os 120
       (1902), p. 119 (as in 1); 3. Blake, COP (1973), pp. 101-2 (as in
       1).

       See 281.

298   Here foloweth a rule howe a mann stondyng in a playne by a steple or
       such another thynge of height by lokyng vponn it shal knowe the
       certentie of the height thereof

       "A Method for Measuring Altitudes", s. xv (?).

       1. Halliwell, Rara (1839), pp. 27-28 (BL Lansdowne 762, f.
       23v).

299   Here foloweth the answers that the enfant sage the whiche ne had but
       thre yeres of age and was called lytell sone vnto the emperour

       Wyse Chylde of Thre Yere Olde, answers of little boy to every-
       thing asked of him by Emperor Adrian, s. xv ex. (?).

       1. W. de Worde, [1520?] (STC 5136).

300   Here foloweth the copye of a lettre whyche maistre Alayn Charetier
       wrote to his brother whyche desired to come dwelle in Court

       William Caxton, Curial, letter of advice not to come to court
       translated from the French of Alain Chartier, ca. 1484.

       1. W. Caxton, 1484? (STC 5057); 2. 1549 (STC 5058), frag-
       ment; 3. EETS es 54 (1888), pp. 1-16 (as in 1).

       Here folowethe the evident Examples and the Resons of comfort for a
       reformacion to be had uppon the piteous complaintes and dolorous
       lamentacions   Incipit to text proper of 190.

       Here folowythe the namys of the Bayles and Sheryfys of London in the
       cytte of Kynge Richarde the Fryste aftyr the Conqueste of Englonde
       Incipit to version C of 365.

301   Here foloweth the said Tullius de Amicicia translated in to our mater-
       nall Englissh tongue by the noble famous Erle The Erle of wurcestre

       William Caxton, prologue to John Tiptoft's translation, Tullius
       de Amicicia, ca. 1481.

       1. W. Caxton, 1481 (STC 5293, Part 2); 2. [W. Rastell, 1530?]
       (STC 5275); 3. Oldys (1737), pp. 258-59 (as in 1); 4. Ames
       (1749), p. 26 (as in 1); 5. Herbert, I (1785), 32-33 (as in 1); 6.
       Blades, Life, I (1861), 162 (as in 1); 7. Aurner (1926), p. 247
       (as in 1); 8. EETS os 176 (1928), pp. 44-5 (as in 1); 9. Blake,
       COP (1973), p. 123 (as in 1); 10. (1977) (facsimile of 1).

       See 555.

       Here folowyng been the names of Kepers and Baillifs in the tyme of
       king Richard the first   Introductory rubric to version A of 365.

       Here I take ye N to my weddid wyfe to hald and to haue at bed and at
       borde   Incipit to edition 2 of 313.

302   Here in thys booke folowyng is determynde the lynage of Coote armuris
       and how gentilmen shall be knowyn from vngentill men

       Liber Armorum, treatise on heraldry based partially on Nicholas

Upton, De Officio Militari, Book IV (ante 1434-40), s. xv (2).

1. [St. Albans Printer, 1486] (STC 3308); 2. W. de Worde, 1496 (STC 3309); 3. J. Dallaway, Inquiries into the Origin and Progress of the Science of Heraldry in England (1793), Appendix, pp. lxvii-cxii (as in 1); 4. Heraldic Miscellanies (1793), pp. 67-112 (as in 1); 5. ed. J. Haslewood (1810-11) (facsimile of 2); 6. Blades, Boke (1881, 1905) (facsimile of 1); 7. (1966) (facsimile of 2); 8. (1969) (facsimile of 1).

Part of what is later called the Boke of St. Albans.

303   Here is a good boke to lerne speke Frensshe Vecy vng bon liure a apprendre parler francoys In the name of the fader and þe sone En nome du pere et du filz And of the holy goost I wyll begynne Et du saint esperit ie vueil commencer

Lytell Treatyse for to Lerne Englysshe and Frensshe, primer, with English and French interspersed, containing within it IMEV 1920 and a letter from an apprentice to his master, s. xv.

1. W. de Worde, [1497] (STC 24866); 2. R. Pynson, [1500?] (STC 24867); 3. P. Mareschal, [ca. 1525] (STC 24868.3); 4. C. van Ruremond, ca. 1530 (STC 24868.7); 5. ed. J. Gessler, Deux Manuels de Conversation imprimés en Angleterre au XVe siècle (1941) (as in 1, with variants from 2).

Cf. 514.

Here is þe book þat spekiþ on a place þat is i-clepid þe abbeye of þe holy gost þe whiche schulde be foundid in clene conscience   Incipit to brief introduction to 590.

Here may þou lere to make aureum musicum   See 622.

Here seweth a souereyn and a notable sentence to comforte a persone that is in temptacion   See 528.

304   Homo quidam erat dives . . . Crist telliþ in þis parable how richessis ben perilouse for liȝtli wole a riche man use hem unto moche lust A parable is a word of stori þat bi þat hydeþ a spirituall witt

Wycliffite sermons, divided into five parts (for the Sunday

105

Gospels, the Commune Sanctorum, the Proprium Sanctorum, the Ferial Gospels, and the Sunday Epistles), s. xiv ex.

1. SEW, I-II (1869-71) (Bodl Bodley 788); 2. ed. A. Hudson and P. Gradon, 1- (1983-) (BL Addl. 40672).

Also in the following MSS, complete or fragmentary: Cambridge Christ's 7, CCCC 336, Cambridge Magdalene Pepys 2616, Cambridge Pembroke 237, Cambridge Peterhouse 69, Cambridge St. John's 58, Cambridge St. John's 190, Cambridge Sidney Sussex 74, TCC B.2.17, TCC B.4.20, TCC B.14.38, CUL Ii.1.40, Chelmsford Essex County Record Office D/DPr554, Edinburgh University 93, Leicester Old Town Hall 3, Leicester Wyggeston Hospital 10.D.34/6, BL Cotton Claudius D. VIII, BL Harley 1730, BL Harley 2396, BL Royal 18 B.ix, BL Addl. 40671, Lambeth Palace 1149, Bodl Don.c.13, Bodl Douce 321, Bodl Laud Miscellaneous 314, Bodl Addl. A. 105, Oxford Hertford 4, Oxford New 95, Princeton Robert H. Taylor MS, and Wisbech Town Museum 8.

Honory bisshop seruant of the servauntis of God to his welbeloued sounys Brother Fraunces and to alle other brotherne   Preface to **697** by Pope Honorius III confirming the Rule.

305   How mony case has yow Sex Whilk er þay þe nominatif genitif datif acusatif vocatif þe ablatif (from 2)

Grammatical treatise, s. xv.

1. Durham University Journal, 17 (1907), 194-96 (Durham Cathedral B.IV.19, f. 1); 2. Thomson (1984), pp. 191-92 (as in 1).

306   How many compoundis hath þis verbe sum es fui Sum cum bis septem componis

Grammatical treatise (on verbs), ca. 1501.

A. Version of ca. 1501: 1. Thomson (1984), pp. 209-13 (BL Arundel 249, ff. 18-20).

B. Version by John Stanbridge, Verba Anomala (s. xvi in.): 1. R. Pynson, [ca. 1505] (STC 23155.4); 2. R. Pynson, [ca. 1505] (STC 23155.6); 3. R. Pynson, [1509?] (STC 23155.8); 4. [W. de Worde, 1509?] (STC 23155.9); 5. R. Pynson, [1510?]

(STC 23156); 6. W. de Worde, [1517?] (STC 23157); 7. W. de Worde, [1518?] (STC 23159.5); 8. W. de Worde, [1519?] (STC 23159a); 9. W. de Worde, [1520?] (STC 23159a.1); 10. W. de Worde, [1520?] (STC 23159a.2); 11. W. de Worde, [1521?] (STC 23159a.3); 12. [W. de Worde, 1522?] (STC 23159a.4); 13. R. Pynson, [1523?] (STC 23159a.5); 14. W. de Worde, [1524?] (STC 23159a.7); 15. W. de Worde, [1525?] (STC 23159a.8); 16. W. de Worde, [1526?] (STC 23159a.9); 17. W. de Worde, 1526 (STC 23159a.10); 18. J. Cousin, [1526?] (STC 23159a.12); 19. W. de Worde, 1527 (STC 23159a.13); 20. W. de Worde, 1527 (STC 23160); 21. W. de Worde, 1527 (STC 23160.3); 22. J. Butler, [1529?] (STC 23160.7); 23. W. de Worde, 1530 (STC 23161); 24. J. Toy, 1531 (STC 23162); 25. P. Treveris, [1531?] (STC 23162.5); 26. W. de Worde, 1532 (STC 23163); 27. T. Godfray, [1534?] (STC 23163.2).

How many degreys of comparson ben þer III Wych iii Þe positiue degre þe comparatiue and þe superlatiue   Incipit to versions C, E, and G of 813.

307   Hov mani maner of wayes schall thou begynne to make Laten and constru V maner off wayes

F. Framton, grammatical treatise closely dependent on earlier texts, s. xvi in.

1. Thomson (1984), pp. 214-20 (BL Harley 1742, ff. 1-11).

How many maners of speche byn þer VIII Whiche viii   Incipit to versions E and J of 308.

308   How many partis of reson be þer VIII Whiche viij Nown pronown verbe aduerbe participill coniunccion preposicion and interieccion (from H)

John Leylond (?), Accedence/Liber Accidencium, grammatical treatise, s. xiv/xv.

A. Early version: 1. Thomson (1984), p. 55 (Bodl Digby 26, ff. 63, 5v, 62v, incomplete).

B. Version of s. xv (1): 1. Essays and Studies in English and Comparative Literature by Members of the English Department at the University of Michigan, 13 (1935), 101-17 (TCC O.5.4, ff.

4v-6v); 2. Thomson (1984), pp. 32-43 (as in 1).

C. Version by Stephen Bukherst (ca. 1416): 1. Thomson (1984), pp. 51-52 (London PRO C. 47/34/13, ff. 22-23, ending imperfectly).

D. Version of s. xv med.: 1. Thomson (1984), pp. 1-8 (Aberystwyth NLW Peniarth 356B, ff. 54v-57v, 48).

E. Version of s. xv med.: 1. Thomson (1984), pp. 9-16 (Aberystwyth NLW Peniarth 356B, ff. 163, 165-67v).

F. Version of s. xv med.: 1. PMLA, 50 (1935), 1019-28 (Cambridge St. John's 163, ff. 1-12); 2. Thomson (1984), pp. 17-31 (as in 1).

G. Version by Walter Pollard (1444-83): 1. Thomson (1984), pp. 61-62 (Bodl Rawlinson D. 328, ff. 124-25).

H. Version of s. xv (2): 1. Thomson (1984), pp. 45-50 (BL Addl. 37075, ff. 1-6v).

I. Version by John Leke (s. xv [2]): 1. Thomson (1984), p. 44 (BL Addl. 12195, f. 66, ending imperfectly).

J. Version of s. xv (2): 1. Thomson (1984), pp. 63-64 (Worcester Cathedral F. 123, f. 99v).

K. Version of ca. 1492-94: 1. PMLA, 50 (1935), 1028-32 (Bodl Douce 103, ff. 53-57); 2. Thomson (1984), pp. 56-60 (as in 1).

L. Long printed version attributed to John Stanbridge (s. xv ex.): 1. W. de Worde, [1495] (STC 7009, 23153.4); 2. W. de Worde, [1499] (STC 7010, 23153.5); 3. [W. Faques, 1504?] (STC 23153.6); 4. J. de Doesborch, [1509?] (STC 23153.7); 5. G. Back, [ca. 1510] (STC 23153.9); 6. W. de Worde, 1513 (STC 23153.10); 7. W. de Worde, [1518?] (STC 23154); 8. H. Pepwell, 1519 (STC 23154.3).

M. Informatio Puerorum (s. xv ex.): 1. R. Pynson, [1499?] (STC 14078); 2. R. Pynson, [1503] (STC 14079).

N. Version of s. xv/xvi: 1. Thomson (1984), pp. 53-54 (Norwich Record Office Colman 111, f. 1v of medieval MS A, beginning and ending imperfectly).

O. Short printed version attributed to John Stanbridge (s. xv/xvi): 1. W. de Worde, [1500?] (STC 23154.5); 2. [W.

108

Faques, ca. 1505] (STC 23154.7); 3. G. Back, [ca. 1510] (STC 23155); 4. J. de Doesborch, [ca. 1515] (STC 23155.2).

P. Version by John Stanbridge (s. xvi in.): 1. R. Pynson, [1505?] (STC 23139.5); 2. [P. Violet, ca 1505] (STC 23140); 3. W. de Worde, [1507?] (STC 23140.5); 4. W. de Worde, [1510?] (STC 23142); 5. R. Pynson, [1510?] (STC 23143); 6. [R. Pynson, ca. 1510] (STC 23143.5); 7. [R. Auzoult, ca. 1515] (STC 23147.2); 8. W. de Worde, [1517?] (STC 23147.4); 9. W. de Worde, 1519 (STC 23147.6); 10. R. Pynson, [1520?] (STC 23147.8); 11. W. de Worde, [1520?] (STC 23148); 12. W. de Worde, 1520 (STC 23148.2); 13. R. Copland, 1522 (STC 23148.3); 14. R. Pynson, [1523?] (STC 23148.4); 15. W. de Worde, 1525 (STC 23148.6); 16. J. Cousin, 1526 (STC 23148.7); 17. [J. Rastell, 1527?] (STC 23148.8); 18. W. de Worde, [1528] (STC 23148.10); 19. W. de Worde, [1529?] (STC 23148.12); 20. W. de Worde, [1529] (STC 23148a); 21. J. Skot, [1529?] (STC 23149); 22. P. Treveris, [1529?] (STC 23149.5); 23. W. de Worde, [1530?] (STC 23150); 24. [W. de Worde? 1530?] (STC 23150.3); 25. J. Skot, [1530?] (STC 23150.5); 26. P. Treveris, [1530?] (STC 23150.7); 27. J. Warwick, 1532 (STC 23151); 28. P. Treveris, [1532?] (STC 23151.3); 29. W. de Worde, 1534 (STC 23151.7); 30. M. Keyser, 1534 (STC 23153.2), considerably abridged; 31. J. Byddell, [1538?] (STC 23152.3); 32. N. Bourman, 1539 (STC 23152.5); 33. J. Michell, [1550] (STC 23153).

How mony partys of spech byn þer VIII Qwech viij   Incipit to versions D, G, and K of **308**.

309   I knowleche me gulti and ȝelde me to God Almihti and to his blessed Moder seynte Marie and to al þe holy cumpanye of heuene and to þe mi gostliche fader here in godes stude

[Richard Rolle], A Good Confession, a form of confession, s. xiv.

1. YW, II (1896), 340-45 (Bodl Eng. poet. a. 1, ff. 366-67); 2. Baugh (1956), pp. 87-95 (BL Addl. 37787, ff. 3-11v).

Also in Bristol Public Library 6, BL Harley 1706, BL Addl. 22283, Bodl Douce 322. Jolliffe C.21.

310   I knowleche that the Sacrament of the autar is verray Goddus body in fourme of brede but it is in another maner Goddus body then it is in

hevene

John Wyclif (?), Prima Confessio Wyclyff de Sacramento, confession on the Eucharist, abstract of the Latin original (1381), 1382-90.

1. Twysden (1652), cols. 2647-48 (BL Cotton Tiberius C. VII, f. 179v); 2. Lewis (1720), pp. 285-86 (as in 1); 3. Lewis, rev. ed. (1820), p. 335 (as in 1); 4. SEW, III (1871), 500 (as in 1 & BL Cotton Claudius E. III, f. 271); 5. Rolls 92 (1895), 2, 157-58 (as in 4); 6. Hudson (1978), p. 17 (as in 1).

Cf. 802.

I knowleche to God of heuene and vnto the blessid Marye   See 135.

311   I knowleche to þe þu hiȝe increate and euerlastynge trinite þat is to sey almiȝti God þe fadir almiȝti God þe sone

A Confession Þat Seynt Brandon Made, a form of confession, s. xv.

1. Archiv, 175 (1939), 41-49 (CUL Hh.1.12, ff. 52-59v); 2. Geibun Kenkyn (Journal of the Keio Society of Arts and Letters), 25 (1968), 12-30 (Lambeth Palace 541, ff. 150v-65).

Also in BL Harley 1706, Bodl Rawlinson C. 699, Oxford Queen's 210, Paris BN anglais 41.

312   I am maker of heuen and erth and see and of all thynges that bene in hem I am on wyth the fader and the holy goste

Revelations of St. Birgitta, translation from Latin, s. xv.

1. EETS os 178 (1929) (Princeton University Garrett 145).

Other versions in BL Arundel 197, BL Cotton Claudius B. I, BL Cotton Julius F. II (with prologue by Matthias, Canon of Linköping, beginning "Wondyr and marvelys are herd in oure cuntre and in oure land yt was a mervelous thinge"), BL Harley 4800, Lambeth Palace 392, Bodl Rawlinson C. 41.

313   I aske þe banes betwen I de B and A de C ȝif any man or woman kan sey or put any lettenge of sybrede wherfor they may not ne owght not to

come togedre (from 10)

English portions of the marriage service from the Manual, s. xv.

1. Surtees Soc. 60 (1874), p. xviii (Hereford Cathedral Welsh Manual); 2. Surtees Soc. 63 (1875), p. xvi (Cambridge (Mass.) Harvard University Widener 1, f. 62r-v); 3. Surtees Soc. 63 (1875), p. xvi (York Minster XVI.M.4, flyleaf); 4. Surtees Soc. 63 (1875), pp. 24-27 (STC 16160); 5. Surtees Soc. 63 (1875), p. 19* (STC 16140); 6. Surtees Soc. 63 (1875), pp. 116*-17* note (Oxford University 78A); 7. Surtees Soc. 63 (1875), pp. 167*-68* (STC 16163); 8. Surtees Soc. 63 (1875), pp. 167*-68* (as in 1); 9. Surtees Soc. 63 (1875), pp. 220*-21* note (Bodl Barlow 5); 10. Maskell, 2nd ed., I (1882), 53-54 note 7 (BL Addl. 30506, ff. 25-27v); 11. EETS es 90 (1903), pp. 5-6 (as in 10).

Also in early printed editions of the Manual (STC 16138-39, 16141-59, 16161).

314   I aske the banes betwix the hyghe and moost myghty prynce kyng of all kynges sone of almyghty god and the virgyne Mary in humanyte Cryste Ihesu of Nazareth of the one partye And A B of the thother partye

John Alcock, Bishop of Ely, Spousage of a Virgyn to Cryste/Desponsacio Virginis Christo, service for the ordination of a nun, ca. 1496.

1. W. de Worde, [1496] (STC 286); 2. W. de Worde, [ca. 1498] (STC 287).

315   I Balthasar by the grace of Mahownd Kyng of Kyngs Lord of Lords Sowdane of Surrey Emperour of Babilon Steward of Hell

Satirical proclamation by Lucifer to Henry VI, s. xv med.

1. Camden Soc. 86 (1863), pp. 166-67 (Emral MS); 2. EETS os 15 (1866), pp. 12-14 (BL Cotton Vespasian B. XVI, f. 5); 3. MLN, 52 (1937), 173-74 (BL Addl. 34193, f. 203v).

Cf. 101.

I bileve as Crist and his apostels have tauȝt us þat þo sacrament of þe auter whyte and rownde   Incipit to editions 5 and 7 of 802.

111

316 I bileve in God fadir almichty sshipper of hevene and of eorþe and in
Jhesus Crist his onlepi sone (from 3)

"Apostles' Creed", various dates from s. xiii to s. xv.

1. Rel. Ant., I (1841), 22-23 (BL Cotton Cleopatra B. VI, f.
201v); 2. Rel. Ant., I (1841), 42 (BL Arundel 57, f. 94); 3.
Rel. Ant., I (1841), 57 (BL Harley 3724, f. 44r-v); 4. Rel.
Ant., I (1841), 282 (Cambridge Gonville and Caius 52/29); 5.
Maskell, II (1846), 240 (as in 1); 6. Maskell, II (1846), 240 (as
in 3); 7. Maskell, II (1846), 241 (BL Harley 2343, f. 2); 8.
Maskell, II (1846), 241 (Bodl Douce 246); 9. Maskell, II
(1846), 242, paraphrased version (BL Royal 17 B.xvii); 10.
EETS os 23 (1866), pp. 262-63 (as in 2); 11. EETS os 34 (1868),
p. 217 (BL Cotton Nero A. XIV, f. 131r-v); 12. Mätzner, I, 2
(1869), 3 (as in 4); 13. Mätzner, I, 2 (1869), 4 (as in 3); 14.
Mätzner, I, 2 (1869), 4 (as in 1); 15. ES, 1 (1877), 215
(Salisbury Cathedral 126, f. 5); 16. Maskell, 2nd ed., III
(1882), 251 (as in 1); 17. Maskell, 2nd ed., III (1882), 251 (as
in 3); 18. Maskell, 2nd ed., III (1882), 252 (as in 7); 19.
Maskell, 2nd ed., II (1882), 252 (as in 8); 20. Maskell, 2nd
ed., II (1882), 253 (as in 9); 21. MLN, 4 (1889), 276 (Blickling
Hall MS, f. 35); 22. EETS os 23, rev. ed. (1965), pp. 262-63
(as in 2).

Also included in 157 and various other ME works.

317 Ic ileue on enne god fæder almihti wurchend heouene and eorþe and alle
iseienliche þing and vniseienliche and on enne crist

Worcester Master, Nicene Creed, s. xiii in.

1. Anglia, 1 (1878), 286 (Bodl Junius 121, f. vi); 2. Anglia, 52
(1928), 5 (as in 1).

I byleue stedfastely in my lord god almyȝhty   Incipit to editions 9
and 20 of 316.

318 I Beseche þe brethren in the lorde Christ Iesu and for the loue of hys
spirite to praye with me that we may be vessels to his laude and praise

John Wyclif (?), "Wycklyffes Wycket", a treatise on the sacra-
ments, s. xiv ex.

1. [J. Day?], 1546 (STC 25590); 2. [J. Day?], 1546 (STC

25590.5); 3. [J. Day?, 1548?] (STC 25591); 4. [J. Day?, 1548?] (STC 25591a); 5. J. Barnes, 1612 (STC 25592); 6. ed. T.P. Pantin (1828) (as in 1).

319 I beseke þe reuerent doctour to informe me þe way of goode lyfyng & how I sal dispose me to cum to euerlastyng lyfe þe whilk is ordand for þaim þat here dewly lufs & serfys almyghty god

Of Actyfe Lyfe and Contemplatyfe Declaracion, tract on contemplative life, s. xv.

1. MS, 37 (1975), 88-111 (BL Addl. 37049, ff. 87v-89v).

Cf. 784.

I bitake in to thine hondes and in to thine hondis of thine halwen
See 352.

320 I charge þee and I beseche þee wiþ as moche power and vertewe as þe bond of charite is sufficient to suffre what so euer þou be þat þis book schalt haue in possession ouþer bi propirte ouþer by keping

Clowde of Unknowyng, devotional treatise in epistle form, s. xiv ex.

1. EETS os 218 (1944), pp. 1-133 (BL Harley 674, ff. 17v-91v);
2. Hodgson (1982), pp. 1-74 (as in 1).

Also in Ampleforth Abbey 42, CUL Ff.6.41, CUL Ii.6.39, CUL Kk.6.26, Downside Abbey 10, Downside Abbey 11, TCD 122, BL Harley 959, BL Harley 2373, BL Royal 17 C.xxvi, BL Royal 17 C.xxvii, BL Royal 17 D.v, Bodl Bodley 576, Bodl Douce 262, Oxford University 14, St. Hugh's Charterhouse (Sussex) Parkminster D. 176, Thropton All Saints MS.

I cristen þe in þe nayme of þe fadyr and þe sone   Incipit to edition 7 and similar to that of edition 1 of 468.

I comaunde ow godfadre and godmodre on holy chirche bihalue that ye chargen the fadur and the modur of this child   Incipit to editions 3 and 10 of 468.

I creature ymaad of þe maker bi me þe maker haþ maad of him þis
booke   Incipit to text proper of 732.

321 I desyrede thre graces be the gyfte of god The fyrst was to have mynde
of cryste es passion the seconde was Godelye syekenes and the thryd
was to haue of goddys gyfte thre woundys

Julian of Norwich, A Vision Schewed be the Goodenes of God to
a Devoute Woman (A)/A Revelacion of Love That Jhesu Christ
Our Endles Blisse Made in XVI Shewynges (B), devotional
treatise, 1373-1393.

A. First, shorter version (1373): 1. MET 8 (1978) (BL Addl.
37790, ff. 97-115); 2. Colledge and Walsh (1978), I, 201-78 (as
in 1).

B. Second, longer version (ca. 1393): 1. ed. Serenus de Cressy
(1670) (Wing C6903) (Paris BN anglais 40); 2. Cressy, 2nd ed.,
ed. G.H. Parker (1843) (as in 1); 3. ed. G. Tyrrell (1902) (as in
1); 4. ed. G. Tyrrell, 2nd ed. (1920) (as in 1); 5. ed. M.
Glasscoe (1976) (BL Sloane 2499); 6. Colledge and Walsh
(1978), II, 281-734 (as in 1).

B also in BL Sloane 3705; excerpts in London Westminster
Archdiocesan Archives MS and Upholland (Lancashire) St. Joseph's College MS.

322 I fynde nomore of this werke to fore sayd For as fer as I can
vnderstonde This noble man Gefferey Chaucer fynysshyd at the sayd
conclusion

William Caxton, epilogue to Chaucer's House of Fame, ca.
1484.

1. W. Caxton, 1484? (STC 5087); 2. R. Pynson, [1526?] (STC
5088), slightly revised; 3. Ames (1749), p. 61 (as in 1); 4.
Herbert, I (1785), 81-82 (as in 1); 5. Blades, Life, II (1863),
Plate XLI and pp. 165-66 (as in 1); 6. Blades, Biography
(1877), p. 292 (as in 1); 7. Chaucer Soc., 1st Series 57 (1878),
p. 241 (as in 1); 8. Blades, Biography, 2nd ed. (1881), pp. 294-
95 (as in 1); 9. Spurgeon (1914), p. 61 (as in 1); 10. Aurner
(1926), pp. 267-68 (as in 1); 11. EETS os 176 (1928), p. 69 (as
in 1); 12. PBSA, 42 (1948), 142 (as in 1); 13. Blake, COP
(1973), p. 103 (as in 1); 14. Brewer (1978), p. 75 (as in 1).

323   I fynde wretyn & rede in holy mennys wrytyng þat aftur oure ladys assumpcyon Seynt Ion þe euungeliste gretely desyryd to se þat blessyd ladi

"The Vision of St. John on the Sorrows of the Virgin", meditation on the five sorrows of the Virgin, s. xiv.

1. Baugh (1956), pp. 151-52 (BL Addl. 37787, ff. 161-62v).

Also in CUL Addl. 6686 and San Marino Huntington HM 147, following Contemplacyons of the Drede and Love of God (362).

324   I have joy fully to telle to alle treue men þo bileve þat I holde and algatis to þo pope for I suppose þat if my fayth be riȝtful and gyven of God þo pope wil gladly conferme hit (from 6)

[John Wyclif], letter to Pope Urban VI, translation and amplification of the Latin original (1384) by followers of Wyclif, s. xiv ex.

1. Lewis (1720), pp. 283-85 (Bodl Bodley 647, f. 107); 2. Lewis, rev. ed. (1820), pp. 333-35 (as in 1); 3. Vaughan, Life (1828), II, 455-56 (as in 1); 4. Vaughan, Life, 2nd ed. (1831), II, 435 (as in 1); 5. Vaughan, John (1853), p. 576 (as in 1); 6. SEW, III (1871), 504-6 (as in 1); 7. Winn (1929), pp. 75-77 (as in 1).

Also in Oxford New 95. The Latin original in Bodl e Mus. 86 is edited in Rolls 5 (1858), pp. 341-42.

I Haue shewyd to yow in thys booke a foore how gentilmen began and how the law of armys was first ordant   Incipit to Part 2 of 302.

I Iack vplande make my mone to very god   Incipit to text proper in edition 1 of 782.

325   I Iohn Arderne fro the first pestilence that was in the ȝere of our lord 1349 duellid in Newerk in Notyngham shire vnto the ȝere of our lord 1370 and ther I helid many men of fistula in ano

John Arderne, Fistula in Ano, medical treatise, s. xiv (after 1370).

1. EETS os 139 (1910) (BL Sloane 6, ff. 141-74v, and BL Sloane

2002, ff. 79-80v).

Also in BL Sloane 76, BL Sloane 277, BL Sloane 563, BL Sloane 8093.

I Johon Schep som tyme Seynte Marie prest of York   Incipit to edition 2 of 425.

326   I N by the grace of God electe ordeyned and chosen Abbesse of this Monastery of N of the order of N promyse here afore God and all holy sayncts

"Benedictio Abbatissae Electae", a form of consent for an elected abbess, s. xv (2).

1. Surtees Soc. 61 (1875), 248-49 (BL Lansdowne 388).

I N take the N to my wedded wif to haue and to holde fro this day forward for bettere for wers for richere for pouerer   Incipit to edition 5 and similar to incipits in editions 1, 6, and 8 of 313.

I N underfynge ye N for my vvedded vvyf for betere for vvorse Incipit to edition 7 of 313.

I rede in Genesi the firste book of holi write 12 16 & 17 capitulis See 24.

327   I rede in olde storiys this matere folwyng the qwyche was kept off as a kalendere off experte men off the dysposycion off the yere

John Metham, prognostications based on Christmas day, s. xv.

1. EETS os 132 (1916), pp. 146-47 (Princeton University Garrett 141, f. 78r-v); 2. EETS os 132 (1916), pp. 157-58 (Princeton University Garrett 141, f. 87r-v).

328   I rede in the boke the qwyche ys clepid the Pryuyte off Phylosophyrs the qwyche was made be the excellent philysophyr Arystotyl the qwyche endytyd this boke be meruulus kunnyng off very knowlech

John Metham, treatise on physiognomy, s. xv.

116

1. EETS os 132 (1916), pp. 118-45 (Princeton University Garrett 141, ff. 57-75v).

I Romulus sone of thybere of the Cyte of Atyque gretyng Esope man of grece subtyle and Ingenyous techeth in his fables how men ought to kepe and rewle them well   Incipit to Fables of 179.

I schall schryve to þee Lord for þou art wraþþ to me turnyd is þi breeþ and þou cumfortidst me   See 134.

Hi true in God fader hal-michttende þat makede heven and herdeþe Incipit to editions 1, 5, 14, and 16 of 316.

329   Y William Stavnton born in þe bisshopryche of Dereham of englond bi goddes grace entred in to þe purgatorie of seint Patrik in the bisshopriche of Cleghire in Irlande

þe Revelacion the Which William Staunton Saw in Patrik Is Purgatorie, legend, 1409.

1. ed. G.P. Krapp, The Legend of Saint Patrick's Purgatory (1900), pp. 58-77 (BL Royal 17 B.xliii, ff. 133-48v).

Also in BL Addl. 34193.

330   I wounder syr noble knyghte that in fewe dayes tymes be changed right is buryed lawes be ouerturned and statutes be trodde vnder foote

John Trevisa, Dialogus inter Clericum et Militem, translation of a work attributed to William of Ockham, s. xiv (2).

1. [T. Berthelet, 1533] (STC 12511); 2. T. Berthelet, [1540?] (STC 12511a); 3. EETS os 167 (1925), pp. 1-37 (upper halves only) (BL Harley 1900, ff. 1-5); 4. EETS os 167 (1925), pp. 1-38 (lower halves only) (as in 1).

Also in Cambridge St. John's 204, BL Stowe 65, BL Addl. 24194, Manchester Chetham 11379, San Marino Huntington HM 28561.

331   3if a man were siker þat he schulde to morowe come bifore a juge and oþer lese or wynne alle þe godes þat he hadde and also hys lif to he

117

wolde drede þis jugement

Þe Seven Werkys of Mercy Bodyly, Wycliffite tract, s. xiv ex.

1. SEW, III (1871), 168-82 (Oxford New 95, ff. 127v-35).
Also in Cambridge (Mass.) Harvard University English 738,
TCD 245, New York H.P. Kraus MS, and York Minster
XVI.L.12.

332 Iff it be possible that of vyce myght growe vertue it wolde please me
well in this partie to be passioned as a woman (from 2)

The Body of Polycye, translation of Christine de Pisan's Livre du
corps de policie (1404-7), guide for princes, s. xv med.

1. J. Skot, 1521 (STC 7270); 2. MET 7 (1977) (CUL Kk.1.5,
ff. 1-79v).

333 If it plese ony man spirituel or temporel to bye ony pyes of two and thre
comemoracions of salisburi vse enpryntid after the forme of this present
lettre

William Caxton, advertisement of ca. 60 words for Ordinale
issued ca. 1477.

1. W. Caxton, 1477 (STC 4890); 2. Dibdin, TA, I, 2 (1810),
cii (facsimile of 1); 3. Dibdin, BS, IV (1815), 350 (as in 1); 4.
Catalogue of the Books and Manuscripts Bequeathed by Francis
Douce, Esq. to the Bodleian Library (1840), p. 305 (facsimile of
1); 5. Blades, Life, I (1861), 64 (as in 1); 6. Blades, Life, II
(1863), 101 (as in 1); 7. Price (1877), Plate II (facsimile of 1);
8. Blades, Biography (1877), pp. 71, 237 (as in 1); 9. Blades,
Biography, 2nd ed. (1882), pp. 72, 239 (as in 1); 10. ed. F.
Proctor and C. Wordsworth, Breviarium ad Usum Insignis Ecclesiae Sarum, III (1886), lxix-lxx (as in 1); 11. ed. E.W.B.
Nicholson (1892) (facsimile of 1); 12. ed. C. Wordsworth, The
Tracts of Clement of Maydeston (1894), p. 97 (as in 1); 13. ed.
W.A. Copinger, Supplement to Hain's Repertorium Biblio-
graphicum, II, I (1898), 4, no. 32 (as in 1); 14. Duff, WC
(1905), Plate V and p. 42 (as in 1); 15. ed. K. Burger,
Buchhändleranzeigen des 15. Jahrhunderts (1907), Plate 21 (facsimile of 1); 16. The Bibliophile, 1 (1908), 22 (facsimile of 1);
17. Duff (1917), p. 22 (as in 1); 18. Aurner (1926), p. 41 and
Plate V (as in 1); 19. Gesamtkatalog der Wiegendrucke, 6
(1934), 354, n. 6440 (as in 1); 20. Kaiser (1958), plate facing p.

118

341 (facsimile of 1); 21. Blake, Caxton (1969), Plate 8 (facsimile of 1); 22. Blake, COP (1973), p. 55 (as in 1).

334　If it thonder in Januarij then it betokeneth that yere moche ffrute & great warre

Off the Thonder, prognostic, s. xv ex.

1. Archiv, 128 (1912), 288 (Bodl Ashmole 189, f. 102r-v).

Cf. 510.

ʒyf seynt Paules day be fayre and clere it ys token of goode tyme of þe ʒere　　Incipit to fifth item in 687.

335　If þat þou hauyst stedfolys to kepe and to noryschin the ferst ʒer wyl þat thei ben ʒonge do hem to howse in cold wedyr

Boke of Marchalsi, treatise on horse breeding and veterinary medicine, with verse prologue, s. xv.

1. ed. B. Odenstedt (1973) (BL Harley 6398, ff. 1-58).

Also in TCC R.14.51, BL Harley 5086, Oxford Balliol 354, Bodl Ashmole 1437, Bodl Douce 291, Bodl Wood empt. 18.

Yf the Tryangle of the hand be of ʒeuun lynes that the lynes go nere to on quantite in leynthe　　Incipit to text proper of 566.

336　ʒef þou coueite to be maad cleene in soule as it may be heere of al þe stathel of synne the which wol alweies leeue in þee after þi confession

A Ful Good Meditacioun for Oon to Seie by Him-self Al-oone, s. xiv.

1. YW, II (1896), 441-43 (Oxford University 97, ff. 153-55v).

Also in Cambridge Magdalene Pepys 2125, TCC B.14.53, Edinburgh University 93, BL Arundel 197, BL Addl. 22283, Bodl Laud Miscellaneous 174.　Jolliffe I.18.

Gif þow desiris tobe cleyn of syn and tobe riche of verteuis and to haue

119

victory of thy ennemes to haue oftymes conpuncioun of þi synnis
Incipit to introduction to 670.

337   Yef þou dremyst of Armery it be-tokenyth chaunge of sum þinge Yef
þou dremyst þou bere armour it by-tokenyth worship

Danyelles Dremys, dream book, extract from a translation of
Somnia Danielis circulating separately, s. xv.

1. Anglia, 80 (1962), 266-67 (BL Lansdowne 388, f. 372v); 2.
Bühler (1973), p. 557 (as in 1).

For another translation see 100.

338   Iffe þou sey to me þis ys an harde worde whiche þou spekeste who may
forsake þe worlde as þou seyest and hate hys flessche

Augustinus de Contemptu Mundi, treatise on the vanity and
transitoriness of worldly conditions, s. xiv.

1. YW, II (1896), 374-75 (BL Harley 1706, ff. 149-50).

Also in TCC B.15.39, TCD 516, BL Cotton Titus C. XIX, BL
Harley 1706 (again), BL Addl. 14408, BL Addl. 37788, Bodl
Rawlinson A. 381, San Marino Huntington HM 774. Jolliffe
I.20.a.

339   If þou wole be weel with god And haue grace to reule þi lijf And come
to þe ioie of loue Þis name ihesu fastne it so fast in þin herte

[Richard Rolle], "On the Name of Jesus", short exhortation
extracted and expanded from Chapter 9 of the Forme of Lyvyng,
s. xiv.

1. EETS os 24 (1867), p. 40 (Lambeth Palace 853, pp. 88-89);
2. YW, I (1895), 106 (Bodl Rawlinson C. 285, f. 59r-v).

Also in CUL Ff.5.40 and Bodl Rawlinson A. 389 (fragment).
Jolliffe I.21. For MSS of the Forme of Lyvyng see 351.

340   Yf thou wylt do thy saluacyon benygnely thou shalt obey vnto god &
vnto his commaundementes as here after thou shalt here

Andrew Chertsey, The Floure of the Commaundementes of God,

translation from French, treatise on the ten commandments and other religious topics, s. xv ex. (?).

1. W. de Worde, 1510 (STC 23876); 2. W. de Worde, 1521 (STC 23877).

341   Iff ye desire or covytt to gete or cum into many menys favour and have true and trusty love trust not to mych in youre fayrnes strenght wytt

English prose passages, with model Latin translations, for the use of students, ca. 1495.

1. ed. W. Nelson, A Fifteenth Century School Book (1956) (BL Arundel 249, ff. 9-61; English passages only, rearranged).

In a Monasterye callyd Euyssham there was a certein yong man turnyd wyth feythfull deuocyon fro thys worldys vanyte to the lyfe of a Monke Incipit to text proper of 695.

In all the wordes þat er stabillede and sett to say in erthe þan es þe Pater noster þe beste and þe hegheste and þe halyest   See 533.

342   In Apryll take the tayle off a rede worme that ys wyth owt the knotte and breke of the hede

Medicina Piscium, fishing treatise, s. xv.

1. Braekman (1980), pp. 54-56 (Bodl Rawlinson C. 506, ff. 298-99).

343   In drede of almighty god Religyous suster a short pistle I sende you the mater of temptacions whiche pystle as me thenketh maye reasonably be cleped The Chastisyng of Goddes Childern Of this mater ye haue desyred to knowe in comforte of youre soule

Chastysing of Goddes Chyldern, mystical text for female religious, ca. 1382.

1. [W. de Worde, ca. 1492] (STC 5065, Part 1); 2. Bazire and Colledge (1957), pp. 91-258 (Bodl Bodley 505, ff. 1-92).

Also in Cambridge Magdalene Pepys 2125, Cambridge St. John's 128, TCC B.14.19, Liverpool University Library F. 4. 10, BL

Harley 1288 (extracts), BL Harley 6615, BL Addl. 33971 (beginning imperfectly), Bodl Ashmole 41, Bodl Eng. th. c. 57, Bodl Laud Miscellaneous 99, Bodl Rawlinson C. 57, Oxford Jesus 39.

In eche synneful man or woman   See 351.

In erthe ben three degrees of folk and alle schulden love god over al thing   Incipit to text proper of 563.

344   In Ynglond ther ys a schepcote the whiche schepekote hayt ix dorys and at yevery dor standet ix ramys and every ram hat ix ewys

   "An Arithmetical Question", s. xv.

   1. Rel. Ant., I (1841), 161 (CUL Ee.4.35).

345   In euery manys herte dwellyng in wrecchid vale of teris is nedful to ben foundyn gostly labour & trauayle in telyng of his concyens þis holy tyme of Lent

   John Drury, Tractatus de Modo Confitendi, notes on instruction for true confession in Lent, ca. 1434.

   1. Speculum, 9 (1934), 76-79 (CUL Addl. 2830, ff. 80-83v).

346   In first ye shall swere that ye shall be trewe to oure high and excellent prince oure soverayn lord that here is and to hym that makys yow herold

   A form of oath for a herald, s. xv med.

   1. Archaeologia, 57 (1900), 70 (New York Morgan M 775, ff. 279v-80).

347   In fraunce somtyme there was a noble man and a ryche the whiche loued and worshypped well god and holy chirche and specyally oure blessyd lade saynt Mary

   Myracles of Oure Blessyd Lady, s. xv.

   1. W. de Worde, [1496] (STC 17539); 2. W. de Worde, 1514 (STC 17540); 3. W. de Worde, 1530 (STC 17541).

348 In honorem dei omnipotentis gloriamque . . . Thanked be the highe
name of oure Lorde and sauiour Criste Jhesu excellent glorie and
eternall reuerence to his blessid moder Seinte Marie

Robert Ricart, "Mayor's Kalendar", chronicle containing
abridgments of other chronicles, a book of instructions for
officers of the city of Bristol, a charter, etc., s. xv ex-s. xvi in.

1. Camden Soc., n.s. 5 (1872), pp. 2-113 passim (Bristol
Corporation Archives MS).

349 In how mone maners shal þu begynne to make a Latyn an to construe In
foure Qweche foure First be a vocatif case

John Leylond, Informacio, grammatical treatise, ca. 1401-28.

A. Early version (ca. 1414): 1. Thomson (1984), pp. 105-10
(Lincoln Cathedral 88, ff. 91v-95).

B. Version of s. xv med.: 1. Thomson (1984), p. 104 (Aberystwyth NLW Peniarth 356B, ff. 167v-68, ending imperfectly).

C. Version of s. xv med.: 1. Thomson (1984), pp. 122-30 (Bodl
Rawlinson D. 328, ff. 8-15v, 73v).

D. Version by Thomas Pennant, Introduccio Puerorum (s. xv
[2]): 1. Thomson (1984), pp. 93-103 (Aberystwyth NLW Peniarth 256B, ff. 1-9v).

E. Version by John Rede and William Slingsby, Regule Latisandi
(1467-ca. 1480): 1. Thomson (1984), pp. 111-21 (Bodl Hatton
58, ff. 46-54v).

F. Version by John Edwards of Chirk (1480's): 1. Thomson
(1984), pp. 82-92 (Aberystwyth NLW 423D, ff. 11v-17).

G. Long printed version attributed to John Stanbridge, Longe
Parvula (s. xv ex.): 1. [T. Rood, 1482?] (STC 23163.13); 2.
R. Pynson, [1496] (STC 23163.14); 3. [W. de Worde, 1499?]
(STC 23163.16); 4. [R. Pynson, 1505?] (STC 23163.17); 5.
W. de Worde, 1509 (STC 23164); 6. [G. Bac, ca. 1510] (STC
23164.1); 7. Festschrift (1906), pp. 453-60 (as in 5).

H. Standard printed version attributed to John Stanbridge, Per-
vula (s. xv ex.): 1. [W. de Worde, 1496?] (STC 23163.6); 2.
W. de Worde, [1497?] (STC 23163.7); 3. [R. Pynson, 1497?]
(STC 23163.8); 4. N. Marchant, [1500] (STC 23163.9); 5.

[W. de Worde, 1501?] (STC 23163.11).

I. Version by John Stanbridge, Parvulorum Institutio (s. xvi in.): 1. W. de Worde, [1507?] (STC 23164.2); 2. W. de Worde, [1508?] (STC 23164.4); 3. [W. de Worde, 1510?] (STC 23164.6); 4. W. de Worde, [1511?] (STC 23164.8); 5. W. de Worde, [1513?] (STC 23165.5); 6. W. de Worde, [1514?] (STC 23166); 7. R. Pynson, [1515?] (STC 23166.5); 8. W. de Worde, [1518?] (STC 23167.3); 9. W. de Worde, [1519?] (STC 23167.5); 10. W. de Worde, 1520 (STC 23167.7); 11. W. de Worde, 1521 (STC 23168); 12. R. Pynson, [1524?] (STC 23168.3); 13. W. de Worde, [1525?] (STC 23168.5); 14. W. de Worde, 1526 (STC 23168.7); 15. W. de Worde, 1526 (STC 23169); 16. [W. de Worde, ca. 1526] (STC 23169.5); 17. J. Butler, [1528?] (STC 23172); 18. W. de Worde, 1528 (STC 23173); 19. W. de Worde, 1529 (STC 23174); 20. [W. de Worde?], 1529 (STC 23174.3); 21. W. de Worde, 1530 (STC 23174.5); 22. P. Treveris, [1531?] (STC 23174.6); 23. W. de Worde, 1534 (STC 23174.7); 24. R. Lathum, [1539?] (STC 23175); 25. T. Petit, [ca. 1545] (STC 23175.5).

350   In how many maners schalt thou by gynne to make Latyn Byfoure by ryghtfull order of construccyon

Grammatical treatise, s. xv.

1. Essays and Studies in English and Comparative Literature by Members of the English Department of the University of Michigan, 13 (1935), 98-101, 118-25 (TCC O.5.4, ff. 4, 6v-7v); 2. Thomson (1984), pp. 178-85 (as in 1).

351   In ilk a synful man or woman þat es bunden in dedly syn er thre wrechednes þe wylk brynges þam to þe dede of hell Þe first es defaute of gastly strength

Richard Rolle, Forme of Lyvyng, epistle written to the recluse Margaret Kirkeby, 1348-49.

1. YW, I (1895), 3-49 (CUL Dd.5.64, ff. 1-22v); 2. YW, I (1895), 3-49 (Bodl Rawlinson C. 285, ff. 40-57v); 3. Allen, English (1931), pp. 85-119 (as in 1).

Also in Beeleigh Abbey Foyle MS, Cambridge Gonville and Caius 669/646, Cambridge Magdalene Pepys 2125, TCC B.14.38, TCC B.15.17, TCC O.1.29 (adaptation), CUL Ff.5.40, CUL Ff.5.45, CUL Hh.1.12, CUL Ii.4.9, CUL

Ii.6.55, TCD 154, TCD 155, Edinburgh University 107, Hereford Cathedral P.I.9, BL Arundel 507 (extracts), BL Harley 1022, BL Lansdowne 455, BL Addl. 22283, BL Addl. 37790, Lambeth Palace 853 (extract), London Westminster School 3, Longleat Marquis of Bath 29, Longleat Marquis of Bath 32, Manchester Chetham 6690, New York Morgan M 818, Bodl Ashmole 1393 (extract), Bodl Ashmole 1524, Bodl Bodley 110, Bodl Bodley 938, Bodl Digby 18, Bodl Douce 302 (extract), Bodl Douce 322, Bodl Eng. poet. a. 1, Bodl Laud Miscellaneous 210, Bodl Laud Miscellaneous 524, Bodl Rawlinson A. 389, Oxford University 97, Paris Bibl. Ste.-Geneviève 3390, San Marino Huntington HM 127, San Marino Huntington HM 502. For a verse version see IMEV 1442; a Latin version appears in Cambridge Gonville and Caius 140/80 and BL Harley 106.

352   In manus tuas Lord I bitake in to thine hondes and in to thine hondis of thine halwen in this nyght my soule and my bodi

Prayer at night, s. xv.

1. Maskell, II (1846), 283 (Cambridge St. John's 256); 2. Maskell, 2nd ed., III (1882), 305 (as in 1).

353   In Marche þou shalt lern for to angul I vndurstande with þi hoke & þi lyne to take þe fysche þat is fletande (from 2)

De Arte Piscandi, treatise on angling, s. xv.

1. Braekman (1980), pp. 33-38 (BL Sloane 1698, ff. 12-13); 2. English Studies, 62 (1981), 110-12 (as in 1).

Erroneously called verse in IMEV 1502.5.

354   In monte te saluum fac . . . Thise wordes were sayd vnto Loth by an angell by the commaundement of almyghty god whan the citees of Sodome and Gomor edifyed in the vale sholde be dystroyed for theyr synne and demerytes

John Alcock, Bishop of Ely, Hyll of Perfeccion/Mons Perfeccionis, ca. 1496.

1. W. de Worde, 1496 (STC 278); 2. W. de Worde, 1497 (STC 279); 3. R. Pynson, [1497-98] (STC 280); 4. W. de Worde, 1501 (STC 281).

Jn nomine domini amen Tahpostle saynt poul sayth that All they that wyll liue surely in Ihesu cryst shall suffre persecucion   Incipit to "Diverse Sayings of Sain Paul," devotional tract (Part 9) incorporated into 751.

355   In nomine Iesu omne genu flectatur . . . Iesu Iesu Iesu Mercy . . . Iesu haue mercy on me & forgiue me the great offences which I haue done (from 5)

Psalter of Jesu, fifteen prayers, s. xv.

1. R. Copland, 1529 (STC 14563); 2. J. Foulerum, 1575 (STC 14563.3); 3. J. Foulerum, 1575 (STC 14563.5); 4. [W. Carter?, 1579?] (STC 14563.7); 5. H. Mareschalum, 1580 (STC 14564); 6. [Greenstreet House Press, 1580-81] (STC 14568); 7. [Fr. Parsons' Press], 1583 (STC 14566); 8. [English secret press, 1595-1600?] (STC 14566.5); 9. [J. Danter?], 1596 (STC 14567); 10. [P. Auroi], 1604 (STC 14568.3); 11. [P. Auroi], 1611 (STC 14568.5); 12. [P. Auroi], 1618 (STC 14569); 13. P. Auroi, 1624 (STC 14570); 14. [St. Omer, English College Press], 1624 (STC 14570.3); 15. ed. H.G. (1885) (Marquis of Abergavenny MS); 16. STS, 3rd series 23 (1955), pp. 194-204 (BL Arundel 285, ff. 107-16).

Also in BL Lansdowne 379 (first ten prayers only) and London Westminster Abbey 39; included in some early printed editions of the Sarum Primer and in some editions of the Manual of Prayers (STC 17263-17278.6).

356   In nomine patris etc. In þe honour of oure lord Jesu Crist and oure ladye seynt Marie and seynt Jop and seynt Jopes fader sowle

A Charme for þe Farsynes, s. xv.

1. Chaucer and Middle English Studies (1974), p. 65 (BL Royal 17 A.xxxii, f. 129v).

357   In olde tyme the realme of Englande was greatly troubled with the danes so þat in many kynges dayes there coude no peas be made

The Lyfe of Seinte Edward Kyng and Confessour, saint's life, s. xv (1).

1. W. de Worde, 1523 (STC 7500); 2. Moore (1942), pp. 75-106 (BL Addl. 35298, ff. 48-53).

The version in BL Addl. 35298 is unique to that copy of the Gilte Legende (1438). For other ME prose versions see 357, 577, and 803. Also in 682. For a verse version see IMEV 2888.

558 In oone techynge acordyth and in oone verite Shewyth the moste wyse clerkes and Maysteris of renoune that haue beyn afor vs in al tymys

James Yonge, Boke of the Governaunce of Prynces, book of instruction translated from the Latin Secreta Secretorum, 1422.

1. EETS es 74 (1898), pp. 121-248 (Bodl Rawlinson B. 490, ff. 28v-72).

559 In ure lauerdes luue þe feader is of frumscheft ant iþe deore wurðmunt of his deorewurðe sune ant iþe heiunge of þe hali gast þe of ham be glideð (from 2)

Þe Liflade ant te Passiun of Seinte Juliene, saint's life, s. xiii in.

1. EETS os 51 (1872), even pages (BL Royal 17 A.xxvii, ff. 56-70); 2. EETS os 51 (1872), odd pages (Bodl Bodley 34, ff. 36v-52); 3. ed. S.R.T.O. d'Ardenne (1936), even pages (as in 1); 4. ed. S.R.T.O. d'Ardenne (1936), odd pages (as in 2); 5. EETS os 248 (1961), even pages (as in 1); 6. EETS os 248 (1961), odd pages (as in 2); 7. ed. K. Sperk, Medieval English Saints' Legends (1970), pp. 21-40 (as in 2); 8. d'Ardenne (1977), pp. 94-127 (as in 2).

For verse versions see IMEV 2951 and 2952.

In primis pro oculis Aqua facialis preciosa dicta   See 23.

In Principio Veteris Rhetorice scribit tulius . . . Tulius þ gret orature of rome in þ begynnyng of his rethoric writis þat Eloquens without wissdome js richt dangerus   Incipit to introduction to 565.

560 In rome bethe ijc paresche churchs & vij & xc chapellis and v The Cytty his about þe wallys xlij myllys and ouer them byn ijc & lx tourris

The Stacyons of Rome, description of Roman churches, s. xv.

1. EETS os 25 (1867), pp. 30-34 (Aberystwyth NLW Porkington 10, ff. 132-36v).

127

For a verse version see IMEV 1962.

361   In the autentyke and noble cyte of Anthyoche in the partyes of Syrye
       was somtyme a myghty kynge the whych hadde to name Anthiogus

       Robert Copland, Kynge Apollyn of Thyre, romance translated
       from French, s. xvi in.

       1. W. de Worde, 1510 (STC 708.5); 2. ed. E.W. Ashbee (1870)
       (facsimile of 1).

362   In the begynnynge and endynge of all good werkes worshyp and
       thankynge be to almyghty god maker and byer of al mankynde

       [Richard Rolle], Contemplacyons of the Drede and Love of
       God/Fervor Amoris, epistle for lay readers, s. xiv (2).

       1. W. de Worde, 1506 (STC 21259); 2. W. de Worde, [1519?]
       (STC 21260); 3. YW, II (1896), 71-205 (as in 1).

       Also in TCC B.15.39-40, CUL Ii.6.40, CUL Addl. 6686,
       Durham University Cosin V.IV.6, BL Arundel 197, BL Harley
       1706 (with last chapter repeated in a different hand), BL Harley
       2409, BL Royal 17 A.xxv, BL Sloane 1859, Maidstone Corpora-
       tion Museum Mus. 6, New York Morgan M 861, Bodl Ashmole
       1286, Bodl Bodley 423, Philadelphia University of Pennsylvania
       English 2, Philadelphia University of Pennsylvania English 8,
       San Marino Huntington HM 127. Jolliffe H.15.

363   In the begynnyng of all werkes men oughten first of alle to calle the
       name of the creatour of all Creatures (from 2)

       Noble Hystorye of Melusyne, romance translated from French,
       ca. 1500.

       1. [W. de Worde, 1510] (STC 14648), fragment; 2. EETS es 68
       (1895) (BL Royal 18 B.ii, ff. 1-219v).

       In þe bisshoperiche of Leody in a toun þat is callid Niuelle þere was a
       ʒonge mayden in lyfe & name gloryous þe whiche highte Mary   Inci-
       pit to text proper of 853.

364   In the cyte of Room ben iiic parysch churchis Off the which vii ben

previlegid above all other and thaye be of more pardon and holynesse

An advertisement of Rome, s. xv.

1. MP, 20 (1923), 411 (BL Addl. 35298, ff. 65-66v).

6

In the cite of Seene in Italye and of the prouynce of Tuskane ther was a
man his name was James or Jacob   Incipit to text proper of **96**.

365 In the day of the coronacion of the kyng ther was grete sleyng of Jewes
of all tho that myght be founde bothe with Iron and fire

Chronicle of London beginning in 1189 and originally ending in
the reign of Henry IV, s. xv in.

A. "Great Chronicle of London" in two parts to 1496 (to 1439:
s. xv med.; 1439-96: s. xv/xvi): 1. ed. A.H. Thomas and
I.D. Thornley (1938), pp. 1-273 (London Guildhall 3313, ff.
1-245, 247-51v, with later additions to 1512 by Robert Fabian).

7

B. Chronicle to 1483 (s. xv ex.): 1. ed. N.H. Nicolas and E.
Tyrrell (1827) (BL Harley 565, supplemented by BL Cotton Julius
B. I).

C. Chronicle to 1470 erroneously attributed to William Gregory
(s. xv [2]): 1. Camden Soc., n.s. 17 (1876), pp. 57-239 (BL
Egerton 1995, ff. 113-222).

D. Chronicle to 1465 (ca. 1465): 1. Camden Soc., n.s. 28
(1880), pp. 31-80 (Lambeth Palace 306).

E. Chronicle to 1432 (ca. 1435): 1. Kingsford, Chronicles
(1905), pp. 1-116 (BL Cotton Julius B. II, ff. 4-101).

F. Fragmentary chronicle from 1414-43 (s. xv med.): 1. Kingsford, Chronicles (1905), pp. 117-52 (BL Cotton Cleopatra C.
IV, ff. 22-61v, beginning and ending imperfectly).

G. Abbreviated chronicle by Richard Arnold (s. xv ex.): 1. [A.
van Berghen, 1503?] (STC 782); 2. [P. Treveris, 1521] (STC
783); 3. ed. F. Douce, The Customs of London (1811) (as in 1).

London chronicles also in TCC O.9.1, CUL Hh.6.9, Chicago
University 254, TCD 509, former Eshton Hall MS, Hatfield
House Marquis of Salisbury 281, BL Cotton Vespasian A. XXV,
BL Cotton Vitellius A. XVI, BL Cotton Vitellius F. IX, BL

A Latin translation in Bodl e Mus. 86 (ed. W.W. Shirley as Fasciculi Zizaniorum, Rolls 5, 1858, p. 319).

372   In the name of God and of oure ladi and Job iii pater noster and iii aueʒ

Charm for parasites, s. xv.

1. Chaucer and Middle English Studies (1974), p. 65 (BL Royal 17 A.xxxii, f. 127v).

In the name of God I Henry of Lancastre chalenge this reiaume
Incipit to edition 4 of **369**.

373   In the name of god pitos & merciable seide [leyk] the largere þat thow makest this instrument the largere ben thi chef deuisiouns

Geoffrey Chaucer (?), "The Equatorie of the Planetis", astrono-mical treatise, ca. 1392.

1. ed. D.J. Price (1955) (Cambridge Peterhouse 75, ff. 71v-78v); 2. Fisher (1977), pp. 938-48 (as in 1).

In the name off the blissed trinite in whom at alle tymes I putt my dispocicioun and werkes I intende to transpose and for myne owne lernynge a trettesse from latyn into englysche   Preface to **846**.

In the name of the fadre . . . And of the soone . . . And of the holy
ghoost   See **514**.

374   In the noble lande of Surrye ther was a noble kyng and myghty & a man of grete renoun þat me called Dyoclician þat wel and worthily hym gouernede

Brut, chronicle of England originally ending in 1333, translated from Anglo-Norman, s. xiv ex.

A. Original version, with continuations to 1479: 1. EETS os 131 (1906) and 136 (1908) (Bodl Rawlinson B. 171, supplemented by fifteen other MSS).

B. Cronycullys of Englonde, abridged version (ca. 1465): 1. Camden Soc., n.s. 28 (1880), pp. 1-28 (Lambeth Palace 306, ff. 1 ff.).

C. Chronicles of England, based largely on the Brut down to 1461, with additions by William Caxton (?) (ca. 1480): 1. W. Caxton, 1480 (STC 9991, Part 1), with brief prologue by Caxton; 2. W. Caxton, 1482 (STC 9992), with prologue as in 1: 3. [W. de Machlinia, 1486] (STC 9993); 4. G. de Leeu, 1493 (STC 9994).

D. Chronicles of Englonde, the Brut with interpolations on ecclesiastical history (s. xv ex.): 1. St. Albans Printer, [1485] (STC 9995); 2. W. de Worde, 1497 (STC 9996, Part 1); 3. W. de Worde, 1502 (STC 9997, Part 1); 4. J. Notary, 1504 (STC 9998, Part 1); 5. R. Pynson, 1510 (STC 9999, Part 1); 6. J. Notary, 1515 (STC 10000, Part 1); 7. W. de Worde, 1515 (STC 9985, Part 1; 10000.5); 8. W. de Worde, 1520 (STC 10001, Part 1); 9. W. de Worde, 1528 (STC 10002, Part 1).

Also in Aberystwyth NLW Peniarth 343A, Aberystwyth NLW Peniarth 396D, Aberystwyth NLW Peniarth 397C, Aberystwyth NLW Peniarth 398D, Aberystwyth NLW Addl. 442D, Alnwick Castle Duke of Northumberland 457A, Ann Arbor University of Michigan 225, Bethlehem (Pennsylvania) Lehigh University MS (fragments), Brussels Bibl. Royale IV.461, CCCC 174, CCCC 182, Cambridge Fitzwilliam Museum Bradfer-Lawrence Deposit 11, Cambridge Fitzwilliam Museum McClean 186, Cambridge Peterhouse 190, TCC O.9.1, TCC O.10.34, TCC O.11.11, TCC R.5.43, CUL Ee.4.31-Ee.4.32, CUL Ff.1.6, CUL Ff.2.26, CUL Hh.6.9, CUL Kk.1.3, CUL Kk.1.12, CUL Ll.2.14, CUL Addl. 2775, Cambridge (Mass.) Harvard University English 530, Cambridge Harvard University English 587, Cambridge Harvard University English 750, Cambridge Harvard University English 938, Cambridge Harvard University Richardson 35, Chapel Hill Robert G. Heyneman MS, Charlottesville University of Virginia 38-173, Chicago University 253-254, Cleveland Public Library W q091.92-C468, TCD 489-490, TCD 505-506, TCD 5895, Edinburgh NLS 6128, Edinburgh University 184-185, Glasgow University Hunterian 61, Glasgow University Hunterian 74, Glasgow University Hunterian 83, Glasgow University Hunterian 228, Glasgow University Hunterian 230, Glasgow University Hunterian 443, Hamburg Staats- und Universitätsbibliothek Cod. 98 in scrin., Holkham Hall Earl of Leicester 669-670, Leicester University 47, Lincoln Cathedral 70, Lincoln Cathedral 98, BL Cotton Claudius A. VIII, BL Cotton Galba E. VIII, BL Egerton 650, BL Harley 24, BL Harley 53, BL Harley 63, BL Harley 266, BL Harley 753, BL Harley 1337, BL Harley 1568, BL Harley 2182, BL Harley 2248, BL Harley 2256, BL Harley 2279, BL Harley 3730, BL Harley

3945, BL Harley 4690, BL Harley 4827, BL Harley 4930, BL Harley 6251, BL Harley 7333, BL Royal 17 D.xxi, BL Royal 18 A.ix, BL Royal 18 B.iii-18 B.iv, BL Sloane 2027, BL Stowe 68-71, BL Welbeck Abbey Duke of Portland 29/331, BL Addl. 12030, BL Addl. 24859, BL Addl. 26746, London College of Arms Arundel 8, London College of Arms Arundel 58, London College of Arms Vincent 421, London Inner Temple Petyt 511 Vol. 11, Lambeth Palace 6, Lambeth Palace 84, Lambeth Palace 259, Lambeth Palace 264, Lambeth Palace 331, Lambeth Palace 491, Lambeth Palace 738, London Sion College Arc. L.40.2/E.42, London Society of Antiquaries 93, London Society of Antiquaries 223, Manchester Rylands English 102-105, Manchester Rylands English 206-207, New Haven Yale University 323, New Haven Yale University 494, New York Columbia University Plimpton 261-262, New York Mrs. J.D. Gordan 63, Nottingham Nottinghamshire County Council DDFS 3/1, Bodl Ashmole 791, Bodl Ashmole 793, Bodl Bodley 231, Bodl Bodley 754, Bodl Bodley 840, Bodl Digby 185, Bodl Digby 196, Bodl Douce 290, Bodl Douce 323, Bodl e Mus. 39, Bodl Hatton 50, Bodl Laud Miscellaneous 550, Bodl Laud Miscellaneous 571, Bodl Laud Miscellaneous 733, Bodl Lyell 34, Bodl Rawlinson B. 166, Bodl Rawlinson B. 173, Bodl Rawlinson B. 187, Bodl Rawlinson B. 190, Bodl Rawlinson B. 196, Bodl Rawlinson B. 205, Bodl Rawlinson B. 216, Bodl Rawlinson C. 155, Bodl Rawlinson poet. 32, Bodl Tanner 11, Bodl Tanner 188, Oxford Jesus 5, Oxford Lincoln Lat. 151, Oxford Trinity 5, Oxford University 154, Paris BN anglais 30, Philadelphia Free Library Lewis 238, Princeton Robert H. Taylor MS, Princeton University Garrett 150, San Marino Huntington HM 113, San Marino Huntington HM 131, San Marino Huntington HM 133, San Marino Huntington HM 136, Sydney University Nicholson 13, Tokyo Takamiya 12, Tokyo Takamiya 18, Tokyo Takamiya 29, University Park Pennsylvania State University 3A, Urbana University of Illinois 82, Urbana University of Illinois 116, Victoria (Australia) Geelong Church of England Grammar School MS, Washington Folger 725.2, Washington Folger 1232-3, Woburn Abbey Duke of Bedford 18. BL Addl. 10099 is a copy of Caxton's copytext for edition C.1.

In the noble londe of Surrye was some tyme a greate kynge and a myghty that was named Dioclesyan and he was the moste worthiest kynge than levinge on erthe   Incipit to version B of 374.

In þe prouince of Leody bisyde a famous abbey of Nunnys of Cistens ordir þat is callyd Herkenrode   Incipit to text proper of 78.

375 Inn the tenthe yere of my sorowfull exile aftir many troubles and aftir
many mortale perillis and the daungers which I haue passid vnto this
tyme thankid be Allmyghty God (from 2)

"The Treatise of Hope", translation of Alain Chartier's Le Traité
de l'esperance (1428), s. xv (1).

1. Clermont (1869), I, 483-90 (BL Cotton Vitellius E. IX, ff.
176-81v, beginning and ending imperfectly); 2. EETS os 270
(1974), pp. 3-132 (Bodl Rawlinson A. 338, ff. 33v-111).

Also in Cambridge St. John's 76, Chicago Newberry f. 36 Ry.
20, London Sion College Arc. L.40.2/E.43.

376 In þe þursday aftur þe closyng of Eestur In þe ȝere regnyng of oure kyng
Harry þe sixte þe ix ȝere at Abyndon in þe Counte of Berkes

Nicholas Bishop, historical notes on the Short Metrical Chronicle
(IMEV 1105), s. xv.

1. PMLA, 49 (1934), 457-59 (CUL Dd.14.2, ff. 286-90).

377 In the tyme of kynge Charles of Fraunce the yere of our lord Ihesu
Cryst M CC lxxj was in the londe of vyennoys a ryche baron daulphyn
and lord of the lond that was named syr Godefroy

William Caxton, Th' Ystorye of the Noble and Valyaunt Knyght
Parys and the Fayr Vyenne, ("Paris and Vienne"), romance
translated from French, 1485.

1. W. Caxton, 1485 (STC 19206); 2. G. Leeu, 1492 (STC
19207); 3. [W. de Worde, ca. 1505] (STC 19207a); 4. [W. de
Worde, ca. 1505] (STC 19208); 5. ed. W.C. Hazlitt, Roxburghe (1868) (as in 1); 6. Kentfield/Allen (1956) (as in 1); 7.
EETS os 234 (1957) (as in 1).

378 In the tyme of the full worthi Josue as the story reherceth by þe writing
of þe noble clerke Boas that King Alphioun founded and first bigan

Sege of Thebes, romance, ca. 1450.

1. Archiv, 130 (1913), 47-52, 268-72 (Bodl Rawlinson D. 82,
ff. 1-10v).

379   In the tyme that Alexander was born it is red so as the histories berith
       witnes that the nyght tended to the more part of the day

       Parva Recaputalio of Alexander the Great, s. xv.

       1. N&Q, 27 (1980), 16-18 (Worcester Cathedral F. 172, ff.
       146v-48).

380   Yn the tym that the kynge henry þat was the kynges fadyr Richard &
       the kynges fadyr Iohn regned in englaund well & heighe man in Irland
       þat het dermod Macmorgh (from 2)

       Of the Conqueste of Irland by Englysh Men, translation based on
       the Expugnacio Hibernica of Giraldus Cambrensis (1166-85), s.
       xv in. (?).

       1. ed. J.S. Brewer and W. Bullen, Calendar of the Carew
       Manuscripts, 5 (1871), 261-317 (Lambeth Palace 598, ff. 1-31);
       2. EETS os 107 (1896), even pages (TCD 592, ff. 1-27v); 3.
       EETS os 107 (1896), odd pages (Bodl Rawlinson B. 490, ff. 1-
       28); 4. ed. W. Heuser, Die Kildare-Gedichte (1904), pp. 221-
       22, extract (Bodl Laud Miscellaneous 526, last leaf).

       Also in TCD 593. A later translation (16th c.) is in the Book of
       Howth (Lambeth Palace 623).

381   In þe xx ȝere of Kyng Edward þe þridde Abbot Thomas Cudelyngton
       Abbot of Oseney by a chanon of hys oon sire Andrew Colesbourne

       Nicholas Bishop, De Diversis Querelis, a memoir of alleged
       wrongs committed by the Abbot of Oseney, s. xv.

       1. PMLA, 49 (1934), 453-56 (CUL Dd.14.2, ff. 32v-35v).

382   In the west ende of grete Britayn whiche now is callyd Englond is a
       prouynce whiche is named walys This said prouynce was somtyme
       inhabyted of sayntes

       William Caxton, Lyf of the Holy and Blessid Vyrgyn Saynt
       Wenefryde, translation from the Latin of Robertus, Prior of
       Shrewsbury, followed by Latin prayers to St. Winifred, ca.
       1485.

       1. W. Caxton, 1485? (STC 25853); 2. Anglia, 3 (1880), 295-
       313 (Lambeth Palace 306, ff. 188-201v, which is a copy of 1

bound into the MS).

Another ME prose version in BL Addl. 35298, where it is unique to this MS of the Gilte Legende.

383   In the yere and date aforesaid the King and the Quene coming owt of the Whyt hall to Westmester hall unto the King's benche all upon red clothe

Coronacion of King Rychard the IIIde & Quene Anne (1483), s. xv ex.

1. Bentley (1833), pp. 379-83 (BL Harley 2115).

Also in London College of Arms I.18.

384   In ye ȝere arn xxxij perlouse dais in qwich if a man falle seke he xalle not liue

Introduction to a list of perilous days, s. xv (1).

1. Hanna (1984), p. 38 (San Marino Huntington HM 1336, f. 35r-v).

Cf. 723.

In the yere of grace 1471 aftar the comptinge of the churche of England the ij day of Marche endynge the x yere of the reigne of our soveraign Lord   Incipit to version B of 602.

385   In the yere of oure Lord a M thre honderd lxxj as I was in a gardyn vnder a shadowe as it were in thyssue of Aprylle all moornyng and pensyf But a lytel I reioysed me in the sowne and songe of the fowles sauuage

William Caxton, Book Which the Knyght of the Toure Made, instructions for women translated from the French of Geoffrey de la Tour Landry, 1483.

1. W. Caxton, 1484 (STC 15296); 2. EETS ss 2 (1971) (as in 1).

Cf. 387.

137

386 In the yere of thyncarnacion of our lord Ihesu crist M CCCC lxxx And
in the xx yere of the Regne of kyng Edward the fourthe Atte request of
dyuerce gentilmen

William Caxton, brief prologue to Cronicles of Englond (version
C of 374), ca. 1480.

1. W. Caxton, 1480 (STC 9991, Part 1); 2. W. Caxton, 1482
(STC 9992); 3. Lewis (1737), p. 28 (as in 1); 4. Ames (1749),
p. 20 (as in 1); 5. Herbert, I (1785), 26 (as in 1); 6. Blades,
Life, II (1863), 109 (as in 1), 120 (as in 2); 7. Blades,
Biography (1887), pp. 245-46 (as in 1); 8. Blades, Biography,
2nd ed. (1882), p. 247 (as in 1); 9. Blake, COP (1973), pp. 68-
69 (as in 1).

387 In the yere of the incarnacion of oure lord Mle iiijc lxxj as y was in a
gardin al heui and fulle of thought in the shadow about the ende of the
month of Aprille

"Book of the Knight of La Tour Landry", instructions for women
translated from the French of Geoffrey de la Tour Landry, s. xv
med.

1. EETS os 33 (1868) (BL Harley 1764, ff. 1-54v, supplemented
by Caxton's translation); 2. EETS os 33, rev. ed. (1906) (as in
1).

Cf. 385.

In this abbaye Charyte shall be Abbesse Wysdome Pryouresse Mekenes
suppryouresse And thyse ben in the Couent   Incipit to editions 1-3
of 590.

In this begynnyng so wyl I writte of the xv Tokens they whiche shullen
be shewed afore the drefull daye off dome of our lorde Ihesu criste
Brief introduction to 65 (edition 1 only).

In þis book he techyt for to knowe þe planete seknesse lyf and deth and
þe times þer of First seyth ypocras þat a leche xal take kep of þe mone
wanne he is atte þe full   Preface to 629.

In this booke is Conteyned the names of þe baylifs Custos mairs and
sherefs of the cite of london from the tyme of king richard the furst and

138

als thartycles of the Chartur and liberties of the same Cyte   Incipit
to version G of 365.

388   In this historye ben wreton the parables goode lerynge and dyuerse
       poyntes to be merkyd by whiche poyntes men maye lerne to come to the
       subtyl knoweleche of suche thynges as dayly ben vsed

       William Caxton, Historye of Reynard the Fox, translated from
       Dutch, 1481.

       1. W. Caxton, 1481? (STC 20919); 2. W. Caxton, 1489? (STC
       20920) (as in 1); 3. [R. Pynson, 1494] (STC 20921) (as in 1); 4.
       [R. Pynson, ante 1506] (STC 20921.5) (as in 1); 5. [W. de
       Worde, ca. 1525] (STC 20921a) (as in 1); 6. T. Gaultier, 1550
       (STC 20922) (as in 1); 7. anonymous edition (1560?, 1586?) (as
       in 1); 8. ed. W.J. Thoms (1844) (as in 1); 9. ed. E. Arber
       (1878) (as in 1); 10. ed. E. Goldsmid (1884) (as in 1); 11. ed.
       H.H. Sparling (1892) (as in 1); 12 The Booke of Raynarde the
       Foxe (1969) (as in 6); 13. EETS os 263 (1970) (as in 1); 14. ed.
       J.A.W. Bennett (1976) (facsimile of 2).

       Many modernizations beginning in the seventeenth century and
       continuing into the twentieth. For edition 7 and two possible
       Wynkyn de Worde editions before 1525 see K. Varty, "The
       Earliest Illustrated Editions of 'Reynard the Fox'" in J. Goossens
       and T. Sodmann, eds., Reynaert, Reynard, Reynke (1980), pp.
       160-95.

       In this tretyce that is cleped Gouernayle of helthe What is to be sayd
       wyth crystis helpe of some thynges that longen to bodily helthe
       Incipit to brief preface to 407.

389   In two dayes 6 howris and 40 minutis the mone gothe thorowe a signe
       and euery signe gothe 30 degres

       Notes on the zodiac, s. xv ex.

       1. Hanna (1984), p. 3 (San Marino Huntington HM 64, f. 17v).

390   In as moche as it is straytly commaundyd by the Constitucionus
       Prouynciall that euery man hauynge Cure and charge of mannys soule
       shall iiij tymes in the yere declare and shewe

       Articles of Oure Fayth, translated from Latin by a doctor of divinity, s. xv ex. (?).

1. R. Pynson, [1520?] (STC 3359).

390.5 Induite vos armatura Dei . . . Þes beÞ Þe wordys of seynt Paule Þe
apostel Þat beÞ nedeful to every Crysten man to understande and to
note hem in werke

Milicia Christi, amplified translation of Pseudo-Anselm, Simili-
tudo Militis, s. xv in.

1. Journal of the Warburg and Courtauld Institutes, 45 (1982),
47-68 (BL Arundel 286, ff. 20-81v).

Also in BL Egerton 842 (fragment); Jolliffe H.33.

391 In so much that gentill men and honest persones haue greete delite in
haukyng and desire to haue the maner to take haukys

[Juliana Berners], Booke of Hawkyng, treatise on hawking, s. xv
(2).

1. [St. Albans Printer, 1486] (STC 3308); 2. W. de Worde,
1496 (STC 3309); 3. H. Tab, 1540 (STC 3310), without preface; 4. J. Waley, [1550?] (STC 3316), without preface; 5. W.
Copland, [1561] (STC 3312), without preface; 6. A. Vele,
[1563?] (STC 3311), without preface; 7. E. Allde, 1586 (STC
3313), without preface; 8. A. Islip, 1596 (STC 3315), without
preface; 9. Haslewood (1810-11) (facsimile of 2); 10. Blades,
Boke (1881, 1905) (facsimile of 1); 11. (1966) (facsimile of 2);
12. (1969) (facsimile of 1); 13. Hawking (1972) (facsimile of 8);
14. ed. R. Hands, English Hunting and Hawking (1975), pp. 3-
55 (facsimile of 1).

Part of what is later called the Boke of St. Albans. The author
probably made use of both 194 and 741.

[I]n so myche that it is necessari to all creaturis of criston religyon or of
fals religyon os gentyles and machomytes to knaw theer prince or
prynces that regne a pon them   Incipit to version D of 374.

Instauntly required vii yeres ago to translate this holy rule of saynt
Augustyne out of the latyn in to englysshe   Incipit to preface added
to edition B.2 of 268.

392 Ipse Ihesus apropinquans ibat cum illis Thyse wordes ben conteyned in the xxiiij chapytre of Luke and rad in the holy gospel of this day To say in englyssh tonge The same Ihesus nyghynge walkyd with mankynde

Richard FitzJames, Sermo Die Lune in Ebdomada Pasche, sermon, s. xv ex.

1. W. de Worde, [1495?] (STC 11024).

393 Ysodor seyth be auctoryte of Ypocras þat þer arn iii dayes no man owyth to be lete blood

"Directions for Bloodletting", s. xv (2).

1. Louis (1980), pp. 157-61 (Bodl Tanner 407, ff. 11v-13).

See IMEV 3848 for a verse version.

394 Hit befel in the dayes of Vther pendragon when he was kynge of all Englond and so regned that there was a myȝty duke in Cornewaill that helde warre ageynst hym long tyme

Thomas Malory, Le Morte d'Arthur, romance based on the life of King Arthur, 1469-70.

1. W. Caxton, 1485 (STC 801); 2. W. de Worde, 1498 (STC 802); 3. W. de Worde, 1529 (STC 803), beginning imperfectly; 4. W. Copland, [1557] (STC 804); 5. T. East, 1578 (STC 805); 6. Southey (1817) (as in 1 supplemented by 2); 7. Sommer, I (1889) (as in 1); 8. Mott (1933) (as in 2); 9. Vinaver, Works (1947) (BL Addl. 59678); 10. Vinaver, Malory (1954) (as in 9); 11. Vinaver, Works, 2nd ed. (1967) (as in 9); 12. Vinaver, Malory, 2nd ed. (1971) (as in 9); 13. Needham (1976) (facsimile of 1); 14. Spisak and Matthews (1983) (as in 1).

Often modernized in the nineteenth and twentieth centuries.

395 It befell in the xix yere of þe Synorye of Cybarye cesarye Emperour of Rome And in þe synorye of herodis that was þe sone of herodys whiche was kynge of Galyce

Treatys of Nycodemus Gospell, translation from French, s. xv ex. (?).

1. J. Notary, 1507 (STC 18565); 2. W. de Worde, 1509 (STC

18566); 3. W. de Worde, 1511 (STC 18567); 4. W. de Worde, 1512 (STC 18567a); 5. W. de Worde, 1518 (STC 18568); 6. J. Skot, 1529 (STC 18569); 7. W. de Worde, 1532 (STC 18570); 8. J. Skot, [1537?] (STC 18570a); 9. J. Wilson, 1767; 10. W. Garrett, 1775 (?).

For other translations see 397.

396   It befel in tyme past that there was a duke in normandye whiche was called ouberte the whiche duke was passynge ryche of goodes and also vertuous of lyuynge

Lyfe of Robert the Devyll, romance, s. xv.

1. W. de Worde, [1500?] (STC 21070); 2. [R. Pynson?, 1510?] (STC 21071.5); 3. W. de Worde, [1517?] (STC 21071); 4. Thoms (1828), I, 3-56 (as in 1); 5. Thoms, 2nd ed. (1858), I, 3-56 (as in 1); 6. Morley (1889), pp. 169-206 (as in 1); 7. Thoms, enlarged ed. (1906, 1907), pp. 169-206 (as in 1).

Itt fallethe ofte tymes that a deuoute man louethe another deuout man or ellys a deuoute woman in good honeste loue   Incipit to edition 4 of 677.

397   Yt felle yn the xvth yere that Thybery Cesar had ben emperoure of Roome and yn the xixth yere of Herode sone to Herode whych was kynge of Galylee

Nichodemus His Gospell, translation from French sources, s. xv (2).

1. ed. B. Lindström (1974) (BL Harley 149, ff. 255-76).

For another translation see 395. There are six other prose translations in thirteen MSS: (1) BL Egerton 2658, Manchester Rylands English 895, Bodl Bodley 207, Stonyhurst College B.xliii, (2) Cambridge Magdalene Pepys 2498, Leeds University Brotherton 501, San Marino Huntington HM 144; (3) by Trevisa, BL Addl. 16165, Salisbury Cathedral 39, Winchester College 33; (4) CUL Mm.1.29; (5) Washington Library of Congress 4; (6) Worcester Cathedral F. 172. For another translation see 396. For verse translations see IMEV 130 and 512; for an OE prose translation see Ker 20, 209, 215.

It is convenient and reson requireth that every Prince estate or greete lord have and will observe III profitable consideracions   Incipit to text proper of 136.7.

Hit is good to schriuen to vre lord and singen to þi name þou allerhiȝest See 115.5.

It is not lyght for euery man to drawe eny longe thyng from latyn in to oure Englyshe tongue   Incipit to second prologue to 798.

398   Hyt is ofte sene þat lewed men quich ben of mony wordes and prowde of hor wytt will aske prestis diuerse questions of thyngis þat towchen þer seruice of Holy Church

John Mirk (?), Deus Expediat Me, a tract on the liturgy for Maundy Thursday and Holy Saturday for the use of parish priests inserted in the Festivall, s. xv in.

1. Speculum, 11 (1936), 225-30 (BL Harley 2250, f. 85r-v).

For other MSS and editions of the Festivall see 734.

399   It is ordeined and decreed by holy chyrche that euery Curate hauynge cure of Soule shall shewe and declare vnto his parysshen Foure tymes in the yere the xiiii artycles of the fayhte (from 2)

Exornatorium Curatorum, translation of Peckham's Constitutions, s. xv ex. (?).

1. [W. de Worde, 1515?] (STC 10628), beginning and ending imperfectly; 2. J. Notary, 1519 (STC 10629); 3. R. Pynson, [1520?] (STC 10630); 4. W. de Worde, [1520?] (STC 10631); 5. H. Pepwell, [1530?] (STC 10632); 6. [P. Treveris, 1530?] (STC 10633); 7. T. Godfray, [1532?] (STC 10634).

400   Hit is redde in bokes that Evax the kyng of Arabye sente a booke to Nero the Emperour of Rome the whiche tolde hym þe strenkthis and vertues of the stonys and here names & here coloures

Lapidarie, lapidary translated from Anglo-Norman, s. xv.

1. ed. A. Zettersten, A Middle English Lapidary (1968) (Bodl Eng. misc. e. 558, ff. 2-10).

Hit es seyde in the Crede that Athanasie made Quicumque vult Who-so-euer wyl be saue it es nedful be-forne al thynges that be holde the feyth of al-holy chyrche   Incipit to text proper of 6.

401   Hit is seide þat thre þinges stourblen þis reume and specialy heresie þat hafs thre parties bot of blasphemye þat is þo worste is bot litel spoken

"De Blasphemia Contra Fratres", Wycliffite tract, s. xiv (2).

1. SEW, III (1871), 402-29 (Bodl Bodley 647, ff. 37-57v).

402   Hit is so that in many and diuerse places the comyn cronicles of englond ben had and also now late enprinted at Westmynstre

William Caxton, prologue to the Descripcion of Britayne, ca. 1480.

1. W. Caxton, 1480 (STC 13440a, 9991 Part 2); 2. W. de Worde, 1498 (STC 13440b, 9996 Part 2); 3. W. de Worde, 1502 (STC 9997, Part 2); 4. J. Notary, 1504 (STC 9998, part 2); 5. R. Pynson, 1510 (STC 9999, Part 2); 6. J. Notary, 1515 (STC 10000, Part 2); 7. W. de Worde, 1515 (STC 9985, Part 2); 8. W. de Worde, 1520 (STC 10001, Part 2); 9. W. de Worde, 1528 (STC 10002, Part 2); 10. Lewis (1737), p. 40 (as in 1); 11. Ames (1749), p. 20 (as in 1); 12 Herbert, I (1785), 27 (as in 1); 13 Blades, Life, I (1861), 164 (as in 1); 14. Aurner (1926), p. 250 (as in 1); 15. EETS os 176 (1928), p. 40 (as in 1); 16. Blake, COP (1973), p. 72 (as in 1).

See 177.

403   Hyt ys soþ þat beleve is ground of alle vertues and þerfore eche Cristyn man schulde be sad in beleve Þer be þre credys in þe Chirche

Exposition of the Apostles' Creed, Wycliffite tract, s. xiv (2).

1. SEW, III (1871), 114-16 (Lambeth Palace 408, ff. 3v-4v); 2. EETS os 118 (1901), pp. 14-18 (as in 1).

Also in CUL Nn.4.12, TCD 245, Paris Bibl. Ste.-Geneviève 3390, and York Minster XVI.L.12.

404   It is to be knawen to vs dere breþer how þat God in þe begynyng made heuen & erthe & by hym al þinges ar formed & how he made man

144

Of þe Begynyng of þe Warld and of þe Endyng, translation of a work attributed to Methodius, s. xv (1).

1. EETS os 167 (1925), pp. 94-112 (lower halves only) (BL Addl. 37049, ff. 11-16v).

Cf. **221**.

405   Hit is to vnderstonde that in the eclipsis of the sonn and the mone is to knowe wahat party of the body schal be derke

Explanation of a drawing and tables containing eclipses, s. xv ex.

1. Hanna (1984), p. 10 (San Marino Huntington HM 64, f. 12).

It is to vnderstand that ther be three maner of Psalters The fyrste is called Dauid psalter vvhich conteineth thries fifty Psalmes   Incipit to 16th-c. editor's preface to **355**.

406   It is to wite that on peny rounde and withouten tonsure owe to weye xxxij whete cornes in the middes of the ere

"Assize of Bread", s. xv med.

1. Archaeologia, 57 (1900), 59-60 (New York Morgan M 775, ff. 12-13).

It yt [sic] may also be vnderstondyt be the vii moneth of the ȝear be iiii sayssons the qwych ar that ys to wnderstond Prymtym sommer antom [sic] et wynter   Incipit to text proper of **474**.

407   It nedyth hym that woll haue longe lyff to knowe the crafte of holsome gouerneyle And so for to kepe contynuelly the helthe of his body for els he maye not com to his naturell ende

[John Lydgate], Governayle of Helthe, medical and moral treatise translated from Latin, with brief preface, s. xv.

1. W. Caxton, 1489? (STC 12138); 2. W. de Worde, [n.d.] (STC 12139); 3. ed. W. Blades (1858) (as in 1).

Also in BL Harley 2390, BL Sloane 989, BL Sloane 3215, Bodl

Ashmole 1481, Bodl Ashmole 1498. In the three printed editions a <u>Medicina</u> <u>Stomachi</u> in verse, really Lydgate's "Dietary" (<u>IMEV</u> 824), is appended to the <u>Governayle</u>.

408 Hit semes medeful to susteyne prestis to-gedre for so did Crist mayster best of alle But men shulden be war of hom in þese thre poyntis

[Richard Rolle], <u>Epistola</u> <u>ad</u> <u>Simplices</u> <u>Sacerdotes</u>, advice for establishing a religious body, s. xiv.

1. <u>YW</u>, II (1896), 62-63 (BL Royal 17 B.xvii, f. 96v).

409 It was a saul and askyd clennes of saul of our lorde And he sayd to hir Whate-sa þou dose luke I be þi cause

[Richard Rolle], "Sentences", extract from the <u>Documento</u> of St. Catherine of Siena, s. xiv.

1. <u>YW</u>, I (1895), 108 (Bodl Rawlinson C. 285, f. 61r-v).

Also in CUL Ff.5.40. Jolliffe I.7.b. For two other versions see Jolliffe I.7.a and I.7.c.

410 Hit was an holi mon and bi-souȝte god sende him grace such vertues for to vse þat weore best to lyf and to soule

[Richard Rolle], "Points Best Pleasing to God", treatise on the nine virtues, s. xiv (2).

1. <u>YW</u>, I (1895), 110-11 (Bodl Eng. poet. a. 1, f. 333); 2. <u>YW</u>, I (1895), 110-11 (BL Harley 1704, ff. 48v-49).

Also in TCC O.2.53, CUL Dd.11.89, BL Royal 8 F.vii, BL Addl. 22283, BL Addl. 60577, Bodl Douce 141. Jolliffe I.12.e; cf. 256; also cf. 847 (another version of same); for a verse version see <u>IMEV</u> 1188; see Allen, <u>Writings</u> (1927), pp. 317-20 for a discussion and other versions.

411 It was wont to be douted of sum whi tithes bien yeven to holichirche It is in reproef of al wikked and cursed spirites of al the feithful men

"The Origin of Tithe Giving", s. xv.

1. Hulme (1918), pp. 21-22 (Worcester Cathedral F. 172, f.

16r-v).

Item quha þat will say þir prayeris and artickillis efter following euery
Sonday till þe honour of þe haly croun of thorne off our Lord Iesu Crist
Incipit to introduction to **496**.

412   Jakke Carter prayes ȝowe alle that ȝe make a gode ende of that ȝe hane
begunnen and doþ wele and ay bettur and bettur

Jack Carter (John Ball?), address, 1381.

1. Twysden (1652), col. 2637; 2. Rolls 92 (1895), 2, 139 (BL
Cotton Claudius E. III and BL Cotton Tiberius C. VII); 3.
Dobson (1970), p. 382 (as in 2); 4. Dobson, 2nd ed. (1983), p.
382 (as in 2).

413   Iamys þe seruaunt of God and of oure Lord Iesu Criste to þe twelue
kynredis þat beþ spred a-brode gretynge wel My deere breþeren wite
ȝee and hopeþ alle ioye whanne þat ȝe been in many temptacyonus

Catholic Epistles (omitting 2-3 John and Jude), s. xiv.

1. Paues (1904), pp. 209-25 (Bodl Douce 250, ff. 58-77v
passim).

For another version of the Catholic Epistles see the relevant part
of **263**.

414   Janeuere þonder toneth grete wynd and plente of all kyn frute and
battell þat ilke yer Feuerel þonder toneth manes quellyng

Prognostications, s. xv.

1. Archiv, 128 (1912), 287-88 (Bodl Ashmole 342, f. 134r-v).

Ieronimus In the begynnyng of euery werk deuoutly sey the praer of
oure lord the pater noster and enprynte the sygne of the cros   Incipit
to introductory prayer to **6**.

415   Ihesu Criste Goddes sun of heuen kyng of kynges and lorde of lordes mi
lorde and my Godd For þe mekenes of þi clene incarnacione

"A Prayer to Christ", s. xv (?).

1. EETS os 26, rev. ed. (1914), p. 87 (Lincoln Cathedral 91, f. 212).

416   Iesu crist godes sune soð godd and soð mon of þe eadie meiden iboren maria þet is meiden and bute make moder ich of alle sunfulle am on mest ifuled of sunne

"On Lofsong of Ure Loverde", mystical prayer to Christ, s. xiii in.

1. EETS os 34 (1868), pp. 209-17 (odd pages only) (BL Cotton Nero A. xiv, ff. 128-31); 2. EETS os 241 (1958), pp. 10-15 (as in 1).

417   Iesu Christ that was ybore of the mayde Marye haue on thy poore seruauntes mercy and pytie and helpe hem in her gret nede to fight ayenst sine

Prayer and Complaynt of the Ploweman unto Christ, Wycliffite attack on abuses of the church, s. xiv in. (?).

1. [M. de Keyser, 1531?] (STC 20036); 2. [T. Godfrey, ca. 1532] (STC 20036.5); 3. Harleian Miscellany (1744-46), 6, 84-106 (as in 1).

Perhaps first printed before 1531, by W. de Worde, according to Duff (1917), p. 97.

418   Ihesus clamabat Qui habet aures audiendi audiat . . . Thyse Wordes ben wryten in the gospell of this daye And thus to be englysshyd Ihesu our sauyour made a proclamacion with a highe and grete voyce to the people

John Alcock, Bishop of Ely, Sermo on Luke viii, ca. 1497.

1. W. de Worde, [ca. 1497] (STC 284); 2. W. de Worde, [ca. 1498] (STC 285).

Iesu Iesu Iesu Mercy . . . Iesu haue mercy on me & forgiue me   See 355.

Ihesu mercye withdrawe nowe thy rodde of ryghtwysnes beneme
nought thye grace of vnderstandynge for peyne of my synne   Introductory prayer to 658.

418.3 Ihesu my lord ihesu my god ihesu my creature ihesu my sauour ihesu my
blis ihesu my succour ihesu my helpe

Prayer to the name of Jesus, s. xv.

1. ed. F.M.M. Comper, The Life of Richard Rolle (1928), pp.
142-43 (BL Addl. 27948, f. 63).

419 Ihesu soð god godes sone ihesu soð goð soð mon Mon Maidene bern
Ihesu min hali loue min sikere spetnesse Ihesu min heorte Mi sel mi
saule hele

On Wel Swuþe God Ureisun of God Almichti ("On Ureisun of
Ure Loverde"), mystical prayer to Christ, s. xiii in.

1. EETS os 34 (1868), pp. 183-89 (odd pages only) (Lambeth
Palace 487, ff. 65v-67, ending imperfectly); 2. EETS os 34
(1868), pp. 200-3 (BL Cotton Nero A. XIV, ff. 123v-26v); 3.
EETS os 241 (1958), pp. 1-4 (as in 1); 4. EETS os 241 (1958),
pp. 5-9 (as in 2).

420 Ihesu swete ihesu mi druð mi derling mi drihtin mi healend mi huniter
mi haliwei Swetter is munegunge of þe þen mildeu o muðe

Wohunge of Ure Laverd, mystical prayer to Christ, s. xiii in.

1. EETS os 34 (1868), pp. 269-87 (odd pages only) (BL Cotton
Titus D. XVIII, ff. 127-33); 2. EETS os 241 (1958), pp. 20-38
(as in 1); 3. Blake, MERP (1972), pp. 61-72 (as in 1).

421 Jeshu that was in Bedeleme bore and baptyste in flom Jorden and stynte
the water on the stone stynte the blode of this man N

A Charm to Staunche Bloode, s. xv.

1. Rel. Ant., I (1841), 315 (BL Sloane 88).

422 Job lay on a dongehill and in a dongehill he lay and cride vppon oure
lord Jesu Crist ix wormeȝ ete my fflesshe and my blode

149

Charm for worms, s. xv.

1. Chaucer and Middle English Studies (1974), p. 65 (BL Royal 17 A.xxxii, f. 120).

423   Johannes de vetrioto seythe þat þer was som tyme a wicked man in a
       countrey þat lyved be rabeyn and robere

       Exemplum attributed to Jacques de Vitry, s. xv.

       1. NM, 72 (1971), 102-4 (BL Royal 18 B.xxiii, f. 69v).

424   John Alleynys rent furre is a good ȝemen Johannis Aleyn lacerata
       penula est bono effedi

       John Drury, Parve Latinitates de Termino Natalis Domini, par-
       allel English and Latin sentences for instructing schoolboys,
       1434.

       1. Speculum, 9 (1934), 82-83 (CUL Addl. 2830, f. 97r-v).

425   Johon Schep som tyme Seynte Marie prest of ȝork and now of
       Colchestre greteth wel Johan Nameles and Johan the Mullere and Johon
       Cartere

       John Sheep (John Ball?), letter, 1381.

       1. Rolls 28, 2 (1864), 33-34 (London College of Arms Arundel
       7); 2. Rolls 28, 2 (1864), 34 note (BL Royal 13 E.ix, f. 287); 3.
       Rolls 64 (1874), p. 322 (BL Harley 3634); 4. ed. O. Eberhard,
       Der Bauernaufstand vom Jahre 1381 in der englischen Poesie
       (1917), p. 23 (as in 1); 5. Dobson (1970), p. 381 (as in 1); 6.
       Dobson, 2nd ed. (1983), p. 381 (as in 1).

       Modernized versions in R. Holinshed, Chronicles, 3 (1587),
       437b (STC 13569) and J. Stow, Annales (1580-1631; STC
       23333-23338, 23340).

426   . . . Iule shalbe temperate ynough after his nature but about the
       begynnynge shalbe grete raynes and wynde with hayle thonder and
       lyghtnynge and namely about the iii daye

       Prognostication for 1498, translated from a foreign language,
       1497.

1. [W. de Worde, 1497] (STC 385.3, 20414), fragment.

427 Kynge Salomone sais in his buk of his contemplacione and detestacione
of this warld that al this warld is bot vanite of vanite₃

Dicta Salomonis, a paraphrase of Ecclesiastes, s. xv.

1. EETS os 43 (1870), pp. 11-25 (CUL Kk.1.5.6, ff. 5-12); 2.
STS, 3rd series 11 (1939), pp. 177-92 (as in 1).

428 Knowe ₃ee Cristen men that as Crist God and man is bothe weye trewth
and lif as seith the gospel of Jon weye to the errynge trewth to the
unknowyng and doutyng lif to the strynge

A Tretise of Miraclis Pleyinge, Wycliffite sermon, s. xiv ex.

1. Rel. Ant., II (1843), 42-57 (BL Addl. 24202, ff. 14-21); 2.
ed. W.C. Hazlitt, The English Drama and Stage under the Tudor
and Stuart Princes 1543-1664 (1869), pp. 73-95 (as in 1); 3.
Mätzner, I, 2 (1869), 224-42 (as in 1); 4. ed. C. Davidson, A
Middle English Treatise on the Playing of Miracles (1981) (as in
1).

429 Knowest thou not doughter who thou arte and who I am If thou knowe
well thyse two wordes thou arte and shal be blessyd Thou arte she yt
arte nought

Dyvers Doctrynes Devoute and Fruytfull, selected passages from
the Lyf of Saint Katherin of Senis circulating separately, s. xv
ex.

1. H. Pepwell, 1521 (STC 20972, Part 2).

In BL Royal 17 D.v, ff. 59-62. Cf. 96.

Lady ffor thy Ioyes fyve Wysse me the waye of Rightwys lyffe amen
See 479.

430 Laudate pueri dominum . . . Prayse ye children almyghty god as þe
phylosopre sayth in dyuerse places Tho thinges that haue the habite of
perfite cognicion maye moue themselfe and conueye themselfe to theyr
ende

John Alcock, Bishop of Ely, Sermo pro Episcopo Puerorum, sermon, followed by indulgences in Latin granted by Pope John XXII, ca. 1497.

1. [W. de Worde, ca. 1498] (STC 282); 2. [W. de Worde, ca. 1499] (STC 283).

431 Lay þi ballokes in aysell or in cald water and þe blode sall staunche

Charm for stanching blood, s. xv.

1. Chaucer and Middle English Studies (1974), p. 62 (BL Royal 17 A.viii, f. 48v).

432 Legimus in ewangelio mt xii Quia de omni uerbo occioso . . . Mi leue frend wilde wimmen & gol me[n] i mi contereie wan he gon of þe ring among manie oþere songis (from 2)

Sermon using IMEV 445 as its text, s. xiii.

1. Anglia, 42 (1918), 152-54 (TCC B.1.45, ff. 41v-42); 2. Bulletin of the Modern Humanities Research Association, 2 (1928), 106-7 (as in 1).

433 Let alle men be warned þat seruen ʒou and warnyng be ʒeue to alle men that be of howseholde to serue god and ʒou trewly and diligently

Statuta Familie Bone Memorie, translation of household ordinances perhaps written to Robert Grosseteste by Adam de Marisco, s. xv (2).

1. Rolls 4, 1 (1858), 582-86 (BL Sloane 1986, pp. 193-97); 2. EETS os 32 (1868, 1904), pp. 328-31 (as in 1); 3. Lamond (1890), pp. 147-50 (as in 1).

434 Lettyng of blode is to be consydered on 2 wyse On is þat if þe passion of þe sekenes be olde þe blode lettyng schall be on þe same syde þat þe sekenes aperys in

Of Blode Lyttyng, treatise on bloodletting, s. xv (1).

1. Voigts and McVaugh (1984), pp. 54-55 (Cambridge Gonville and Caius 84/166, pp. 205-6).

435   Liberauit nos . . . Crysten peple thier wordis þat I af take to speke of
at this tyem þay er þe wordis of Seynt Powl

Sermons (2), s. xv (?).

1. Grisdale (1939), pp. 22-80 (Worcester Cathedral F. 10, ff. 42-52v).

A third sermon follows on ff. 52v-53v, but it is fragmentary.

Leue frend þese woordys been the woordys of Salomon þe wyse þus
mechil to seyne at зoure vnderstondyng   English incipit to edition 4
of 156.

436   Lincolniensis generaliter describat sic claustralem egressum de claustro
. . . Þere is he seis a deed caryone cropun of his sepulcre wrapped wiþ
clothes of deul and dryven wiþ þe devel for to drecche men

"Lincolniensis", Wycliffite tract, s. xiv ex.

1. SEW, III (1871), 230-32 (Bodl Bodley 647, ff. 62v-63); 2.
Winn (1929), pp. 38-40 (as in 1).

437   Lyne owre holy fadyr pope of Rome he ordeyned thys rewle to all
solytary men that takys the degre of an heremyзte

Thomas Scrope (?), "Rule of St. Linus", translation of a Latin
original (probably s. xiii ex.), s. xv (2).

1. Antonianum, 9 (1954), 263-65 (Lambeth Palace 192, f. 46).

438   Litel Lowys my sonne I perceyue wel by certayne euydences thyn
abilite to lerne sciences touching nombres and proporcions

Geoffrey Chaucer, Tretyse of the Astrolabe, astronomical treatise, ca. 1391.

1. Thynne (1532; STC 5068); 2. Thynne, 2nd ed. (1542; STC
5069); 3. Thynne, 3rd ed. ([1545?]; STC 5071); 4. Stow (1561;
STC 5075); 5. Speght (1598; STC 5077); 6. Speght, 2nd ed.
(1602; STC 5080); 7. Speght, 3rd ed. (1687); 8. Urry (1721);
9. Chalmers (1810); 10. ed. A.E. Brae (1870) (BL Sloane 261,
ff. 6-66, supplemented by BL Sloane 314 and BL Addl. 23002);
11. EETS es 16 (1872) (CUL Dd.3.53, ff. 1-27); 12. Chaucer

Soc., 1st series 29 (1872) (as in 11); 13. Skeat, Complete (1894), 3, 175-232 (as in 11); 14. Ellis (1896); 15. Globe (1898) (Bodl Bodley 619, ff. 1-70v); 16. Lounsbury (1900); 17. Skeat, Complete, 2nd ed. (1900) (as in 11); 18. Thynne (1905) (facsimile of 1); 19. MacCracken, College (1913); 20. Shakespeare Head (1929) (as in 15); 21. Robinson (1933), pp. 641-62 (as in 15); 22. ed. P. Pintelon (1940) (Brussels Bibl. Royale 4862-69, ff. 75-96v); 23. Robinson, 2nd ed. (1957), pp. 545-63 (as in 15); 24. Winterich (1958) (facsimile of 14); 25. Scolar Press (1969) (facsimile of 1); 26. Fisher (1977), pp. 908-34 (as in 11).

Also in Aberdeen University 123, Aberystwyth NLW 3049D, Aberystwyth NLW 3567B, Aberystwyth NLW Peniarth 359, Alnwick Castle Duke of Northumberland 460, CCCC 424, Cambridge St. John's 105, TCC R.15.18, CUL Dd.12.51, Cambridge (Mass.) Harvard University English 920, BL Egerton 2622, BL Addl. 29250, London Institution of Electrical Engineers Thompson 1, New York Columbia University Plimpton 254, New York H.P. Kraus Bute 13, Bodl Ashmole 360, Bodl Ashmole 391, Bodl Ashmole 393, Bodl Bodley 68, Bodl Digby 72, Bodl e Mus. 54, Bodl e Mus. 116, Bodl Rawlinson D. 3, Bodl Rawlinson D. 913, Tokyo Takamiya 9.

Lo bretheren we are comen here before God and his angels and all his halowes   Incipit to edition 4 of 313.

139   Lowe my god I desyre to laude the for I knowe myselfe to be made to laude þe Open my mouth in thy laude þat I may synge Ioye to thi name

Simon Appleby of London Wall, Fruyte of Redempcyon, s. xv ex.

1. W. de Worde, 1514 (STC 22557); 2. W. de Worde, 1517 (STC 22558); 3. W. de Worde, 1530 (STC 11407, 22559); 4. R. Redman, 1531 (STC 22559.5); 5. W. de Worde, 1532 (STC 22560); 6. ed. C. Welch (1912) (facsimile of 1).

Lo sustren I haue schewid ʒou what ympis & trees I haue founde and gaderid to plaunte & sette in ʒoure goostly orcherd   Incipit to original prologue to 561.

139.5 Lo thus is seid of þat Citee in a place There-in is no sorwe heuynesse ne waymentynge what is more blisful than þat lyf is where no dreede is of pouerte

Thomas Hoccleve, conclusion to <u>Ars Utilissima Sciendi Mori</u> (IMEV 3121), translated from the Ninth Lesson for All Saints' Day from the <u>Sarum Breviary</u>, ca. 1422.

1. EETS es 61 (1892), pp. 213-15 (Durham University Cosin V.III.9, ff. 75-77); 2. EETS es 61, rev. ed. (1970), pp. 213-15 (as in 1).

Also in Coventry Corporation Record Office MS, BL Harley 172, BL Royal 17 D.vi, Bodl Bodley 221, Bodl Laud Miscellaneous 735, Bodl Selden Supra 53, San Marino Huntington HM 144.

Lord as thou made me of noʒt J be seche the ʒeue me grace to serue the with alle my herte   Incipit to edition B.3 of **618**.

440 Lord als wissely as þis is þe first corne þat god let sow and setten on erthe

Charm to protect a horse from diseases, s. xv.

1. <u>Chaucer and Middle English Studies</u> (1974), p. 64 (BL Sloane 962, f. 135).

441 Lord be Thou pleased with the prayeres of thy Cherche and graunte that alle erroures and adversities be destroyed that thy Cherche mowe serve to Thee in siker pees

<u>Orisone Ecclesie Tue</u>, prayer, s. xv.

1. Coxe (1840), pp. 27-28 (Bodl Douce 246, f. 57).

Lord god graunte us helpe of tribulacion To þe soule þat art distroublid and temptid to þe is purposed þat þou schalt lerne wherof tribulacions seruen   See **142**.

442 Lord haue mercy on vs crist haue mercy on vs ande graunt vs strength of soule inwarde and outwarde that we may serue the to the pleasure of thi wyll (from 3)

<u>The Golden Letany off the Lyeff and Passion of Cryste</u>, s. xv.

1. R. Copland, 1531 (STC 15707); 2. J. Skot, [1536?] (STC

15707.5); 3. Maskell (1846), II, 244-54 (Lambeth Palace 546, ff. 29-52); 4. Maskell, 2nd ed. (1882), III, 263-74 (as in 1); 5. Trans. of the Royal Society of Literature, 27 (1905), 124-33 (Bodl Douce 42); 6. STS, 3rd series 23 (1955), 205-12 (BL Arundel 285, f. 116v-25).

Frequently found in early printed editions of Horae and the Primer.

Lord I bitake in to thine hondes and in to thine hondis of thine halwen in this nyght   See 352.

Lauerd seið godes spuse to hire deore wurðe spus   See 559.

Lord þat madist me of nouȝt I biseche þee to ȝeue me grace to serue þe wiþ al myn herte wiþ al my myȝt wiþ al my strenkþe   Incipit to edition B.1 of 618.

Lord thou schalt opyne myn lippis And my mouth schal schewe thi prisyng   See 157.

443   Loys by the grace of god kyng of Fraunce Vnto alle theym that thies present lettres shall see gretyng Be it knowen that betwene the most Cristen Prynce the kyng of Fraunce aforeseyd and the most noble Prince the Kyng of England hys moost dere cousyn true entier and perfite amyte ys couenaunted

Documents of King Louis of France, including Promisse of Matrimonie, Lettre of Annuelle Port, Obligacion of Nisi, and Articles, 1475.

1. [W. de Machlinia, 1485?] (STC 9176).

444   Lucifer lord and prince of the depe donion of derkenes rewlour of the regne of the infernall empyre kyng of the contre of cumbryd

Lettre of the Infernall Emperour Lucifer, translation of Peter Ceffons' Epistola Luciferi (1352), attack on the clergy, s. xiv (2).

1. Medieval Literature and Civilization, ed. D.A. Pearsall and R.A. Waldron (1969), pp. 235-47 (San Marino Huntington HM

114, ff. 319-25).

Cf. 587.

445　Make a bag of twede thick sewed and take a quantite of groute malte

A Bate fir Tenches or All Maner Flote Fish, recipes for catching fish, s. xv.

1. Braekman (1980), p. 32 (BL Sloane 1201, f. 3).

446　Mak lye of verueyne of betayne and of werwod and wassh þi hed thries in þe woke

Medicynis, medical recipes (76), s. xiv.

1. Henslow (1899), pp. 105-20 (BL Harley 2378, ff. 229-96 passim).

Cf. 447 and 647.

447　Make þer for lye of verveyne or ellys of betenye ether of wormod and þer with wasshe thyne hede thrise in þe weke

Leechbook (1074 recipes), s. xv.

1. ed. W.R. Dawson (1934), pp. 18-329 (even pages only) (London Medical Society 136, ff. 1-95v).

Cf. 446.

448　Man and womman þat wilneþ to fle synne and lede clene lyfe taketh hede to þis litul tretys þat is y write in englisch tong for lewed men

Memoriale Credencium, compilation of theology for lay people, s. xv (1).

1. ed. J.H.L. Kengen (1979) (Bodl Tanner 201, ff. 7-106v).

Also in CUL Dd.1.1, BL Harley 211 (fragment), BL Harley 535, BL Harley 2250 (fragment), BL Harley 2398, BL Sloane 1009 (fragment), Bodl Rawlinson C. 89 (fragment), Philadelphia University of Pennsylvania 6 (fragment). Jolliffe A.4.

449 Mannes mynde þat is ofte robbid of þe tresour of kunnyng bi þe enemye
of science þat is forȝetyng is greetly releeued bi tablis maad bi lettre
aftir þe ordre of ABC

Preface to a Wycliffite concordance to the New Testament, s. xv
in.

1. Franciplegius (1965), pp. 290-92 (BL Royal 17 B.i, ff. 3-7);
2. Speculum, 43 (1968), 270-73 (as in 1).

450 Many men in þis world aftyr her pilgrimage haue left memoriales of
swech þingis as þei haue herd and seyn þat nowt only here eres schuld
ber witnesse but eke her eyne (from 2)

John Capgrave, Solace of Pilgrimys, description of Rome, ca.
1450.

1. Rolls 1 (1858), 357-66 (Oxford All Souls 17 and Oxford
Balliol 190, both fragments only); 2. ed. C.A. Mills (1911)
(Bodl Bodley 423, ff. 355-414).

451 Many men there ben that with eeres openly sprad so moche swalowen
the delyciousnesse of iestes and of ryme by queynt knyttyng coloures

Thomas Usk, The Testament of Love, ca. 1387.

1. Thynne (1532; STC 5068); 2. Thynne, 2nd ed. (1542; STC
5069); 3. Thynne, 3rd ed. ([1545?]; STC 5071); 4. Stow (1561;
STC 5075); 5. Speght (1598; STC 5077); 6. Speght, 2nd ed.
(1602; STC 5080); 7. Speght, 3rd ed. (1687); 8. Urry (1721);
9. Chalmers (1810); 10. Skeat, Chaucerian (1897), pp. 1-145
(as in 1); 11. Thynne (1905) (facsimile of 1); 12. Scolar Press
(1969) (facsimile of 1).

Many there ben þat knowe and vnderstonde many other thynges and yet
they knowe not theyr owne self They take moche hede to other but they
loke not well to themself   Incipit to text proper of 245.

452 Marmaduke þe sone of Patryke þe sage of alle langages fonde in þe
regioun of Grece with-inne þe temple of þe Solayle þe whiche þat
famous and gret philosophre Euscalabinus made

Decretum Aristotelis/Secrete of Secretes and Tresore Incompera-
ble, book of instruction translated from a French version of the

Secreta Secretorum, s. xv (1).

1. EETS os 276 (1977), pp. 203-4 (Bodl Ashmole 59, ff. 1-12v).

453   Mary Magdaleyn was surnamed of Magdalon the castell and she was
       born of the kynred that were descendid of ryal kynne and hir fadir
       highte Syrus

       The Lyfe of Marye Magdaleyn, saint's life from the Gilte Legen-
       de, circulating separately, s. xv.

       1. Archiv, 91 (1893), 210-24 (Durham University Cosin
       V.II.14, ff. 106-11v, ending imperfectly).

       Also in TCD 319, BL Harley 4775, BL Addl. 35298, Bodl Douce
       372.

       Mayster Alberte Archebysshop of Coleyne sayd thyse wordes in the
       persone of Jhesu cryst The fyrste is this Gyue a peny for my loue in thy
       lyfe   Incipit to "Master Albert of Cologne's Nine Articles," devo-
       tional tract (Part 8) incorporated into 751.

454   Master tel me what thynge is god My chylde he is a thyng spyrytuall in
       þe whiche is all dygnyte and all perfeccyon

       Andrew Chertsey, Lucydary, translation of Honorius of Autun's
       Lucidarium, s. xv ex. (?).

       1. W. de Worde, [1508?] (STC 13686).

       Mathew of Jewerye born as he is putt first in ordre so first he wrote the
       gospel in Jewes langage   Incipit to New Testament in Version A of
       119.

       Matheu that was of Judee as he is set first in ordre of the gospelleris
       Incipit to New Testament in Version B of 119.

       Memorare nouissima et in eternum non peccabis . . . Ecclesiasticus
       saith in his seuenth chapiter thise wordes folowyng Bere wel in thy
       mynde the last things and thou shalt neuer fal in synne   Incipit to
       text proper of 47.

Memoriam fecit mibilium suorum miseri cors . . . These wordes of
Dauyd in the psaulter said in prophecye longe tyme before the Incarnacion of oure lord Ihesu   Incipit to short treatise added to 553.

Men ar hyghly bounde of a congruence vnto these wrytars of maters &
histories that by their laborious estudye haue pourchaced hye enprow-
mentes vnto the lyf of man   Incipit to text proper of 457.

455   Men greten comynli oure Ladi Goddis Moder and we supposen þat þis
gretynge saveþ many men For we taken as bileve þat sche is blessid in
hevene

Exposition of the "Ave Maria", Wycliffite tract, s. xiv (2).

1. SEW, III (1871), 111-13 (Bodl Bodley 789, f. 97); 2. EETS
os 118 (1901), pp. 11-14 (Lambeth Palace 408, ff. 2v-3v).

Also in CUL Nn.4.12, TCD 245, BL Harley 2385, and York
Minster XVI.L.12.   Cf. 276.

Miȝtfull god þat euermore is wondirful in hys seyntis & glorious in his
werkis many wondirful þingis wrouȝt and schewed to all his holy
seyntis   Incipit to edition 7 of 290.

Myn owne simple vnderstondyng I fele wele how it fareth by other that
ben in the same degree and hauen charge of soules   Incipit to
prologue in edition 2 of 734 and in all subsequent editions before 1500.

456   Mollificant olera durissima crusta Fryndis this is to saye to your lewde
undurstandyng that hoote wordes erased crusstes makeyn sofft harde
wortes

Burlesque, s. xv.

1. Rel. Ant., I (1841), 82-84 (Edinburgh NLS Advocates Jac.
V. 7, 27).

Mor haue I meruayled þen I schewe fforsothe when I felt fyrst my hert
wax warme and treuly not ymagynyngly   Incipit to text proper of
92.

457 Most reuerent Holy Fader ther ne hath be wryter of maters in tyme of seasons passid were he neuer so famous a scribe that so desyrous hath ben vnto ony Prynce his werke to arette

John Skelton, <u>Diodori Siculi Historiarum Priscarum</u>, translation of Poggio's partial Latin translation of Diodorus Siculus's <u>Biblio-theca Historica</u>, ca. 1485.

1. EETS os 233 (1956) (CCCC 357, ff. 1-256v).

458 Mothir of God quhilk hes consauit and borne our saluiour Iesu be vertu of þe Haly Gaist without seid of man perpetualie abiding in haly virginite

The <u>Lang Rosair</u>, rosary of prayers to the Virgin, s. xv.

1. STS, 3rd series 23 (1955), pp. 322-34 (BL Arundel 285, ff. 213v-24).

459 Mogworte or moderwort is clepid arthemesia for þat she is modir of alle oþer herbes or for þi þat þe modir of herbes hauyþ ȝouyn her name (from 3)

John Lelamour, <u>Þe Trettice of Macer</u>, herbal translated from the Latin <u>De Viribus Herbarum</u> by Macer Floridus, s. xiv.

1. R. Wyer, [1530?] (STC 17172); 2. R. Wyer, [1535?] (STC 17173); 3. ed. G. Frisk (1949) (Stockholm Kungliga Biblioteket X.91, ff. 1-45).

Also in CUL Ee.1.15, BL Sloane 2269, BL Sloane 2527, BL Addl. 37786, Bodl Digby 95, Bodl Hatton 29, Bodl Rawlinson C. 81.

My dere brother and sister I se weel that many wolde ben in religioun but they mowe nowt   Incipit to edition 7 of 39.

My dere ferendis ȝe shullen vndirstonde þat Crist Ihesus auctour and doctour of trewþe   See 560.

460 My dere sone in God thou hiest fast the wai to Godward there thou shalt see alle thi former faderis apostils martiris confessoris virginis and alle men and wommen that be sauid

168.

My soule is wery of the lyfe For there I see no thynge   See 653.

466   My souerayn frende Attitus how be it that I knowe certaynly that thou
art bothe nyght and day pensif and careful ffor the gouernement of the
comyn profyte of the Romayns callyd in latyn Res publica

Tullyus de Senectute/Tullye of Olde Age, translation made at the
request of Sir John Fastolf of Premierfait's French version of
Cicero's De Senectute (with prologue by Caxton), s. xv med.

1. W. Caxton, 1481? (STC 5293, Part 1); 2. ed. H. Susebach
(1933) (as in 1); 3. (1977) (facsimile of 1).

467   My soverayne maistres certen evydens have done me to vnderstonde
ʒour abylyte to lerne scyens partyculere and als wele consyder I ʒour
desyre in specyal

Preface to a calendar for 1430, s. xv (1).

1. Halliwell, Rara (1839), pp. 89-93 (BL Harley 937).

468   N I cristene þe in þe name of þe fader and of þe sone and of þe holy
gost . . . Godfaderis and godmoderis I charge ʒow and þe fader and þe
moder that þis child be kept þis seuen ʒer fro water (from 11)

English portions of the service of baptism from the Manual, s.
xv.

1. Maskell, I (1846), cxx (STC 16160); 2. Maskell, I (1846),
14, 28 (STC 16150); 3. Maskell, I (1846), 25-26 note 32 (BL
Royal 2 A.xxi); 4. Surtees Soc. 63 (1875), pp. 18, 20 (as in 1);
5. Surtees Soc. 63 (1875), p. 18 note (Cambridge (Mass.)
Harvard University Widener 1, f. 60); 6. Surtees Soc. 63
(1875), p. 11* (STC 16140); 7. Fifth Report (1876), p. 305 (as
in 5); 8. Maskell, 2nd ed., I (1882), ccli (as in 1); 9. Maskell,
2nd ed., I (1882), 15, 31 (as in 2); 10. Maskell, 2nd ed., I
(1882), 28 note 39 (as in 3); 11. EETS es 90 (1903), p. 5 (BL
Addl. 30506, ff. 23-24).

Also in early printed editions of the Manual (STC 16138-39,
16141-49, 16151-59, 16161).

169   Nature was not my frende þat suffrede me to be bore of vnsemeli schap
RESOUN Nature was not þyn enemye for þat þou wantes þi deliȝt he
dede it for þi profiȝt

"A Dialogue Between Reason and Adversity", adaptation of Pet-
rarch's De Remediis Utriusque Fortunae, s. xv.

1. ed. F.N.M.Diekstra (1968), odd pages (CUL Ii.6.39, ff.
177v-88v).

170   Nicholas bysshop seruaunt of the seruauntes of god To our welbeloued
sonnes and to our welbeloued doughters in Cryste þe brethern and
systers of the order of þe brethern of penaunce

Reule of the Living of the Brethrene and Susters of the Order of
Penitentis, translation of the third version (1289) of the Rule for
the Third Order (Penitents) of St. Francis, s. xv (2).

1. W. de Worde, 1510 (STC 19596), preceded by a renewal by
Pope Urban V or VI of the privileges granted by Pope Nicholas
IV; 2. EETS os 148 (1914), pp. 45-55 (formerly R.W. Cham-
bers MS, ff. 2-15v).

171   Nym clene Wete and bray it in a morter wel that the holys gon al of and
seyt yt til it breste and nym yt up and lat it kele

Universa Servicia Tam de Carnibus Quam de Piscibus, recipes
for cooking, 1381.

1. Pegge (1780), pp. 91-122 (Pegge MS ?).

172   Nym resons and do out ye stones and bray it in a morter with pepir and
gingiuer and salt and wastel bred tempre hit with wyn boille hit dresse
hit forth

Recipes (25) for various foods, s. xv.

1. EETS os 91 (1888), pp. 112-14 (Bodl Laud Miscellaneous
553, ff. 5-6v).

173   Nammore ne is be-tuene ane manne and ane beste bote ine onderstond-
ynge Naȝt of oþre þinge ne glorefye þe

Dan Michel of Northgate, treatise on the difference between men and beasts., ca. 1340.

1. EETS os 23 (1866), pp. 270-71 (BL Arundel 57, f. 96v); 2. EETS os 23, rev. ed. (1965), pp. 270-71 (as in 1).

Noble and worshipfull among the ordre of cheualrie renommeed ffor in as much as ye and such othir noble knyghtes and men of worchip haue exerciced and occupied   Incipit to the prose prologue dedicating the work to Sir John Fastolf in edition 1 of 513 (in contrast to the verse prologue dedicating the work to the Duke of Buckingham in edition 2).

Nomina Custodum et Balliuorum tempore Regis Ricardi primi . . . In this same yere that is to say the yere off oure Lord Ml CCij there were greete Reynes   Incipit to version E of 365.

Nomina custodum London tempore Reg Rici primi . . . The same day that the king was crowned and the nyght folwynge alle the Jewes that myghte be founden weren for the moste partie slayne and brent Incipit to version B of 365.

474   Non shyppart lrepāt [sic] hys sheyp in the feyldys qwych was not clerlr [sic] et had no wnderstondyng of wryttys bot oonly be hys naturel wyt et wnderstondyng

Antoine Verard (?), Kalendayr of the Shyppars, translation into Scottish of the French Compost et Kalendrier des Bergiers, s. xv ex. (?).

1. [A. Verard], 1503 (STC 22407); 2. R. Wyer, [1530?] (STC 20480), extracts.

STC 22408 (Pynson, 1506) is a new translation from the French into English made because of the incomprehensibility of STC 22407.

475   Notandum þat by takyns off þe Element þat falles In þe moneth a man schall knawe Plenteth and darke By þe monethes

"What Thunder Signifies in Different Months", s. xv ex. (?).

1. EETS os 26, rev. ed. (1914), p. 114 (Lincoln Cathedral 91, f. 50r-v).

166

Nowe deuout reders you must ymagen that the selfe heretikes done
speke for ye reasons that done folowe   Incipit to text proper of **267**.

476   Now I wolle you tell a noble storye wherof a man may lerne many
goode ensamples and yonge men may here the goode dedes of aunciente
people that dide muche goode and worschip in their days

"King Ponthus and the Fair Sidone", romance translated from
French, s. xv (1).

1. PMLA, 12 (1897), 1-150 (Bodl Digby 185, ff. 166-203).

Also in Bodl Douce 384 (fragment). For another translation see
609.

477   Now Ihesu goddis sonne giffere of all vertus vouche þou safe to giffe
me the seuene giftys of þe haly gaste

Oracio in Inglys, prayer, s. xv (?).

1. YW, I (1895), 380 (Lincoln Cathedral 91, f. 177v).

478   Nou let heere here and vnderstonde ententyflyche myne wordes what-
euere heo beo þat haþ fursake þis wordle and ychose solytarye lyf

Thomas N., Informacio Alredi Abbatis Monasterii de Rievalle
ad Sororem Suam Inclusam, translation of Ailred's Latin, s. xiv.

1. ES, 7 (1884), 305-44 (Bodl Eng. poet. a. 1, ff. iii verso-vi);
2. EETS os 287 (1984), pp. 26-60 (as in 1).

For another translation see **607.5**.

479   Now mekest and ioyfulleste lady saynt Marye ffor þe Ioye þou hadde
whene þou conceyuede thy dere sonne of þe haly gaste in the gretynge
of the angell

A Preyere off the Fyve Joyes of Owre Lady, prayer on the five
joys and the five sorrows, s. xv (?).

1. YW, I (1895), 377-79 (Lincoln Cathedral 91, f. 177v).

480   Now open þi hert wyde to thynke on þase paynes þat Cryst for þe

thoolede and thynke þaim in þi hert rygth als he þaim thoolede

[Richard Rolle], Meditacione de Passione Ihesu Christi, s. xiv.

1. YW, I (1895), 112-21 (Bodl Rawlinson C. 285, ff. 64-68v).

Related to the Forme of Lyvyng (351); cf. 502, into which it is
incorporated; Jolliffe I.30.

481 Now passid al maner sightis of descant & with him wel replesshid yt
natural appetide not saturate sufficientli

Chilston, Tretises Diverse of Musical Proporcions, s. xv.

1. Speculum, 10 (1935), 265-69 (BL Lansdowne 763, ff. 116-
21v).

Also in New York C.F. Bühler MS.

482 Now pray I to hem alle that herkene this litil tretyse or rede that yf ther
be ony thing that liketh hem that therof they thanke oure lord Ihesu
Crist

Geoffrey Chaucer, "Retraction" to the "Canterbury Tales", s.
xiv ex.

1. W. Caxton, [1477?] (STC 5082); 2. W. Caxton, [1483?]
(STC 5083); 3. R. Pynson, [1492?] (STC 5084); 4. W. de
Worde, 1498 (STC 5085); 5. R. Pynson, 1526 (STC 5086); 6.
Thynne (1532; STC 5068); 7. Thynne, 2nd ed. (1542; STC
5069); 8. Thynne, 3rd ed. ([1545?]; STC 5071); 9. Stow (1561;
STC 5075); 10. Speght (1598; STC 5077); 11. Speght, 2nd ed.
(1602; STC 5080); 12. Speght, 3rd ed. (1687); 13. Urry (1721);
14. Morell (1737); 15. Tyrwhitt (1775); 16. J. Bell (1782); 17.
Anderson (1793); 18. Tyrwhitt, 2nd ed. (1798); 19. Chalmers
(1810); 20. Aldine (1845); 21. Wright (1847-51) (BL Harley
7334); 22. R. Bell (1854-56), 4 (as in 21); 23. Aldine, rev. ed.
(1866); 24. Chaucer Soc., 1st series 49 (1877) (BL Harley 1758,
BL Lansdowne 851, BL Addl. 5140, Bodl Selden Arch. B. 14
supplemented by Bodl Hatton Donat. 1, Petworth House Lord
Leconfield 7, San Marino Huntington EL 26 C 9); 25. Chaucer
Soc., 1st series 50 (1877) (San Marino Huntington EL 26 C 9);
26. Chaucer Soc., 1st series 51 (1877) (BL Addl. 5140); 27.
Chaucer Soc., 1st series 52 (1877) (BL Harley 1758); 28.
Chaucer Soc., 1st series 53 (1877) (Bodl Selden Arch. B. 14
supplemented by Bodl Hatton Donat. 1); 29. Chaucer Soc., 1st

series 54 (1877) (Petworth House Lord Leconfield 7); 30. Chaucer Soc., 1st series 55 (1877) (BL Lansdowne 851); 31. R. Bell, rev. ed. (1878); 32. Gilman (1880); 33. Poetical ([1880]); 34. Blackwood (1880?); 35. Pollard (1886-87); 36. Skeat, Complete (1894), 4, 644; 37. Ellis (1896); 38. Globe (1898); 39. Lounsbury (1900); 40. Skeat, Complete, 2nd ed. (1900); 41. Chaucer Soc., 1st series 96 (1902) (BL Egerton 2726); 42. Thynne (1905) (facsimile of 6); 43. Works of Chaucer (1906); 44. Burrell (1908); 45. Burrell, rev. ed. (1912); 46. Koch (1915) (as in 25); 47. MacCracken, CT (1928); 48. ed. J.M. Manly, Canterbury Tales by Geoffrey Chaucer (1928), pp. 491-92 (as in 25); 49. Shakespeare Head (1929), 4; 50. Geoffrey Chaucer (1929-30); 51. Complete Works (1930); 52. Pollard, 2nd ed. (1931); 53. Robinson (1933), p. 314 (as in 25); 54. Manly-Rickert (as in 25, etc.), 4, 476-77; 55. Robinson, 2nd ed. (1957), p. 265 (as in 25); 56. Cawley (1958); 57. ed. E.T. Donaldson, Chaucer's Poetry (1958), pp. 421-22 (as in 25); 58. Winterich (1958) (facsimile of 37); 59. ed. A.C. Baugh, Chaucer's Major Poetry (1963), p. 533 (as in 25); 60. ed. R.A. Pratt, Geoffrey Chaucer Selections from The Tales of Canterbury and Short Poems (1966), pp. 385-86 (as in 25); 61. Scolar Press (1969) (facsimile of 6); 62. (1972) (facsimile of 2); 63. Pratt (1974), pp. 557-58 (as in 25); 64. ed. E.T. Donaldson, Chaucer's Poetry, 2nd ed. (1975), pp. 582-83 (as in 25); 65. Fisher (1977), p. 397 (as in 25); 66. Blake, CT (1980), pp. 660-61 (as in 25).

Also in Austin University of Texas 46, Austin University of Texas 143, Cambridge Fitzwilliam Museum McClean 181, Cambridge Magdalene Pepys 2006, TCC R.3.15, CUL Ii.3.26, CUL Mm.2.5, Chatsworth Duke of Devonshire MS (Christie's 6 June 1974 to L.D. Feldman), Chicago University 564, Glasgow University Hunterian 197, Lichfield Cathedral 29, BL Egerton 2864, BL Harley 7333, BL Royal 18 C.ii, Manchester Rylands English 113, Bodl Bodley 414, Bodl Rawlinson poet. 223, Oxford New 314, Oxford Trinity 49.

Nowe take hede that whan oure lorde god had made heuene and erthe and alle the Ornamentis of hem God sawe that thei wer goode   Incipit to edition B.1 of 25.

483   Now þese chapitles of þis book ben yordeyned I wole fulfille my purpos pursuynge ech chapitle bi ordre and confermynge my wordis aftir þe auctorite of myn auctoris and wiþ experiment þat I haue longe tyme used

Book of Lanfrank, translation of Lanfranc's surgical treatise
(1296), 1380.

1. EETS os 102 (1894) (Bodl Ashmole 1396, ff. 1-272v); 2.
EETS os 102 (1894), pp. 1-157 (bottoms of pages only) (BL
Addl. 12056, ff. 33-86v, ending in II,iv).

484   Now þou says þat þou may noght kepe þe fra vanytese of heryng ffor
diuerse men werldly and othir comes oft for to speke with þe and tellis
þe talis

Walter Hilton, How ane Ankares Sal Haf Hir to Þaim Þat Comes
to Hir, Chapter 82 of the Ladder of Perfeccion circulating as a
separate item, s. xiv (2).

1. YW, I (1895), 106-7 (Bodl Rawlinson C. 285, ff. 59v-60).

See 255.

Now to speke of hawkys first thay been Egges and afterwarde they bene
disclosed hawkys and communeli goshawkys been disclosed   Incipit
to text proper of 391.

485   Nowe we will begynne at the hare and wherefore at the hare rather then
at eny other best for why it is the most merveylous beste

"The Craft of Venery", treatise on hunting translated from
Guillaume Twiti, Le Art de Venerie (ca. 1327), s. xv in.

1. ed. A. Dryden, The Art of Hunting, or Three Hunting MSS
(1908), pp. 106-12 (Paul Mellon MS, formerly Phillipps 12086,
ff. 37-40); 2. Baillie-Grohman (1904), pp. 247-48 (BL Lansdowne 285, ff. 215-16, copied from 1 by Sir William Dethick);
3. Tilander (1956), pp. 51-58 (as in 1); 4. ed. B. Danielsson,
William Twiti The Art of Hunting 1327 (1977), pp. 40-58 (even
only) (as in 1 supplemented by 2); 5. ed. J.B. Podeschki, Book
on the Horse and Horsemanship (1981), pp. 5-8 (as in 1).

Another translation in 763.

Now wylle we begynne atte hare and why she is most merveylous best
of the world   Incipit to text proper of 763.

486 O blissit Trinite Fathir Sone and Haly Gaist thre personis and ane God
     I beseik the with myne hert and confessis with my mouth all þat haly
     kirk belevis and haldis of þe

     Prayers, s. xv.

     1. STS, 3rd series 23 (1955), pp. 238-54 (BL Arundel 285, ff.
     144-59v).

     Also found in early printed editions of Horae.

487 Oh Gloriouse angell to whom our blessyd lord of his most mercyfull
     grace hath taken me to kepe to thee I synful creature crye and calle

     To the Propre Angell a Devoute Prayer, prayer to guardian angel,
     s. xv.

     1. Maskell, II (1846), 269-70 (BL Harley 2445, f. 138); 2.
     Maskell, 2nd ed., III (1882), 291 (as in 1).

     One of the prayers appended to 489. Cf. 40.

488 O Glorious Ihesu O mekest Ihesu O mooste swettest Ihesu I praye the
     that I may haue trewe confession contricion and satisfaction or I dye

     Deathbed prayers, s. xv.

     1. W. Caxton, ca. 1484 (STC 6442, 14554); 2. Blades, Life, II
     (1863), Plate XXXVII (facsimile of 1); 3. English Incunabula in
     the John Rylands Library (1930), Plate 3 (facsimile of 1).

     Frequently found in early printed editions of Horae and the
     Primer.

     O her ageynes wartþe monie remedies frowern a muchel floch and
     mistliche boten   Incipit to edition 6 of 559.

489 O Ihesu endles swetnes of louyng soules O Ihesu gostly ioye passing &
     excedyng all gladnes and desires

     XV Oos, English version of Latin prayers on the passion of
     Christ attributed to St. Bridget of Sweden, with five other
     prayers appended, s. xv.

171

1. W. Caxton, 1491 (STC 20195); 2. R. Copland, 1529 (STC 20196); 3. R. Wyer, [ca. 1545] (STC 20196.5); 4. Ayling (1869) (facsimile of 1).

XV <u>Oos</u> common in early printed editions of the Sarum Primer and <u>Horae</u>, beginning with STC 15875 and especially between ca. 1527 and ca. 1550 (STC 15959-16051); cf. the version of 1527 printed in Maskell, II (1846), 255-61 and Maskell, 2nd ed., III (1882), 275-82. Two of the five appended prayers are **487** and **494**. For another version see **490**.

490   O lorde iesu crist euerlasting swetnes a ioyful gladnes of hem þat louen the passinge alle ioyes and alle desyris

"Fifteen O's", English version of Latin prayers on the passion of Christ attributed to St. Bridget of Sweden, s. xv med.

1. <u>MP</u>, 68 (1971), 358-61 (Canberra National Library of Australia Clifford 2, ff. 77-88v).

For another version see **489**.

491   O Man know thy selfe know what thou art knowe thy beginning why thou were borne vnto what vse or ende thou were gotten

<u>The Gadered Counseyles of Seynte Isodre</u>, tract on vices and virtues, s. xiv.

1. T. Berthelet, 1534 (STC 14270); 2. T. Berthelet, 1539 (STC 14270.5); 3. T. Berthelet, 1544 (STC 14271); 4. T. Berthelet, 1546 (STC 16932, last item); 5. J. Kyng, 1560 (STC 16933, last item); 6. <u>YW</u>, II (1896), 367-74 (BL Harley 1706, ff. 140-42v).

Also in TCC B.15.39, TCC O.1.74, BL Cotton Titus C. XIX, BL Harley 1706 (again), BL Harley 2371, BL Royal 17 C.xviii, BL Addl. 14408, BL Addl. 37788, Bodl Bodley 220, Bodl Laud Miscellaneous 23, Bodl Rawlinson A. 381, Bodl Rawlinson C. 894, San Marino Huntington HM 744. See also Jolliffe I.22c.

492   O maist marcifull lady and sweitest virgin Sanct Mary mother of God maist fulfillit of all piete virgin befor thy birth virgin into thy birth and virgin efter thy birth

<u>Orisouns</u>, a series of prayers to the Virgin, s. xv.

1. STS, 3rd series 23 (1955), pp. 279-89 (BL Arundel 285, ff. 178v-90).

493   O my lorde iesu crist as it hath pleasede the to assigne an angell to
       wayte on me dayly and nyghtly with greate attendance and diligence

       The Collect, a prayer to one's good angel, s. xv ex. (?).

       1. Legg (1899), p. 27 (San Marino Huntington EL 34 B 7, f. 81r-
       v); 2. Hanna (1984), p. 48 (as in 1).

       O My lorde Iesu cryst eternal trouthe these wordes beforesayd be thy
       wordes Albeit they haue not ben sayd in one selfe tyme   Incipit to
       text proper of Margaret Countess of Richmond's translation of Book 4
       of De Imitatione Christi (838).

494   O mi souerayne lord Jhesu the vary sone of all myghtye Gode and of þe
       moste cleyne & gloryous virgyne Mary

       Prayer to Jesus, s. xv.

       1. MLN, 52 (1937), 556-57 (New York Morgan M 486, roll).

       Also common in early printed editions of the Sarum Primer and
       Horae; one of the prayers appended to 489.

495   O nobil king if thou wilt diligently rede and vnderstonde this litil booke
       and tretice and rule thi selfe aftir the doctrine rulis and preceptis in this
       booke

       Booke of Goode Governance and Guyding of þe Body, book of
       instruction translated from Johannes Hispaniensis's Latin version
       of the Secreta Secretorum, s. xv.

       1. EETS os 276 (1977), pp. 3-9 (Bodl Rawlinson C. 83, ff. 1v-
       8v).

496   O sueit Iesu Crist sone of God of life I synfull and vnworthy creatour
       desires now hertlie with gret blithnes and sueitnes to hals ȝour kinglie
       heid

       Ane Dewoit Exercicioun, sixteen prayers, s. xv.

173

1. STS, 3rd series 23 (1955), pp. 182-93 (BL Arundel 285, ff. 94v-106v).

497   O swete iesu gyve me thy loue and grace forto keepe thy commaunde-
       mentes pater noster aue maria

       Prayer, s. xv ex. (?).

       1. Legg (1899), p. 29 (San Marino Huntington EL 34 B 7, f. 82r-
       v); 2. Hanna (1984), p. 48 (as in 1).

497.5 O þouȝ merciful lord god I beseche þe graunt un to me what so evere be
       plesing unto þe fervently to desiren wysely for to seken & sergen

       Oracio Thome de Alquin, translation of a Latin prayer attributed
       to Thomas Aquinas, s. xiv ev.

       1. Dominican Studies, 1 (1948), 235, 237-38 (CUL Ii.6.39, ff.
       163v-65).

       Also in CUL Ii.6.39 (again).

498   O what good welthe and prosperite shulde growe to the Reaume of
       Englande yif suche a counsell be oones perfitely stablisshed and the
       king guided therby (from 2)

       John Fortescue, Example What Good Counseill Helpith, perhaps
       an alternative version of Chapter 16 of "On the Governance of
       England", s. xv (2).

       1. Clermont (1869), I, 475-76 (BL Harley 542); 2. Plummer
       (1885), pp. 347-48 (BL Addl. 48031).

       O what is a comparison A liknes of diuerse thyngis   Incipit to
       edition A.1 of 813.

499   O yee so noble and worthi pryncis and princesse oþer estatis or degrees
       what-euer yee beo

       John Shirley, introduction to Chaucer's Knight's Tale, s. xv (1).

       1. Brewer (1978), p. 66 (BL Harley 7333, f. 37).

500 ... octa iohan bap [. . .] litari in mar [. . .] trans [. . .] trans
[. . .] saynt [. . .]

Part of an almanac, s. xv ex. (?).

1. [W. de Worde, ca. 1500] (STC 386), fragment.

Odiui ecclesiam malignantium et cum impiis non sedebo psalmo vicesi-
mo v God the creatour spekynge by þe mouthe of the prophete royall
Dauyd agaynst the synners   Incipit to text proper of 464.

501 Of al þe feiþ of þe gospel gederen trewe men wiþ opyne confescioun of
þes newe ordris þat men shulden rette hem eretikis and so not comyne
wiþ hem for þei denyen þe gospel

De Sacramento Altaris Corpus Domini, Wycliffite tract, s. xiv
(2).

1. EETS os 74 (1880, 1902), pp. 357-58 (Bodl Bodley 788, ff.
96v-97).

Also in Cambridge Pembroke 237, TCD 244, Leicester Wyggeston Hospital 10.D.34/6, and BL Addl. 40672.

502 Off Goddis grace stirrand and helpand and þat na thyng may be done
with-owttene grace Þat is Gracia dei vita eterna (from 3)

[Richard Rolle], Þe Holy Boke Gratia Dei, devotional treatise,
s. xiv.

1. YW, I (1895), 112-21, 132-36, 136-56, (BL Arundel 507,
ff. 41-48, 54v-66, beginning imperfectly), abridged version; 2.
YW, I (1895), 300-21 (Lincoln Cathedral 91, ff. 237-50v,
ending imperfectly); 3. ed. M.L. Arntz (1981) (as in 2, supplemented by 1 and San Marino Huntington HM 148, ff. 1-22v,
ending imperfectly).

Also in Edinburgh NLS 6126 (fragment); Jolliffe H.34a-c,
I.29a, M.8.

503 ... of our lorde I haue had forgyuenes Also I haue offended of ye
power of ye fader by frayle & grete mocions of line the which I haue
felt in my self

"The Serche of Confessyon", devotional tract, s. xv ex. (?).

1. R. Copland, 1529 (STC 22141), beginning imperfectly.

Of the autorite of god almychty fadyr and sone and haly gast and of the
blissyte virgynne Mary   Incipit to edition I.3 of **122**.

Of þe auctoris or ellis þe makeris of rome or of hem þat first dwelt þere
are many opynyones   Incipit to text proper of **450**.

504   Of your charyte in the worshyp of þe v wondes of our lord and þe v
ioyes of oure lady say Pater noster and Aue

Indulgence, s.xv (?)

1. [W. de Worde?, ca. 1505] (STC 14077c.15); 2. <u>Walpole</u>
<u>Soc</u>., 17 (1929), Plate XXXVI(c) (as in 1); 3. Dodgson, <u>English</u>
(1936), p. 10 and Plate 18 (as in 1).

505   Ofte he bið efter wroð þet nule beon biuore war Wis is þet war is Ofte
he bið bicherred þet alle men ileueð God is skile

Proverbs (4), s. xiii.

1. <u>N&Q</u>, 224 (1979), 5 (BL Harley 47, f. 6v margin).

The second proverb is in <u>Proverbs of Hendyng</u> (Whiting W 392).

Oyle oute-ʒettyd es þi name Þe name of Ihesu comes in to þo worlde &
als sone it smelles oyle out-ʒettyd   See **506**.

Old auctours seyene that this yle was clepyd Albyoun peraventure of
the white Craggis and Clyffis abowt the see-bankys   Incipit to text
proper of **224**.

506   Oleum effusum nomen tuum Þat es on Inglyssch Oyle oute-ʒettyd es þi
name Þe name of Ihesu comes in to þo worlde & als sone it smelles oyle
out-ʒettyd (from 3)

[Richard Rolle], <u>Of the Vertuʒ of the Haly Name of Ihesu</u>
("Oleum Effusum"), translation of part of the fourth section of

Rolle's Latin commentary on the Canticles, s. xiv (2).

1. EETS os 20 (1866), pp. 1-5 (Lincoln Cathedral 91, ff. 192-93v); 2. Mätzner, I, 2 (1869), 120 (as in 1); 3. YW, I (1895), 186-91 (BL Harley 1022, ff. 62ff.); 4. YW, I (1895), 186-91 (as in 1); 5. Kluge (1904, 1912), pp. 30-33 (as in 1); 6. EETS os 20, rev. ed. (1921), pp. 1-5 (as in 1).

Also in TCD 155 (perhaps a different version) and BL Stowe 38 (fragment).

507 Omni custodia serua cor tuum . . . With alle warde kep þin hert for of hit lyfe goþe þese are þe wordys of Salomon

William Lichfield (?), Tractus de V Sensibus, treatise based on Parts II and III of Ancrene Wisse, s. xv med.

1. EETS os 232 (1956) (BL Royal 8 C.i, ff. 122v-43v).

See 559.

508 On a day whan saynt Elisabeth was in preuy prayer and sought her spouse Ihesu Cryste wyth deuoute herte and drery spyryte and founde hym not

The Revelacions of Saynt Elysabath, translation from the Latin of Raimundus de Vineis, s. xv.

1. W. de Worde, 1492? (STC 24766, Part 2); 2. W. de Worde, [1500?] (STC 24766.3); 3. Archiv, 76 (1886), 392-400 (as in 1).

509 On Christmas day the King our soueraigne lorde Edward the iiijte after the conqueste was crowned at Westmester and ye quene also (from 2)

Bluemantle Pursuivant, account of the events of 1471-72, s. xv ex.

1. Archaeologia, 26 (1836), 265-86 (BL Addl. 6113, ff. 101-7, beginning imperfectly); 2. Kingsford, EHL (1913), pp. 379-88 (BL Cotton Julius C. VI, ff. 255-59).

510 On Ianuari monðe ȝyf hit þunreð hit bodeð toweard mycele windes & wel ȝewænde eorðe wæstme

177

Emb Þunre, prognostic, s. xiii.

1. Anglia, 10 (1888), 185 (BL Cotton Vespasian D. XIV, f. 103v).

Cf. 334.

511 Opyn techynge and Goddis lawe old and newe opyn ensaumple of
     Cristis lif and his glorious apostlis and love of God drede of peynes and
     Goddis curs and hope of grete reward in þe blisse of hevene

     For Þre Skillis Lordis Schulden Constreyne Clerkis to Lyve in
     Mekeness ("Church Temporalities"), Wycliffite tract, ca. 1377-
     78.

     1. SEW, III (1871), 213-18 (CCCC 296, pp. 221-24).

     Also in TCD 244 and San Marino Huntington HM 503.

512 [O]thea in greke langage mey be take for womans wysedom & for as
     myche as somtyme old peymyngs nott havyng yett þe lyght of þe feyth
     wurschypped many goddes

     Anthony Babyngton, Epistola of Othea to Hector, glosses and
     moralities to his verse translation (IMEV 3377) of Christine de
     Pisan, Lepistre Othea, s. xv ex.

     1. ed. J.G. Gordon (1942) (BL Harley 838, ff. 67-91v).

     For another translation, by Stephen Scrope, see 513.

513 Othea vppon the Greke may be taken for the wisedome of man or
     woman and as ancient pepill of olde tyme not hauyng yit at that tyme
     lyght of feith wurschiped many goddes (from 2)

     Stephen Scrope, Pistell of Othea, glosses and allegories to his
     verse translation (IMEV 2766) of Christine de Pisan, Lepistre
     Othea, s. xv med.

     1. Roxburghe (1904), pp. 1-114 (Longleat Marquis of Bath 253,
     ff. 2-75v); 2. EETS os 264 (1970), pp. 3-120 (Cambridge St.
     John's 208), with the later dedication to Sir John Fastolf on pp.
     121-24 (as in 1).

     Also in New York Morgan M 775. For another translation, by

Anthony Babyngton, see 512.

514 Ov nom du pere In the name of the fadre Et du filz And of the soone Et
du saint esperite And of the holy ghoost Veul commencier I wyll
begynne Et ordonner vng liure And ordeyne this book

Prouffytable Lernynge ("Vocabulary"), dialogues in French and
English interspersed, adaptation of the French Livre des Mestiers
and a Flemish wordbook, occasionally in verse, ca. 1465-66.

1. W. Caxton, 1480? (STC 24865); 2. EETS es 79 (1900) (as in
1); 3. ed. J. Gessler, Le Livre des Mestiers de Bruges et ses
dérivés, III (1931) (as in 1); 4. ed. J.C.T.Oates and L.C.
Harmer (1964) (facsimile of 1).

515 Oure euil dedes are oure awne as oure propre catell bot þe gode when
we it do es oddes

Note on evil deeds and good deeds, s. xiv ex.

1. YW, I (1895), 156 (BL Arundel 507, f. 36v, bottom margin).

Oure Fader that art in heuenes and in alle holy men hallewed be thi
name in us   Incipit to editions 5 and 11 of 171.

516 Oure fadir þat art in heuenes halwid be þi name þi reume or kyngdom
come to þe be þi wille don in herþe as it is doun in heuene

Pater Noster, Wycliffite exposition of the Pater Noster, s. xiv
(2).

1. EETS os 74 (1880, 1902), pp. 198-202 (CCCC 296, pp. 172-
75).

Also in Cambridge Sidney Sussex 74. Cf. 171.

Hure wadur þat is in euene þyn name beyn ahd   Incipit to edition 9
of 171.

Our fader whiche arth in heofnai halowid be thi name   Incipit to
edition 14 of 171.

517   Owr god imperator et makar of hewen et erth and in the begynnyng of
      tyme and of al thingys of noth wyth owt ony mater lyeng tharto

      Antoine Verard, Art of Good Lywyng and Good Deyng, transla-
      tion from his own edition of the French version (1493), s. xvi in.

      1. A. Verard, [1503] (STC 791).

518   Our holy fadre the Pope Innocent the viij To the perpetuall memory of
      this here after to be hade by his propre mocion without procurement of
      our souerayn lord the Kyng or of any other person

      Bull issued by Pope Innocent VIII confirming the succession of
      Henry VII and his marriage to Elizabeth of York, 1486.

      1. [W. de Machlinia, 1486] (STC 14096); 2. Camden Soc. 39
      (1847), pp. 5-7 (as in 1).

      Cf. 586.

519   Vre hlaford almihtiȝ god wile and us hot þat we hine lufie and of him
      smaȝe and spece naht him to mede ac hus to freme and to fultume

      Sermons (4), s. xiii (1).

      1. EETS os 34 (1868), pp. 217-45 (odd pages only) (BL Cotton
      Vespasian A. XXII, ff. 54-59v).

520   Owre Lord gave vnto me brother Frauncis thys to begynne and doo
      penaunce for why when I was in the bondage of synne yt was bitter to
      me and lothesomme to se

      The Testament of Oure Holy Fadre Seynt Frauncis, translation
      from St. Francis's Latin, with glosses, s. xv.

      1. Rolls 4, 1 (1858), 562-66 (BL Cotton Faustina D. IV, ff. 25-
      33).

      For another translation see 522.

521   Oure Lord God Almyȝty spekiþ in his lawe of tweie matrimoneys or
      wedlokis þe first is gostly matrimonye bitwixe Crist and holy Chirche
      þat is Cristene soules ordeyned to blisse

"Of Weddid Men and Wifis and of Here Children Also", Wycliffite tract, s. xiv (2).

1. SEW, III (1871), 188-201 (CCCC 296, pp. 224-35).

Also in CUL Dd.12.39, CUL Ii.6.55, BL Harley 2398, BL
Addl. 24202, London Westminster School 3, Bodl Bodley 938.

522   Houre lord haþ ȝouen to me fraunseis to bigynne to do penaunce &
whanne I was in ouere myche synnes it semyd to me bittrere

    Testament of Seynt Fraunseis, Wycliffite version, with commen-
tary, s. xiv (2).

    1. EETS os 74 (1880,1902), pp. 45-51 (CCCC 296, pp. 35-39).

    Also in TCD 244, Bodl Bodley 647. See 698; for another
translation see 520.

523   Oure lorde Ihesu criste hathe shewed and made open his grace to the
people in his feythfull seruaunte Seynt Frauncis for our Lorde sente
hym for to teche the folke the ryght waye

    The Lyfe of the Gloryous Confessoure of Oure Lorde Jhesu Criste
Seynte Frauncis, s. xv ex. (?).

    1. R. Pynson, [1515?] (STC 3270).

524   Oure Lord Jesus Crist techiþ us to preie evermore for alle nedful þingis
boþe to body and soule For in þe gospel of Seynt Luk Crist seiþ þat is is
nede to preie evermore

    How Preire of Good Men Helpiþ Moche ("De Precationibus
Sacris"), Wycliffite tract, s. xiv (2).

    1. SEW, III (1871), 219-29 (CCCC 296, pp. 145-57).

    Also in TCD 244, TCD 246 (two copies), BL Addl. 37677, Bodl
Bodley 540.

525   Oure Lord Jhesu Crist very God and very man seith in the gospel
Blessid ben they that heren Goddis word and kepen it

    John Purvey (?), tract used as prologue to an English translation of Clement of Llanthony's Unum ex Quattuor, ca. 1390.

1. Forshall and Madden (1850), I, xiv-xv note (BL Arundel 254, f. 2).

Also in BL Harley 1862, BL Harley 6333, BL Royal 17 C.xxxiii, BL Royal 17 D.viii, Manchester Rylands English 77, New York Columbia University Plimpton 268, Phillipps 7157, and others.

526   Oure lord saiþ he þat folowiþ me goþ not in darkenes These are þe wordes of crist in þe whiche we are amonysshed to folowe his lyf and his maners

Musica Ecclesiastica, translation of Books 1-3 of the Latin De Imitatione Christi attributed to Thomas à Kempis, s. xiv ex.

1. EETS es 63 (1893), pp. 1-150 (TCD 678, ff. 1-121).

Also in Cambridge Magdalene F. 4. 19, CUL Gg.1.16, Glasgow University Hunterian 136. For another translation see **838**.

527   Our lord til his chosin makis þe day scharpe þat þai delite nogth in þe gate and forgete þe Ioy of heeuen If temptacyoun pute vs nogth we suld trow þat we war of sum vertu

[Richard Rolle], "Sentences from Gregory", s. xiv.

1. YW, I (1895), 106 (Bodl Rawlinson C. 285, f. 59v).

Also in CUL Ff.5.40. Jolliffe J.12.

528   Oure merciful lord god chastyseth hese childirn and suffereth hem to ben tempted for many profytable skeles to here soule profiȝte (from 5)

A Sovereyn and a Notable Sentence to Comforte a Persone That Is in Temptacion ("Remedy Against the Troubles of Temptation"), translation (expanded) of William Flete's De Remediis contra Temptaciones, s. xiv med.

1. W. de Worde, 1508 (STC 20875.5, Part 1; 21262, Part 1); 2. W. de Worde, 1519 (STC 20876, Part 1; 21263, Part 1); 3. [W. de Worde, ca. 1525] (STC 20876.5, Part 1); 4. YW, II (1896), 106-23 (as in 1); 5. Archivio Italiano per la storia della pieta, 5 (1968), 221-40 (CUL Hh.1.11, ff. 10-16).

182

Also in TCD 154, BL Harley 1706, Bodl Holkham misc. 41, Worcester Cathedral F. 172. Jolliffe K.8.c. TCD 154, BL Harley 1706, and editions 1-3 contain an extract from Chapter 3 of Rolle's Forme of Lyvyng (351) preceding the text of the work; editions 1-3 bound with 679. Two other English translations: (1) 230 and (2) in Beeleigh Abbey Foyle MS, BL Harley 6615, BL Harley 2409, BL Royal 18 A.x, and Bodl Bodley 131 (Jolliffe K.8.a).

Oure moste holy faders the popes aboue specified that is to say pope Innocent of blessyd memorie the viii   See 586.

529   Ovr swete lord god of heuene that noman wil perisshe but wil that we comen alle to the knowleching of him and to the blisful lyf that is perdurable

Geoffrey Chaucer, The Persouns Tale, from the "Canterbury Tales", s. xiv ex.

1. W. Caxton, [1477?] (STC 5082); 2. W. Caxton, [1483?] (STC 5083); 3. R. Pynson, [1492?] (STC 5084); 4. W. de Worde, 1498 (STC 5085); 5. R. Pynson, 1526 (STC 5086); 6. Thynne (1532; STC 5068); 7. Thynne, 2nd ed. (1542; STC 5069); 8. Thynne, 3rd ed. ([1545?]; STC 5071); 9. Stow (1561; STC 5075); 10. Speght (1598; STC 5077); 11. Speght, 2nd ed. (1602; STC 5080); 12. Speght, 3rd ed. (1687); 13. Urry (1721); 14. Morell (1737); 15. Tyrwhitt (1775); 16. J. Bell (1782); 17. Anderson (1793); 18. Tyrwhitt, 2nd ed. (1798); 19. Chalmers (1810); 20. Aldine (1845); 21. Wright (1847-51) (BL Harley 7334); 22. R. Bell (1854-56), 4 (as in 21); 23. Aldine, rev. ed. (1866); 24. Chaucer Soc., 1st series 49 (1877) (Aberystwyth NLW Peniarth 392 supplemented by BL Addl. 5140 and Oxford Christ Church 152, CUL Gg.4.27 supplemented by BL Harley 1758, BL Lansdowne 851, Oxford CCC 198 supplemented by Bodl Selden Arch. B. 14, Petworth House Lord Leconfield 7, San Marino Huntington EL 26 C 9); 25. Chaucer Soc., 1st series 50 (1877) (San Marino Huntington EL 26 C 9); 26. Chaucer Soc., 1st series 51 (1877) (Aberystwyth NLW Peniarth 392 supplemented by BL Addl. 5140 and Oxford Christ Church 152); 27. Chaucer Soc., 1st series 52 (1877) (CUL Gg.4.27 supplemented by BL Harley 1758); 28. Chaucer Soc., 1st series 53 (1877) (Oxford CCC 198 supplemented by Bodl Selden Arch. B. 14); 29. Chaucer Soc., 1st series 54 (1877) (Petworth House Lord Leconfield 7); 30. Chaucer Soc., 1st series 55 (1877) (BL Lansdowne 851); 31. R. Bell, rev. ed. (1878); 32. Gilman (1880); 33. Poetical ([1880]); 34. Blackwood (1880?); 35.

Pollard (1886-87); 36. Skeat, Complete (1894), 4, 570-643; 37. Ellis (1896); 38. Globe (1898); 39. Lounsbury (1900); 40. Skeat, Complete, 2nd ed. (1900); 41. Chaucer Soc., 1st series 96 (1902) (BL Egerton 2726); 42. Thynne (1905) (facsimile of 6); 43. Works of Chaucer (1906); 44. Burrell (1908); 45. Burrell, rev. ed. (1912); 46. Koch (1915) (as in 25); 47. MacCracken, CT (1928); 48. Shakespeare Head (1929), 4; 49. Geoffrey Chaucer (1929-30); 50. Complete Works (1930); 51. Pollard, 2nd ed. (1931); 52. Robinson (1933), pp. 273-314 (as in 25); 53. Manly-Rickert (as in 26, etc.), 4, 364-476; 54. Robinson, 2nd ed. (1957), pp. 229-64 (as in 25); 55. Cawley (1958); 56. Winterich (1958) (facsimile of 37); 57. Scolar Press (1969) (facsimile of 6); 58. (1972) (facsimile of 2); 59. Pratt (1974), pp. 490-557 (as in 25 supplemented by 26); 60. Fisher (1977), pp. 349-96 (as in 25); 61. Ruggiers (1979), pp. 938-97 (as in 26); 62. Blake, CT (1980), pp. 596-660 (as in 26 supplemented by 25).

Also in Alnwick Castle Duke of Northumberland MS, Austin University of Texas 46, Austin University of Texas 143, Cambridge Fitzwilliam Museum McClean 181, Cambridge Magdalene Pepys 2006, TCC R.3.3, TCC R.3.15, CUL Ii.3.26, CUL Mm.2.5, Chicago University 564, Chatsworth Duke of Devonshire MS (Christie's 6 June 1974 to L.D. Feldman), Geneva Bodmer Foundation Cod. 48, Glasgow University Hunterian 197, Lichfield Cathedral 29, Lincoln Cathedral 110 (imperfect), BL Egerton 2863 (imperfect), BL Egerton 2864, BL Harley 7333, BL Royal 17 D.xv, BL Royal 18 C.ii, BL Sloane 1685, BL Addl. 35286 (imperfect), London Royal College of Physicians 388 (imperfect), Longleat Marquis of Bath 29, Manchester Rylands English 113, New York Morgan M 249 (imperfect), Bodl Bodley 414, Bodl Hatton Donat. 1, Bodl Laud Miscellaneous 600, Bodl Rawlinson poet. 149, Bodl Rawlinson poet. 223, Oxford New 314, Oxford Trinity 49, Philadelphia Rosenbach Foundation 1084/1 (Phillipps 8137, imperfect), Philadelphia Rosenbach Foundation MS (fragment), Princeton University 100. The Parson's Tale circulated separately in Longleat Marquis of Bath 29. Many reprints of the various editions appeared in the 18th, 19th, and early 20th centuries.

530   Ovre suete lord Jhesu Crist vpe his godhede he was tofore all creatures
        for whi he made alle creatures þorouȝ his owen suete miȝht

        Gospels an Hundreþ and Sex, a harmony of the gospels narrating
        the life of Christ, translated from French, s. xv.

        1. EETS os 157 (1922) (Cambridge Magdalene Pepys 2498, pp.

1-43).

531 Ovtalmus ys a stoune yf he be wrappyd yn a loryll leue and bere it on
thy wryste hytt schall make the ynvysebell

Vertus of Stounys, lapidary, s. xv.

1. EETS os 190 (1933), pp. 58-59 (Bodl Ashmole 1447, pp. 37-
38).

532 Parce michi Domine . . . Spare me Lord forsoþe my dayes ben nouȝt
What is man þat þou magnifiest hym or wherto settiste þou þin herte
towardis hym

Lessons from the Dirige, circulating separately, s. xiv/xv.

1. EETS os 155 (1921), pp. 59-64 (BL Addl. 39575, ff. 45-51).

For verse paraphrases of the same lessons see <u>IMEV</u> 251 and
1854; the Office for the Dead may be found in the Primer (157).

533 Pater noster qui es in celis In all the wordes þat er stabillede and sett to
say in erthe þan es þe Pater noster þe beste and þe hegheste and þe
halyeste

<u>Tractatus</u> <u>de</u> <u>Dominica</u> <u>Oracione</u>, treatise on the Pater Noster, s.
xiv.

1. <u>YW</u>, I (1895), 261-64 (Lincoln Cathedral 91, ff. 209v-10v).

A similar treatise in BL Harley 4712.

534 . . . Patryarke with all the solempnyte that he myght doo by the leue of
the chyrche theym wedded And whan the masse was done they tourned
agayne to the palays to theyr dyner (from 2)

"William of Palermo", romance adapted from the alliterative
"William of Palerne" (<u>IMEV</u> 3281.5), s. xv ex. (?).

1. [W. de Worde, ca. 1515] (STC 25707.5), fragment; 2.
<u>Archiv</u>, 118 (1907), 323-25 (as in 1).

535 Poule and Myȝel praied to oure lord Jesu Crist of his gret grace to

schewe þe peynes of helle to his disciple Poule þat he myȝt declare hem

A Questioun of þe Peynes of Helle, vision of St. Paul, s. xiv.

1. ES, 22 (1896), 134-37 (BL Addl. 10036, ff. 81-84v).

Poule seruaunt of iesu cristi callid apostil   See 536.

536   Paulus seruus Iesu cristi vocatus apostolus . . . Poule seruaunt of iesu cristi called apostil departid in to þe ewangelye of god þe whiche bifore he hadde bihiȝt bi his prophetis in holy writtes of his sone

        "Pauline Epistles", translation of the fifteen epistles, with Latin interspersed, s. xiv ex.

        1. EETS es 116 (1916) (CCCC 32, ff. 155-208v).

537   Per multas tribulaciones oportet introire in regnum dei Thus sayth the apostole saynt Poule in the boke of actes and dedes that is to saye in englysshe By many trybulacions we muste entre in to þe kyngdome of god (from 2)

        Rote or Myrour of Consolacyon and Conforte, didactic treatise, s. xv ex.

        1. [W. de Worde, 1496] (STC 21334); 2. W. de Worde, [ca. 1499] (STC 21335); 3. W. de Worde, 1511 (STC 21336); 4. W. de Worde, 1530 (STC 21337).

538   Per proprium sanguinem introiuit . . . Be his awne propre blode he entred in Blode kyndely maketh a tree þat is drie fruteful Hit maketh mennes bodies þat bene seke heleful

        John Gregory, Bonus Sermo, sermon, s. xiv ex.

        1. ed. H.G. Pfander, The Popular Sermon of the Medieval Friar in England (1937), pp. 54-64 (Oxford University 97, pp. 324-39).

539   . . . [p]erylle the whiche bene lyke to falle withoute a direccion be had in this behalfe So that yf ye tender my desyres ye shall procure an universalle quyet

"Somnium Vigilantis", a defense of the proscription of the Yorkists, 1459/60.

1. EHR, 26 (1911), 513-23 (BL Royal 17 D.xv, ff. 302-10, beginning imperfectly).

540 Petir Alfons seruaunt of Jhesu Crist maker of this booke saith Thankynges I do to god the whiche is first and without bigynnyng to whom is the bigynnyng and the end

Litel Epistil, translation of Peter Alphonse's Disciplina Clericalis, exempla, s. xv.

1. Western Reserve University Bulletin, n.s. 22, 3 (1919) (Worcester Cathedral F. 172, ff. 118v-38).

541 Philosofus puttyn 9 speris vndirewritten but Diuinis puttin þe tenþe spere where is heuyn empire in þe whiche angelis & sowlis of seyntis seruen god

Notes on the spheres and planets, s. xv.

1. EETS os 16, rev. ed. (1889), p. 26 (BL Sloane 73, f. 26).

542 Please it to our most Noble and most Worthy King Richard king both of England and of France and to the Noble Duke of Lancastre and to other great men of the Realme

John Wyclif (?), "A Petition to the King and Parliament", 1382.

1. ed. T. James (J. Barnes, 1608; STC 25589, Part 1) (CCCC 296, pp. 288-98, 170-71); 2. SEW, III (1871), 507-23 (as in 1).

Also in TCD 244; Latin version in Florence Biblioteca Laurenziana Plut. XIX, cod. XXXIII, ff. 23v-26v, s. xiv ex. (edited Speculum, 7 [1932], 88-94).

Pape Innocent hes grantit iiic dais of indulgence till all þame þat sayis þat orisoun followand in þe honour of þe blist virgin Mary   Incipit to introduction to 492.

543 Pope Innocent hath grauntit to what man or woman that dayly

worchyppeht the v pryncypall woundes of oure Lorde Jhesu Cryste
(from 2)

Indulgence, s. xv.

1. Bliss (1857), p. 193 (London Wellcome Historical Medical
Library 632); 2. Bliss, 2nd ed., I (1869), 194 (as in 1); 3.
Doble, II (1886), 375-76 (as in 1); 4. JBAA, 48 (1892), 38-39
(as in 1); 5. Buchanan-Brown (1966), pp. 95-96 (as in 1).

544   Pope Innocent the viij hath grauntyd that who so euer man or woman
       that beth deryth the lenght of this naylis upon hym & worshipith
       deuoutly the iiij naylis of our Lord Ihesu Crist

       Indulgence, s. xv.

       1. JBAA, 48 (1892), 52 (BL Harley Rot. T.11); 2. Speculum,
       39 (1964), 277 (as in 1); 3. Bühler (1973), p. 573 (as in 1); 4.
       Louis (1980), p. 295 (Bodl Tanner 407, f. 51).

       Also in New York Morgan Glazier 39.

545   Pope Sixtus ordeyned that masse schuld be sungun on Awters which
       was not doon bifore in þe ȝere of our lord CCC iijxx x2 ȝer Pope Gayus
       ordeyned þat ordris in þe chirch schuld stiȝe vp

       [John Wyclif], chronicle of the papacy, ca. 1379.

       1. JEGP, 41 (1942), 175-93 (Cambridge Emmanuel 85, ff. 1-
       29).

       Prayse ye children almyghty god as þe phylosopre sayth in dyuerse
       places   See 430.

546   Pray god þat he wil gif to þe compungcion & wepyng in þi hert with
       mekenes & ay luke on þi nawene synnes & deme nogth other bot be
       vnderloute to all

       [Walter Hilton], "Sayings of the Fathers", compilation, s. xiv.

       1. YW, I (1895), 125-28 (Bodl Rawlinson C. 285, ff. 71-73v).

547   Preyeth for þe saul of frere Ion lacy Anchor and Reclused in þe new

castell upon tynde þe wiche þat wrooth þis book and lymned hit to his
awne use

John Lacy, invocation preceding a series of prayers, 1420-34.

1. SP, 6 (1910), 9 (Oxford St. John's 94, ff. 101v-2); 2.
Dominican Studies, 1 (1948), 230-31 (as in 1).

548   Prayng es a gracyous gyfte of owre lorde godd tyll ylk mane diuysed as
he vouches-safe till sum mare delyttabyll till sum lesse as all oþer
gudnes & gyftes ere gyffene

[Richard Rolle], "On Prayer", treatise on prayer, s. xiv.

1. YW, I (1895), 295-300 (Lincoln Cathedral 91, ff. 233-36v,
ending imperfectly).

Also in Liverpool University F. 4. 10, BL Royal 18 A.x (last part
only), Bodl e Mus. 35. Jolliffe M.11.

549   Prelatis sclaundren pore prestis and oþere cristen men þat þei wolen not
obesche to here souereynes ne dreden curs ne drede ne kepe þe lawe

Hou Men Owen Obesche to Prelatis Drede Curs, Wycliffite
tract, s. xiv (2).

1. EETS os 74 (1880, 1902), pp. 29-38 (CCCC 296, pp. 23-
29).

Also in TCD 244.

550   Preestis dekenis other curatis shulden not be lordis bi worldli manere
To this vndirstondinge that preestis and clerkis shulden fighte bi
material swerd neithir pleete neithir stryue agens temporal lordis

"Remonstrance Against Romish Corruptions"/"Ecclesiae Regi-
men", commentary on 37 conclusions ascribed to Wyclif, ca.
1395.

1. ed. J. Forshall (1851) (BL Cotton Titus D. I).

Also in TCD 246, Norwich Castle Museum 159.926 4g.3, and
Bodl Bodley 540. The 37 conclusions only, along with the
corresponding Latin versions from which they may have been
translated, are printed in EHR, 26 (1911), 741-49 (from BL

Cotton Titus D. I).

Principium evangelii . . . As men shulden trowe in Crist þat he is boþe God and man so men shulden trowe bi hise wordis þat þei ben soþe and wordis of liif   Incipit to Ferial Gospels series of **304**.

Pro salfo fleumate   See **642**.

551   Propyr wille þat is forsakyn and made commen þan is it acordant wyht goddis wylle and alle gode mens wille and principaly ouer alle thynge

[Walter Hilton], "Proper Will", treatise on self-will, s. xiv.

1. YW, I (1895), 173-75 (CUL Dd.5.55, ff. 91v-94v).

Also in CUL Ff.5.40 and CUL Ff.6.31(1).   Jolliffe F.22.

552   Quamdiu fuero memor ero laborum . . . Alse longe as i liue i þis werld i schal þenkin of þe michele suink þat Iesu Crist þolede in spellinge (from 2)

Sermon, preceded by IMEV 1917 and 2285, s. xiii.

1. Anglia, 42 (1918), 148, 150 (TCC B.1.45, f. 24r-v); 2. Anglia, 42 (1918), 149, 151 (BL Cotton Cleopatra C. VI, f. 56v); 3. Bulletin of the Modern Humanities Research Association, 2 (1928), 104-5 (as in 1).

553   Quecunbque scripta sunt ad nostram doctrinam scripta sunt . . . These ben the wordes of the grete doctour and holy apostel saynte Poule consyderynge that the ghostly lyuyng of alle trew Cristen creatures in thys world stant specyally in hope of the blysse and the lyf that is to comen (from 2)

Nicholas Love, Mirroure of the Blissid Lyf of Jesu Criste/Speculum Vite Christi, translation of Pseudo-Bonaventure's Meditationes Vite Christi, a series of meditations for each day of the week, followed by a short treatise and a prayer on the holy sacrament, s. xv in.

1. W. Caxton, 1486? (STC 3259), beginning and ending imperfectly; 2. W. Caxton, 1490? (STC 3260); 3. W. de Worde, 1494 (STC 3261); 4. R. Pynson, [1494] (STC 3262); 5. R.

Pynson, [1506] (STC 3263); 6. W. de Worde, 1517 (STC 3264),
beginning imperfectly; 7. W. de Worde, n.d. (STC 3265); 8.
W. de Worde, 1525 (STC 3266); 9. W. de Worde, 1530 (STC
3267); 10. ed. L.F. Powell (1908, two identical editions) (Oxford Brasenose 9).

Also in Beeleigh Abbey Foyle MS, CCCC 142, CCCC 143,
Cambridge Fitzwilliam Museum Bradfer-Lawrence Deposit 9,
Cambridge Fitzwilliam Museum McClean 127, TCC B.2.18
(parts), TCC B.15.16, TCC B.15.32, CUL Hh.1.11, CUL
Ii.4.9 (extracts), CUL Ll.4.3, CUL Mm.5.15, CUL
Oo.7.45(i) (fragment), CUL Addl. 6578, CUL Addl. 6686,
Columbia University of Missouri Fragmenta Manuscripta 174
(fragment), Edinburgh NLS Advocates 18.1.7, Glasgow University Gen. 1130, Glasgow University Hunterian 77, Hastings
East Sussex County Record Office MS (fragment), Leeds Diocesan Archives MS, BL Arundel 112, BL Arundel 364, BL Harley
4011 (extracts), BL Royal 18 C.x, BL Addl. 11565, BL Addl.
19901, BL Addl. 21006, BL Addl. 30031, Lambeth Palace 328,
London PRO Exchequer K.R. Misc. Book 1.26 (fragment),
Longleat Marquis of Bath 14, Manchester Chetham 6690, Manchester Rylands English 94, Manchester Rylands English 98,
Manchester Rylands English 413, New Haven Yale University
324, New Haven Yale University 535, New York Morgan M
226, Bodl Bodley 131, Bodl Bodley 207, Bodl Bodley 634, Bodl e
Mus. 35, Bodl Eng. th. c. 58 (extracts), Bodl Eng. th. f. 10
(fragment), Bodl Hatton 31, Bodl Rawlinson A. 387B, Oxford
University 123, Oxford Wadham 5, Princeton University Kane
21, San Marino Huntington HM 149, San Marino Huntington
HM 1339, Tokyo Takamiya 4 (Phillipps 8820), Tokyo Takamiya
8, Tokyo Takamiya 20, Urbana University of Illinois 65, Worcester Cathedral C.1.8 (fragment). Cf. 837; for adaptations
and other translations see E. Salter's article in Middle English
Prose: Essays on Bibliographical Problems, ed. A.S.G. Edwards and D. Pearsall (1981), pp. 115-27.

54 Qui habitat in adiutorio altissimi . . . Alle men þat wol liuen in þis
world cristenliche schall suffre persecucions as þe Apostel seiþ or from
withouten be malice of men or from withinne bi temptacion of þe fend

Walter Hilton (?), Qui Habitat, commentary on Psalm 90, s. xiv
(2).

1. Wallner (1954) (Bodl Eng. poet. a. 1, ff. 338v-40v).

Also in CUL Dd.1.1, CUL Hh.1.11, Lambeth Palace 472.
Cf. 115.5.

191

555 Quintus Mucius Augur Seuola This was his name whiche was wonte to telle many thinges merely And by mynde of Celius Lelyus his fader in lawe

John Tiptoft, _Tullius_ _de_ _Amicicia_, translation from a French version of Cicero's work (with prologue and epilogue by Caxton), before 1470.

1. W. Caxton, 1481 (STC 5293, Part 2); 2. [W. Rastell, 1530?] (STC 5275); 3. (1977) (facsimile of 1).

556 [Q]uum appropinquasset ihesus ierosolimam . . . Gode men hit is an heste dei to dei þe is on xii monþe þis godspel sed hu þe helend nehlechede to-ward ierusalem

Sermon collection, s. xii ex.

1. EETS os 29 (1867) and os 34 (1868), pp. 3-159 (odd pages only) (Lambeth Palace 487, ff. 1-59v).

557 Rede this as it foloweth afore the seke persone ye shall vnderstonde that none shall haue the kyngdome of heuen but suche as fyghteth for it and specyally agaynst theyr body in tyme of temptacyon and sekenes

The _Doctrynalle_ _of_ _Deth_, treatise to be read to a man or woman at the point of death, with prayers, s. xv ex.

1. W. de Worde, [1498] (STC 6931); 2. W. de Worde, 1532 (STC 6932).

558 Recipe iij sponfull of the galle of a barough swyne and for a woman of a gilte and iij Sponfull of homelok the Juce

Anaesthetic recipe, s. xv.

1. _Bulletin_ _of_ _the_ _History_ _of_ _Medicine_, 8 (1940), 1247 (Montreal McGill University Osler 7591, p. 42).

559 Recti diligunt te . . . Lauerd seið godes spuse to hire deore wurðe spus þeo richte luuieð þe þeo beoð [þe] richte þe liuieð efter riwle (from 10)

Ancrene _Wisse_ ("Ancrene Riwle"), guide for nuns, s. xiii in. (probably 1215-22).

1. Camden Soc. 57 (1853) (BL Cotton Nero A. XIV, ff. 1-
120v); 2. Journal of Germanic Philology, 2 (1898), 199-202
(Bodl Eng. th. c. 70, f. 1r-y, fragment); 3. ed. J. Pahlsson,
The Recluse, in Lunds Univ. Arsskrift, N.F., Afd. 1, Bd. 6, r.
1 (1911) (Cambridge Magdalene Pepys 2498, pp. 371a-449a),
Wycliffite revision of s. xiv (2); 4. ed. J. Pahlsson, The
Recluse, 2nd ed. (1918) (as in 3); 5. EETS os 225 (1952) (as in
1); 6. EETS os 229 (1954) (Cambridge Gonville and Caius
234/120, pp. 1-185), extracts, rearranged; 7. EETS os 249
(1962) (CCCC 402, ff. 1-117v), rev. version; 8. EETS os 252
(1963), pp. 1-160 (BL Cotton Titus D. XVIII, ff. 14a-105b,
beginning imperfectly at end of Part I); 9. EETS os 252 (1963),
pp. 166-67 (as in 2); 10. EETS os 267 (1972) (BL Cotton
Cleopatra C. VI, ff. 4-198v); 11. EETS os 274 (1976) (as in 3).

Also in Bodl Eng. poet. a. 1, ff. 339vb-93b. French transla-
tions in BL Cotton Vitellius F. VII (EETS os 219 [1944]) and
TCC R.14.7, Bodl Bodley 90, and Paris BN français 6276 (EETS
os 240 [1958]); Latin translation in BL Cotton Vitellius E. VII,
BL Royal 7 C.x, Oxford Magdalen 67, and Oxford Merton 44
(EETS os 216 [1944]).

560   Redde racionem villacacionis tue . . . My dere ferendis ʒe shullen
vndirstonde þat Crist Ihesus auctour and doctour of trewþe in his book
of þe gospel liknyng þe kyngdom of Heuene to an housholdere (from 24)

       Thomas of Wimbledon, "Redde Racionem Villacacionis Tue",
       sermon, 1388.

       1. [J. Mayler? 1540?] (STC 25823.3); 2. E. Whytchurche, ca.
       1548 (STC 25823.7); 3. R. Kele, [ca. 1550] (STC 25824); 4. J.
       Kynge, [1561?] (STC 25825.3); 5. Foxe (1563 and 8 later
       editions to 1684), pp. 175-83; 6. J. Awdely, 1572 (STC
       25825.7); 7. J. Awdely, 1574 (STC 25826); 8. J. Awdely, 1575
       (STC 15827); 9. J. Awdely, 1575 (STC 25827.5); 10. J.
       Charlewood, 1579 (STC 25828); 11. J. Charlewood, 1582 (STC
       25830); 12. J. Charlewood, 1584 (STC 25831); 13. J. Charle-
       wood, 1588 (STC 25832); 14. J. Charlewood, 1593 (STC
       25833); 15. J. Roberts, 1599 (STC 25834); 16. J. Roberts, 1603
       (STC 25834.5); 17. W. Jaggard, 1617 (STC 25835); 18. W.
       Jaggard, 1617 (STC 25836); 19. T. and R. Cotes, 1629 (STC
       25837); 20. T. Cotes, 1634 (STC 25838); 21. T. Cotes, 1635
       (STC 25839); 22. J. Morgan, Phoenix Britannicus (1731-32), I,
       1-17; 23. ed. K.F. Sunden, A Famous Middle English Sermon
       (1925) (Bodl Hatton 57, pp. 1-32); 24. MS, 28 (1966), 178-97
       (CCCC 357, ff. 270-82v); 25. ed. I.K. Knight, Wimbledon's
       Sermon (1967) (as in 24).

Also in Cambridge Magdalene Pepys 2125, Cambridge Sidney Sussex 74, TCC 322, TCD 155, Durham Cathedral Hunter 15.2, Gloucester Cathedral 22 (extracts), Helmingham Hall Lord Tollemache LJ.II.2, Leeds University Brotherton 501, Lincoln Cathedral 50 (extracts), BL Harley 2398, BL Royal 18 A.xvii, BL Royal 18 B.xxiii, BL Addl. 37677, Bodl Eng. th. f. 39, Bodl Laud Miscellaneous 524, Oxford University 97, San Marino Huntington HM 502. A Latin translation from the English in Cambridge Gonville and Caius 334/727 and CUL Ii.3.8.

561   Religyous modir & deuoute sustren clepid & chosen bisily to laboure at the hous of Syon in the blessid vyneʒerd of oure holy Saueour his parfite rewle which hymsilf enditide to kepe contynuly (from 2)

Þe Orcherd of Syon, devotional treatise translated from St. Catherine of Siena's Dialogue, s. xv in.

1. W. de Worde, 1519 (STC 4815); 2. EETS os 258 (1966) (BL Harley 3432, ff. 2-192).

Also in Cambridge St. John's 75, New York Morgan M 162; extracts in Manchester Rylands Latin 395, Oxford University 14.

562   Relygyous syster for as moche as þou arte now planted in the gardyn of holy relygyon yf thou wylt at the last be a tree of þat heuenly paradyse thou must vertuously growe here and bryng forthe good goostly fruyte

Letter of Religious Governaunce and Letter of þe Twelve Fruites of þe Holy Gost ("Devout Treatyse Called the Tree and XII Frutes of the Hooly Goost"), two letters to a female religious, s. xv.

1. R. Copland, 1534 and R. Copland and M. Fawkes, 1535 (STC 13608); 2. ed. J.J. Vaissier (1960), pp. 1-35, 36-164 (Cambridge Fitzwilliam Museum McClean 132, ff. 94-117, 117v-98v).

Also in Durham University Cosin V.III.24, BL Addl. 24192. Jolliffe H.27/0.39 (second letter only).

Relygyus syster in the begynnynge of these symple medytacyonys I pray ʒow firste to wythdrawe ʒoure thowgth fro alle othyr thowghtys Incipit to text proper of 254.

Relygious syster it is not longe a goo that I wrote to the a pystle of relygious exhortacyon how thou sholdest growe in relygyon vertuously as a goostly tree   Incipit to second letter in 562.

563   Respicite volatilia celi Biholde ye the foulis of hevene for bi hem men lerne how thei schulden love god

"A Treatise of the Three Estates", extract from Wycliffite epistle sermons for 21 and 22 Trinity circulating separately, s. xv.

1. Dominican Studies, 3 (1950), 351-58 (BL Harley 2339, ff. 72v-78).

Cf. 304.

564   Recharde hermyte reherces a dredfull tale of vn-perfitte contrecyone þat a haly mane Cesarius tellys in ensample He says þat A ʒonge mane a chanone at parys vn-chastely and delycyously lyfande and full of many synnys laye seke to þe dede

Richard Rolle (?), De Inperfecta Contricione, an exemplum of imperfect contrition from Cesarius of Heisterbach's Dialogus Miraculorum, extracted from Rolle's Judica B, s. xiv.

1. EETS os 20 (1866), pp. 6-7 (Lincoln Cathedral 91, f. 194); 2. Mätzner, I, 2 (1869), 125-26 (as in 1); 3. Wülcker, 1 (1874), 116 (as in 1); 4. YW, I (1895), 192-93 (as in 1); 5. Kluge (1904, 1912), pp. 33-34 (as in 1); 6. EETS os 20, rev. ed. (1921), pp. 6-7 (as in 1).

Cf. 58; also 126.

565   Richt Hie and mychty prince and Souuerane lorde as writtis the gret and devin philosophoure plato Tunc Beate sunt res publice

John of Ireland, Meroure of Wysdome, guide for princes written for King James IV of Scotland, 1490.

1. STS, 2nd series 19 (1926) (Edinburgh NLS Advocates 18.2.8).

566   Ryʒt noble and Reuerent Ladi As Poetys dyties recorden the prayer of the souereyn is a violent maner of commawndement which semeth not ʒe soiet in no wyse disobey

Lytill Tretis Draw Owt of the Sciens of Ciromanci, treatise on palmistry, s. xv.

1. ed. D.J. Price, An Old Palmistry (1953), even pages only (Bodl Digby Roll IV).

567 Right nobill and worthy lady and my full reuerent and dere goestly doughter in oure lord Jhesu I haue in mynd how on seint Jeromys day (from 2)

Simon Wynter (?), Vita Beati Ieronimi Confessoris/Lyff of Seint Jerome, saint's life translated from the Legenda Aurea, followed by two Latin prayers to St. Jerome, s. xv.

1. [W. de Worde, 1499?] (STC 14508), without prologue; 2. Anglia, 3 (1880), 328-60 (Lambeth Palace 432, ff. 1-37).

Also in Cambridge St. John's 250, Lambeth Palace 72, New Haven Yale University 317.

Ryght welbelouyd brother and persone Eloquent thou admonestest and exhortest me to prepare and make redy place and entree for the vnto the lyf Curiall whyche thou desirest   Incipit to text proper of 300.

568 Ryse Richard Rise Richard Rise Richard quia genuisti regem orbis Vox in sompnis Anno domini 1454 mensis augusti die 13

John Piggot, "Memoranda" on the events of 1450-54, s. xv med.

1. Kingsford, EHL (1913), pp. 370-73 (BL Harley 543, f. 144).

569 Robert Steward the kyng of Scotis hadde ii sonnys of the whiche the eldere was a semely mane of persone and knyght clepid the duke of Roseye

John Shirley, The Dethe of the Kynge of Scotis, chronicle of the murder and death of James I of Scotland, ca. 1440.

1. ed. J. Pinkerton, The History of Scotland (1797), I, 462-75 (BL Addl. 5467, ff. 72v-82v); 2. Miscellanea Scotica, 2 (1818), 3-29 (as in 1); 3. ed. J. Stevenson, Maitland Club (1837), pp. 47-67 (as in 1).

570   Seynt adryan was abbot of the monastery of viridian that is a lytle fro napuls And for his vertue and cunnynge vitalian the pope wolde haue made him archebussope of Caunterbury

        Kalendre of the Newe Legende of Englande, English epitome of John Capgrave's Latin compilation Nova Legenda Anglie, s. xv ex. (?).

        1. R. Pynson, 1516 (STC 4602, Part 1).

571   Seynt albert the byschop seyth thes wordis folowynge Fyrst when ye receyue oure lord in forme of bred ye receyve v partis The fyrst ys the same body that he toke of the vurgyn marie

        A God Seying of Seynt Albert the Bysshop What Ye Resceve When Ye Resceve the Blessed Sacrament of the Auter, instruc-tions for receiving the Eucharist translated from Latin, s. xv.

        1. Ampe (1964), pp. 169-71 (Bodl Laud Miscellaneous 517, ff. 181-82).

        For another translation see 572.

572   Seynt Albert the byschopp thou man he sayth whan thou takest goddys body thou takyst v partyes The fyrst part ys the body that he toke of the mayde

        The Sacrament of the Auter, instructions for receiving the Eu-charist translated from Latin, s. xv.

        1. Ampe (1964), pp. 168-69 (BL Harley 665, ff. 297v-98).

        Also in TCC R.3.21, BL Harley 1706, Lambeth Palace 546, and Bodl Douce 322. For another translation see 571.

573   Saynt Ancelyne ersbiscop of Cantyrbery says þat a seke man languys-sand to þe dede sulde of his prest þus be askide and þus he answer

        [Richard Rolle], a form of death-bed confession translated from St. Anselm's Admonitio Morienti, s. xiv.

        1. YW, I (1895), 107-8 (Bodl Rawlinson C. 285, ff. 60v-61);
        2. ed. R.W. Southern and F.S. Schmitt, Memorials of St. Anselm (1969), pp. 353-54 (as in 1).

Also in CUL Ff.5.40, CUL Ff.6.21, Oxford Trinity 86. Jolliffe L.6/N.12.

574 Seynt Austyne the holy doctour techeth thorough declaracion of holy wryte that the synfulle mane for noo synne falle in despeyre ffor more ys the mercy of gode to mane thane any mannes synne

Meditacio Sancti Augustini, treatise on the infinite mercy of God translated from a Latin piece of Pseudo-Augustine, s. xiv.

1. YW, II (1896), 377-80 (BL Harley 1706, ff. 81-83).

Also in CUL Hh.1.12, Glasgow University Hunterian 520, Manchester Rylands English 412, Bodl Douce 322, Bodl Laud Miscellaneous 23, Bodl Addl. C. 87. Jolliffe I.32.

575 Seynt Bernard spekis of þo comyng of oure lord Ihesu Crist & saies I wil not breþer ʒe forgete þo tyme of ʒoure visytacion

[Richard Rolle], Of the Double Comminge of Christ, translation of St. Bernard's De Adventu Domini Sermo VI, s. xiv.

1. YW, II (1896), 60-62 (BL Royal 17 B.xvii, ff. 67-69).

576 Seynt Birget was of the stok and lynage of the noble kyng of Gothis of the kyngdome of Swecia hir Faders name was Byrgerus

[Thomas Gascoigne], Lyfe of Seynt Birgetta, saint's life followed by two Latin prayers to St. Bridget, s. xv med. (?).

1. R. Pynson, 1516 (STC 4602, Part 2); 2. EETS es 19 (1873), pp. xlvii-lix (as in 1).

Other prose versions of the life in BL Cotton Claudius B. I and BL Cotton Julius F. II.

577 Seynt Edward þe good kynge oughte devoutly to be hade in remembraunce he was borne in England of þe blood royalle Afore hys dayes þer was in Englande oft-tymes werre and bloode-scheed

"Life of Edward the Confessor", saint's life, s. xv.

1. Moore (1942), pp. 108-30 (Oxford Trinity 11, ff. 1-51v).

198

For other ME prose versions of the life of Edward the Confessor see 357 and **803**; for the verse version from the <u>South</u> <u>English</u> <u>Legendary</u> see <u>IMEV</u> 2888.

78   Saynt Frauncis in the IIIIth chapiter of his rewle saith these wordis that folowe I commaunde stedfastly to all my bretherne that in noo wise they resceiue coyne or money

John Howell (?), notes to the Franciscan Rule, s. xv.

1. Rolls 4, 1 (1858), 567-74 (BL Cotton Faustina D. IV, ff. 34,42, 56).

See **697**.

79   Seynt Gregori Sent Syluester and Sent Leon that were popys of Rome reseyved þis writyng and sayd Hosoeuer bere þis writyng abowte hym he thar not drede hym

Introduction to charm (in Latin) received by the popes, s. xv (2).

1. Louis (1980), pp. 247-48 (Bodl Tanner 407, f. 36r-v).

80   Seynt Gregore with oþire popes and bisshoppes yn seere Haue graunted of pardon xxvj dayes and xxvj Mill yeere To þeym þat before þis fygure on þeire knees

Indulgence, s. xv.

1. [ca. 1490] (STC 14077c.9).

Saynt Ierome came of noble kinne and in his childhode he was sent to rome to lerne And ther he lerned Trew latyn and Ebrew   Incipit to text proper of **567**.

81   Seynt Leon the pape of Rome wrote this letter and sende hyt to kyng Charles the gode kyng of Frawnce whyche an angell of heuyn browȝt hym

Letter from heaven acting as a kind of charm, ca. 1470.

1. <u>Anglia</u>, 42 (1918), 219 (Göttingen Universität philol. 163, f. 72v).

Also in Edinburgh NLS Advocates 19.3.1, BL Harley 586, BL Royal 17 A.xvi, BL Addl. 37677, Bodl Rawlinson C.814.

582　Saynt Poul doctour of veryte sayth to vs that al thynges that ben reduced by wrytyng ben wryton to our doctryne and Boece maketh mencion that the helthe of euery persone procedeth dyuercely

William Caxton, Th' Ystorye and Lyf of the Noble and Crysten Prynce Charles the Grete, romance translated from the French prose Fierabras (1478) attributed to Jean Bagnyon, 1485.

1. W. Caxton, 1485 (STC 5013); 2. EETS es 36, 37 (1880-81) (as in 1).

583　Sanct paul sais that rycht as our lord Ihesu cryst is mar worthi and mar preciouss than ony vthir creatur that god maid

Vertewis of the Mess, comments by Jesus, the evangelists, and church fathers, s. xv.

1. EETS os 43 (1870), pp. 113-15 (CUL Kk.1.5.6, ff. 53-54); 2. STS, 3rd series 11 (1939), pp. 192-94 (as in 1).

584　Seint Poule þapostle seiþ þat alle þoo þat willen pytiuosli leuen in iesu crist shullen suffre persecuciouns & anguisshes Ac oure swete lorde Iesus crist ne wil nouȝth þat his chosen failen in tribulacioun

Apocalips of Jesu Crist, translation from Norman French, with commentary, s. xiv.

1. ed. E. Fridner, An English Fourteenth Century Apocalypse Version (1961), pp. 1-206 (BL Harley 874, ff. 2-31).

Also in Cambridge Gonville and Caius 231/117, Cambridge Magdalene Pepys 2498, Cambridge St. John's 193, TCD 69, BL Harley 3913, BL Royal 17 A.xxvi, Manchester Rylands English 92, New York Columbia University Plimpton Add. 3, Bodl Laud Miscellaneous 33, Bodl Laud Miscellaneous 235, Bodl Rawlinson C. 750. Another prose version in Cambridge Magdalene F. 4. 5, BL Harley 171, BL Harley 1203.

585　Salue regina mater Heil qweene modir of merci heil lijf swetnesse & oure hope to þee we crien outlawid sones of eue we siȝen weymentynge and wepinge

Antym of Oure Lady, hours of the Virgin, s. xiv.

1. MLN, 30 (1915), 231 (Bodl Ashmole 1288, f. 49v).

586 . . . [s]ancte matris ecclesie filius ad quos presentes . . . Oure moste
holy faders the popes aboue specified that is to say pope Innocent of
blessyd memorie the viii and Alexandre the sext the pope that nowe is

Reissue of bulls by Popes Innocent VIII and Alexander VI confirming the succession of Henry VII and other matters, in English
and Latin, ca. 1497.

1. [R. Pynson, 1497] (STC 14099).

Cf. 518.

587 Sathanas kyng of sorowe prince off darkenes duke and lorde of all hell
abbott and prior of all apostatais from Crist of the order of ypocrysie
and president of pride to all þe brethern of our ordre the coventis of
lyers

Sathanas Commyssion unto His Wel Belovyde Sectis of Perdi-
cion, Wycliffite satire in the form of an "epistola Sathane ad
cleros", s. xiv ex.

1. Hudson (1978), pp. 89-93 (CUL Ff.6.2, ff. 81-84v).

Cf. 444.

588 Satera is a thyng that bygynnythe goodely and so endithe commede is he
that begynnythe loborusly and wickidly and endithe ioyfully

Notes on Latin words, s. xv ex.

1. Hanna (1984), p. 2 (San Marino Huntington HM 64, f. 14v).

589 Sei me where was god whanne he made heven and erthe Maister I sey
the in the forthere ende of the wynde (from 4)

Questiones By-twene the Maister of Oxenford and His Clerke,
modernization of the Old English prose dialogue "Salomon and
Saturn" in BL Cotton Vitellius A. XV, s. xv.

1. Rel. Ant., I (1841), 230-32 (BL Lansdowne 762, f. 3v); 2.

Kemble (1848), pp. 216-20 (as in 1); 3. Wülcker, 2 (1879), 191-94 (as in 1); 4. ES, 8 (1885), 284-87 (BL Harley 1304, f. 100).

590   Sciant presentes & futuri . . . Wetiþ ȝe þat ben now here & þei þat schulen comen after ȝou þat almiȝti god in trinite fader & sone & holy gost haþ ȝouen & graunted (from 4)

Þe Chartre of þe Abbeye of þe Holy Gost, devotional treatise, s. xiv (2).

1. W. de Worde, [1496]; 2. W. de Worde, 1497 (STC 13609); 3. W. de Worde, [1521] (STC 13610); 4. YW, I (1895), 337-62 (Bodl Laud Miscellaneous 210, ff. 136-46v, supplemented by Bodl Eng. poet. a. 1, ff. 360b-63a).

Also in Aberystwyth NLW Peniarth 334A, Cambridge Jesus 46, Cambridge Magdalene Pepys 2125, TCC O.1.29, CUL Ii.4.9, CUL Ll.5.18, Hopton Hall Chandos-Pole-Gell MS, BL Egerton 3245, BL Harley 1704, BL Harley 2406, BL Harley 5272, BL Addl. 22283, BL Addl. 36983, Longleat Marquis of Bath 4, Maidstone Corporation Museum Mus. 6, New York Columbia University Plimpton 263, Bodl Douce 323, Stonyhurst College B.xxiii, Stonyhurst College B.xliii, Winchester College 33. Jolliffe H.9. Cf. 39, which is usually joined in MS with the Chartre. On the early printed editions see Allen, Writings (1927), p. 336.

Scyence hath many enemyes for as moche as there is a grete multitude of them that be ygnorant of it Of whom the peasyble kynge Salomon sayth that the nombre of ffoles ben Infenyte   Incipit to prologue of 783.

Scientes quia hora est . . . We taken as bileve þat epistlis of apostlis ben gospelis of Crist for he spak hem alle in hem and Crist mai not erre Incipit to Sunday Epistles series of 304.

591   Sedechias was the first Philosofer bi whom as it was the wille of god lawe was founded and Receyued and wisdome vndrestand

Stephen Scrope, Doctrine of Wisdom of the Wise Auncient Philosophurs ("Dicts and Sayings of the Philosophers"), moral pronouncements attributed to old philosophers translated from the French Dits Moraulx by Guillaume de Tignonville, 1450.

202

A. Original version: 1. ed. M. Schofield (1936), pp. 49-205 (Bodl Bodley 943 supplemented by CUL Dd.9.18); 2. EETS os 211 (1941), pp. 2-292 (even pages only) (Bodl Bodley 943).

B. Revised version, by William Worcester (1472): 1. EETS os 211 (1941), pp. 2-92, variants (even pages only) (TCC O.5.6, ff. 38-64v, CUL Gg.1.34.2, and interlineated in Cambridge Emmanuel 31).

C. Anonymous abbreviated version entitled Liber de Moralibus Philosophorum (s. xv [2]): 1. EETS os 211 (1941), pp. 297-320 (Bodl Rawlinson poet. 32, ff. 194-204).

Another MS of A: Cambridge Emmanuel 31. Cf. 834, 864, and also the metrical paraphrase made directly from the Latin Liber Philosophorum Moralium Antiquorum by George Ashby in the third quarter of the 15th c. (see IMEV 738; ed. EETS es 76 (1899), pp. 43-100, from CUL Mm.4.42).

Sedechias was the first Philosophir by whoom through the wil and pleaser of oure lorde god Sapience was vnderstande and lawes resceyued   Incipit to text proper of 834.

Sentite a domino in bonitate . . . These wordis that I haue seyd here of euerlastynge wysdom ben thus moche to seye in englysshe Felyth oure lorde in goodnes   Incipit to text proper of 465.

Sepcies in die Laudem dixi tibi These ar the wordes of the prophete Dauid saynge thus to our lorde Seuen times on the day I haue sayde praysynges to the   Incipit to text proper of 798.

592   She desyred many tymes that her hede myght be smyten of with an axe vpon a blocke for the loue of our lorde Ihesu

Shorte Treatyse of Contemplacyon, extracts from the "Book of Margery Kempe", s. xv ex. (?).

1. W. de Worde, [1501] (STC 14924); 2. H. Pepwell, 1521 (STC 20972, Part 3) (as in 1); 3. EETS os 212 (1940), pp. 353-57 (as in 1).

Cf. 288.

593 Schort hors sone y-whyped lytell mete sone y-flypyd Curtus equus sito
     strigillatur et modicus sibus illico liguritur Hyt ys grete feleny a mon to
     say a word

     Thomas Schort, "Vulgaria", English sentences with Latin equi-
     valents for use in school, 1427-65.

     1. Traditio, 38 (1982), 314-26 (Oxford Lincoln Lat. 129, ff.
     92-99).

     Cf. 270.

     Si quis habet anelitum uel nasum fetentum   See 625.

594 Si sciret paterfamilias qua hora fur uenturus esset . . . Ure hauerd i þe
     godspel teacheð us þurh abisne hu we ahen wearliche to biwiten us
     seoluen wið þe unwiht of helle

     Sawles Warde, sermon on Matthew 24.43 derived from Hugh of
     St. Victor's De Anima, Book 4, s. xiii in.

     1. EETS os 34 (1868), pp. 245-67 (odd pages only) (Bodl Bodley
     34, ff. 72-80v, supplemented by BL Royal 17 A.xxvii, f. 10r-
     v); 2. Kluge (1904, 1912), pp. 8-15 (Bodl Bodley 34 only, as in
     1); 3. ed. W. Wagner (1908) (BL Royal 17 A.xxvii only, as in
     1); 4. Hall (1920), 1, 117-28 (as in 1); 5. ed. A. Brandl and O.
     Zippel, Mittelenglische Sprach- und Literaturproben (1917,
     1927, 1949), pp. 227-35 (as in 1); 6. ed. R.M. Wilson (1938),
     even pages (upper parts) (as in 2); 7. ed. R.M. Wilson (1938),
     even pages (lower parts) (as in 3); 8. ed. R.M. Wilson (1938),
     odd pages (BL Cotton Titus D. XVIII, ff. 105v-12v); 9. ed.
     J.A.W. Bennett and G.V. Smithers, Early Middle English
     Verse and Prose (1966, 1968), pp. 247-61 (as in 2); 10. d'Ar-
     denne (1977), pp. 165-85 (as in 2).

595 Sicut enim corpus sine spiritu moritur ita opera sine fide . . . For it is
     seide in holdynge of oure haly day þat we schulde ocupie þe tyme in
     prechynge and preiynge and deuoute herynge of þe lawe of god

     Feiþ, Hope, and Charite, Wycliffite tract, s. xiv (2).

     1. EETS os 74 (1880, 1902), pp. 347-55 (Oxford New 95, ff.
     124-27v).

     Also in TCD 245 and York Minster XVI.L.12; a slightly different version is in Paris Bibl. Ste-Geneviève 3390.

596 Siþ byleve teches us þat everiche yvel is ouþer synne or comes synne synne schulde be fled as al maner of yvel And siþ no þing is fled by wisdome of mon bot if þo harme of þat þing be knowen

Synne Is for to Drede, Wycliffite tract, s. xiv (2).

1. SEW, III (1871), 119-67 (Bodl Bodley 647, ff. 1-37).

Also in Cambridge (Mass.) Harvard University English 738, TCD 245, Bodl Bodley 938, and Bodl Douce 273.

597 Siþ ilche cristen man is holdon to sewe Crist and who euer fayliþ in þis is apostata it is likliche to many men þat þe mor part of men bi her viciose lijf ben combred in þis heresye

Tractatus de Apostasia Cleri, Wycliffite tract, s. xiv (2).

1. Todd (1851), pp. lxxxi-cxii (TCD 245, ff. 76-80v); 2. SEW, III (1871), 430-40 (as in 1).

598 Siþen it is so þat in þe first and secund parties of þe donet into cristen religiioun bifore goyng þis present book ben alle þe poyntis of goddis lawe ful openli vndir a compendi and ful profitabli expressid

Reginald Pecock, Folower to þe Donet, ca. 1453-54.

1. EETS os 164 (1924) (BL Royal 17 D.ix, ff. 2-100v).

599 Sen yt es so þat þe land beȝond þe see þat es to say þe land of repromission þat men calles þe Haly Land amanges all oþer landes es þe maste worthy land

Þe Buke of John Maundevill, travel literature, conflation of two earlier English translations, s. xv in.

1. Roxburghe (1889) (BL Egerton 1982, ff. 3-132v).

For other translations see 232, 233, and 239. Verse translations in IMEV 248.5 and 3117.6.

Sen it is sa that apon this mater the quhilk may be lyknyt till a tree that

may bere na fruyte bot fruyte of dolour and dises   Incipit to text
proper of 774.

600   Siþ many falce gloseris maken goddis lawe derk and letten seculere men
to susteyne it and kepen it of siche falce gloseris schulde ech man be
war

"Of Dominion", Wycliffite tract, s. xiv (2).

1. EETS os 74 (1880, 1902), pp. 284-93 (TCD 244, ff. 188-
93v).

Sithe of þese þree worschipfull kynges alle þe worlde from þe risyng of
þe sonne to his downe-goynge ys full of preisyng and merites   Incipit to edition 6 of 290.

Syth that I haue aplyed me to declare and publysshe to alle crysten
people the siege of the noble and invyncyble cytee of Rhodes   Incipit to text proper of 776.

601   Siþen þat þe trouþe of God stondiþ not in oo langage more þan in
anoþer but who so lyueþ best and techiþ best plesiþ moost God of what
langage þat euere it be

Wycliffite treatise justifying translation of the Bible into the
vernacular, s. xiv ex.

1. Hudson (1978), pp. 107-9 (CUL Ii.6.26, ff. 41v-46).

602   Sethe the departynge of our souereyne lorde the king Edwarde the iiijth
oute of the contree of Zeland and there toke the see the xth day of
Marche (from A)

The Arryvaile of Kynge Edward the Fourthe, chronicle of the
events of 1471 translated from French, 1471-72.

A. Short version: 1. Speculum, 56 (1981), 326-32 (London
College of Arms 2M.16, ff. 33v-36).

B. Longer, official account: 1. Camden Soc. 1 (1838), pp. 1-40
(BL Harley 543, ff. 31-49v).

A also in BL Addl. 46354.

603   Sen the passage of this vrechit warlde the quhilk is callit dede semys harde perelus ande rycht horreble to mony men

Craft of Deyng, translation from Latin, s. xv.

1. EETS os 43 (1870), pp. 1-8 (CUL Kk.1.5.6, ff. 1-4); 2. STS, 3rd series 11 (1939), pp. 166-74 (as in 1).

For another translation see 234.

604   Syþþe þe Pater Noster is þe beste prayer þat is for in it mot alle oþer prayers be closed yf þey schulle graciouslyche be hurde of God þerfore scholde men kunne þis prayour and studie þe wyt þerof

Þe Pater Noster, Wycliffite exposition of the Pater Noster, s. xiv (2).

1. SEW, III (1871), 98-110 (BL Harley 2398, ff. 166v-73).

Also in TCC B.14.38 (part only), CUL Nn.4.12, Manchester Rylands English 85, Manchester Rylands English 90, Norwich Castle Museum 158.926.4g.3, Bodl Bodley 938, Princeton Robert H. Taylor MS. This text shares material with 601.

605   Syth the tyme that the grete and high tour of babilone was bylded men haue spoken with dyuerse tonges In such wise that dyuerse men be strange to other and vnderstand not others speche

John Trevisa, Bookes of Cronykes/Polychronycon, translation of Ranulph Higden's Polychronicon, 1398, enlarged by William Caxton ca. 1482.

1. W. Caxton, 1482 (STC 13438); 2. W. de Worde, 1495 (STC 13439); 3. P. Treveris, 1527 (STC 13440); 4. Rolls 41, 8 vols. (1865-1882), odd pages, upper halves (Cambridge St. John's 204 supplemented by 1).

Other MSS (without the Caxton additions): Aberdeen University 21, CCCC 354, Cambridge St. John's 204, Glasgow University Hunterian 367, Liverpool Public Library f909HIG, BL Cotton Tiberius D. VII, BL Harley 1900, BL Stowe 65, BL Addl. 24194, Manchester Chetham 11379, former Penrose 12, Princeton Robert H. Taylor MS, Princeton University Garrett 153, San Marino Huntington HM 28561. New Haven Yale University Osborn 1.20 copied from edition 2. Another translation in 35.

605.3 Sythen witte stondis not in langage but in groundynge of treuthe for þo
same witte is in laten þat is in Grew or Ebrew

> "Tractatus de Regibus", Wycliffite tract on the relations between
> church and state, s. xiv ex.
>
> 1. Genet (1977), pp. 5-19 (Bodl Douce 273, ff. 37v-53).

Sincipit et vertex caput occipur et coma crinis   Incipit to vocabulary
preceding 270.

Syr I besyche yow and alle the convent   See 674.

606   Sire It is wele knowe to ʒowe that ther was a Parlement somond of all
the States of the Reaume for to be at Westmynstre and to begynne on
the Teusday

> Announcement of King Richard's deposition, 1399.
>
> 1. Twysden (1652), cols. 2760-62; 2. Hearne (1729), pp. 214-
> 16 (BL Cotton Tiberius C. IX and BL Cotton Claudius B. IX);
> 3. Rotuli Parliamentorum (1783), 3, 424a-b; 4. Rolls 28, 3
> (1866), 284-86 (CCCC 7).
>
> Also in BL Cotton Faustina B. IX, BL Cotton Nero D. VII,
> Bodl Bodley 462; circulates separately in BL Stowe 66, BL Addl.
> 48031, London College of Arms Arundel 29, Lambeth Palace
> 738, and Woburn Abbey Duke of Bedford 181.

607   Sires I thank God and ʒowe Spirituel and Temporel and all the astates
of the Lond

> Speech by King Henry IV, 1399.
>
> 1. Twysden (1652), col. 2759; 2. Hearne (1729), p. 212 (BL
> Cotton Tiberius C. IX and BL Cotton Claudius B. IX); 3.
> Rotuli Parliamentorum (1783), 3, 423b; 4. Rolls 28, 3 (1866),
> 282 (CCCC 7).
>
> Also in BL Cotton Faustina B. IX, BL Cotton Nero D. VII,
> Bodl Bodley 462.

607.5 Suster thou hast ofte axed of me a forme of lyuyng accordyng to thyn estat inasmuche as thou art enclosed

> A Tretys That Is a Rule and a Forme of Lyvynge Perteynyng to a
> Recluse, translation of Ailred of Rievaulx's De Institutione
> Inclusarum, s. xv (1).
>
> 1. EETS os 287 (1984), pp. 1-25 (Bodl Bodley 423, ff. 178-92).
>
> For another translation see 478.

608 Sex wapunde makiet j ledpounde xij ledpunde j fotmel xxiiij fotmel j
fothir of Bristouwe ys have cc and xxviij wexpound

> "Measures of Weight", s. xiv.
>
> 1. Rel. Ant., I (1841), 70 (BL Cotton Claudius E. VIII, f. 8).

So Bretherne here is my maister I N whiche of his clene deuocioun that
he hath to god and of a speciall desire to us askyth to be amitted
See 787.3.

609 . . . So befell it as fortune it wolde one of the thre sones came as ye
wynde brought his navy by grete tourment that he passed besyde
Croyne in galyce (from 3)

> Henry Watson (?), Hystory of the Moost Excellent and Myghty
> Prynce and High Renowmed Knyght Ponthus of Galyce and of
> Lytell Brytayne, romance translated from French, s. xvi in.
>
> 1. [W. de Worde, 1509?] (STC 20107, 23435a), fragment; 2.
> [R. Pynson? ca. 1510] (STC 20107.5), fragment; 3. W. de
> Worde, 1511 (STC 20108), beginning imperfectly; 4. Archiv,
> 118 (1907), 326-27 (as in 2).
>
> Cf. 476.

610 Sol ys ingendred of pure fix mercury and of sulphre red fix and cler &c
luna is engendred of mercury almost fix

> Alchemical notes, s. xv (2).
>
> 1. Hanna (1984), p. 52 (San Marino Huntington HU 1051, f.
> 51).

611   Salomon in his parablys sayth that a good spyryte makyth a flourynge
      aege that is a fayre aege and a longe

      Treatyse of Fysshynge wyth an Angle, s. xv (1).

      1. W. de Worde, 1496 (STC 3309); 2. W. de Worde [1533?]
      (STC 3313.5, 24243); 3. H. Tab, 1540 (STC 3310); 4. J.
      Waley, [1550?] (STC 3316); 5. W. Copland, [1561] (STC
      3312); 6. W. Copland, [n.d.] (STC 3313.7, 24244); 7. A.
      Vele, [1563?] (STC 3311); 3. E. Allde, 1586 (STC 3313); 9. A.
      Islip, 1596 (STC 3315, 12412); 10. Haslewood (1810-11) (fac-
      simile of 1); 11. ed. W. Pickering (1827) (as in 1); 12. ed.
      G.W. Van Siclen (1875) (as in 1); 13. ed. M.G. Watkins (1880)
      (facsimile of 1); 14. ed. T. Satchell (1883), pp. 1-37 (New
      Haven Yale University Wagstaff 18, ending imperfectly); 15. ed.
      "Piscator" (1885) (as in 1); 16. ed. M.G. Watkins (1894) (as in
      1); 17. ed. St.J. Hornby and M. Turton (1903) (as in 1); 18.
      Origins of Angling (1963), pp. 135-73 (odd pages only) (as in
      14); 19. Origins of Angling (1963), pp. 184-229 (facsimile and
      transcript of 1); 20. (1966) (facsimile of 1); 21. Hawking (1972)
      (facsimile of 9); 22. Braekman (1980), pp. 57-83 (as in 1).

      Part of what is later called the Boke of St. Albans.

612   Summe causes meuen summe pore prestis to resceyue not benefices þe
      friste for drede of symonye þe secunde for drede of myspendynge pore
      mennus goodis (from 2)

      Whi Pore Prestis Han None Benefice, Wycliffite tract, s. xiv (2).

      1. Lewis (1720), pp. 287-98 (CCCC 296, pp. 203-9); 2. EETS
      os 74 (1880, 1902), pp. 245-53 (as in 1).

      Also in TCD 244.

      Som dayes þer bene unhappy and perilous as þe auctoures of Grekes
      seyne   Incipit to second item in 687.

613   Somtyme in þe Cyte of Rome was an Emperour named Poncianus a man
      of grete wysdome He toke to his wyfe a kynges doughter that fayre and
      goodly was (from 2)

      Th' Ystorye of þe VII Wyse Maysters of Rome/Treatyse of the
      Seven Sages of Rome, romance, s. xv.

                                    210

1. [R. Pynson, 1493] (STC 21297), fragment; 2. W. de Worde, [1506?] (STC 21298); 3. W. Copland, [ca. 1555] (STC 21299); 4. ed. G.L. Gomme (1885) (as in 2).

Many modernized and chapbook versions from the late 16th to the 19th centuries. For a verse version see IMEV 3187.

614 Sum-tyme olde wise clerckus þe whiche knewe kyndes and complexcio-nes of men and of bestus þei fonden and writoun many grete resounus in helpynge of bestus

Horse Leechynge, a treatise on medicines for horses, s. xiv.

1. ed. A.C. Svinhufvud, A Late Middle English Treatise on Horses (1978) (BL Sloane 2584, ff. 102-17v).

615 Sym tyme there was in the land of Cecile a king that was called Melhagerie the which was the wysest and the moste iuste king that men knowe euer ouer all in his tyme

"Ipomedon", romance translated from Hue de Rotelande's Anglo-Norman poem (ca. 1190), ca. 1460.

1. ed. E. Kölbing (1889), pp. 323-58 (Longleat Marquis of Bath 257, ff. 90-106v).

For verse versions see IMEV 2142 and 2635.

Son Herkyn þe commandementis of þe mastir   See 83.

Spare me Lord   See 532.

Specyally I haske God mercy that I haue not kepytt his commandments See 136.

Stabat Johannes . . . Þis gospel telliþ in storie how Crist gederide his disciplis and seiþ þat Joon stood and two of Joones disciplis   Incipit to Proprium Sanctorum series in 304.

Sum es fui esse futurus Indicatiuo modo tempore presenti sum   Latin incipit to version B of 306.

616 Swete ihesu cryst for thy blody wounds kepe me fro synne and fendys
    ylle and to lyue aftyr thes viii rulys geue me grace and hartely wyll

    [Richard Rolle], Prayer, s. xiv (2) (?).

    1. Allen, Writings (1927), p. 344 (Lambeth Palace 546, ff. 53v-
    55).

617 Swete lefdi seinte marie meiden ouer meidnes þu bere þat blisfule bern
    þe arerde mon cun þat wes adun ifallet þurh adames sunnen (from 2)

    Oreisun of Seinte Marie ("On Lofsong of Ure Lefdi"), mystical
    prayer to the Virgin freely translated from the Latin poem Oratio
    ad Sanctam Mariam by Bishop Marbod of Rennes, s. xiii in.

    1. EETS os 34 (1868), pp. 205-7 (odd pages only) (BL Cotton
    Nero A. XIV, ff. 126v-28); 2. EETS os 34 (1868), p. 305 (BL
    Royal 17 A.xxvii, f. 70r-v, ending imperfectly); 3. ed. G.
    Sampson, Cambridge Book of Prose and Verse (1924), I, 196-98
    (as in 1); 4. EETS os 241 (1958), pp. 16-18 (as in 1); 5. EETS
    os 241 (1958), p. 19 (as in 2).

618 Swete lord Jesu Cryst I thanke þe and ʒelde þe graces of þat swete
    prayere and of þat holy orysoun þat þou madest

    Richard Rolle, Meditacio de Passione Domine (A)/Devoute Me-
    ditaciouns of þe Passioun of Christ (B), s. xiv (1).

    A. Original text: 1. ES, 7 (1884), 454-63, with corrections in
    ES, 12 (1889), 463-68 (CUL Ll.1.8, ff. 201-7v); 2. YW, I
    (1895), 83-91 (as in 1).

    B. Longer, revised version: 1. YW, I (1895), 92-103 (CUL
    Addl. 3042, ff. 26-78v); 2. ed. H. Lindkvist, Skrifter utgifna
    af K. Humanistiska Vetenskaps-Samfundet i Uppsala, 19,3
    (1917) (Uppsala Universitetsbiblioteket C 494 ff. 1-32, begin-
    ning imperfectly); 3. ed. M.F. Madigan, The Passio Domini
    Theme in the Works of Richard Rolle (1978), pp. 236-77 (BL
    Cotton Titus C. XIX, ff. 92v-117v).

    B also in Bodl e Mus. 232, ff. 1v-18v, partially edited in Allen,
    English (1931), pp. 27-36 (a partial edition of A is also in this
    volume, on pp. 19-27). Cf. 749, which is apparently an imita-
    tion; also cf. 367.

Take   See also Accipe

619   Take a dark stone and chave it to powder and geve it to the traveling
woman to drinke with wyne and she shalbe deliverid anon

Medical recipes, s. xv.

1. ed. T. Vallese, Un ignoto ricettario medico inglese del xiv
secolo (1940), pp. 19-55 (odd pages only) (Naples Biblioteca
Nazionale XIII.B.29, pp. 1-20).

620   Take a long lyne and put on a greate corke then put on ye cord a
forkeyd stycke

To Catch a Pyke at All Tymes, fishing treatise, s. xv.

1. Braekman (1980), pp. 39-42 (BL Harley 2389, f. 73).

621   Take a moldwerp and sethe it wele in wax and wryng it thurgh a clathe

Recipe for ointment for the gout, s. xv.

1. Chaucer and Middle English Studies (1974), p. 60 (BL Royal
17 A.viii, f. 28v).

Take a small Ele that ys qwycke and put yt on your hoke throwgh the
skynne and so yt wyll leve ij or iij days   Incipit to edition 1 of 634.

622   Take a viole of glas and lute it wele or a longe erþen pot and take I
pounde of salt armonyac

Medical recipes (primarily), s. xiv.

1. Henslow (1899), pp. 123-31 (BL Sloane 2584, ff. 5-180
passim).

Tak and mak pouder of palma christi and frankencens   Incipit to
edition 2 of 639.

623   Tak and write in thre hostys thre clausis In the furst hoyst write in the
compas

Charm for fevers, s. xv.

1. Chaucer and Middle English Studies (1974), p. 59 (BL Sloane 2457, f. 29).

Take benes and dry hem in a nost or in an Ovene and hulle hem wele and wyndewe out þe hulkes and wayshe hem clene   Incipit to text proper of 238.

624   Take beeff and merybones and boyle yt in fayre water þan take fayre wortys and wassche hem clene in water and parboyle hem in clene water

Cookbook, divided into three parts, containing 258 recipes, followed by bills of fare for seven banquets, s. xv (1).

1. EETS os 91 (1888), pp. 1-64 (BL Harley 279).

Also in Bodl Ashmole 1439.

625   Take blac mynte and wos of the rewe of boþe y-lych moche and do hit in þe nostrell

Medical recipes (223) and a charm, s. xiv.

1. Henslow (1899), pp. 8-73 (MS in Henslow's possession, ff. 159-258 passim).

626   Tac brasyl ant seoþ in dichwater to þe halfendel oþer to þe þridde partie and seþþe tac a ston of chalk

Recipes, s. xiv.

1. Archiv, 207 (1971), 96-97 (BL Harley 2253, f. 52v).

627   Take clene qwete and bray hit wele in a morter that tho holles gone alle of and then seth hit that hit breke in faire watur

Recipes (199) for cooking, followed by a medicinal recipe, s. xv.

1. Proceedings of the Society of Antiquaries of London (1790), 425-73 (BL Arundel 334, pp. 275-445); 2. Warner (1791), pp. 51-92 (as in 1).

628   Take Colys and stripe hem faire fro the stalkes Take Betus and Borage
auens Violette Malvis parsle betayn pacience þe white of the lekes and
þe croppe of þe netle

A Boke of Kokery, cookbook containing 182 recipes, preceded
by bills of fare for two banquets, s. xv (1).

1. EETS os 91 (1888), pp. 69-107, 115-17 (BL Harley 4016, ff.
1-28, supplemented by Bodl Douce 55 passim).

629   Take croppes of the rede coole of the rede netle tansey hemp and of
sparge of iche Ilyche mychil and do ther-to as mychyl of mader as of
alle othere herbes

Booke of Ypocras, 91 recipes, primarily medical, with preface,
s. xiv.

1. Henslow (1899), pp. 76-105, 120-22 (BL Harley 2378, ff. 5-
227, 301-24 passim).

630   Tak felettes of pork or of befe well betten in a mortair rawe and in
betteinge alay the fleshe with egges then tak up the fleshe (from 2)

A Noble Book of Cookry, collection of 253 recipes, preceded by
a list of feasts, s. xv (2).

1. R. Pynson, 1500 (STC 3297); 2. ed. Mrs. A. Napier (1882)
(Holkham Hall Earl of Leicester 164).

631   Take flowr and powder of peper and powder of gynger and graynys and
menge þese

And Ye Wyll Kyll Many Fysches in a Pole, instructions for
catching fish, s. xv.

1. Braekman (1980), pp. 30-31 (Bodl Rawlinson C. 506, ff.
299-300).

632   Take gallys coporose and gumme of rabyk of iche aleke mekyll be wyte

Recipes for ink, glue, and tempering, s. xv (2).

1. Louis (1980), pp. 170-73 (Bodl Tanner 407, ff. 15v, 16v).

215

633   Take gysers and lyuers and hert of Swanne and if þe guttys ben fat slyt them and caste þem þer-to and boile þem in faire watre

Sauces pur Diverse Viaundes, recipes (19) for sauces, s. xv (1).

1. EETS os 91 (1888), pp. 108-10 (Bodl Ashmole 1439, ff. 36-37v).

634   Take grondit walle yat ys senclion and hold yt yn yi handes in ye water (from 3)

"Recipes for Anglers", s. xv.

1. Rel. Ant., I (1841), 324 (BL Sloane 4, ff. 2v-58 passim, 1 recipe); 2. N&Q, 3rd series 6 (1884), 4-5 (as in 1, 3 recipes); 3. Braekman (1980), pp. 27, 51-54 (as in 1, 2 recipes).

635   Take ħ and beate it as thin as yow can then take aqua vitae viniger distilled that is that is [sic] Rectefyed and putt these thynne plates

[Geoffrey Chaucer], Galfridus Chauser His Worke, alchemical treatise, s. xv (?).

1. Ambix, 13 (1965), 13-20 (TCD 389, ff. 96-104v).

636   Take henbanesede and caste it in to a ponde wher fishe

For to Kill Fishe, fishing recipe, s. xv.

1. Braekman (1980), p. 27 (BL Harley 3831, f. 14).

637   Take merlyn soden or raw or uede wod yat wyll shyne qwycke syluer or glowe

Bates for Hope Nettes, fishing treatise, s. xv.

1. Braekman (1980), pp. 44-50 (BL Sloane 4, ff. 39v-41).

638   Take on chyld of yonge age þat is betwyxen vii and xiiii and in the sonne set hym betwyxen þi leggis And than knytte a red sylke thred abowte his ryght thombe

"Procedure for Divination", example of onimancy, s. xv (2).

216

1. Louis (1980), pp. 169-70 (Bodl Tanner 407, f. 15).

639 Tak palma Christi and frankandsence and medul hem togedir and put hit in a fome clowte and hold the pouder on thi finger that a gold ryng is upon

To Make Alle the Fisches in a Pont to Come to Thy Hand, recipe for catching fishes, s. xv.

1. Rel. Ant., I (1841), 56 (J.O. Halliwell 8, f. 50); 2. Braekman (1980), p. 26 (BL Sloane 3153, f. 67v).

640 Take rue and betanye of eche a porcion bray hem wel to-geder in a morter aftyr temperid vp with old ale

Medical recipes (26), s. xiv.

1. Henslow (1899), pp. 133-39 (BL Sloane 521, ff. 200-26v passim).

641 Take smythis synder & make yt rede hote in the ffyre Than put in a vesselle

For the Tothe Ache, medical recipe, s. xv (2).

1. Studies in Medieval Literature in Honor of Professor Albert Croll Baugh, ed. M. Leach (1961), p. 288 (New York C.F. Bühler 21, f. 15); 2. Bühler (1973), p. 547 (as in 1).

642 Tak stronge vinegre of whit wyne and anoynte euery day þryes or foure times þe vysage þer hit is saucefleme

Medical recipes, preceded by index of topics, s. xiv.

1. ed. F. Heinrich, Ein mittelenglisches Medizinbuch (1896) (BL Addl. 33996, ff. 76v-148v).

Also in BL Harley 1600, BL Royal 17 A.iii, BL Sloane 405, BL Sloane 3153, BL Addl. 19674.

643 Take the blode of his litle fynger & wryte these ij verses folowynge & hange it abowt his necke

217

Charm, s. xv.

1. N&Q, 207 (1962), 48 (BL Harley 2389, f. 42).

644   Tak þe heued of a stork and þe fete and all þat es wyth in þe stork bot þe body ane

Recipe for a powder for the canker, s. xv.

1. Chaucer and Middle English Studies (1974), p. 60 (BL Royal 17 A.viii, f. 35v).

645   Take þe leywys of egremony and sethe heme in honny

For þe Molde Þat Ys Fallonn Doun, medical recipes (10), s. xv.

1. NM, 54 (1953), 49-50 (Aberystwyth NLW Porkington 10, ff. 89v-90v).

646   Take the poudre of ii unces of salpetre and half an unce of brymston and half an unce of lyndecole and temper togidur in a mortar with rede vynegre

To Make Goode Gonepoudre, recipe for gunpowder, s. xv.

1. Rel. Ant., I (1841), 14-15 (London Society of Antiquaries 101, f. 76).

647   Take veruayne or vetoyn or filles of wormod and make lee þer-of and wasche þi heued þer-with thrys in a weke

Liber de Diversis Medicinis, compendium of medical remedies, s. xv.

1. EETS os 207 (1938) (Lincoln Cathedral 91, ff. 28-314v).

Cf. 446 and 447.

648   Take vervayne rites and sethe hem in suete wort a good whille

Fishing recipe, s. xv.

1. Braekman (1980), p. 27 (BL Sloane 3160, f. 135).

649 Take your best coloured pippins and pare them then make a piercer and
bore a hole thorow them then make syrrup for them

Recipes (8) for preserving fruit, s. xv.

1. Warner (1791), pp. 91-92 (unspecified MS).

650 Takuth heed & ȝe mow undurstonde þat god has gifen us ten com-
mawndementis þat is þat ille a cristen man religeus & seculer awt for to
kepe parfitly

Treatise on the ten commandments, s. xv (1).

1. SP, 6 (1910), 9-35 (Oxford St. John's 94, ff. 119-26).

Cf. 48 and 49.

651 Tarie the noght man to be conuerted vnto thi lord god nother delay the
noght from day to day For sodainly he revisshith wrecchis with greuous
deth

[Richard Rolle], The Libel of Richard Hermyte of Hampol of the
Amendement of Mannes Lif, translation of Richard Rolle's De
Emendacione Vite, s. xv.

1. Hulme (1918), pp. 29-58 (Worcester Cathedral F. 172, ff.
17-32v).

For other translations see 652 and notes to that entry.

652 Tary þou not to oure lorde to be turnyd ne put it not fro day to day for
oft tymes cruelte of deed rauischis wrechis and þame þat irkis now to
be turnyd

Richard Misyn, Of Mendynge of Lyfe, translation of Richard
Rolle's De Emendacione Vite, 1434.

1. EETS os 106 (1896), pp. 105-31 (Oxford CCC 236, ff. 45-
56).

Also in BL Addl. 37790 and New Haven Yale University 331.
Other translations: (1) 651; (2) in CUL Ff.5.30, TCD 432, BL
Harley 1706, Bodl Digby 18, and Bodl Douce 322; (3) in CUL
Ff.5.40 and BL Harley 2406; (4) in Cambridge Gonville and
Caius 669/646, and Edinburgh University 93; (5) in Cambridge

Fitzwilliam Museum Bradfer-Lawrence Deposit 10; (6) in BL
Lansdowne 455; and (7) in Longleat Marquis of Bath 32.

653   Tedet animam meam vite mee My soule is wery of the lyfe For there I
see no thynge but mater of sorowe myserye and synne

Complaynt of the Soule, didactic literature, s. xv.

1. W. de Worde, [1510?] (STC 5609); 2. W. de Worde, 1532
(STC 5610).

654   Tempur rug plom or vermyloun with gleyr of egges or with gummed
watir or thynne cole that is to say the clere therof

Recipes (seven) for colors and removing stains, s. xv.

1. Rel. Ant., I (1841), 109-9 (BL Sloane 1313, f. 126v).

Tenor vero dictorum articulorum . . . Furst alle they ar accursed that
presume to take a wey or to pryve any churche of the ryght that longeth
therto   Incipit to edition C.3 of 122.

655   Thales Mylesyes the qwyche was the fyrst phylosophyre in the cyte of
Atene be the ansqwere off god Apollo fyrst dyd wryte the syens off
cyromancy in the langage of Parce

John Metham, Syens of Cyromancy, treatise on palmistry translated from Latin, s. xv.

1. EETS os 132 (1916), pp. 84-116 (even pages only) (Princeton
University Garrett 141, ff. 1-11v); 2. EETS os 132 (1916), pp.
85-117 (odd pages only) (Oxford All Souls 81, ff. 202-11v).

Thanked be the highe name of oure Lorde and sauiour Criste Jhesu
See 348.

656   Þat prelatis leuen prechynge of þe gospel and ben gostly manquelleris of
mennys soulis And sathanas transfigurid in to an aungel of liȝt and ben
gostly sodomytis worse þan bodily sodomytis

Of Prelatis, Wycliffite tract, ca. 1383-84.

1. EETS os 74 (1880, 1902), pp. 55-107 (CCCC 296, pp. 65-103).

Also in TCD 244.

. . . that the Kinges of Englande so comyn of a dawghter of Fraunce maie not enjoy the sayde Lande of France by suche title   Incipit to edition 1 of 15.

That tyme when the Right happy wele of peas flowrid for the most parte in all cristen Realmes And that moche peple dyde moche peyne to gadre and multyplye vertues   Incipit to text proper of 795.

The Auncyent hystoryes saye that Eracles was a good crysten man and gouernour of thempyre of Rome   Incipit to text proper of 681.

The apostel seinte poule seyth the fulfyllyng of the lawe ys loue and Seynte gregory seyth Quicquid precipitur in sola caritate solidatur Incipit to text proper of 751.

The autour of this buke rehersis how it befell in a contree quhare a worthy wyse anciene knycht that lang tyme had bene in the excercisioun of honourable weris   Incipit to text proper of 90.

657   The bee has thre kyndis Ane es þat scho es neuer ydill and scho es noghte with thaym þat will noghte wyrke bot castys thaym owte and puttes thaym awaye

Richard Rolle, Moralia de Natura Apis, exemplum, s. xiv (1).

1. EETS os 20 (1866), pp. 8-9 (Lincoln Cathedral 91, f. 194r-v); 2. Mätzner, I, 2 (1869), 126-28 (as in 1); 3. Wülcker, 1 (1874), 117 (as in 1); 4. Zupitza (1874 and later editions), pp. 87-88 (as in 1); 5. ed. G.E. MacLean, An Old and Middle English Reader (1893), pp. 95-96 (as in 1); 6. YW, I (1895), 193-94 (as in 1); 7. Kluge (1904, 1912), pp. 34-35 (as in 1); 8. Emerson (1905, 1915, 1932), p. 143 (as in 1); 9. EETS os 20, rev. ed. (1921), pp. 8-9 (as in 1); 10. Sisam (1921), pp. 41-42 (as in 1); 11. Allen, English (1931), pp. 54-56 (as in 1); 12. ed. F. Mossé, Manuel d'anglais du moyen âge des origines au xive siècle, II, 1 (1949, 1952), 260-62 (as in 1); 13. ed. R.L. Hoffman, History of the English Language (1968), pp. 87-89 (as

in 1); 14. ed. J.H. Fisher and D. Bornstein, In Forme of Speche Is Chaunge (1974), pp. 158-61 (as in 1); 15. Garbaty (1984), pp. 795-96 (as in 1).

Also in Durham University Cosin V.I.12. The exemplum appears in a Latin form in BL Harley 268, f. 40v.

658   The benignite ande humanyte of oure lorde Godde and oure sauyour whiche fulle mercyfullye apperede to mankynde be his incarnacion ȝitt plesis hitt to þat same lorde eche daye more ande more

The Booke of Gostlye Grace, translation of the Liber Spiritualis Gracie of Mechtild of Hackeborn, s. xv.

1. ed. T.A. Halligan (1979) (BL Egerton 2006, ff. 1-212).

Also in Bodl Bodley 220.

The boke of generacioun of Jhesu Crist the sone of Dauyd the sone of Abraham   Incipit to text proper of the New Testament in 119.

The church is a place which Cristen men ben much holdun to luff Which is thi principall verbe in this reson   Incipit to version C of 349.

The cyte of Ierusalem standes fayr emange hylles And þer is no ryuer ne welles but watyr cummes be condeth fro Ebron   Incipit to epitome in edition 26 of 233.

659   The clerk seith in the first chaptre that for ye default of good rulyng ane dyetyng in mete an drynke men fallen ofte (from 4)

A Noble Tretis for Medicina Agenst the Pestilence, plague tract translated from the shorter version of John of Burgundy's Latin (ca. 1390), s. xv in.

1. ed. W.B.D.D. Turnbull, Fragmenta Scoto-monastica (1842), No. 15, pp. xcii-xcvi (Kelso Abbey Cartulary); 2. Liber S. Marie de Calchou (1846), II, 448-51 (as in 1); 3. ed. D. Murray (1891), pp. 30-33 (as in 1); 4. Archiv für Geschichte der Medizin, 5 (1911), 73-75 (BL Sloane 2320, ff. 16-17v); 5. EETS os 207 (1940), pp. 51-54 (Lincoln Cathedral 91, ff. 300v-2), abridged.

Also in Cambridge Gonville and Caius 336/725, Cambridge Jesus 43, TCC O.1.77, TCC R.14.32, CUL Kk.6.33, BL Cotton Caligula A. II, BL Egerton 2433, BL Egerton 2572, BL Lansdowne 285, BL Royal 13 E.x, BL Sloane 7, BL Sloane 405, BL Sloane 433, BL Sloane 443, BL Sloane 706, BL Sloane 963, BL Sloane 983, BL Sloane 1764, BL Sloane 2507, BL Sloane 3489, BL Sloane 3566, BL Addl. 14251, Bodl Ashmole 1481, Bodl Rawlinson A. 429. An English translation of John of Burgundy's longer original Latin (1365) is in BL Sloane 965, BL Sloane 2320 (again), BL Sloane 3449, BL Sloane 3566, Bodl Ashmole 1400 (fragment), Bodl Ashmole 1443, Bodl Ashmole 1444, Bodl Ashmole 1481 (again). A conflated translation is in Holywell Mostyn Hall 221, BL Arundel 334, BL Sloane 2320 (again), BL Sloane 3489 (again), BL Sloane 3566 (again), Bodl Digby 196.

60   Þe comawndement of god es þat we lufe oure lorde In al oure hert In all oure saule In al oure thoght In al oure hert þat es in al oure vnderstandyng withowten erryng

Richard Rolle, "The Commandment", epistle on the commandment of God written to a nun of Hampole, s. xiv (1).

1. YW, I (1895), 61-71 (CUL Dd.5.64, ff. 29-34); 2. YW, I (1895), 61-71 (Bodl Rawlinson A. 389, ff. 81-85); 3. Allen, English (1931), pp. 73-81 (as in 1).

Also in Cambridge Fitzwilliam Museum Bradfer-Lawrence Deposit 10, Cambridge Magdalene Pepys 2125, TCC B.15.39-40, TCC O.1.29, CUL Dd.5.55, CUL Ff.5.40, CUL Ii.6.40, BL Addl. 22283, Longleat Marquis of Bath 29, Longleat Marquis of Bath 32, Bodl Eng. poet. a. 1, San Marino Huntington HM 148.

Tho cros of Oure Lord Iesu Crist was a lengthe viii cubites and that was ouerthwert had in lenthe iii cubites and a halfe   Incipit to first extract in edition 27 of 233.

61   The Duc of Clarance Stywarde of Englond ryding in the hall on horsebak his courser rychely trapped hede and body to the grounde

The Coronacon of the Queene, account of the coronation of Elizabeth Woodville, queen of Edward IV, 1465.

1. ed. G. Smith (1935), pp. 14-25 (Great Bedwyn (Wiltshire) George Smith MS).

662 The Duke of Suffolk hath marryed his nese His Suster Dowghter to þe Capdawe &c And yaf hym wt here the Revenewes þat come fro Bordiaux

"Collections of a Yorkist Partisan" relating to the troubles of 1447-52, s. xv med.

1. Kingsford, EHL (1913), pp. 360-68 (BL Cotton Roll II.23).

663 Þe egypta [cyning] þe Idpartus wæs hatan Octauiano þan casere hys frunde hælo bodede þis wordum þus cweþende

De Singlis Feris Medicamentum ("Medicina de Quadrupedibus"), instructions for medical uses of animals, ca. 1150.

1. ed. J. Delcourt, Medicina de Quadrupedibus (1914), even pages only (BL Harley 6258b, ff. 44-51); 2. EETS os 286 (1984), pp. 235-73 (odd only) (as in 1).

663.3 Themperour þat y spake of aboue is oure lord god þat hath iij sones By the firste sone we shul vndirstonde Angels to whiche god yaf swich confirmacion þat they may nat synne

Thomas Hoccleve, "Moralization" to Fabula ad Instanciam Amici Mei Predilecti Assiduam ("Tale of Jonathas", IMEV 4072), ca. 1422.

1. EETS es 61 (1892), pp. 240-42 (Durham University Cosin V.III.9, ff. 93v-95); 2. EETS es 61, rev. ed. (1970), pp. 240-42 (as in 1).

Also in BL Royal 17 D.vi, Bodl Bodley 221, Bodl Digby 185, Bodl Eng. poet. d. 4, Bodl Laud Miscellaneous 735, Bodl Selden Supra 53.

The excellent and ryght gloriouse virgyn seynt Kateryn was of þe noble kynrede of þe Emperours of Rome by hir Faders syde   Incipit to text proper of 28.

664 The famous doctour Iohan gerson Chaunceler of Parys takynge his grounde of holy scripture and accordynge with all other doctours sayth thus Ovre moost mercyfull fader lord god knowyng our freelte and redynes to all synnes

Thomas Betson, Ryght Profytable Treatyse, an exposition of various prayers compiled from various writings, ca. 1500.

1. [W. de Worde, 1500] (STC 1978); 2. ed. F. Jenkinson (1905) (facsimile of 1).

665   The ffadir in his old age seithe to his sonne leve wisely and discretly aftur god & þe world & thynke on the harde change off ffortune (from 2)

[Robert Grosseteste], Tretyce off Housbandry, translation of Walter of Henley's Dité de Hosebondrie, s. xv (?).

1. [W. de Worde, 1508?] (STC 25007); 2. Lamond (1890), pp. 41-58 (BL Sloane 686, ff. 1-15v); 3. ed. F.H. Cripps Day, The Manor Farm (1931) (facsimile of 1).

Also in Aberystwyth NLW Peniarth 92, TCC O.1.13, London Society of Antiquaries 282 (a 19th-c. copy of an unidentified MS), London Society of Antiquaries 287, Bodl Digby 88 (fragment). Another translation made in 1557 by William Lambarde in Bodl Rawlinson B. 471.

The fader the sone the holy ghost be thre persones by personall proprytees but thabsolute propritees be comune to all thre persones but some of thyse proprytees ben more appropred to oone thanne to one other   Incipit to text proper of 785.

666   The fend sekiþ many weyes to marre men in bileve and to stoppe bodily þis þat no bookis ben bileve For ʒif þou spekist of the Bible þanne seyen Antecristis clerkis

"On the Sufficiency of Holy Scripture", Wycliffite tract, s. xiv (2).

1. SEW, III (1871), 186-87 (TCD 244, ff. 210v-11).

The firste article put saynt Peter saynge I beleue in god Fader almighty creatour and maker of Heuen and Erthe   Incipit to text proper of 390.

The fyrste chylde that Lya conceyued of Iacob is Ruben þat is drede and therfore it is wryten in the psalme The begynnynge of wysdome is þe drede of our lorde   Incipit to text proper of **4**.

667   The fyrste comandement es Thy Lorde God þou sall loute and til Hym
      anely þou sall serue In this comandement es forboden all mawmetryse
      all wychcrafte and charemynge

      Richard Rolle, A Notabill Tretys off the Ten Comandementys,
      commentary, s. xiv (1).

      1. EETS os 20 (1866), pp. 9-11 (Lincoln Cathedral 91, ff. 195v-
      96); 2. Mätzner, I, 2 (1869), 128-30 (as in 1); 3. YW, I
      (1895), 195-96 (as in 1); 4. Emerson (1905, 1915, 1932), pp.
      145-47 (as in 1); 5. EETS os 20, rev. ed. (1921), pp. 10-12 (as
      in 1).

      Also in Bodl Hatton 12.

      Þe ffirst commaundement of God is þis the Lorde spake of þes wordes I
      am þi Lord God   Incipit to editions B.2 and B.4 of **49**.

668   Þe first comaundement þat God comaundide was þis þou ne schalt not
      haue dyuerse goddes þat is to seie þou schalt haue no God but me

      Bok of Vices and Vertues, devotional treatise translated from the
      French Somme le roi by Friar Lorens d'Orléans, ca. 1375.

      1. EETS os 217 (1942), pp. 1-290 (San Marino Huntington HM
      147, ff. 1-113v).

      Also in BL Addl. 17013 and BL Addl. 22283.   Other transla-
      tions in 55, 824, and CCCC 494, BL Royal 18 A.x, BL Addl.
      37677, Bodl Ashmole 1286, Bodl Bodley 283, Bodl Douce 322,
      and Bodl e Mus. 23.

669   Þe first general poynt of pore prestis þat prechen in engelond is þis þat
      þe lawe of god be wel knowen tauȝt meyntened magnyfied

      "Of Poor Preaching Priests", Wycliffite tract, s. xiv ex.

      1. EETS os 74 (1880, 1902), pp. 276-80 (CCCC 296, pp. 234-
      38).

670   The first goldin garland is maid of þe cumyng and bringing vp of þe

226

blest barne Iesus and in the honour of his blist and glorius hert

Þe Thre Rois Garlandis of the Glorius Virgin Mary, rosary of prayers, s. xv.

1. STS, 3rd series 23 (1955), pp. 299-321 (BL Arundel 285, ff. 197-213).

Þe verste heste þet God made and het is þis þou ne selt habbe vele godes þet is to zigge þou ne sselt habbe God bote Me ne worssipie ne servi Incipit to text proper of 55.

571 The first is that he beleve of the Catholyk feith the IIde is that he be suspecte of no erroure the IIIde is that he be not bounde to matrimony

The Generalle Statutis Made in the Generall Chapitre Callid Bercynonde, summary of the statutes of the Franciscan order assembled at the general chapter in Barcelona (1451), including a summary of the Rule of the Observants, s. xv (2).

1. Rolls 4, 1 (1858), 574-78 (BL Cotton Faustina D. IV, item 6).

572 The first is turnyng fra synne to vertu The secound Crist makis a vertius man of a vicius The thirt Crist makis peace betuix þe fader of hevin and þat man

Þe XII Fruttis Þat Cumis of þe Remembrance of þe Passion of Crist, meditations on Christ's passion, s. xv.

1. STS, 3rd series 23 (1955), pp. 213-37 (BL Arundel 285, ff. 125-44).

573 The first man Adam was mad on a Friday withoute modir withoute fader in the feld of Damask and fro that place led into Paradise to dwell there

John Capgrave, Abbreviacion of Cronicles, chronicle of England to 1417, ca. 1438-63.

1. Rolls 1 (1858) (CUL Gg.4.12); 2. EETS os 285 (1983) (as in 1).

Also in CCCC 167.

The friste maistir seyde þat if eni þinge hadde be bettir to eny mannis lyuynge in þis world þan tribulacioun god wolde haue ʒeue it to his sone Incipit to text proper of **287**.

The fyrst mesure of thy lyf whiche is so shorte that unnethes it is ony thynge for we lyue here but in a poynte that is the leest thynge þat may be   Incipit to extract from Forme of Lyvyng prefixed to editions 1-3 of **528**.

674   The fyrst petycion in the colloquium Syr I besyche yow and alle the convent for the luffe of god owr Ladye Marye sant John of baptiste and alle the hoyle cowrte of hevyne

Form for receiving a novice into a Charterhouse, s. xv (2).

1. Maskell, I (1846), cxxi-cxxii note 5 (BL Cotton Nero A. III, f. 130); 2. Maskell, 2nd ed., I (1882), cxl note 26 (as in 1); 3. Henry Bradshaw Soc. 27 (1904), p. 99 (as in 1); 4. Analecta Cartusiana, 31 (1977), p. 125 (as in 1).

The firste prouffite of tribulacion is vnderstonde þat is a trewe socoure or helpe sente fro god to deliuer the soule fro the hand of his enemyes Incipit to text proper of **142**.

675   Þo firste þat þis pope Urban þe sixte bereþ not þe strenght of Seint Petur in erþe but þai affermen hym to be son of Anticriste

Þo Poyntus Þat Worldely Prelatis Putten on Pore Cristen Men ("On the Twenty-Five Articles"), Wycliffite tract, ca. 1388.

1. SEW, III (1871), 455-96 (Bodl Douce 273, ff. 1-37).

Also in TCD 245 (parts only).

676   The ffirst the brede or the oost in the auter sacrid of the prest it is very Goddis body but it is the same bred in kynde that it was before

"Sixteen Points on Which the Bishops Accuse Lollards", Wycliffite tract, s. xv in.

1. Deanesly (1920), pp. 462-67 (TCC B.14.50, ff. 30v-34); 2. Hudson (1978), pp. 19-24 (as in 1).

677 The firste tokene of loue is þat þe louier submytte fully his wille to þe
wille of him þat he loueþ And þis special loue haþ þre worchyngis

> Walter Hilton, Eiȝte Chapitris Necessarie for Men and Wommen
> Þat ȝeven Hem to Perfeccioun, devotional treatise translated
> from Latin, s. xiv ex.
>
> 1. ed. F. Kuriyagawa (1958) (Paris BN Anglais 41, 140v-56); 2.
> ed. F. Kuriyagawa, rev. ed. (1967) (as in 1); 3. ed. F.
> Kuriyagawa (1971) (London Inner Temple Petyt 524, ff. 4-11);
> 4. Poetica, 12 (1979), 144-46 (BL Addl. 60577, ff. 146v-50);
> 5. Takamiya (1980), pp. 14-32 (as in 3).
>
> Also in CUL Hh.1.12 (extracts), BL Harley 993, BL Harley 6615
> (fragment), BL Royal 17 C.xviii, BL Addl. 10053, Lambeth
> Palace 472, Lambeth Palace 541 (fragment), Bodl Rawlinson C.
> 894, Oxford St. John's 94 (extracts).

678 The Friday the xviij day of June the viijth yere of the Reygne of our said
soverayne Lorde the sayd Princesse went from a place in London

> Mariage of the Duc of Burgoigne with the Princesse Margarett
> (1468), s. xv (2).
>
> 1. Bentley (1833), pp. 227-39 (BL Cotton Nero C. IX, ff.
> 173v-77v).
>
> Also in BL Addl. 6113. Cf. 699.

The galeye of myn engyn floting not long syn in the depnes of the sees
of diuerce auncient histories in suche wise as I wolde haue brought myn
esperite vnto the port or hauen of rest   Incipit to text proper of 226.

679 The gloryous mayster Iohn of the mounte in his moryall telleth whiche
also I founde in þe boke of frere Thomas of the temple

> A Devoute Medytacion in Sayenge Devoutly þe Psalter of Our
> Lady, translation of Alanus de Rupe's Tractatus Mirabilis de
> Ortu atque Progressu Psalterii Christi et Marie, s. xv.
>
> 1. W. de Worde, 1508 (STC 20875.5, Part 2; 21262, Part 2); 2.
> W. de Worde, 1519 (STC 20876, Part 2; 21263, Part 2); 3. [W.
> de Worde, ca. 1525] (STC 20876.5, Part 2); 4. YW, II (1896),
> 123-28 (as in 1).

Bound with 528 in editions 1-3.

680 The gospel telleþ þat in a tyme whanne oure lord Ihesu Crist was heere vpon eerthe a man com to hym and askede hym ȝef þat fewe men shulden be sauued

John Clanvowe, "The Two Ways", s. xiv ex.

1. EPS, 10 (1967), 36-56 (Oxford University 97, ff. 114-23v); 2. ed. V.J. Scattergood, The Works of Sir John Clanvowe (1975), pp. 57-80 (as in 1).

Also in BL Addl. 22283 (fragment), for which see EPS, 11 (1968), 54-56.

Þe grace & þe goodnes of vr lord Ihesu þat he haþ schewed to þe in wiþdrawyng of þin herte from loue & lyking of worldli vanyte   Incipit to edition 7 of 147.

Þe grace of ure louerd Iesu Crist & te helpe of ure Lauedi seinte þe milde be mid us nu and eueremore   Brief invocation, following the Latin, to 432.

The hare is a common beest I-now and þerfore me nedeþ not to telle of here makyng for þer be fewe men that ne han seye some of hem Incipit to text proper of 775.

The helpe and þe grace of Almyghty God thorw þe be sekyng of Hys blissyd modyr and maydyn Mary   See 435.

The helpe and the grace of almyghty god thourgh the be sechyng of his blessyd modyr seint mary   Incipit to introductory prayer in edition 2 of Mirk's Festivall (734) and in all subsequent editions before 1500.

681 The hye couragyous faytes And valyaunt actes of noble Illustrous and vertuous personnes ben digne to be recounted put in memorye and wreton

William Caxton, Laste Siege and Conquest of Jherusalem, chronicle containing the histories of Heraclius and Godfrey of Bouillon translated from French, 1481.

230

1. W. Caxton, 1481 (STC 13175); 2. EETS es 64 (1893) (as in 1); 3. ed. H.H. Sparling, The History of Godefroy of Boloyne (1893) (as in 1); 4. The Boke Intitulede Eracles (1973) (facsimile of 1).

BL Royal 18 B.xxvi contains a condensation of Caxton's edition.

682 The holy and blessed doctour saynt Ierom sayth thys auctoryte do alweye somme good werke to thende that the deuyl fynde the not ydle

William Caxton, Golden Legend, saints' lives and biblical translation from Latin, French, and English versions of the Legenda Aurea, ca. 1483.

1. W. Caxton, 1483? (STC 24873); 2. W. Caxton, 1487? (STC 24874); 3. [W. de Worde], 1493 (STC 24875); 4. W. de Worde, 1498 (STC 24876); 5. [W. de Worde, 1500?] (STC 24880.5), extract; 6. J. Notary, 1503 (STC 24877); 7. W. de Worde, 1507 (STC 24878.3); 8. W. de Worde, 1512 (STC 24879); 9. W. de Worde, 1521 (STC 24879.5); 10. W. de Worde, 1527 (STC 24880); 11. ed. F.S. Ellis, 3 vols. (1892) (as in 1).

Bodl Bodley 952 (s. xv ex., incomplete) made from edition 1. The earlier Middle English prose translation, Gilte Legende (1438), used by Caxton and made from Jehan de Vignay's Legende Dorée, exists in twelve MSS: CCCC 142, TCC O.9.1, TCD 319, Gloucester Cathedral 12, BL Egerton 876, BL Harley 630, BL Harley 4775, BL Lansdowne 350 (fragment), BL Addl. 11565, BL Addl. 35298, Lambeth Palace 72, Bodl Douce 372; only selections have as yet been printed.

The holy appostle and doctour of the peple saynt Poule sayth in his epystle Alle that is wryten is wryten vnto our doctryne and for our seruyng   Incipit to new prologue in edition 2 of 62.

Þe holy doctour seynt austyn spekyng in þe persone of crist vnto synful men seiþ in þis wise I schal reproue þe   See 97.

683 The holi prophete Dauid seith in the persone of a iust man Lord how swete ben thi spechis to my chikis that is to myn vndirstondyng and loue

"The Holi Prophete David Seith", Wycliffite tract, s. xiv (2).

1. Deanesly (1920), pp. 446-56 (CUL Ff.6.31, ff. 1-16v).

684   The kynge asked by what maners tokyns and fassyon myghte a man
       knowe the maners and condycyons of good folkes and of euyl

       Certayne Questions of Kynge Bocthus ("Sydrac and Boctus"),
       dialogue, s. xv (?).

       1. R. Wyer, [1535?] (STC 3188); 2. R. Wyer, [after 1536]
       (STC 3188a).

       For verse versions see IMEV 772 and 2147.

685   The Kyng lay in the Palois of York and kept his astate solemply and tho
       there create he Sir John Nevelle Lord Mowntage Erle of Northumber-
       land

       Anno Edwardi Quarti Quarto, brief chronicle, s. xv (2).

       1. Camden Soc. 10 (1839), pp. 36-39 (London College of Arms
       L.9).

       The kynge our souerayne lord callynge to hys remembraunce the duety
       of allegeaunce of his subgettes of his reawme and that they bi reason of
       the same are bounde to serue theyr prynce and souereyne lord   Inci-
       pit to text proper of 11 Henry VII (as in edition 4) of 686.

686   The kynge our souereyn lorde henry the seuenth after the conquest by
       the grace of god kyng of Englonde and of Fraunce and lorde of Irlonde
       at his parlyament holden at westmynster the seuenth daye of Nouembre
       in the first yere of his reigne

       Statutes/Statuta of Henry VII before 1500, 1486-97.

       1. W. Caxton, 1489? (STC 9348), 1, 3, 4 Henry VII; 2. W. de
       Worde, [n.d.] (STC 9349), 1, 3, 4 Henry VII; 3. W. de
       Worde, [n.d.] (STC 9350), 7 Henry VII; 4. [W. de Worde,
       1496] (STC 9352), 11 Henry VII; 5. [W. de Worde, 1496] (STC
       9353), 11 Henry VII; 6. [W. de Worde, 1496] (STC 9354), 11
       Henry VII; 7. [R. Pynson, 1496] (STC 9355), 11 Henry VII; 8.
       J. Notary, 1507 (STC 9351), 7, 11, 12 Henry VII; 9. W. de
       Worde, 1508 (STC 9351a), 1, 3, 4, 7 ,11, 12 Henry VII; 10.
       ed. J. Rae (1869) (facsimile of 1).

587   The man þat falleþ syke þe fyrste day of eny moneþ þe þirde day folowynge he schall be hole

        Six short prognostics (five English, one Latin), s. xv.

        1. NM, 54 (1953), 38-41 (Aberystwyth NLW Porkington 10, ff. 1-2).

588   The marshall in the mornyng ought to come into þe hall and se þat it be clene of all maner thyng þat may be fond vnhoneste þer In

        A Generall Rule to Teche Every Man That Is Willynge for to Lerne to Serve a Lorde or Mayster, courtesy book, s. xv.

        1. EETS os 148 (1914), pp. 11-17 (BL Addl. 37969, ff. 2-8).

589   The Mayster of Sentence in the second book and the first distynction sayth that the souerayn cause why God made al creatures in heuen erthe or water was his oune goodnes

        Quattuor Sermones, adaptation of Lay Folks Catechism in three parts, s. xv.

        1. W. Caxton, 1483-84? (STC 17957, Part 2); 2. W. Caxton, 1484? (STC 17957, Part 3); 3. W. Caxton, 1491? (STC 17959); 4. R. Pynson, [1493] (STC 17960); 5. R. Pynson [1493] (STC 17961); 6. [W. de Worde], 1494 (STC 17962, Part 2); 7. J. Ravynell, 1495? (STC 17963, Part 2); 8. W. Hopyl, 1495 (STC 17964); 9. [W. de Worde], 1496 (STC 17965); 10. M. Morin, 1499 (STC 17966); 11. R. Pynson, 1499 (STC 17966.5); 12. [W. de Worde], 1499 (STC 17967); 13. J. Notary, 1499 (STC 17968); 14. R. Pynson, 1502 (STC 17969); 15. J. Notary, [1506?] (STC 17970); 16. [R. Pynson, 1507?] (STC 17970.5); 17. W. de Worde, 1508 (STC 17971); 18. W. de Worde, 1511 (STC 17971.5); 19. W. de Worde, 1515 (STC 17972); 20. R. Faques, [ca. 1512] (STC 17973); 21. W. de Worde, 1519 (STC 17973.5): 22. W. de Worde, 1528 (STC 17974); 23. W. de Worde, 1532 (STC 17975); 24. Roxburghe (1883) (as in 1); 25. MET 2 (1975) (as in 1).

        TCC B.14.19 contains similar though not identical material to Quattuor Sermones; Cambridge St. John's 187 contains a copy of edition 10. Cf. 734.

The most excellent and dowȝty lord oure lege Lord the Kyng and to alle the Lordys of the reme of this present Parlement   Incipit to edition 1 of 777.

The most learned Egyptians who know of the size of the earth the waves of the sea and the order of the heavens   Modern English incipit, translated from the Latin, of 158.

The names of the Kepers and Baylyffes of the Cite of London in the tyme of Kynge Richarde the fyrst   Incipit to version D of 365.

690   The olde fadres a-fore tymes made fro bigynnyng the festyuites of holy apostles and martires whiche were before hem to be louyd and halowed

Speculum Sacerdotale, collection of sermons de tempore et de sanctis translated from Latin, s. xv.

1. EETS os 200 (1936) (BL Addl. 36791, ff. 1-142v).

691   The pardon for v pater nosters v aues and a crede is xxvj m yeres and xxvj dayes

Indulgence, s. xv.

1. [ca. 1490] (STC 14077c.10); 2. ca. 1490 (STC 14077c.11); 3. H. Pepwell?, 1521? (STC 14077c.11C); 4. R. Copland?, ca. 1525 (STC 14077c.11A); 5. M. Fawkes?, 1534? (STC 14077c. 11B); 6. Cambridge Antiquarian Communications, 3 (1879), 150 (as in 1); 7. Bradshaw (1889), p. 97 (as in 1); 8. Cooke and Wordsworth (1902), p. 649 (as in 1); 9. Walpole Soc., 17 (1929), 97 (as in 2); 10. Walpole Soc., 17 (1929), 99, note 2 (as in 1); 11. Dodgson, English (1936), p. 8 and Plate 7 (as in 1); 12. Dodgson, English (1936), Plate 8 (as in 2).

692   Þo peril of freris is þo laste of eght þat falles to men in þis waye as Seynt Poule telles and Austyne nootis þis is þo moste And for drede doynge shewes more þo sothe

Vita Sacerdotum, Wycliffite tract, s. xiv ex.

1. SEW, III (1871), 233-41 (Bodl Bodley 647, ff. 57v-62v).

The pore synner begynneth in saynge deuoutly O My ryght benygne

234

ryght pyteful and ryght mercyful lorde and redemptour   Incipit to
text proper of **746**.

693   The preste going to masse signifythe and representyd the Sauyour off
      the world our moost swett Redemer Cryst Iesu whyche cam from
      hewyn to the vaile of myserie

          B. Langforde, Meditatyons for Goostly Exercyse in the Tyme of
          the Masse, suggestions for meditations for each part of the mass,
          s. xv.

          1. Henry Bradshaw Soc. 27 (1904), pp. 19-29 (Bodl Wood
          empt. 17, ff. 1-27).

          Also in BL Harley 494.

      The prophet Ieremie considerynge the freylte and miserie of mankinde
      by maner of lamentacion in writyng saith thus Alas I poore creature
      wherfore was I borne out of þe wombe of my moder   Incipit to text
      proper of **704**.

      The Prophete saith thise wordes I shall mount to the appultree & take
      of the frute   Incipit to "The Branches of the Appletree," devotional
      tract (Part 5) incorporated into **751**.

694   [T]he purpos forsoth of þis present besynes yt ys forto tret shortly in
      which maner sekenes flebotomie ys competent and of which veynis

          Of Phlebotomie, treatise on bloodletting translated from a Latin
          text attributed to Henry of Winchester, ca. 1400.

          1. Voigts and McVaugh (1984), pp. 37-53 (odd pages only)
          (Cambridge Gonville and Caius 176/97, pp. 1-11).

695   The reuelacion that foloweth here in this boke tretyth how a certeyn
      deuowt person the wiche was a monke in the abbey of Euishamme was
      rapte in spirite by the wille of god and ladde by the hand of seint
      Nycholas

          Revelacion, translation of Adam of Eynsham's Latin visio, s. xv
          (?).

          1. [W. de Machlinia, 1483] (STC 20917); 2. ed. E. Arber

(1869, 1901) (facsimile of 1).

696 The right gloriouse virgyn seint Dorothee came downe of the noble
blode off the senatours of Rome Hir ffadir hight Dorotheo and her
modir hight Theodera

"Life of St. Dorothy", saint's life, s. xv.

1. Anglia, 3 (1880), 325-28 (Lambeth Palace 432, ff. 90-94).

Other Middle English prose versions in BL Royal 2 A.xviii and
Manchester Chetham 8009.

697 The rewle and lif of the bretherne minorys is this to obserue and kepe
the holy gospelle of our Lord Jhesu Christ in lyving in obedience
without propre and in chastite

The Rewle and Lif of the Bretherne Minoris, translation of the
Franciscan Rule, with glosses and notes, perhaps by John Howell, and preface by Pope Honorius III confirming the Rule, s. xv
in. (?).

1. Rolls 4, 2 (1882), 65-78, supplemented by Rolls 4, 1 (1858),
567-74 (BL Cotton Faustina D. IV, ff. 10-24v, 34, 42, 56).

Cf. 578 and 698.

698 Þe reule and þe lyuynge of frere menours is þis to kepe þe holy gospel of
oure lord ihesu crist lyuynge in obedience wiþ-outen propre and in
chastite

Reule of Seynt Fraunseis, Wycliffite version, followed by the
Testament with commentary, s. xiv (2).

1. EETS os 74 (1880, 1902), pp. 40-45 (CCCC 296, pp. 29-
34).

Also in TCD 244, Bodl Bodley 647. See 522 and cf. 697.

699 The Satturday the xviiith daye of June the viiith yere of the rainge of
our soveraigne lorde the saide Princesse went from a place in London

The Marriage of the Ducke of Bourgogne with Princesse Marge-
ret, account of the marriage of Margaret of York to Charles of

Burgundy (1468), ca. 1468.

1. Archaeologia, 31 (1846), 327-38 (London College of Arms MS).

Cf. **678**.

700 Þe seuene gyftes of þe Haly Gaste þat ere gyfene to men and wymmene þat er ordaynede to þe joye of heuene and ledys thaire lyfe in this worlde ryghtwysely

Richard Rolle, Of the Gyftes of the Haly Gaste, short treatise on the seven gifts of the Holy Ghost, s. xiv (1).

1. EETS os 20 (1866), p. 12 (Lincoln Cathedral 91, f. 196r-v); 2. Mätzner, I, 2 (1869), 131-32 (as in 1); 3. YW, I (1895), 45-46 (CUL Dd.5.64, where it is Chapter 11 of the Forme of Lyvyng); 4. YW, I (1895), 136 (BL Arundel 507, f. 43); 5. YW, I (1895), 196-97 (as in 1); 6. EETS os 20, rev. ed. (1921), p. 13 (as in 1); 7. Sisam (1924), pp. 42-43 (as in 1); 8. ed. C.W. Dunn and E.T. Byrnes, Middle English Literature (1973), pp. 233-34 (as in 1).

701 The solecytouriz and causerys of the feld takyng at Seynt Albonys ther namys shewyn her aftyr The Lord Clyfford Rauff Percy Thorpe

Brief account of the first battle of St. Albans (1455), s. xv (2).

1. Gairdner (1872-75; rptd. 1908), I, 332-33 (Phillipps 9735, no. 278); 2. Gairdner, rev. ed. (1904), III, 29-30 (as in 1).

Cf. **103**.

The tyme of thaduent or comyng of our lord in to this world is halowed in holy chirche the tyme of iiij wekes in betokenynge of iiij dyuerse comynges   Incipit to text proper of **682**.

702 The xij day of December ys the shortest day of the yere for the son aryseth a quarter of an owre after viij and goth downe iij quarters after iij

"Treatise on the Length of the Days in the Year", s. xv.

1. Rel. Ant., I (1841), 318-20 (BL Harley 941).

703 The Wennesday nexte aftir the solempne & devoute feste of the
Resurrexion of oure blessid Savyoure & Redemptour Jhu Criste for
soome of my besynesse

> The Actes of the Fulle Honorable & Knyghtly Armes, account of
> combat between Anthony Woodville and the Bastard of Burgundy
> at Smithfield in June 1467, ca. 1467.

> 1. Bentley (1833), pp. 176-212 (BL Lansdowne 285, ff. 29v-
> 43).

> Also in London College of Arms L.5.

704 The wise man in his boke named Ecclesiastes consideringe the miserye
and fraylete of the worlde saith that it is vanite of all vanites (from 2)

> Margaret Countess of Richmond, Mirroure of Golde to þe Sinfull
> Soule, translation from the French version of the Speculum
> Aureum, with a brief introduction by Wynkyn de Worde (?), s.
> xvi in.

> 1. W. de Worde, [1506?] (STC 6894.5); 2. W. de Worde, 1522
> (STC 6895); 3. J. Skot, 1522 (STC 6896); 4. W. de Worde,
> 1526 (STC 6897); 5. R. Pynson, [n.d.] (STC 6898).

705 The wyseman tawht hys chyld gladly to rede bokys and hem well
vndurstonde for in defaute of vndyrstondyng is ofttymes caused necly-
gence (from 2)

> Prologe of the Englyssh Register and Chronicle of the Hows and
> Monasteri of Godstow, introductory pieces to the English Regis-
> ter of Godstow Nunnery, ca. 1460.

> 1. ed. W. Dugdale, Monasticon Anglicanum, IV (1823), 369
> (Bodl Rawlinson B. 408, f. 13r-v); 2. EETS os 129 (1905), pp.
> 25-27 (as in 1).

706 Þe word of þe Apostele ffalleþ to Men of Religion and to alle gode
cristene men Seoþ þe stat wherto ȝe beoþ clept

> Þe Mirour of Seint Edmound, devotional treatise translated from
> Anglo-Norman and Latin versions of the Speculum Ecclesie of
> Edmund of Abingdon, s. xiv.

> 1. YW, I (1895), 241-61 (Bodl Eng. poet. a. 1, ff. 355 ff.).

For other translations see **800**.

707   The ȝere from the begynnynge of þe world þat was þat tyme þe XVIII
       day of Marche VM Co IVxx and XIXo The fryday þe XXV day of
       Marche was Cryste Jhesu conseyuyd

       Treatise on time, s. xv.

       1. ES, 10 (1887), 34-41 (BL Harley 4011, ff. 164 ff.).

708   Þe be-hovys to know þy fyve wyttys þe uttyr and þe ynnyr and to spend
       hem in good use and in þe lovynge of God Þe fyrst ys syȝt of eye þe
       toþer heryng of ere

       "Exposition on the Five Outer Wits", Wycliffite tract, s. xiv
       (2).

       1. SEW, III (1871), 117 (Lambeth Palace 408).

       Þe þat lyste luf held þine ere & here of luf In þe sang of luf I fynde it
       writen þat I haue sett at þe begynnynge of my wrytynge I slepe and my
       hert wakes   Incipit to edition 2 and similar to edition 3 of **160**.

       Thanne as Innocencius tercius seiþ alon and verrey God withoute
       beginnenge and ende is greet and passeþ alle met and mesure   Incipit
       to text proper of edition 4 of **785**.

       Thenne folowyng this fore wreton boke of Prolicronycon I haue
       emprysed to ordeyne this newe booke by the suffraunce of Almyghty
       god to contunue the sayd werk bryefly   Incipit to Liber Ultimus
       added by Caxton to Trevisa's translation of the Polychronicon (see
       758).

709   Ther been also sex principal thoughtes that euery man and woman shuld
       haue in mynd first is to delite in god

       Short devotional text appended to Here begynneth a lytill shorte
       treatyse, s. xv (2).

       1. Hanna (1984), p. 16 (San Marino Huntington HM 140, f.
       169).

710 Þere ben eiȝte Þingis bi whiche simple Cristene men ben disceyved Þat
ben Þes eiȝte holy Chirche lawe religion obedience cursynge

"Octo in Quibus Seducuntur Simplices Christiani", Wycliffite
tract, s. xiv (2).

1. SEW, III (1871), 447-53 (CCCC 296).

Also in TCD 244, TCD 246, Bodl Bodley 540.

711 Ther been in Englond xxxvj shires lij ml and lxxx townes xlv ml and xj
parisshes lx ml cc xv knightes fees

Computatio Suscripto de Feodis Militum, data on Britain during
the reign of Henry V, s. xv in.

1. Rel. Ant., I (1841), 232 (BL Lansdowne 762, f. 2v).

712 There ben many men at this daye the whiche alleggeth and groundeth
theyr wordes and treasons on the gospelles of the dystaues and knoweth
full lytell of what importaunce and auctoryte they ben of

Henry Watson (?), Gospelles of Dystaves, proverbial stories told
by six women on six days translated from earlier writings, s.
xv/xvi.

1. W. de Worde, n.d. [1507-15] (STC 12091).

There bene iij dayes in Þe ȝere before oÞer to be kept   Incipit to
third item in 687.

713 Therre ben iij Fryydays in the yere that who that euer fast hem
devoutely and be oute of dedely synns and clene shryvyn he shall be
savyd be fore god

"List of Egyptian Days", s. xv.

1. ELN, 13 (1975), 89-90 (Bodl Ashmole 59, ff. 135v-36).

714 There been thre thinges full harde to be knowen which waye they wole
drawe The first is of a birde sitting upon a bough

Proverb, s. xv.

1. Rel. Ant., I (1841), 233 (BL Lansdowne 762, f. 16v).

Whiting T 185.

715 Þer ben two maner of heretikis of whiche Englond schuld be purgid and symonieris ben þe first And alle siche ben symonieris þat occupien bi symonye þe patrimonye of Crist

"Simonists and Apostates", Wycliffite tract, s. xiv (2).

1. SEW, III (1871), 211-12 (Oxford New 95, ff. 122v-23).

716 Þer ben two offisis þat fallen to purging of þe chirche þe toon falliþ to knyʒtis and kyngis wiþ oþere lordis þat shulde defende wiþ strengþe þe lawe of crist in his boundis

John Purvey (?), De Officio Pastorali, Wycliffite tract, s. xiv ex.

1. EETS os 74 (1880, 1902), pp. 460-82 (Manchester Rylands English 86, ff. 1-21v).

717 Ther bith ij kyndes off kyngdomes of the wich that on is a lordship callid in laten dominium regale and that other is callid dominium politicum et regale (from 4)

John Fortescue, "On the Governance of England", 1471-76.

1. ed. J. Fortescue-Aland, The Difference Between an Absolute and Limited Monarchy (1714) (Bodl Digby 145, ff. 131-59); 2. ed. J. Fortescue-Aland, The Difference Between an Absolute and Limited Monarchy, 2nd ed. (1719) (as in 1); 3. Clermont (1869), I, 449-74 (as in 1); 4. Plummer (1885), pp. 109-57 (Bodl Laud Miscellaneous 593).

Also in CUL L1.3.11, BL Cotton Claudius A. VIII, BL Harley 542, BL Harley 1757, BL Addl. 48031, Lambeth Palace 262, Bodl Digby 198, Bodl Rawlinson B. 384. A Latin epitome is in TCC R.5.18.

Þere is he seis a deed caryone cropun of his sepulcre wrapped wiþ clothes of deul and dryven wiþ þe devel for to drecche men   See 436.

718   Ther is no courser vnto poyle Nor no folower vnto almayne Nor no palfrey vnto Englonde Nor no geldynge vnto scotland Nor no hoby vnto Irlonde

The Proprytees and Medycynes for Hors, s. xv ex. (?).

1. W. de Worde, 1502? (STC 20439.3); 2. W. de Worde, ca. 1525 (STC 20439.5); 3. W. Copland, 1565? (STC 20439.7); 4. MÆ, 41 (1972), 238 (Bodl Wood empt. 18, f. 60).

Editions 1, 2, and 3 contain 3 as Chap. 2; combined with 3 in edition 4.

There is no more of this foresaid worke for as it may be wele vnderstande this noble man Geffray Chaucer fynisshed it at the said conclusyon   Incipit to Caxton's epilogue in edition 2 of 322.

There was a man in the vale of Dispolite which was named Perse lombarde and betwene hym and his wyfe was goten & brought forthe a childe   Incipit to text proper of 523.

There was a parlyament at London whiche began about the octave of St. George   See 67.

Ther was an holy woman namyd mawdlen of good and lawdabulle lyff with chaste maners or werkys indued and fulfylled euer with effecte of herte   Incipit to introduction concerning Mary Magdalen to 442.

719   There was in Brytayne a kyng the moost Cristen prynce whose name was Nothus vel Maurus that hadde a doughter named Vrsull

"Life of St. Ursula", saint's life, s. xv.

1. RES, n.s. 9 (1958), 355-60 (San Marino Huntington HM 140, ff. 154-55v).

Also in Southwell Minster VII.

720   Ther was some tyme in Parise a man þat vsid with gret devocion to sey euery day in a chirchyard de profundis for al cristen soules

Exemplum, s. xv.

1. N&Q, 222 (1977), 297 (Coughton Court Throckmorton MS, f. 79).

Item 1464 in F.C. Tubach, Index Exemplorum (1969).

There were sixe mayster togyder and one askyd to a-nother what thyng they shold say of god & began to speke of trybulacion   Incipit to another translation of **287** incorporated into **751**.

Therefore Euere new discipull Ascende to the perfeccioun of this scyence fro degre to degre Fyrst þou sal ascende by the way þat is purgatyfe   See **784**.

These are ye wordes of the appostle the whiche dothe parteyne to men and women of relygion   See **799**.

721   Þese ben also þy fyve inwyttys Wyl Resoun Mynd Ymaginacioun and Thogth Lok þat þy wyl be good and holy and loke þat þy resoun rewle þe and nat þy fleschly lust

"Exposition on the Five Inner Wits", Wycliffite tract, s. xiv (2).

1. SEW, III (1871), 117-18 (Lambeth Palace 408).

These ben the lewed questions of Freres tytes and obseruaunces the whych they chargen more than Goddes lawe   Incipit to brief intro-duction in edition 1 of **782**.

722   These ben the xxii rightousnesses that a very kynge must have vse and holde in hymselfe for they maken the welfare of a realme

John Fortescue, The Twenty-Two Rightwisnesses Belongynge to a Kynge, s. xv (2).

1. Clermont (1869), I, 477-78 (BL Harley 542).

These ben the wordes of Salomon   See **156**.

These ben the wordes of the grete doctour and holy apostel saynte Poule consyderyng that the ghostly lyuyng of alle trew Cristen creatures

243

See 553.

723 These ben III perlous monedayes in þe ȝere on ys þe fyrst monday of
Feuerere and oþer is þe last monday of May

"Three Perilous Days", s. xv.

1. Studies in English Philology: A Miscellany in Honor of
Professor Frederick Klaeber, ed. K. Malone and M.B. Ruud
(1929), pp. 276-77 (Bodl Ashmole 342, f. 136v); 2. Isis, 33
(1942), 612 (as in 1); 3. Bühler (1973), p. 587 (as in 1).

Cf. 384.

Þes beþ þe wordys of seynt Paule þe apostel þat beþ nedeful to every
Crysten man to understande and to note hem in werke   See 390.5.

724 Thiese prayers tofore wreton ben enprinted bi the commaundementes of
the moste hye and vertuous pryncesse our liege ladi Elizabeth

William Caxton, brief epilogue to the XV O's, ca. 1491.

1. W. Caxton, 1491 (STC 20195); 2. Blades, Life, II (1863),
225 (as in 1); 3. Ayling (1869) (facsimile of 1); 4. Blades,
Biography (1877), pp. 348-49 (as in 1); 5. Blades, Biography,
2nd ed. (1882), pp. 352-53 (as in 1); 6. Duff (1917), p. 41 (as
in 1); 7. Aurner (1926), p. 296 (as in 1); 8. EETS os 176 (1928),
p. 111 (as in 1); 9. Blake, COP (1973), p. 83 (as in 1).

See 489.

These revelations were shewed to a simple creature that cowde no letter
the yeere of our lord 1373 the viiith day of May   Incipit to edition
B.3 of 321.

These wordes are writen in holy scripture and are thus to say in
englyshe The doughtres of Syon haue sene hyr   See 798.

Thyse wordes ben conteyned in the xxiiij chapytre of Luke and rad in
the holy gospel of this day To say in englyssh tonge The same Ihesus
nyghynge walkyd with mankynde   See 392.

244

Thyse Wordes ben wryten in the gospell of this daye And thus to be englisshyd Ihesu our sauyour   See **418**.

This wordes sayse Saynte Paule in his pistyll and thay are thus mekill to saye one ynglysche Seese ȝowre callynge   See **800**.

Thise wordes were sayd vnto Loth by an angell by the commaundement of almyghty god   See **354**.

Þai þat lyste lufe herken and here of luf In the sang of luf it es writen See **160**.

725   . . . þin hawke and sclyt þer þe sore is and þu sal finde þer-in als it wer þe maner of a mawe of a pygyoun and gedir it owte all hole and tak a payr of sesurs and cut away sumwhate on euery syde of þe wound

"Treatise of Falconry", book of instructions and remedies for hawks, s. xv (1).

1. Stockholm Studies in Modern Philology, n.s. 4 (1972), 22-36 (even pages only) (Durham County Record Office D/X 76/7, beginning imperfectly).

726   Þenkiþ wisly ȝe men þat fynden prestis þat ȝe don þis almes for Goddis love and helpe of ȝoure soulis and helpe of Cristene men and not for pride of þe world

How Men Schulden Fynde Prestis ("De Stipendis Ministrorum"), Wycliffite tract, xiv (2).

1. SEW, III (1871), 202-8 (CCCC 296, pp. 144-46).

Also in TCD 244.

727   This blyssed virgyn saynt Katheryn was by the dyscent of the lyne and of the noble kynrede of the Emperoure of Rome

The Life of Saincte Katheryne (of Alexandria), saint's life based on group B of the MSS of the Gilte Legende, s. xv ex. (?).

1. R. Pynson? 1510? (not in STC), fragment; 2. J. Waley, 1555 (STC 4817) (as in 1).

Cf. **28** and **138**.

728   This book comprehendiþ al þe oolde and newe testament and techiþ pleynli þe [mysteries] of þe trynytee and of cristis incarnacioun

John Purvey (?), excerpt from the General Prologue to the Wycliffite Bible circulating separately, s. xv (1).

1. Hanna (1984), p. 27 (San Marino Huntington HM 501, f. 22r-v); 2. Hanna (1984), p. 27 (San Marino Huntington HM 501, f. 24).

See **119**.

729   This boke is called þe boke of algorym or Augrym after lewder vse And þis boke tretys þe Craft of Nombryng þe quych crafte is called also Algorym Ther was a kyng of Inde þe quich heyth Algor & he made þis craft And after his name he called hit algorym

Boke of Algorym, arithmetic translated from Alexander of Villa Dei's De Algorismo, s. xv.

1. EETS es 118 (1922), pp. 3-32 (BL Egerton 2622, ff. 136-65).

730   This book is intituled confessio amantis that is to saye in englysshe the confessyon of the louer maad and compyled by Iohan Gower squyer

William Caxton, prologue to John Gower's Confessio Amantis, ca. 1483.

1. W. Caxton, 1483? (STC 12142); 2. Ames (1749), p. 35 (as in 1); 3. Herbert, I (1785), 45 (as in 1); 4. Aurner (1926), pp. 270-71 (as in 1); 5. Blake, COP (1973), pp. 69-70 (as in 1).

In Bodl Hatton 51, f. i (transcribed from edition 1).

731   This book is thus translated out of frenshe into our maternal tonge by the noble and vertuouse lord ANTHOINE Erle Ryuiers Lord Scales

William Caxton, epilogue to Woodville's Cordyal, 1479.

1. W. Caxton, 1479 (STC 5758); 2. [W. de Worde, n.d.] (STC 5759); 3. Ames (1749), pp. 14-15 (as in 1); 4. Herbert, I (1785), 19-21 (as in 1); 5. Blades, Life, I (1861), 149-50 (as in

1); 6. Aurner (1926), pp. 278-80 (as in 1); 7. EETS os 176 (1928), pp. 38-40 (as in 1); 8. ed. J.A. Mulders ([1962]), pp. 150-52 (as in 1); 9. Blake, COP (1973), pp. 70-72 (as in 1).

732   This boke þe whiche is clepid þe Myrour of Symple Soules I moost vnworþi creature and outcast of all oþire many ʒeeris goon wrote it out of French into Englisch after my lewide kunnynge

        M[ichael] N[orthbrook] (?), Þe Mirour of Simple Soules, translation from Margaret Porete's original French, s. xiv med.

        1. Archivio Italiana per la Storia Pieta, 5 (1968), 247-355 (Cambridge St. John's 71, ff. 1-104v).

        Also in BL Addl. 37790, Bodl Bodley 505.

        This chepture declaris hou necessare this dominicall orisone js to ws Gustate et Videte quoniam suauis est dominus   Incipit to text proper of 565.

733   Thys crosse xv tymys metyn ys the lenght of oure Lorde Jhesu Cryst and what day ye locke theron and blesse yow therewith there schall no wycked spryte have no power to hurte yow (from A.2)

        Charm based on the measurement of the length of the body of Jesus, s. xv.

        A. 1. Bliss (1857), p. 195 (London Wellcome Historical Medical Library 632); 2. Bliss, 2nd ed., I (1869), 196 (as in 1); 3. Doble, II (1886), 376 (as in 1); 4. JBAA, 48 (1892), 39 (as in 1); 5. Buchanan-Brown (1966), p. 97 (as in 1).

        B. 1. JBAA, 31 (1875), 105 (BL Harley Rot. A.43); 2. Trans. of the Royal Society of Literature, 2nd series, 11 (1878), 470, 472 (as in 1); 3. JBAA, 48 (1892), 41 (as in 1); 4. Speculum, 39 (1964), 274-75 (as in 1); 5. Bühler (1973), pp. 569-70 (as in 1).

        C. 1. JBAA, 48 (1892), 50-51 (BL Harley Rot. T.11); 2. MLR, 13 (1918), 228-29 (Bodl Bodley 177, f. 61v).

        D. 1. Speculum, 39 (1964), 275 (New York Morgan Glazier 39); 2. Bühler (1973), pp. 570-71 (as in 1).

        E. 1. ed. S.A.J. Moorat, Catalogue of Western Manuscripts on Medicine and Science in the Wellcome Historical Medical Library, I (1962), 492 (London Wellcome Historical Medical Library 632).

734   This day is callyd the first sonday of aduent that is the sonday in cristys comyng Therfore holy chirche this day maketh mencion of ij comynges The first comynge was to bye monkynde out of bondage of the deuyll

John Mirk, Liber Festialis/Festivall, collection of sermons derived primarily from the Legenda Aurea, s. xv in.

1. W. Caxton, 1483? (STC 17957, Part 1); 2. [T. Rood and T. Hunt], 1486 (STC 17958), with introductory prayer and prologue (printed from a MS different from that used for 1); 3. W. Caxton, 1491 (STC 17959); 4. R. Pynson, [1493] (STC 17960); 5. R. Pynson, [1493] (STC 17961); 6. [W. de Worde], 1493 (STC 17962, Part 1); 7. J. Ravynell, 1495 (STC 17963); 8. W. Hopyl, 1495 (STC 17964); 9. [W. de Worde], 1496 (STC 17965); 10. M. Morin, 1499 (STC 17966); 11. R. Pynson, 1499 (STC 17966.5); 12. [W. de Worde], 1499 (STC 17967); 13. J. Notary, 1499 (STC 17968); 14. R. Pynson, 1502 (STC 17969); 15. J. Notary, [1506?] (STC 17970); 16. [R. Pynson, 1507?] (STC 17970.5); 17. W. de Worde, 1508 (STC 17971); 18. W. de Worde, 1511 (STC 17971.5); 19. W. de Worde, 1515 (STC 17972); 20. R. Faques, [ca. 1512] (STC 17973); 21. W. de Worde, 1519 (STC 17973.5); 22. W. de Worde, 1528 (STC 17974); 23. W. de Worde, 1532 (STC 17975); 24. EETS es 96 (1905) (Bodl Gough Eccl. Top. 4, ff. 1-164 with extracts from BL Cotton Claudius A. II and BL Harley 2403).

Also in Cambridge Gonville and Caius 168/89, CUL Dd.10.50, CUL Ee.2.15 (extracts), CUL Ff.2.38 (extracts), CUL Nn.3.10 (extracts), TCD 201 (extracts), Durham University Cosin V.III.5, Hatfield House Marquis of Salisbury 280, Leeds University Brotherton 502, Lincoln Cathedral 133 (extracts), BL Harley 1288 (extracts), BL Harley 2250 (extracts), BL Harley 2371, BL Harley 2391, BL Harley 2417, BL Harley 2420 (extracts), BL Lansdowne 392, BL Royal 18 B.xxiii (extracts), London New College Anc. 1, Bodl Douce 60, Bodl Douce 108, Bodl Hatton 96, Bodl Rawlinson A. 381, Oxford University 102, Southwell Minster MS. Edition 10 is copied in Cambridge St. John's 187. All editions beginning with 3 printed before 1500 follow the text in 2, as does the modern edition (24); in the same editions "A shorte exhortacyon ofte to be shewed to the peple" follows the Festivall (beginning "Doo to a nother"). Extra service material is added in the 15th- and 16th-c. editions as time goes as on. A 15th-c. revision of the Festivall appears in TCD 428, Gloucester Cathedral 22 (pp. 1-44), BL Harley 2247, and

BL Royal 18 B.xxv, parts of which are edited in MET 13 (1981), and Festivall-related sermons appear in Durham University Cosin V.IV.3, Gloucester Cathedral 22 (pp. 45-722), Lincoln Cathedral 50-51, BL Lansdowne 379, Bodl e Mus. 180, and Bodl Greaves 54. Cf. **398** and **689**.

735   This Edward erle of the Marche son and heire of Richard duke of Yorke was borne at Roane in Normandy his fadir then being regent there

Chronicle of the events of the reign of Edward IV, s. xv ex.

1. ed. T. Hearne, Thomæ Sprotti Chronica (1719), pp. 283-306 (unspecified MS, ending imperfectly).

736   This Emperour þat y spak of aboue is our lord Ihesu Cryst his wyf is the soule Themperoures brothir is man

Thomas Hoccleve, Moralizacio of the Fabula de Quadam Emperatrice Romana ("Tale of Jereslaus' Wife", IMEV 1561), s. xv in.

1. EETS es 61 (1892),pp. 175-78 (Durham University Cosin V.III.9, ff. 50-52v); 2. EETS es 61, rev. ed. (1970), pp. 175-78 (as in 1).

Also in CCCC 496, Coventry Corporation Record Office MS, BL Royal 17 D.vi, New Haven Yale University 496, Bodl. Arch. Selden Supra 53, Bodl Bodley 221, Bodl Digby 185, Bodl Eng. poet. d. 4, Bodl Laud Miscellaneous 735.

737   This gloryous and blessyd confessour & true relygyous keper called saynt Nycholas of tollentyne was borne in a countree called Pycen

Life of Saint Nicholas of Tollentino (died 1305), saint's life, s. xv (?).

1. W. de Worde, [1525?] (STC 18528); 2. [W. de Worde, 1525?] (STC 18528.5), fragment.

738   Þis gospel telliþ mouche wisdom þat is hid to many men and speciali for þis cause þat it is not al red in þe Chirche

Of Mynystris in þe Chirche, Wycliffite exposition of Matthew 24, s. xiv ex.

1. SEW, II (1871), 393-423 (Bodl Bodley 788).

Also in CCCC 336, Cambridge Magdalene Pepys 2616, Cambridge Pembroke 237, Cambridge St. John's 193, TCC B.2.17, TCC B.4.20, TCD 245, Leicester Old Town Hall 3, Leicester Wyggeston Hospital 10.D.34/6, BL Cotton Claudius D. VIII, BL Harley 1203, BL Royal 18 B.ix, BL Addl. 40672, Lambeth Palace 1149, Bodl Don.c.13, and Princeton Robert H. Taylor MS.

739   This is resonable to wryght the mervelus dedes done by Virgilius within the cytie of Rome and in other places Rome hath be at all tymes of grete name and fame

The Lyfe of Virgilius, romance, s. xv.

1. J. Doesborch, 1518? (STC 24828); 2. W. Copland, 1562? (STC 24829); 3. ed. E.V. Utterson (1812) (as in 1); 4. ed. W.J. Thoms (1827) (as in 1); 5. Thoms (1828), II, 2-41 (as in 1); 6. Thoms, 2nd ed. (1858), II, 20-59 (as in 1); 7. Morley (1889), pp. 209-35 (as in 1); 8. Thoms, enlarged ed. (1906, 1907), pp. 209-36 (as in 1).

740   This is þe boke þat euax kyng of Arabe sent to tyberi off rom of all maner of precius stones as well of her names vertues as of here colours and her contreys

Lapidary, s. xv.

1. EETS os 190 (1933), pp. 63-118 (Peterborough Cathedral 33, ff. 1-16v).

Thys ys þe firste of godys comaundementys þou schalt not worschype fals goddys Alle þo þat leue in gret synne as pryde Couetyse Gloteny Incipit to edition B.1 of 49.

741   This is the maner to kepe hawkes but not al maner of hawkes but only goshaukes and sperhaukes First to speke of haukes they beth egges and afterward they be disclosed hawkes

[Edward Plantagenet], Booke of Haukynge, treatise on hawking perhaps translated from French or Latin, s. xv.

1. Rel. Ant., I (1841), 293-308 (BL Harley 2340, ff. 1-22v); 2.

SN, 16 (1943-44), 5-21 (as in 1).

Also in Lambeth Palace 306 (rearranged), London York House (Kensington) Duke of Gloucester 45, Bodl Ashmole 1432 (fragment), Bodl Rawlinson C. 506. For another translation see **194**. Both translations were probably used by the author of **391**.

742   This is the mesur of the blessyd wound that our Lord Ihesu Crist had in hs [sic] right side the whiche an angell brought to Charlamayn

      Supplication connected with the wound made by Longinus in the side of Jesus, s. xv.

      1. JBAA, 48 (1892), 52-53 (BL Harley Rot. T.11); 2. Speculum, 39 (1964), 277 (as in 1); 3. Bühler (1973), p. 573 (as in 1).

      Also in New York Morgan Glazier 39.

743   Thys ys þe medesyn þat þe kyngis grace vsythe every day for The raynyng seknys þat now raynthe

      Recipe for King Edward IV's plague medicine, s. xv (2).

      1. N&Q, 5th series 9 (1878), 343 (San Marino Huntington HM 144, f. 150v).

744   This Pagent sheweth the birth of the famous knyght Richard Beauchamp Erle of Warrewik which was born in the Maner of Salwarp in the Counte of Worcester (from 2)

      "Pageant of the Birth, Life, and Death of Richard Beauchamp, Earl of Warwick", s. xv (2).

      1. Roxburghe (1908), even pages (BL Cotton Julius E. IV, part 6); 2. ed. Viscount Dillon and W.H. St. John Hope (1914) (as in 2).

      A copy of the Cotton MS made by William Dugdale in 1636, ed. Hearne (1729), pp. 359-71 (unidentified Bodl Dugdale MS).

Thys planet Saturnus goþ aboute in xxx ȝere þis planet is hoote and drye and malicyous   Incipit to sixth item in **687**.

745   This presente boke is called the Mirroure of golde to þe sinfull soule the whiche hath ben translated at parise oute of laten in to frenche (from 2)

Wynkyn de Worde (?), brief introduction to Margaret Countess of Richmond's Mirroure of Golde to þe Sinfull Soule, s. xvi in.

1. W. de Worde, [1506?] (STC 6894.5); 2. W. de Worde, 1522 (STC 6895); 3. J. Skot, 1522 (STC 6896); 4. W. de Worde, 1526 (STC 6897); 5. R. Pynson, [n.d.] (STC 6898).

See 704.

746   This present treatyse conteyneth a deuoute contemplacyon and oreyson the whiche who so euer it say and it wyll ymagen deuoutly with very repentaunce of his synnes

Boke of Conforte Agaynst All Tribulacione, didactic treatise, s. xv.

1. W. de Worde, [1505?] (STC 3295); 2. R. Pynson, [n.d.] (STC 3296).

This reuelation was made to a symple creature vnlettyrde leving in deadly flesh the yer of our lord a thousannde and three hundered and lxxiij the xiij daie of May   Incipit to edition B.4 of 321.

747   This table was made þe xxvi day of march the ȝere of oure lord mlccclxxxvi and þanne ȝede þe prime by xx

Introduction to a table for finding the date of Easter, s. xv (1).

1. Hanna (1984), pp. 33-34 (San Marino Huntington HM 744, f. 1).

748   This that is writen in this lytyl boke ought the prestres to lerne and teche to theyr parysshens And also it is necessary for symple prestes that vnderstonde not the scriptures And it is made for symple peple and put in to englissh

William Caxton, Doctrinal of Sapyence, didactic treatise on the essentials of faith translated from the French Doctrinal aux simples gens, 1489.

1. W. Caxton, 1489 (STC 21431).

Þilke tyme Moyses and aaron were y send thurgh goddus owne mouthe to kyng Pharao þat was kyng of Egypt to bid him þat he lete þe children of Ysraell   Incipit to text proper of **448**.

749   Þis tretys Is a talkyng of þe loue of God and is mad forto sturen hem þat hit reden to louen him þe more and to fynde lykyng and tast in his loue

A Talkyng of þe Love of God, mystical treatise, s. xiv.

1. YW, II (1896), 345-66 (Bodl Eng. poet. a. 1, ff. 367-71);
2. ed. M. Salvina Westra (1950) (as in 1).

750   This tretis is contriuid vpon the gamme for hem þat will be syngers or makers or techers For þe ferst thing of all þei must know hou many cordis of discant þer be

Lionel Power, treatise on counterpoint, s. xv in.

1. Speculum, 10 (1935), 242-58 (BL Lansdowne 763, ff. 104v-12).

751   This tretyse is of loue and spekyth of iiij of the most specyall louys that ben in the worlde and shewyth veryly and perfitely bi gret resons and Causis how the meruelous & bounteuous loue

Tretyse of Love, compilation of devotional tracts translated from French (based in part on the Ancrene Wisse), 1493.

1. [Wynkyn de Worde, 1493] (STC 24234); 2. EETS os 223 (1951) (as in 1).

Cf. **559**.

This tretis next folewynge maade Sir Johan Clanevowe knyʒt þe laste viage þat he maade ouer the greete see in which he dyede   Incipit to brief introduction to **680**.

This verbe sum es fui with all his compoundys lackyth the gerundiuys and the supynys   English incipit to version B of **306**.

752   Ðis gear com Henri king to þis land Þa com Henri abbot & uureide þe

253

muneces of Burch to þe king forþi ðat he uuolde underþeden ðat mynstre to Clunie (from 6)

Chronicle for the years 1132-54 written at Peterborough, ca. 1154.

1. ed. E. Gibson, Chronicon Saxonicum (1692) (Bodl Laud Miscellaneous 636, ff. 88v-91v); 2. ed. B. Thorpe, Rolls 23, 1 (1861), 381-85 (as in 1); 3. ed. J. Earle, Two of the Saxon Chronicles Parallel (1865), pp. 260-66 (as in 1); 4. ed. C. Plummer, Two of the Saxon Chronicles Parallel, I (1892), 262-69 (as in 1); 5. Emerson (1905, 1915, 1932), pp. 1-8 (as in 1); 6. ed. C. Clark, The Peterborough Chronicle 1070-1154 (1958), pp. 54-60 (as in 1).

753   Þou freend Tymothe what tyme þat þou purposist þee by þe steryng of grace to þe actueel excersise of þi blynde beholdynges loke þou forsake with a stronge & a sleiȝ & a listi contricyon

Deonise Hid Divinite, devotional treatise translated from a Latin translation of the Mystica Theologia of Dionysius the Areopagite, s. xiv ex.

1. EETS os 231 (1955), pp. 2-10 (BL Harley 674, ff. 121-26v); 2. Hodgson (1982), pp. 119-28 (as in 1).

Also in CUL Kk.6.26.

754   Thou shalte be butteler and panter all the fyrst yere and ye muste haue thre pantry knyues one knyfe to square trenchours

Boke of Servyce and Kervynge and Sewynge, handbook of advice for carvers and servers, preceded by a vocabulary of carver's terms, s. xv (?).

1. W. de Worde, 1508 (STC 3289); 2. W. de Worde, 1513 (STC 3290); 3. A. Veale, [1560?] (STC 3291); 4. E. Allde, 1613 (STC 3292); 5. E. Allde, [n.d.] (STC 3293); 6. EETS os 32 (1868, 1904), pp. 261-86 (as in 2).

Thou schalt loue thi lord thi god of al thyn herte of al thy lyf of al thi mynde and of al thi strengthes or myghtes and thyn neighebor as thi-self   See 155.

55   Thow schalt vndirstonde þat eueri religius soule haþ Viij goostly
dwellinge placis The fferste is a temple of deuout preier

"Eight Ghostly Dwelling Places", short allegorical passage, s.
xv.

1. MÆ, 44 (1975), 142 (San Marino Huntington HM 744, ff.
12v-13).

Þou soule tribulid and temptid to þe is þis word shewid þat þou lere
wherof tribulacion serues and þat þou not onely susteyne hom suf-
fraandely but also gladely   See 141.

Þou [Þai in edition 4] þat lyste lufe herken & here of luf In þe sang of
luf it es writen I slepe & my hert wakes   See 160.

Þow ȝernys perauenter gretely for to haue more knawynge & wyssynge
þan þou has of aungels sange and heuenly sown qwat it is & on qwat
wyse it is perceyued   Incipit to edition 4 of 146.

Þou vnbigonne & euerlastyng Wysdome þe whiche in þiself arte þe
souereyn-substancyal Firstheed þe souereyn Goddesse & þe souereyn
Good   Incipit to introductory prayer to 753.

56   Tho the perfecte knawlege of the domes of the crafte of astronomye the
which be the rewlynge of kynde ar browth forthe of the effects of
planetes first it is nedful for to knaw the entrynge of the Sonne

Exafrenon Pronosticationum Temporis, astrological treatise translated from the Latin of Richard of Wallingford (ca. 1317-19), s.
xiv (2).

1. ed. J.D. North, Richard of Wallingford (1976), 1, 183-243
(odd pages only) (Bodl Digby 67, ff. 6-12v).

Also in TCC O.5.26 and Bodl Digby Roll III.

Three degreeȝ of grace are Þe first god gifs til alle creatures til vphald
þaim   Incipit to edition 1 of 502.

57   Thre pontȝ þere are þat kepen vs fro mone sotell desetȝ of þe foule

fende þat mone gostle men begils þorou preway pontȝ of pryde

[Richard Rolle], notes on three points of humility, s. xiv.

1. YW, I (1895), 172 (BL Harley 1022, f. 81).

Jolliffe G. 28.

758   Thus endeth the book uamed [sic] Proloconycon made and compiled by Ranulph monk of chestre whiche ordeyned it in latyn and atte request of the ryght worshipful lord Thomas

William Caxton, epilogue to Trevisa's translation of the Poly-chronicon, followed immediately by a Liber Ultimus through the year 1461, ca. 1482.

1. W. Caxton, 1482 (STC 13438); 2. W. de Worde, 1495 (STC 13439); 3. P. Treveris, 1527 (STC 13440); 4. Lewis (1737), pp. 58-59 (as in 1), epilogue only; 5. Ames (1749), pp. 32-33 (as in 1), epilogue only; 6. Herbert, I (1785), 40-41 (as in 1), epilogue only; 7. Blades, Life, I (1861), 195-265 (as in 1); 8. Rolls 41, 8 (1882), 352-53, 522-87 (as in 1); 9. Aurner (1926), pp. 292-93 (as in 1), epilogue only; 10. EETS os 176 (1928), p. 68 (as in 1), epilogue only; 11. Blake, COP, (1973), pp. 132-33 (as in 1), epilogue only.

See 605.

759   Thus endyth the moost vertuouse hystorye of the deuoute and right renommed lyues of holy faders lyuynge in deserte worthy of remem-braunce to all well dysposed persones

Wynkyn de Worde, epilogue to Caxton's Vitas Patrum, ca. 1495.

1. W. de Worde, 1495 (STC 14507); 2. Ames (1749), p. 73 (as in 1); 3. Herbert, I (1785), 108 (as in 1); 4. Dibdin, TA, II (1812), 45 (as in 1); 5. Dibdin, BS, IV (1815), 397 (as in 1).

760   Thus endeth this boke named Tullius de Amicicia whiche treateth of frendship vtterid and declared by a noble senatour of Rome named Lelyus

William Caxton, epilogue to John Tiptoft's translation, Tullius de Amicicia, ca. 1481.

256

1. W. Caxton, 1481 (STC 5293, Part 2); 2. [W. Rastell, 1530?] (STC 5275); 3. Oldys (1737), p. 259 (as in 1); 4. Ames (1749), p. 26 (as in 1); 5. Herbert, I (1785), 33 (as in 1); 6. Blades, Life, I (1861), 162-3 (as in 1); 7. Aurner (1926), pp. 247-8 (as in 1); 8. EETS os 176 (1928), pp. 45-6 (as in 1); 9. Blake, COP (1973), pp. 123-4 (as in 1); 10. (1977) (facsimile of 1).

See 555.

61 Thus endeth this boke whiche is named the boke of Consolacion of philosophie whiche that boecius made for his comforte and consolacion

William Caxton, epilogue to Chaucer's translation of Boethius, De Consolatione Philosophie, ca. 1478.

1. W. Caxton, 1478? (STC 3199); 2. Ames (1749), pp. 57-58 (as in 1); 3. Herbert, I (1785), 75-76 (as in 1); 4. Blades, Life, I (1861), 151-52 (as in 1); 6. Aurner (1926), pp. 237-38 (as in 1); 7. EETS os 176 (1928), pp. 36-37 (as in 1); 8. Blake, COP (1973), pp. 58-60 (as in 1); 9. Boyd (1978), pp. 172-74 (as in 1); 10. Brewer (1978), pp. 74-75 (as in 1).

Cf. 43.

62 Thus endeth this present boke composed of diuerse fruytfull ghostly maters of whiche the forseyde names folowen to thentent

William Caxton, conclusion to the three-part Boke of Diverse Fruytfull Ghostly Maters, ca. 1491.

1. W. Caxton, 1491 (STC 3305); 2. Blake, COP (1973), p. 102 (as in 1).

Thus sayth the apostole saynt Poule in the boke of actes and dedes
See 537.

63 Tylle alle tho that wyl of venery lere y shall hem teche as y have lernyd of maystris that is disputyd and endyd

Le Venery de Twety and of Mayster Johan Giffarde, treatise on hunting translated from Guillaume Twiti, Le Art de Vénerie (ca. 1327), s. xv (1).

1. Rel. Ant., I (1841), 150-54 (BL Cotton Vespasian B. XII, ff. 5-9); 2. Tilander (1956), pp. 44-50 (as in 1); 3. ed. W. Bowman, England in Ashton-under-Lyne (1960), pp. 51-52 (Ashton-under-Lyne Stamford and Warrington Estates Office MS, fragment).

Another translation in 485.

To alle of you I sende gretynge Wot ye þat I am kyng of alle kynges Lord of alle lordes   Incipit to edition 2 of 315.

764   To alle suche even nombrys the most have cifrys as to ten twenty thirtty an hundred an thousand and suche other but ye schal vnderstonde that a cifre tokeneth nothinge but he maketh other the more significatyf

Treatise on the numeration of algorism, s. xv (?).

1. Halliwell, Rara (1839), pp. 29-31 (J.O. Halliwell MS); 2. EETS es 118 (1922), pp. 70-71 (as in 1).

765   To al them þat deuoutly say v pater nosters v aues and a crede afor such a figur ar graunted xxxij m vij c lv yeres of pardon

Indulgence, s. xv.

1. [W. de Worde, ca. 1500] (STC 14077c.14); 2. [W. de Worde, ca. 1505] (STC 14077c.14A); 3. Dodgson, Woodcuts (1929), p. 34 (as in 1); 4. Walpole Soc., 17 (1929), 103 (as in 2); 5. Walpole Soc., 17 (1929), Plate XXXV(d) (as in 1); 6. Dodgson, English (1936), p. 9 and Plate 13 (as in 1); 7. Dodgson, English (1936), p. 10 and Plate 20 (as in 2).

766   To all verraie contrite and confessid that comen by cause of devocioun tho the cherche or monasterie and ther knelyng saie a pater noster

The Syon Indulgences/Indulgencia Monasterii de Syon, s. xv.

1. Aungier (1840), pp. 421-22 (Bodl Ashmole 750, f. 140).

Also in BL Harley 955.

To comfort a man or a woman yn her laste ende a priste schulde seyȝe thys My dere frende hit semyth that thou hyest faste owte of thys

258

worlde   Incipit to version C of **460**.

To his dere sistir in God Goddis hondemayden and his spouse gretynge in hym   Incipit to introduction to **150**.

To his lord most hegh and in worschippynge of Cristes religioun most noble Guy sothely of Valence of þe Citee of Tripol   Incipit to dedication to **261**.

To his most excellent lord and in worshippyng of Cristen religion hardiest Guy of Valence the gracious Bisshop of Tripolis   Incipit to dedication to **63**.

67   To knowe þe bettere my purpos in þis boke wite ʒe wel þat I desire euerych man and womman and child to be my moder

"Book to a Mother", devotional treatise, s. xiv (2).

1. ed A.J. McCarthy, Elizabethan and Renaissance Studies, 92 (1981) (Bodl Bodley 416, ff. 1-105, supplemented by Bodl Laud Miscellaneous 210, ff. 20-30).

Also in BL Egerton 826 (fragment) and BL Addl. 30897; Jolliffe B.5.

68   To knowe the pulsse laye thy 4 fyngers and towche the pulsse yffe the pulsse vnder the lytill fynger be febill

Ad Cognossendum Pulsum Alicuius, explanation of diagnosis by pulse, s. xv ex.

1. Hanna (1984), p. 3 (San Marino Huntington HM 64, ff. 16v-17).

69   To make an hors þat he schall nat ney or whynye Take a woullen liste & bynde hit about þe myddes of his tonge

Remedy for a horse, s. xv.

1. MÆ, 41 (1972), 237 (Bodl Wood empt. 18, f. 59v).

770   To makynge of the lytel schippe of venyse thre instrumentes at the leste
       beth ful necessarie whiche schul be made Take a Compas & open the
       fete

       Treatise on making a sundial, s. xiv (2).

       1. Journal of the History of Medicine, 15 (1960), 402-7 (TCC
       O.5.26, ff. 121-22v).

       To my Sovereyn Lord Edward be the grace of God Kyng of Ynglond
       and of Frauns Lord of Yrlond   Incipit to dedicatory preface to
       Edward IV to 673.

771   To my wel-beloued in our Lord God maystir of þe order of Sempyng-
       ham wheech ordre is entytled on to þe name of Seynt Gilbert I ffrer I C
       amongis doctouris lest send reuerens

       John Capgrave, Lif of Seint Gilbert, translated from Latin,
       1451.

       1. EETS os 140 (1910), pp. 61-142 (BL Addl. 36704, ff. 46-
       116).

       Also in BL Cotton Vitellius D. XV (fragments).

772   To save yow from theves say thryse Jesus Marya and Disamus save vs
       & kepe vs from al suche as he was

       Charm, s. xv.

       1. N&Q, 207 (1962), 48 (BL Harley 2389, f. 26).

773   To save your clothes from stealynge all nyght Jasper Melcher and
       Balthasar stand ye my enemis

       Charm, s. xv.

       1. N&Q, 207 (1962), 48 (BL Harley 2389, f. 26).

774   To the haly croun of Fraunce in the quhilk this day regnys Charles the
       Sext of that name the quhilk is lufit and redoubtit our all the warld

       Gilbert of the Haye, The Buke of the Law of Armys, translation of Honoré Bonet's Arbre des batailles, 1456.

1. STS, 1st series 44 (1899) (Abbotsford Scott Collection 1-3, ff. 1-85).

75 To the honure and reuerence of yow my ryght worshipfull and dred lord H by the grace of God eldest sone and heire vnto the hie excellent and criston prynce H þe iiij

Edward Duke of York, Maystere of Game, translation of Gaston de Foix's Livre de Chasse, treatise on hunting, 1406-13.

1. Baillie-Grohman (1904) (BL Cotton Vespasian B. XII, ff. 9-105).

Also in CUL Ff.4.15, BL Harley 5086, BL Harley 6824, BL Royal 17 A.1v, BL Royal 17 B.ii, BL Royal 17 B.xli, BL Royal 17 D.iv, BL Royal 17 D.xii, BL Royal 18 C.xviii, BL Sloane 60, BL Sloane 3501, BL Addl. 16165, BL Addl. 18652, London York House (Kensington) Duke of Gloucester 45, London York House (Kensington) Duke of Gloucester MS (fragment), New Haven Yale University 101, New Haven Yale University 163, Bodl Bodley 546, Bodl Digby 182, Bodl Douce 335, Bodl James 11 (extracts), Rome English College 1306, San Marino Huntington EL 1123, Tokyo Takamiya 16, Tokyo Takamiya 19.

To the honour of god almyghty and to the gloryous vyrgyne Marye moder of alle grace and to the vtylyte and prouffyt of all the policye mondayne this present booke compyled by virgyle ryght subtyl and Ingenyous oratour and poete   Incipit to preface to 27.

To the kynge our souerayne lorde Prayen your comyns in this present parlyament assembled that where þe comen wele and profyte of your habytaunces   Incipit to text proper of 12 Henry VII (as in edition 8) of **686**.

76 To the moste excellente moste redoubted and moste crysten Kyng Edward the fourth Iohan kay hys humble poete lawreate and moste lowly seruant knelyng vnto the ground sayth salute

John Kay, Siege of the Noble and Invyncyble Cytee of Rhodes, translation from Gulielmus Caorsin's version, ca. 1482.

1. [W. de Machlinia, ca. 1482] (STC 4594); 2. ed. D. Gray

261

(1975) (facsimile of 1).

777 To the moste excellent redoubte lorde the Kyng and to alle the noble
lordes of this present parlement shewen mekely alle the trewe comvnes
seyynge this sothely (from 3)

A Bille of the Tempereltees Beyng in Religious Handes, Lollard
bill for disendowing worldly clergy presented in Parliament,
1410.

1. Rolls 28, part 5, I (1870), 453-56 (BL Harley 3775, ff. 120-
21v); 2. Kingsford, Chronicles (1905), pp. 65-68 (BL Cotton
Julius B. II, 61-63v); 3. Hudson (1978), pp. 135-37 (as in 2).

A Latin version appears in Bodl Bodley 462 (ed. V.H. Gal-
braith, The St. Albans Chronicle 1406-1420 [1937], pp. 52-55).

778 To the moost high and excellent mageste of princes to the right
honeurable magnificence of nobles circumspection of clerkes and good
instruccion of the comon peeple

The Quadriloge of Aleyn Charietere, translation of Alain Chartier's Le Quadrilogue invectif (1422), s. xv med.

1. EETS os 270 (1974), pp. 135-247 (odd only) (Oxford University 85, ff. 1-35).

For another translation see 779.

779 To the ryght high and excellent mageste of princes to the full honorable
magnificence of nobles to the circumspection of clerkis and to the witty
exercise of the people of Fraunce

Quadrilogum Invectum, translation of Alain Chartier's Le Quadrilogue Invectif (1422), s. xv (1).

1. EETS os 270 (1974), pp. 134-246 (even only) (Bodl Rawlinson A. 338, ff. 1-33v).

For another translation see 778.

To the right noble right excellent and vertuous prince George duc of
Clarence   Dedication to edition 1 only of 62.

To the soule that art delyuered to temptacions and to tribulacions of this lyf is ordeyned the wisdom of this worde   See **143**.

To the worshipe of god and of all holy chirche And for the comen wele and profyt of this reame of England   Incipit to 4 Henry VII of **686**.

780   To þem þat before þis ymage off pyte Deuoutly v tymes say pater noster and aue Pite[ous]ly beholding þies [armes of Chris]tes passion (from 2)

Indulgence, under an image of pity, s. xv.

1. W. Caxton, ca. 1487 (STC 14077c.6), with text cut out; 2. ca. 1490 (STC 14077c.7); 3. W. Caxton, ca. 1490 (STC 14077c.8); 4. ca. 1480-90 (STC 14077c.8A); 5. ca. 1500 (STC 14077c.13); 6. Blades, Biography (1877), p. 318 (as in 2); 7. Blades, Biography (1877), p. 320 (as in 3); 8. Cambridge Antiquarian Communications, 3 (1879), 94 and plate facing 135 (as in 3); 9. Blades, Biography, 2nd ed. (1882), p. 322 (as in 2); 10. Blades, Biography, 2nd ed. (1882), p. 324 (as in 3); 11. Bradshaw (1889), p. 94 and plate facing p. 95 (as in 3); 12. Schreiber, Manuel, 1 (1891), 250 (as in 3); 13. Cooke and Wordsworth (1902), Plate i (as in 3); 14. Duff, WC (1905), Plate XIV (as in 1); 15. Aurner (1926), Plate VIII (as in 1); 16. Schreiber, Handbuch (1926-30), item 866 (as in 3); 17. Dodgson, Woodcuts (1929), pp. 33-34 (as in 2); 18. Walpole Soc., 17 (1929), Plate XXXV(a) (as in 4); 19. Walpole Soc., 17 (1929), Plate XXXV(b) (as in 2); 20. Walpole Soc., 17 (1929), Plate XXXV(c) (as in 5); 21. Dodgson, English (1936), p. 7 and Plate 3 (as in 2); 22. Dodgson, English (1936), p. 8 and Plate 5 (as in 5); 23. Dodgson, English (1936), Plate 1 (as in 4); 25. Dodgson, English (1936), Plate 10 (as in 3).

Often found in early printed editions of the Primer and Horae.

781   To thilke of this regiown whiche han noon hows but alle as seith seynt Poul be thei riche be thei poore be thei wise other fooles be thei kynges other queenes

The Pilgimage of the Lyfe of the Manhode, translation of Le Pélerinage de la vie humaine by Guillaume de Deguilleville, s. xv.

1. Roxburghe 91 (1869) (CUL Ff.5.30, ff. 5-140).

Also in London Sion College Arc. L.40.2/E.44.

263

782 To veri God and to alle trewe in Crist I Iacke Vplond make my moone
þat Anticrist and hise disciplis bi coloure of holynes wasten and
disceiuen Cristis chirche (from 8)

"Jack Upland", Wycliffite tract, s. xv in.

1. J. Gough, [1536?] (STC 5098); 2. Foxe, 2nd ed. (1570 and
later editions), I, 341-45; 3. Speght, 2nd ed. (1602; STC
5080); 4. Speght (1687); 5. Urry (1721) (as in 2); 6. Rolls 14, 2
(1861), 16-39 (as in 2); 7. Skeat, Chaucerian (1897), pp. 191-
203 (as in 1); 8. ed. P.L. Heyworth (1968), pp. 54-72 (BL
Harley 6641, ff. 1-25).

Also in CUL Ff.6.2; a Latin version appears in Bodl Bodley 703.
For Friar Daw's rejoinder see Bodl Digby 41.

To dai is cumen ðe holie tid þat me clepeð aduent þanked be ure louerd
ihesu crist þit haueð isend   See 159.

783   . . . Tofore ye haue herde how Yphis a Doughtir becam a sone and
toke a Wyf The god Hymeneus was at this Wedyng and when he
departed thens he wente by thayr

William Caxton, Ovyde Hys Booke of Methamorphose, translation of the Ovide moralisé, 1480.

1. ed. G. Hibbert, Six Bookes of Metamorphoseos (1819),
Books X-XV (Cambridge Magdalene Pepys 2124); 2. ed. S.
Gaselee and H.F.B. Brett-Smith (1924), Books X-XV (as in 1).

The Prologue and Books I-IX were discovered in a Phillipps MS
(now Cambridge Magdalene F. 4. 34) in 1966 and were reunited
with Pepys 2124 in 1968; see The Metamorphoses of Ovid
(1968), a facsimile edition of the two volumes of the MS.

. . . togeder to þe gappe wtowte more company and þen owre kyng
tourned ayene and led on his hoste and comfortyd hem   Incipit to
version F of 365.

784   Triplex est via ad deum . . . Therefore Euere new discipull Ascende to
the perfeccioun of this scyence fro degre to degre Fyrst þou sal ascende
by the way þat is purgatyfe

Via ad Contemplacionem, tract on contemplative life, s. xv.

1. <u>MS</u>, 37 (1975), 92-110 (BL Addl. 37790, ff. 234-36).

Cf. **319**.

Trowe in god loue holy kirk Trow in holy ewcarist Honoure þo
ewangely   See **786**.

785   True it is that after the noble and experte doctryne of wyse and well
lernyd Philosophers lefte and remaynyng with vs in wrytyng we know
þat the propritees of thynges folowe and ensewe their substaunces

John Trevisa, <u>Liber Bartholomei</u> de <u>Proprietatibus Rerum</u>, translation from the Latin, 1398-99.

1. [W. de Worde, 1495] (STC 1536) (New York Columbia
University Plimpton 263); 2. T. Berthelet, 1535 (STC 1537)
(based on 1, but corrected by reference to Latin texts); 3. ed. S.
Batman (T. East, 1582) (STC 1538) (based on 1, but enlarged
and amended by reference to Latin texts); 4. ed. M.C. Seymour
et alii, 2 vols. (1975) (BL Addl. 27944).

Also in Bristol Public Library 9, CUL Ii.5.41, BL Harley 614,
BL Harley 4789, BL Addl. 45680 (fragments), London Quaritch
(Catalogue 1036 (1984), item 21), New York Morgan M 875,
Bodl e Mus. 16.

Truelye we finde in the gestes and faites of the good kynge Charlemayne that vpon a time at a feast of Penthecoste the sayde kyng
Charlemayne kept a ryght great and solempne court at Parys   Incipit
to text proper of **80**.

786   Trouthe Hope Loue Grace Honoure Reuerence Compassion Mercie
Mildenesse Clennesse Holynesse Stedfastnesse Ad primum Trouth
Trowe in god loue holy kirk Trow in holy ewcarist Honoure þo
ewangely

[Richard Rolle], injunctions to virtuous living, s. xiv.

1. <u>YW</u>, II (1896), 66-67 (BL Royal 17 B.xvii, f. 100).

Jolliffe I.39.

787   Tu es Refugium meum A Tribulacione My worshipfull Maystre Seynt

Bernard taught me that in all pereylles and alle anguysshes and in euery Tribulacion

John Lydgate, translation of St. Bernard's homily Super Missus Est inserted into the "Pilgrimage of the Life of Man" (IMEV 4265), s. xv (1).

1. EETS es 83 (1901), pp. 437-56 (BL Stowe 952, ff.287v-301); 2. Roxburghe (1905) (as in 1).

Also in BL Cotton Vitellius C. XIII. Cf. 244 and 835.

787.3 Tunc surgens a prostratione . . . So Bretherne here is my maister I N whiche of his clene deuocioun that he hath to god and of a speciall desire to us askyth for goddes sake to be amitted

Form for admitting a candidate into a religious fraternity, s. xiv.

1. Maskell, I (1846), cxx-cxxi note 5 (Exeter Cathedral Pontifical); 2. Maskell, 2nd ed., I (1882), cxxxviii-cxxxxix note 26 (as in 1).

788   Two liues are þat cristin men lyues inne Actiue & Comtemplatiue life is mikel outewarde & mare trauail & peril for temptacions þat are in þe werld

"Active and Contemplative Life", treatise extracted from Chapter 12 of Rolle's Forme of Lyvyng, s. xiv.

1. YW, I (1895), 416-17 (BL Arundel 507, f. 43v).

See 351.

789   Too thingys y haue purposyd þorwh goddis grace to don in þis litel tretys Fyrst to schewe schortly þe comoun condicionys of þe seuene dedly synnys as by figure and ensample in general And afterward to reherse be proces and be ordre what bronchis and bowys growyn owt of hem in specyal

Richard Lavynham, Litel Tretys of þe Sevene Dedly Synnys, s. xiv ex.

1. ed. J.P.W.M. Zutphen (1956) (BL Harley 211, ff. 35-46v).

Also in TCC B.14.19, CUL Ff.6.31, Leeds University Brotherton 501, BL Harley 1197, BL Harley 1288, BL Harley 2383, BL Royal 8 C.i, BL Sloane 3160, London Society of Antiquaries 687, London Dr. Williams' Library Anc. 3, Norwich Castle Museum 158.926 4g.5, Bodl Ashmole 750, Bodl Douce 60, Bodl Laud Miscellaneous 23, Bodl Rawlinson C. 288.

790 Two virtues ben in mannes soule by whyche a man shuld be rewled hoolynesse in mannes wille and good kunnyng in his wytt

Tractatus de Confessione et Penitencia, Wycliffite tract, s. xiv (2).

1. EETS os 74 (1880, 1902), pp. 327-45 (TCD 245, ff. 127v-38).

Also in Manchester Rylands English 86.

791 . . . uges than these for englisshemen be nat [n]ecessarye to be knowen And therfore I haue omyt[ted a]nd past ouer the translation of certeyn cytees

Prognostication for 1498 (?), composed shortly before.

1. [R. Pynson, 1500?] (STC 385.7, 20415), fragment.

Vlcus or vlcer after entension of G 4o cerapeutice is a solucion of contynuite in þe flesh   Incipit to Book IV of complete translation of Guy de Chauliac's Inventarium partially edited by B. Wallner (1982); see notes to 31 and 32.

792 Vndirnyme thou biseche thou and blame thou in al pacience and doctrine ije Thi iiije cap THOU3 these wordis weren writen by Seint Poul to Thimothe being a bischop and not a lay person

Reginald Pecock, Represser of Over Myche Blamyng the Clergie, 1449-55.

1. Rolls 19, 2 vols. (1860), pp. 1-565 (CUL Kk.4.26).

793 Unto the noble auncyent and renommed Cyte the Cyte of london in England I William Caxton Cytezeyn and coniurye of the same and of the fraternyte and felauship of the mercerye

267

William Caxton, <u>Caton</u>, moral school text translated from a French prose version of the <u>Disticha Catonis</u>, 1483.

1. W. Caxton, 1484? (STC 4853).

794   Unto the praysynge and dyuyne glorye of god whiche is lord and souerayne kynge aboue and ouer alle thynges celestyal and worldly

William Caxton, <u>Book of the Ordre of Chyvalrye or Knyghthode</u>, translation of a French version of Ramon Lull's <u>Libre del orde de cauayleria</u>, ca. 1484.

1. W. Caxton, 1484? (STC 3326); 2. ed. F.S. Ellis (1892) (as in 1); 3. EETS os 168 (1926), pp. 1-125, upper halves (as in 1); 4. EETS os 168 (1926), pp. 1-125, lower halves (BL Harley 6149, ff. 83-109, a Scots copy of 1 made in 1494); 5. (1976) (facsimile of 1).

795   Vnto the right noble puyssaunt and excellent pryncesse my redoubted lady my lady Margarete duchesse of Somercete Moder vnto our naturel and souerayn lord and most Crysten Kynge henry þe seuenth

William Caxton, "Blanchardyn and Eglantine", romance translated from a fifteenth-century French prose version, ca. 1489.

1. W. Caxton, 1489? (STC 3124), ending imperfectly; 2. EETS es 58 (1890), pp. 1-223 (as in 1 supplemented by a continuation based on a modernization by T.P. Goodwine printed in 1595 (STC 3125) and on a MS of the French original).

796   Upon a season hertofore as king salomon full of wisdome and richesse sate vpon the kinges sete or stole that was his fadres davyd

<u>Dyalogus or Communyng Betwixt the Wyse King Salomon and Marcolphus</u>, perhaps translated from Dutch, s. xv ex.

1. G. Leeu, [1492] (STC 22905); 2. ed. E.G.Duff (1892) (facsimile of 1).

A later version, from French, in STC 22899.

797   Urban bisschop seruaunt of seruantis of god to his bilouid dowtris in crist þe Abbes & þe couent of sustris Menowressis enclosid of þe monestre of oure ladi of þe diocise of Paris

Rewle of Sustris Menouresses Enclosid, translation of amended
Rule for the Second Order (Clares) of St. Francis, with additions, s. xv.

1. EETS os 148 (1914), pp. 81-116 (Bodl Bodley 585, ff. 48-
101).

Urban bysshop seruaunt of the seruauntes of god to all the beloued
brethern and systers of the order of penaunce sendeth gretynge and
blessynge appostolyke   Incipit to renewal of privileges added to
edition 1 of 470.

Ve Vobis scribe et pharisei ipocrite . . . Crist biddiþ vs be war wiþ þes
false profetis þat comen in cloþing of scheepe   Incipit to edition 2 of
127.

Verytably we fynde in the auncient cronicles that the noble and
valiaunt kyng pepyn wedded and toke vnto wyfe Berthe   Incipit to
text proper of 52.

798   Viderunt eam Filie Syon et beatissimam predicauerunt These wordes
are writen in holy scripture and are thus to say in englyshe The
doughtres of Syon haue sene hyr

[Thomas Gascoigne], Myroure of Oure Lady, book of religious
instruction written for the nuns of Syon Abbey, s. xv (1).

1. R. Fawkes, 1530 (STC 17542); 2. EETS es 19 (1873) (as in
1).

In Aberdeen University WPR.4.18 (ending imperfectly), Bodl
Rawlinson C. 941 (beginning imperfectly).

799   Videte vocationem vestram These are ye wordes of the appostle the
whiche dothe parteyne to men and women of relygion

The Myrour of the Chyrche, devotional treatise translated from
the Latin Speculum Ecclesie of Edmund of Abingdon, s. xv.

1. W. de Worde, 1521 (STC 965); 2. W. de Worde, 1527 (STC
966); 3. P. Treveris, [1522-32] (STC 967).

Closely related to Bodl e Mus. 232; also in Bodl Douce 25 and

Earl Beauchamp MS. For other translations see **800**.

800 Videte vocacionem vestram This wordes sayse Saynte Paule in his pistyll and thay are thus mekill to saye one ynglysche Seese ȝowre callynge

The Myrrour of Seynt Edmonde, devotional treatise translated from Anglo-Norman and Latin versions of the Speculum Ecclesie of Edmund of Abingdon, s. xiv.

1. EETS os 26 (1867), pp. 15-47 (Lincoln Cathedral 91, ff. 197-209); 2. YW, I (1895), 219-40 (as in 1); 3. EETS os 26, rev. ed. (1914), pp. 16-62 (as in 1).

Other translations from Anglo-Norman and Latin are in **706** and Aberystwyth NLW Peniarth 395D; a translation from Anglo-Norman only is in BL Addl. 10053, London Westminster School 3, Bodl Bodley 416; for a translation from Latin see **799**; for an interpolated version see **202**; extracts and fragments are in Cambridge Magdalene Pepys 2125, CUL Ff.2.38, CUL Ii.6.43, Coughton Court Throckmorton MS, BL Arundel 286, BL Harley 2398, BL Harley 4012, BL Royal 17 B.xvii, and San Marino Huntington HM 502. For verse versions see IMEV 974 and 1512.

801 Water of pympernel is gud for al maner sekenes aboute ye herte water of betony is gud for ye hedache

Notes on medicinal preparations and their uses, s. xv (2).

1. Harley and Bickley (1928), p. 427 (San Marino Huntington HU 1051, f. 90v); 2. Hanna (1984), p. 53 (as in 1).

802 We beleve as Crist and his Apostolus han tauȝt us that the Sacrament of the Auter white and ronde and like tyl oure bred or ost unsacrede is verray Goddus body in fourme of brede

[John Wyclif], Secunda Confessio Wyclyff, confession on the Eucharist, 1382-90.

1. Twysden (1652), cols. 2649-50 (BL Cotton Tiberius C. VII, ff. 180v-81); 2. Vaughan, Life (1828), II, 454-55 (as in 1); 3. Vaughan, Life, 2nd ed. (1831), II, 433-34 (as in 1); 4. Vaughan, John (1853), pp. 570-71 (as in 1); 5. SEW, III (1871), 502-3 (Bodl Bodley 647, ff. 63v-64v); 6. Rolls 92

(1895), 2, 161-62 (as in 1 & BL Cotton Claudius E. III, ff. 271v-72); 7. Winn (1929), pp. 86-88 (as in 5); 8. Hudson (1978), pp. 17-18 (as in 1).

Cf. 310.

We Crysten oughte moche hertly to Remembre in our hertes & thynke on the rihte grete loue þat the swete childe of bethleem Ihesu crist shewed to vs by the wounde of his precious side   Incipit to "The Seven Signs of Jesus' Love," devotional tract (Part 6) incorporated into 751.

803   We fynde wretyn in the lyfe of Seynt Edwarde kyng whos body lythe in schryne at westmynstyr wheche lyf as for the more autoryte in sothnes wrotte the wurthy clerke & holy abbot of ryuaus Seynt alrede

Narracio de Sancto Edwardo, account of appearance of Christ to Edward the Confessor and Earl Leofric, s. xv.

1. Moore (1942), pp. 132-33 (CUL Ii.4.9, ff. 94-95).

Cf. the lives in 357 and 577.

804   We Herrowdys of Armis beryng scheldis of deviis here we yeve in knowlache un to all Gentill men of name and of armus (from 5)

Justus of Pees, instructions for organizing peaceful jousts, s. xv med.

1. Archaeologia, 17 (1814), 290-94 (BL Lansdowne 285, ff. 9v-10v); 2. Meyrick (1824), II, 188-91 (as in 1); 3. Archaeological Journal, 4 (1847), 231-33 (New York Morgan M 775, ff. 3-4v); 4. Historic Society of Lancashire and Cheshire, 2 (1850), 206-9 (as in 1); 5. Archaeologia, 57 (1900), 39-41 (as in 3); 6. Cripps-Day (1918), pp. xxxiii-xxxiv (as in 1).

Also in BL Addl. 46354.

805   We may likne our fader Seynt Augustyn on to þe holy patriark Iacob for many causes On is for interpretacion of his name for Iacob is as mech for to say a supplanter or a deceyuour

John Capgrave, Tretis on the Augustinian orders abstracted from a sermon preached by him in 1422.

271

1. EETS os 140 (1910), pp. 145-48 (BL Addl. 36704, ff. 116v-19).

806   We ought oftentymes to remembre deuoutly many and greuous paynes that our lorde Ihesu Cryst suffred for our redempcyon that our loue may be the more feruent to hym

Revelacion of the Hundred Pater Noster, prayers for each day of the week based on the seven occasions Christ shed blood, s. xv.

1. W. de Worde, [1500?] (STC 14546); 2. W. de Worde, 1509 (STC 14546.3, 14572); 3. Laudate, 14 (1936), 172-82 (BL Lansdowne 379, ff. 41-54, beginning imperfectly).

Revell 277.

807   We pore men tresoreris of Cryst and his apostlis denuncyn to þe lordis and þe comunys of þe parlement certeyn conclusionis and treuthis

"Twelve Conclusions of the Lollards", 1395.

1. EHR, 22 (1907), 295-304 (Cambridge Trinity Hall 17, ff. llv et passim); 2. ed. H.S. Cronin, Rogeri Dymmok Liber Contra XII Errores et Hereses Lollardorum (1922), pp. 25, 30, 53, 71, 89, 113, 145, 160, 180, 207, 237, 272, 292, 306 (as in 1); 3. Hudson (1978), pp. 24-29 (as in 1).

Also in CUL Ii.4.3, Bodl Lat. th. e. 30, and Paris BN lat. 3381.

808   We purposynge to write þe lyfe of þe memorabil Crystes virgyne Crystyne þat put wee first in þe bigynnynge of oure sermone at worshepeful James byshope of Accone

Þe Lyfe of Seinte Cristin þe Mervelous, saint's life, s. xv.

1. Anglia, 8 (1885), 119-34 (Bodl Douce 114, ff. 12-26v).

809   We rede in the auncient and autentike cronycles yt somtime ther was a noble king in lile fort otherwise named the strong ile (from 2)

Robert Copland, Helyas Knyght of the Swanne, romance translated from French, s. xvi in.

1. [W. de Worde, 1512] (STC 7571); 2. W. Copland, [1550?] (STC 7572); 3. Thoms (1828), 3, 1-149 (as in 2); 4. Thoms, 2nd ed. (1858), 3, 15-149 (as in 2); 5. ed. J. Ashton, Romances of Chivalry (1887) (as in 2); 6. Grolier Club (1901) (facsimile of 1); 7. Thoms, enlarged ed. (1906, 1907), pp. 691-784 (as in 2).

We redeth i þo holi godespelle of te dai ase ure louerd god almichti i-bore was of ure lauedi seinte Marie   See 140.

810   We schal bileve þat þis Pater Noster þat Crist himsilf tauȝte to alle Cristene men passiþ oþere prayers in þese þre þingis in auctorite in sotilte and profit to Christis Cherche

Þe Pater Noster Exponed, Wycliffite exposition of the Pater Noster, s. xiv ex.

1. SEW, III (1871), 93-97 (Bodl Bodley 789, f. 97); 2. EETS os 118 (1901), pp. 7-11 (Lambeth Palace 408, ff. 1v-2v); 3. EETS os 217 (1942), pp. 337-39 (BL Addl. 17013, f. 36).

Also in CUL Dd.12.39, TCD 245, BL Harley 2385, Paris Bibl. Ste.-Geneviève 3390, and York Minster XVI.L.12.

We sall make a speciall prayer unto god all myghty   English incipit to editions 2, 4, 9, and 12 of 857.

Welthe and worship to my worthy and worshipful lord sir Thomas lord of Barkley I Iohan Treuisa youre preest and bedeman obedyent and buxom to werke your wylle   Incipit to dedicatory epistle to 605.

811   Well dysposed men and lawfull that ben not meyntenours of quarelles sholde be Iustyces of the peas et vide statutum inde Anno primo E iii capitulo xviii

Boke of Justices of Peas, a guide to procedure in English and Latin probably based on a pre-1500 original, with short preface, ca. 1505-6 (?).

1. R. Pynson, [1505?] (STC 14862); 2. W. de Worde, 1506 (STC 14863); 2. W. de Worde, 1510 (STC 14864); 4. W. de Worde, 1515 (STC 14864.5); 5. J. Skot, 1521 (STC 14866); 6. R. Pynson, 1521 (STC 14867); 7. R. Redman, 1527 (STC

273

14868); 8. [R. Redman, 1527?] (STC 14869); 9. R. Redman, [1530?] (STC 14870); 10. [J. Rastell, 1526-30?] (STC 14871); 11. T. Berthelet, [ca. 1533] (STC 14871.5); 12. R. Redman, [1533?] (STC 14872); 13. T. Berthelet, [1535-37?] (STC 14873); 14. R. Redman, [1538?] (STC 14875); 15. T. Berthelet, 1539 (STC 14876), with additions; 16. W. Myddelton, [1543?] (STC 14878); 17. T. Berthelet, 1544 (STC 14877); 18. W. Myddelton, [1544?] (STC 14878.3); 19. N. Hill, 1546 (STC 14879); 20. W. Powell, 1550 (STC 14880), with additions; 21. R. Tottel, 1556 (STC 14881); 22. R. Tottel, 1559 (STC 14882); 23. R. Tottel, 1559 (STC 14883); 24. R. Tottel, 1569 (STC 14884); 25. R. Tottel, 1574 (STC 14885); 26. R. Tottel, 1580 (STC 14886).

812   Whatt for ryght what for wrong mony men be made ryche

Aphorism, s. xv ex.

1. RES, n.s. 2 (1951), 119 (BL Harley 1002, f. 72v).

813   Qwhat is a comparison A liknes of diuerse thyngis in a certeyn accidens as Iohn is wys Thomas is wysere þan he William is wysest þan alle (from A.2)

John Leylond, De Comparacionibus, grammatical treatise, ca. 1401-28.

A. Version by John Drury and Hardgrave of Beccles (ca. 1434-35): 1. Speculum, 9 (1934), 79-82 (CUL Addl. 2830, ff. 54v-56v); 2. Thomson (1984), pp. 70-74 (as in 1).

B. Version of s. xv med.: 1. Thomson (1984), pp. 66-69 (Aberystwyth NLW Peniarth 356B, ff. 163-64v, ending imperfectly).

C. Version by Walter Pollard (1444-83): 1. Thomson (1984), pp. 76-80 (Bodl Rawlinson D. 328, ff. 80-83).

D. Version by Thomas Pennant (s. xv [2]): 1. Thomson (1984), p. 65 (Aberystwyth NLW Peniarth 356B, f. 9v).

E. Version of s. xv (2): 1. Thomson (1984), p. 81 (Worcester Cathedral F. 123, ff. 99v-100, ending imperfectly).

F. Version of s. xv/xvi: 1. Thomson (1984), p. 75 (Bodl Douce Printed Book D. 238 (2), ff. B5v-B6).

G. Version by John Stanbridge, <u>Gradus Comparationum</u> (s. xvi in.): 1. R. Pynson, [ca. 1505] (STC 23155.4); 2. R. Pynson, [ca. 1505] (STC 23155.6); 3. R. Pynson, [1509?] (STC 23155.8); 4. [W. de Worde, 1509?] (STC 23155.9); 5. R. Pynson, [1510?] (STC 23156); 6. W. de Worde, [1517?] (STC 23157); 7. W. de Worde, [1518?] (STC 23159.5); 8. W. de Worde, [1519?] (STC 23159a); 9. W. de Worde, [1520?] (STC 23159a.1); 10. W. de Worde, [1520?] (STC 23159a.2); 11. W. de Worde, [1521?] (STC 23159a.3); 12. [W. de Worde, 1522?] (STC 23159a.4); 13. R. Pynson, [1523?] (STC 23159a.5); 14. W. de Worde, [1524?] (STC 23159a.7); 15. W. de Worde, [1525?] (STC 23159a.8); 16. W. de Worde, [1526] (STC 23159a.9); 17. W. de Worde, 1526 (STC 23159a.10); 18. J. Cousin, [1526?] (STC 23159a.12); 19. W. de Worde, 1527 (STC 23159a.13); 20. W. de Worde, 1527 (STC 23160); 21. W. de Worde, 1527 (STC 23160.3); 22. J. Butler, [1529?] (STC 23160.7); 23. W. de Worde, 1530 (STC 23161); 24. J. Toy, 1531 (STC 23162); 25. P. Treveris, [1531?] (STC 23162.5); 26. W. de Worde, 1532 (STC 23163); 27. T. Godfray, [1534?] (STC 23163.2).

814   What is þe kynde of a man in bodi & in soule Thow schalt understonde þat a man is of two kyndis oon bodili anoþer goostli

Treatise on the nature of man, s. xv.

1 <u>N&Q</u>, 212 (1967), 243-44 (Princeton University Garrett 143, ff. 36v-38).

What is to be done whan an englysshe is gyuen to be made in latyn Incipit to version I of **349**.

814.7 What man sayes it deuotly durant insuthfaste penance haf and reuth off ye blyssyng mayden Wete he wele for certayne yat he es in grace

St. Anselm (?), <u>Orison o Sorow & Compassion off Oure Lady Saynt Mary</u>, devotion, s. xv.

1. Surtees Soc. 132 (1919), pp. 178-79 (TCC O.3.10, ff. 143v-44).

What nownys maketh comparison all adiectyues welnere that betoken-yth a thynge that may be made more or lesse as feyre feyrer feyrest blacke blacker blackest   Introductory rubric to version G of **813**.

What noumbre and person is the verbe sum The syngler noumbre
See 161.

815   What rewle of lyuynge to god is to be take to systres in a monastery
Cryste the begynner therof and doctour techeth all vnder the answere of
one in his gospel

> The Rewle of Saynt Jherome, rule for women in Bethlehem, s.
> xv (?).
>
> 1. R. Pynson, ca. 1510 (STC 14505.5).

What schalt thow do whan thow hast on Englysch to make yn Latyn
Incipit to versions E, G, and H of 349.

816   When a freman schall do his homage to his chef lord he halt of his chef
tenement

> "The Manner of Doing Homage and Fealty", forms for swearing
> homage, s. xv (2).
>
> 1. Louis (1980), pp. 145-46 (Bodl Tanner 407, f. 9).

817   Whann a man of craft wyll werkyn ony gret werk þat askyth long
labour dyscretly he ymagyth and castyth be forn in his herte how he
wyll makyn it and endyn it

> Fons Jacob ("Jacob's Well"), collection of homilies, s. xv (1).
>
> 1. EETS os 115- (1900-) (Salisbury Cathedral 103, ff. 6-101v).

817.5 When a pryoresse shall bee made thabbes shall commaunde hyr the Rule
injoyning her that shee bee unto hyr helping and the points of the Rule
to meyntene Religion

> Form for creating a prioress at Barking Abbey, s. xiv/xv.
>
> 1. ed. W. Dugdale, Monasticon Anglicanum, I (1817), 437 note
> k (Bodl Wood F. 30); 2. Maskell, 2nd ed., I (1882), cxl note 26
> (as in 1).

818   Whan ony of lyklyhode shal deye thenne is moste necessarye to haue a

specyall frende the whiche wyll hertly helpe and praye for hym and
therwyth counseyll the syke for the wele of his sowle

William Caxton (?), Ars Moriendi, translation from Latin, s. xv
ex.

1. W. Caxton, 1491? (STC 786); 2. W. de Worde, [1497] (STC
787); 3. W. de Worde, 1506 (STC 788); 4. ed. W. Blades
(1859) (facsimile of 1); 5. ed. E.W.B.Nicholson (1891) (facsimile of 1); 6. (1974) (facsimile of 1).

Whan y behold and knowe the oppynyons of the men nourissyd in ony
synguler hystoryes of Troye and see and beholde also   Incipit to text
proper of 825.

819   Whan I beholde the estate and lyfe þat I haue ben of syns þat I coude
knowe þe good and the yll

Peter of Luxembourg, Next Way to Heven, s. xv (?).

1. W. de Worde, [1502?] (STC 19795).

820   Whan I consydere the condycions and maners of the comyn people
whiche without enformacion and lernyng ben rude and not manerd lyke
vnto beestis brute acordyng to an olde prouerbe

William Caxton, Book of Good Maners, translation from the
French of Jacques Legrand, 1486.

1. W. Caxton, 1487 (STC 15394); 2. R. Pynson, 1494 (STC
15395); 3. W. de Worde, [1498] (STC 15397); 4. R. Pynson,
[1500] (STC 15396); 5. W. de Worde, 1507 (STC 15398); 6. W.
de Worde, [1526?] (STC 15399); 7. R. Wyer, [1531-4] (STC
15399.5), extract.

821   When I had takene my singulere purpos and lefte þe seculere habyte and
I be-gane mare to serue God þan mane it fell one a nyghte als I lay in
my ryste

[Richard Rolle], A Tale, s. xiv.

1. EETS os 20 (1866), pp. 5-6 (Lincoln Cathedral 91, f. 193v);
2. Mätzner, I, 2 (1869), 125 (as in 1); 3. YW, I (1895), 192 (as
in 1); 4. Kluge (1904, 1912), p. 33 (as in 1); 5. EETS os 20,

rev. ed. (1921), pp. 5-6 (as in 1).

Also in BL Harley 1022, where it is appended to 506.

822   Whan I haue þis Englysch at comyng byfore a proper name of a towne
vylage oþer syte noght componyd

Grammatical treatise, s. xv.

1. Thomson (1984), p. 177 (Cambridge Gonville and Caius
417/447, f. 15v).

823   When I profir the pig opin the poke

Proverbs, s. xv ex.

1. ed. M.G. Segar, Some Minor Poems of the Middle Ages
(1917), p. 37 (Oxford Balliol 354).

824   Whan I remembre and take hede of the conuersacion of vs that lyue in
this wretched lyf in which is no surete ne stable abydyng

William Caxton, Ryal Book, or a Book for a Kyng, translated
from the Somme le roi of Friar Lorens of Orléans, 1484.

1. W. Caxton, 1488? (STC 21429); 2. W. de Worde, [1507]
(STC 21430).

For other translations see 55 and 668.

825   Whan I remembre that euery man is bounden by the comandement and
counceyll of the wyse man to eschewe slouthe and ydlenes whyche is
moder and nourysshar of vyces

William Caxton, Recuyell of the Historyes of Troye, historical
romance translated from Raoul Lefevre's French version, 1469-
71.

1. W. Caxton, 1473-4? (STC 15375); 2. W. de Worde, 1502
(STC 15376); 3. W. Copland, 1553 (STC 15378); 4. ed. H.H.
Sparling, 3 vols. in 2 (1892) (as in 1); 5. ed. H.O. Sommer, 2
vols (1894) (as in 1).

Many modernized versions between 1596 and 1738.

26 Whan it ys soo that what a man maketh or doeth it is made to come to
    some ende And yf the thynge be goode and well made it muste nedes
    come to goode ende

    William Caxton, Arte and Crafte to Knowe Well to Dye, trans-
    lation from an abridged French version of the Latin, 1490.

    1. W. Caxton, 1490? (STC 789); 2. R. Pynson, [ante 1500]
    (STC 790); 3. (1875) (facsimile of 1); 4. (1970) (facsimile of 1).

27 Whenne it thundreth in Ariete that is to say whenne the Sonne is in
    Ariete there shall be moche gras

    Astrological prognostications, s. xv.

    1. MLN, 56 (1941), 353-55 (New York Morgan M 775, ff.
    280v-82v); 2. Bühler (1973), pp. 376-78 (as in 1).

28 Whan that I Mary Ihesus moder sate in Iherusalem at the holy feest of
    cester alone in my hous for moche multytude of people that came to the
    cyte

    [John Lydgate], Lamentacion of Oure Lady, s. xv.

    1. W. de Worde, [1509-10?] (STC 17537); 2. Archiv, 79
    (1889), 454-59 (Bodl Bodley 596).

    Also in CUL Ii.4.9, BL Cotton Cleopatra D. VII, Longleat
    Marquis of Bath 29.

    Whan the chyldern of Israel were goon oute of Egypte and had wonne
    Iherusalem and all the londe lienge there abowte and no man was hardy
    in al þat countree   Incipit to text proper of 290.

29 Qwanne the Dominicall lettyr ffallyth vpon the A than schall be a
    warme wynter and a peryyng somer

    "Prognostications According to the Dominical Letter", prophe-
    cies about New Year's Day, s. xv (2).

    1. Louis (1980), pp. 312-14 (Bodl Tanner 407, f. 53r-v).

    For verse prognostications see IMEV 73, 1194, 1538.5.

830   Whan Thempyre of Rome moste fliured And was in the age of his force
and strengthe The fame of one named Fulgeus was right ferre spredde to
his grete worship ffor he was right eurous to richesse honoure and
frendship

John Tiptoft, Oracionis, translation from the French version
(printed Bruges 1475) of Buonaccorso da Montemagno's Contro-
versia de Nobilitate (with epilogue by Caxton), ca. 1460.

1. W. Caxton, 1481? (STC 5293, Part 3); 2. ed. R.J. Mitchell,
John Tiptoft (1427-1470) (1938), pp. 215-41 (as in 1); 3. (1977)
(facsimile of 1).

[W]han þe kynges son had rayede all þyng þat vas for honour to cum
into Irland   Incipit to edition 4 of 380.

831   Whenne the mone is in Tauro hit is good to plante treys of pepyns

Tretice for a Mane to Knowe Wyche Tyme of the 3ere Hit Is Best
to Graffe, treatise on planting, s. xv.

1. Halliwell, Miscellanies (1855), pp. 66-72 (Aberystwyth NLW
Porkington 10, ff. 27-33).

832   When thow hast an englyss reason to be made yn latyn thow shalte
reherse hyt untyll thow mayst sey yt perfytly

Grammatical treatise, s. xvi in.

1. Hermathena, 20 (1930), 353-59 (TCD 130, pp. 3-11); 2.
Thomson (1984), pp. 186-90 (as in 1).

When thou rysist fro slepe in þe morning first stretch thy lymmis þi
leggys thine armis thy shuldris thy necke thyne hed   Incipit to text
proper of 495.

833   Where I had sent forth this poore lesson vnto a pryuate persone and
specyal frende the copy therof came vnto the syght of certeyn deuoute
persones

Richard Whitford, A Werke for Housholders, devotional treatise, s. xv ex./xvi in. (?).

1. W. de Worde, [1530?] (STC 25421.8); 2. W. de Worde, 1530 (STC 25422); 3. P. Treveris, [1531?] (STC 25422.3); 4. R. Redman, 1531 (STC 25422.5); 5. W. de Worde, 1533 (STC 25423); 6. R. Redman, 1537 (STC 25425); 7. J. Waylande, 1537 (STC 25425.5); 8. ed. J. Hogg, Richard Whytford, 5 (1979), 1-62 (as in 1).

Probably also printed before 1530.

834 Where it is so that euery humayn Creature by the suffraunce of our lord god is borne and ordeigned to be subgette and thral vnto the stormes of fortune

Anthony Woodville, Dictes or Sayengis of the Philosophhres, moral pronouncements attributed to old philosophers translated from the French Dits Moraulx by Guillaume de Tignonville (with epilogue by William Caxton), after 1473.

1. W. Caxton, 1477 (STC 6826); 2. W. Caxton, 1480? (STC 6828); 3. W. Caxton, 1489? (STC 6829); 4. W. de Worde, 1528 (STC 6830); 5. ed. W. Blades (1877; rptd. 1974) (facsimile of 1); 6. 1979 (facsimile of 1).

Four MSS made from edition 1: Chicago Newberry f. 36 Ry. 20, BL Addl. 22718 (s. xv ex.), BL Addl. 60577 (extract), and Lambeth Palace 265 (1477). Three MSS made from edition 2: TCD 213 (extract, ed. EETS es 47, 1886, pp. 279-83), BL Addl. 22718, and New York C.F. Bühler 11.

Qweche is þe knoulaching of þe first declinesone Þis is hit of quom þe genitif and þe datif cas singuler   Incipit to version A of 308.

835 Whylome as olde bokes maketh mencion whan the noble and famous Cite of Rome was moste shynynge in hys felicite and flouring in his glory (from 2)

John Lydgate, Serpent of Division/Cronycule of Julius Caesar, a life of Julius Caesar translated from French, followed by a verse declaration (IMEV 3625), 1422-23.

1. P. Treveris, 1521-35?, fragment; 2. R. Redman, [ca. 1535] (STC 17027.5); 3. O. Rogers, [1559] (STC 17028); 4. E. Allde, 1590 (STC 17029); 5. ed. J[oseph] H[aslewood], Censura Literaria, ed. E. Brydges, 9 (1809), 369-73 (as in 1); 6. ed. J[ospeh] H[aslewood], Censura Literaria, 2nd ed., ed. E. Bryd-

281

ges, 5 (1815), 316-19 (as in 1); 7. ed. H.N. MacCracken (1911) (Cambridge Fitzwilliam Museum McClean 182, ff. 1-10, supplemented by BL Addl. 48031, ff. 165-75v).

Also in Cambridge Magdalene Pepys 2006 and Cambridge (Mass.) Harvard University English 530; an 18th-c. transcript in BL Addl. 38179 made from Pepys 2006. Cf. **244** and **787**.

Hwo to-for de verbe ys nominatyf case hwat efter de verbe ys acusatyf case   Incipit to version C of **308**.

Who so beryth thys mesure uppon hym wyth trewe fayth and good devocyon saying v pater nosters v aves and a credo   Incipit to version E of **733**.

836   Who so kane wysely considere the nature of his colours and kyndely make his commixtions with naturale proporcions

The Crafte of Lymnynge of Bokys, treatise on illumination, s. xv.

1. Halliwell, Miscellanies (1855), pp. 72-91 (Aberystwyth NLW Porkington 10, ff. 33-52v).

Also in Paul Mellon MS (Phillipps 12086).

837   Who so desyres to ffynd comforthe and gostely gladnes in þe Passione and in þe croysse of oure lorde Ihesu hym nedis with a besy thoghte ffor to duell in it

Previte off the Passioune of Owre Lorde Ihesu, translation of St. Bonaventure's De Mysteriis Passionis Ihesu Christi, s. xiv (?).

1. YW, I (1895), 198-218 (Lincoln Cathedral 91, ff. 179-89).

Also in TCC B.10.12, Durham University Cosin V.III.8, New York H.P. Kraus Bute F 16. Cf. **553**; also the verse translation in IMEV 248 and 646, a prose version of which is in Bodl Bodley 789.

838   Who so folowith me sayth cryst our sauiour walketh nat in darkenes These be the wordes of Iesu Cryste wherby we be exorted to folowe his lore and doctryn

William Atkynson and Margaret Countess of Richmond, A Full Devoute and Gostely Treatyse of þe Imytacion and Folowynge þe Blessyd Lyfe of Our Most Mercifull Saviour Cryst/Imitatio Christi, translation of Books 1-3 (by Atkynson) of the Latin De Imitatione Christi attributed to Thomas à Kempis and of Book 4 (by Margaret) of a French translation of the same, 1502, 1504.

1. R. Pynson, 1503[-4] (STC 23954.7); 2. R. Pynson, 1517 (STC 23957); 3. W. de Worde, [1518-19?] (STC 23956); 4. W. de Worde, [1528?] (STC 23960), Books 1-3 only; 5. EETS es 63 (1893), pp. 153-283 (as in 1).

For another translation see 526.

839   Wha-so forsakis þe solace & þe ioie of þis werld & takis him to solitarie life til suffire for goddis luf angers & noyes

De Solitaria Vita, treatise extracted from Chapters 2-4 of Rolle's Forme of Lyvyng, s. xiv.

1. YW, I (1895), 419-20 (BL Arundel 507, f. 46r-v).

See 351.

840   . . . whoso loueth þe toode he wenyth yt is þe mone Bufonem cura fiet te iudice luna (from 2)

Proverbs in prose and verse, with Latin equivalents interspersed, alphabetically arranged, s. xv.

1. Festschrift (1906), pp. 44-57 (Bodl Douce 52, ff. 13-31), beginning at end of C; 2. Bulletin of the John Rylands Library, 14 (1930), 92-109 (Manchester Rylands Latin 394, ff. 2-26v), beginning with B.

841   Whoso wyl haue hys desyr fulfyllyt in al godnes he most say a mt aue maria in x dayys

Note, s. xv (2).

1. HLQ, 3 (1940), 445 (San Marino Huntington HM 142, f. 61v); 2. Hanna (1984), p. 17 (as in 1).

842   Who so wol haue in mynde þe dreedful day of doom so þat he mowe be

moeued with dreede to flee fro synne as þe wise man biddeth his sone

Of Þree Arwes Þat Schullen Bee Schot on Domesday, devotional treatise, s. xiv.

1. YW, II (1896), 446-48 (Oxford University 97, ff. 158v-62).

Also in Cambridge Magdalene Pepys 2125, TCC B.14.53, CUL Ff.2.38, CUL Ff.5.45, CUL Ff.6.55, Coughton Court Throckmorton MS, Glasgow University Hunterian 496, Glasgow University Hunterian 520, BL Arundel 197, BL Harley 1706, BL Harley 2339, BL Harley 2385, BL Harley 2388, BL Addl. 10036, BL Addl. 22283, Manchester Rylands English 85, Bodl Bodley 3, Bodl Douce 13, Bodl Laud Miscellaneous 23, Bodl Laud Miscellaneous 174, Bodl Tanner 336.

843   Who so euer beynge in the state of grace þat deuoutly wyll say the sawter of our lady in the worshyp of xv grete passyons

Indulgence issued by William Patten, Bishop of Winchester, s. xv (2).

1. [W. de Worde, ca. 1499] (STC 14077c.148, 19478); 2. Duff (1917), p. 61 (as in 1).

844   Hosoeuer blede on ye rith hande ye xvij day of marche and on ye lifte hande ye xi day of aprille he salle not lese yat ȝere his eyesith

Good Dais to Be Lat Blode, s. xv (1).

1. Hanna (1984), p. 38 (San Marino Huntington HM 1336, f. 35).

845   Who sum euer deuoutly beholdith these armys off cristis passyon hat vj M vij C lv yeris off pardon

Indulgence, s. xv.

1. ca. 1500 (STC 14077c.22); 2. ca. 1500 (STC 14077c.16); 3. Report of the Bodleian Library (1882-87), p. 49 (as in 1); 4. Schreiber, Manuel, 1 (1891), 284 and 6 (1893), Plate XXII (as in 1); 5. Schreiber, Handbuch (1926-30), item 976 (as in 1); 6. Dodgson, Woodcuts (1929), p. 34 (as in 1); 7. Walpole Soc., 17 (1929), 103 (as in 2); 8. Walpole Soc., 17 (1929), Plate XXXV(d) (as in 1); 9. Dodgson, English (1936), p. 9 and Plate

13 (as in 1); 10. Dodgson, English (1936), p. 10 and Plate 20 (as
in 2).

346 Whosoeuer will lyffe in the most perfytt state of the modere holy
chirche fyrst it es necessary that he be a good man and besely actualle

Trettesse of Perfeccioun of the Sonnys of God, translation of Jan
van Ruusbroec's De Perfectione Filiorum Dei, s. xv in.

1. Bazire and Colledge (1957), pp. 229-58 (BL Addl. 37790, ff.
115-30).

347 Will ȝe offe þir poyntis lere þat our lorde es leue and dere How þat man
couaytis whilke es our lord maast likynges

[Richard Rolle], "Points Best Pleasing to God", treatise on the
nine virtues, s. xiv (2).

1. YW, I (1895), 110-12 (Bodl Rawlinson C. 285, ff. 62v-
64v).

For other versions see 256 and 410.

348 Wit thou wele dere ffrende þat þof þou had neuer done syne with thi
bodi dedly ne venyall bot anely this þat es called orygynall for it es þe
firste syne and þat es þe lossyng of thy ryghtwysnes whilke þou was
mad in

[Richard Rolle], "An Epistle on Salvation by Love of the Name
of Jesus", constitutes Chapter 44 in some MSS of the Ladder of
Perfeccion, s. xiv (2).

1. EETS os 20 (1866), pp. 42-45 (Lincoln Cathedral 91, ff.
229v-30v); 2. Mätzner, I, 2 (1869), 150-52 (as in 1); 3. YW, I
(1895), 293-95 (as in 1); 4. EETS os 20, rev. ed. (1921), pp.
44-47 (as in 1).

See 255.

With alle warde kep þin hert   See 507.

349 Wið innoðes sar ȝenim þa wirte þe man artemesiam & oðrum naman
mugwyrt nenneð & ȝecnuca hiȝ to duste & ȝemeng hi wið beor

285

"Herbarium Apuleii", treatise on plants, ca. 1150.

1. ed. H. Berberich (1902) (BL Harley 6258b, ff. 1-44); 2. EETS os 286 (1984), pp. 31-233 (odd only) (as in 1).

850   With þe myȝt wisdom & grace of þe holy trynite I write to ȝou a tretice in englisch breuely drawe out of þe book of quintis essencijs in latyn

Þe Mooste and þe Sovereyneste Secrete of Alle Secretis, treatise on alchemy and medicine translated from Latin, s. xv.

1. EETS os 16 (1866) (BL Sloane 73, ff. 10-15v); 2. EETS os 16, rev. ed. (1889), pp. 1-15 (as in 1).

851   Wythdragh þi þoght fro þi gude dedys & fro þine ill dedys and ynk [sic] þo arte ewere in þe syght of gode & in is presens

[Richard Rolle], prayer, s. xiv.

1. YW, I (1895), 172 (BL Harley 1022, f. 80v).

Jolliffe M.16.

Withholdyng of this blode that þei mowe noȝt haue her purgacions in due tymes comyn in diuerse maners   Incipit to text proper of 235.

Wetiþ ȝe þat ben now here and þei þat schulen comen after ȝou   See 590.

Wondyr and marvelys are herd in oure cuntre and in oure land yt was a mervelous thinge   See 312.

Worsship not only of oon or two dropes but more in the worsship of euery drope of alle his blessed blode must nedes be of excellent vartu Incipit to edition 3 of 806.

852   Worchipfull and reverenteful fadere and modere with lowly subieccion and seruise mekely I comende me to youre worthy reuerence

Ad Patrem et Matrem, model letter for the use of a student, s. xv.

1. Speculum, 56 (1981), 580 (Cambridge (Mass.) Harvard University Law Library 43, f. 130v).

353 Worshypful Jamee byshope of Accone wrote vnto þe byschope of Tholose a longe proheme in to þe lyfe þat heere folowiþ in þe whiche proheme hee writiþ compendiously dyuerse commendacyouns

þe Lyfe of Seint Mary of Oegines, saint's life, s. xv.

1. Anglia, 8 (1885), 134-84 (Bodl Douce 114, ff. 26v-76).

Wonde is solucioun of continuite recent sanguinolent without putrefaccioun made in softe partieʒ   Incipit to Book III of complete translation of Guy de Chauliac's Inventarium partially edited by B. Wallner (1976, 1979); see notes to 31 and 32.

354 ʒe must take wurte and barley and comyn

Recipe, probably for feeding doves, s. xv (2).

1. Louis (1980), p. 260 (Bodl Tanner 407, f. 40v).

Ye ought to knowe that whan Our Lord God made the world and that he had made alle thinges of nought he had no nede of it ffor as moche had he bifore as he had afterward   Incipit to text proper of 137.

355 ʒe schul first pryncypally take hede þat þe pees be kepte in ʒour towne

"Charges to the Peace Officers", forms of charges to constables and the watch, s. xv (2).

1. Louis (1980), pp. 154-57 (Bodl Tanner 407, f. 11r-v).

ʒe shall knell down on your kneis and praie devoutle and mekle Incipit to edition 6 of 857.

ʒe sal mak your prayers specially till our lord god almighti   English incipit to editions 8 and 10 of 857.

856 ʒe scholn soth seyn of alle maner articules þat schal be put to ʒow here

287

of þe Kyngis behalfe

Ad Faciendum Jusiurandum ad Inquisitionem, formulary for administering oaths to jurors, s. xv (2).

1. Louis (1980), pp. 143-44 (Bodl Tanner 407, f. 8v).

857   Ye shulle stonde up and bydde your bedys in the worshepe of our lord Jhesu Christ and his moder Saint Marye and of all the Holy Company of Heaven

Deprecacio, bidding prayers, various dates from s. xiv to s. xv ex.

1. Coxe (1840), pp. 11-25 (unidentified Worcester Cathedral MS); 2. Coxe (1840), pp. 40-50 (STC 16160); 3. Maskell, III (1847), 342-46 (unidentified Salisbury Cathedral MS); 4. Surtees Soc. 63 (1875), pp. 123-27 (as in 2); 5. Surtees Soc. 63 (1875),pp. 220*-23* (Bodl Barlow 5); 6. Surtees Soc. 63 (1875), pp. 223*-25* (BL Harley 335); 7. Surtees Soc. 63 (1875), pp. 225*-26* (Salisbury Cathedral 148, ff. 11v-15v); 8. Fifth Report (1876), p. 306 (Cambridge (Mass.) Harvard University Widener 1, ff. 105-7); 9. EETS os 71 (1879), pp. 64-67 (as in 8); 10. EETS os 71 (1879), pp. 68-73 (York Minster XVI.M.4); 11. EETS os 71 (1879), p. 74 (York Minster XVI.M.4, later addition); 12. EETS os 71 (1879), pp. 75-80 (as in 2); 13. Maskell, 2nd ed., III (1882), 401-5 (as in 3); 14. Wordsworth (1901), pp. 22-32 (as in 7).

Also in Caxton's 1483 edition of the Festivall (734), Quattuor Sermones (Part 3) (689), and the York Manual of ca. 1530 (STC 16161).

858   Ye shall swere that ye shal be good and trew unto our liege Lord kyng of Englond and to his Eyres kynges

Oath for freemen, s. xv.

1. Blades, Life (1861), I, 86 (London Mercers' Company MS of Wardens' Accounts); 2. Blades, Biography (1877), p. 144 (as in 1); 3. Blades, Biography, 2nd ed. (1882), pp. 146-47 (as in 1).

859   Ye shall swere that ye shal be true vnto oure liege lorde the kyng and to his heires kynges

Oath for the issue of apprentices, s. xv.

1. Blades, Life (1861), I, 85-86 (London Mercers' Company MS of Wardens' Accounts); 2. Blades, Biography (1877), pp. 143-44 (as in 1); 3. Blades, Biography, 2nd ed. (1882), pp. 145-46 (as in 1); 4. EETS os 176 (1928), pp. xxxix-xl (as in 1).

360 ʒe schull sweren that ʒe schal with with [sic] alle ʒoure myght and ʒoure pouer kepen pees and reste and tranquillite withinne ʒoure crafte

"Charge to the Masters of Every Guild", responsibilities of guild officers, s. xv (2).

1. Louis (1980), pp. 318-20 (Bodl Tanner 407, f. 61).

361 Ye schal vnderstonde þat wymmen hafe las heete yn þem þen men and more moystenesse

Þe Sekenesse of Wymmen, medical treatise, s. xv.

1. ed. M.R. Hallaert (1982), odd pages (New Haven Yale University Medical Library MS, ff. 60-71v).

362 Ye wise and prudent maydens pure and clene virgyns yn our Lord God prepare and make redy your lyghts Loo your spouse Jesu Cryste the sone of God ys at hand

Consecratyon of Virgins, ritual for the ordination of nuns, s. xv (2).

1. Surtees Soc. 61 (1875), pp. 237-47 (BL Lansdowne 388, ff. 407 ff.).

Cf. 89, 178, and 366.

363 Gernyng and delite of Ihesu Criste þat has na thyng of worldes thoghtes es wondyrfull pure haly and faste and when a man felis hym in þat degre than es a man Circumsysede gastely (from 4)

Richard Rolle, Delyte and ʒernyng of Gode, short treatise, s. xiv (1).

1. EETS os 20 (1866), p. 13 (Lincoln Cathedral 91, f. 196v); 2. Mätzner, I, 2 (1869), 2, 132 (as in 1); 3. YW, I (1895), 197 (as

289

in 1); 4. EETS os 20, rev. ed. (1921), pp. 14-15 (as in 1); 5. Allen, Writings (1927), pp. 271-72 (Longleat Marquis of Bath 29, f. 48v); 6. Allen, English (1931), pp. 57-58 (as in 1).

Yrste   See [F]yrste

864   Zedechye was the first philisophre which by the will of God lawe was first resceiued and wisdam vndirstanden

Booke of Morall Seyenges of Philysophres, moral pronouncements attributed to old philosophers translated from the French Dits Moraulx by Guillaume de Tignonville, ca. 1450.

1. EETS os 211 (1941), pp. 3-293 (odd pages only) (Helmingham Hall Lord Tollemache MS).

Middle English titles are listed according to the modern English spelling of the words involved; the articles A, An, and The are omitted in the alphabetical scheme. Middle English surnames and Latin and French titles are listed as they appear in the printed editions.

"Ancrene Riwle" 559
Ancrene Wisse 507, 559, 751
And Ye Wyll Kyll Many Fysches in a Pole 631
Anno Edwardi Quarti Quarto 685
Anselm, St. 462, 573, 814.7; Pseudo- 219, 390.5
Antym of Oure Lady 585
Antichrist 93
Anwykyll, John 265
Aphorism 812
Apocalips of Jesu Crist 584
"Apology for Lollard Doctrines" 188
"Apostles' Creed" 316, 403
Appleby, Simon, of London Wall 439
Arbre des batailles 774
Arderne, John 325
"Arguam Te Nescis" 97
Arithmetic 115, 729
Arithmetical question 344
Arnold, Richard 365
Arryvaile of Kynge Edward the Fourthe 602
Ars Moriendi 818
Ars Utilissima Sciendi Mori 439.5
Arte and Crafte to Knowe Well to Dye 826
Art de Venerie 485, 763
Art of Good Lywyng and Good Deyng 517
Art of Nombryng 115
Arthur, King 394
Articles 443
Articles of advice 186
Articles of Oure Fayth 390
Ashby, George 591
"Assize of Bread" 406
Aston, John 370
Astrological prognostications 827; treatise 756
Astronomical treatise 201, 373, 438
Atkynson, William 838
Attack on the clergy 444
Augustine, St. 213; Pseudo- 41, 574
Augustinian orders 805
Augustinus de Contemptu Mundi 338
Autobiography 288
Ave Maria 276, 279, 455

Babyngton, Anthony 512
Bagnyon, Jean 582
Bate fir Tenches or All Maner Flote Fish 445
Bates for Hope Nettes 637
Ball, John 412, 425

293

303

307

319

MANUSCRIPT INDEX

Manuscripts are listed alphabetically by city, library, and shelfmark.
For the names of private owners and for former owners and locations,
see the separate section following York.

98   122
Exeter, Cathedral, Pontifical   787.3
Florence, Biblioteca Laurenziana, Plut. XIX, cod. XXXIII   542
Geneva, Bodmer Foundation, Cod. 48   18, 529
Glasgow, University of Glasgow, Gen. 223   49, 119
    Gen. 1130   553
    Hunterian 61   374
    Hunterian 74   374
    Hunterian 77   553
    Hunterian 83   73, 374
    Hunterian 136   526
    Hunterian 176   119
    Hunterian 189   119
    Hunterian 191   119
    Hunterian 197   18, 482, 529
    Hunterian 228   374
    Hunterian 230   374
    Hunterian 258   4
    Hunterian 270   156
    Hunterian 337   119
    Hunterian 367   605
    Hunterian 410   226
    Hunterian 443   374
    Hunterian 472   157
    Hunterian 496   213, 465, 842
    Hunterian 520   213, 230, 574, 842
Gloucester, Cathedral, 12   682
    22   172, 560, 734
    Diocesan Record Office, 8   119
Göttingen, Universität, philol. 163   581
Great Bedwyn, Wiltshire, George Smith MS   661
Hamburg, Staats- und Universitätsbibliothek, Cod. 98 in scrin.   374
Hastings, East Sussex County Record Office MS   553
Hatfield House, Marquis of Salisbury, 280   734
    281   365
    Unidentified MS   75
Helmingham Hall, Lord Tollemache, LJ.II.2   560
    Unidentified MS   864
Hereford, Cathedral, O.VII.1   119
    P.I.9   351
    Welsh Manual   313
Holkham Hall, Earl of Leicester, 164   630
    667   18
    669   374
    670   374
    671   212
    672   263
    Unidentified MS   10

Harley 106	351
Harley 149	156, 397
Harley 171	584
Harley 172	439.5
Harley 211	448, 460, 789
Harley 218	48
Harley 237	460
Harley 247	67
Harley 266	374
Harley 268	657
Harley 272	119
Harley 279	624
Harley 283	21
Harley 326	33
Harley 327	119
Harley 330	255
Harley 335	122, 857
Harley 425	37
Harley 494	693
Harley 535	448
Harley 537	10
Harley 540	365
Harley 541	365
Harley 542	498, 717, 722
Harley 543	105, 181, 186, 365, 568, 602
Harley 545	105
Harley 565	365
Harley 586	581
Harley 614	785
Harley 630	682
Harley 665	122, 572
Harley 674	4, 240, 250, 251, 252, 320, 753
Harley 753	374
Harley 838	512
Harley 874	584
Harley 937	467
Harley 940	119
Harley 941	702
Harley 955	766
Harley 959	320
Harley 984	119
Harley 993	240, 677
Harley 1002	162, 812
Harley 1022	4, 8, 22, 126, 255, 351, 506, 757, 821, 851
Harley 1035	255
Harley 1197	143, 789
Harley 1203	584, 738
Harley 1212	119

```
Harley 1288    343, 734, 789
Harley 1304    589
Harley 1337    374
Harley 1568    374
Harley 1600    642
Harley 1605    238
Harley 1666    119, 205
Harley 1704    11, 25, 39, 290, 410, 590
Harley 1706    11, 76, 120, 142, 166, 213, 234, 287, 309,
   311, 338, 362, 465, 491, 491, 528, 528, 572, 574, 652,
   842
Harley 1730    304
Harley 1742    307
Harley 1757    10, 717
Harley 1758    18, 482, 529
Harley 1764    387
Harley 1806    134, 271
Harley 1862    525
Harley 1896    119
Harley 1900    151, 221, 605
Harley 2115    383
Harley 2182    374
Harley 2247    734
Harley 2248    374
Harley 2249    119
Harley 2250    398, 448, 734
Harley 2253    626
Harley 2254    46, 147
Harley 2256    374
Harley 2261    35
Harley 2276    117
Harley 2279    374
Harley 2309    119
Harley 2320    368
Harley 2324    266
Harley 2330    41
Harley 2339    22, 213, 563, 842
Harley 2340    741
Harley 2343    316
Harley 2346    48, 49
Harley 2371    491, 734
Harley 2373    4, 240, 250, 251, 252, 320
Harley 2378    446, 629
Harley 2383    122, 269, 460, 789
Harley 2385    155, 208, 455, 810, 842
Harley 2386    233
Harley 2387    255
Harley 2388    25, 842
```

```
Harley 2389    620, 643, 772, 773
Harley 2390    407
Harley 2391    734
Harley 2396    304
Harley 2397    115.5, 147, 255
Harley 2398    49, 203, 448, 460, 521, 560, 604, 800
Harley 2399    122
Harley 2403    734
Harley 2406    39, 590, 652
Harley 2409    230, 362, 528
Harley 2415    46
Harley 2417    734
Harley 2420    734
Harley 2421    43
Harley 2445    40, 487
Harley 2869    17
Harley 3432    561
Harley 3634    425
Harley 3724    316
Harley 3730    374
Harley 3774    365
Harley 3775    777
Harley 3831    636
Harley 3840    38
Harley 3903    119
Harley 3913    584
Harley 3945    374
Harley 3954    233
Harley 4011    224, 234, 553, 707
Harley 4012    28, 166, 184, 213, 287, 800
Harley 4016    628
Harley 4027    119
Harley 4172    122
Harley 4690    374
Harley 4712    533
Harley 4775    25, 453, 682
Harley 4789    785
Harley 4800    312
Harley 4827    374
Harley 4890    119
Harley 4930    374
Harley 5017    119
Harley 5086    335, 775
Harley 5259    28
Harley 5272    39, 590
Harley 5767    119
Harley 5768    119
Harley 6097    223
```

```
Royal 18 C.xviii    775
Sloane 4      634, 637
Sloane 6      325
Sloane 7      38, 659
Sloane 60     775
Sloane 73     541, 850
Sloane 76     325
Sloane 88     421
Sloane 120    38
Sloane 135    38
Sloane 213    45, 249
Sloane 249    235
Sloane 261    438
Sloane 277    325
Sloane 297    38
Sloane 314    438
Sloane 351    125
Sloane 405    642, 659
Sloane 433    659
Sloane 443    659
Sloane 521    286, 640
Sloane 563    325
Sloane 686    665
Sloane 706    659
Sloane 779    47, 62
Sloane 962    38, 60, 440
Sloane 963    659
Sloane 965    201, 659
Sloane 983    154, 248, 659
Sloane 989    407
Sloane 1009   5, 18, 448
Sloane 1201   445
Sloane 1313   654
Sloane 1315   38
Sloane 1317   201
Sloane 1609   100, 201
Sloane 1685   18, 529
Sloane 1686   18
Sloane 1698   353
Sloane 1764   659
Sloane 1859   362
Sloane 1986   433
Sloane 2002   325
Sloane 2027   374
Sloane 2269   459
Sloane 2319   233
Sloane 2320   659
Sloane 2453   201
```

344

Hastings, Marquis of   119
Henslow, George   291, 625
Heyneman, Robert G.   See Chapel Hill
Honeyman, formerly San Juan Capistrano, California   12
Kerslake, Thomas, of Bristol   119
Kraus, H.P., New York   331
        Bute 13   438
        Bute F 16   837
Leconfield, Lord   See Petworth House
Leicester, Earl of   See Holkham Hall
Maggs, London   119
Maskell, William   157
Mellon, Paul, Phillips 12086   485, 836
Mostyn, Lord   See Holywell
Northumberland, Duke of   See Alnwick Castle
Pegge, Samuel   471
Penrose, Boies   233; see also Savery, W., and Tokyo, Takamiya
Phillipps, Thomas, 7157   525
        9735   701
        12086   485, 836
        13783   105
        Unidentified MS   783
Plimpton   See New York, Columbia University
Portland, Duke of   See London, British Library
Quaritch, London   119, 785
Richardson, W.K.   See Cambridge, Massachusetts
Rosebery, Lord   See Barnbougle Castle
Rosenbach Foundation   See Philadelphia
Salisbury, Marquis of   See Hatfield House
Savery, W., Texas, Penrose 12   605
Savile, Henry   274
Scheide, William H.   See Princeton, Princeton University
Scott, Mrs. Maxwell   See Abbotsford
Smith, George   See Great Bedwyn
Sotheby's, London, 4 April 1939, lot 295   122
        15-16 October 1945, lots 1034-1036   119
        June 1950, lot 218   119
        3 December 1951, lot 18   119
        4-5 July 1955, lot 87   122
Takamiya, Toshiyuki   See Tokyo
Taylor, Robert H.   See Princeton
Throckmorton, Sir N.W.   See Coughton Court
Todd, J.H., of   College, Dublin   119
Tollemache, Lord   See Helmingham Hall
Uffenbach, Conrad von   119
Unspecified MSS   122, 199, 369, 649, 735
Walton, Harry A., Jr.   See Covington
Welbeck Abbey   See London, British Library

Whalley MS   290
Williams, Dr.   See London